BARACK OBAMA AND THE FUTURE OF AMERICAN POLITICS

PAUL STREET

PARADIGM PUBLISHERS
Boulder • London

green press INITIATIVE

Paradigm Publishers is committed to preserving ancient forests and natural resources. We elected to print this title on 30% post consumer recycled paper, processed chlorine free. As a result, for this printing, we have saved:

24 Trees (40' tall and 6-8" diameter)
8,807 Gallons of Wastewater
17 million BTU's of Total Energy
1,131 Pounds of Solid Waste
2,122 Pounds of Greenhouse Gases

Paradigm Publishers made this paper choice because our printer, Thomson-Shore, Inc., is a member of Green Press Initiative, a nonprofit program dedicated to supporting authors, publishers, and suppliers in their efforts to reduce their use of fiber obtained from endangered forests.

For more information, visit www.greenpressinitiative.org

Environmental impact estimates were made using the Environmental Defense Paper Calculator. For more information visit: www.papercalculator.org.

Published in the United States by Paradigm Publishers,
3360 Mitchell Lane Suite E, Boulder, CO 80301 USA.

Paradigm Publishers is the trade name of Birkenkamp & Company, LLC,
Dean Birkenkamp, president and publisher.

Library of Congress Cataloging-in-Publication Data
Street, Paul Louis.
Barack Obama and the future of American politics / Paul Street.
p. cm.
Includes bibliographical references and index.
ISBN 978-1-59451-631-3 (hardcover : alk. paper)
1. Obama, Barack. 2. Presidential candidates—United States.
3. United States—Politics and government—2001– I. Title.
E901.1.O23S77 2008
328.73092—dc22

2008024297

Printed and bound in the United States of America on acid-free paper that meets the standards of the American National Standard for Permanence of Paper for Printed Library Materials.

12 11 10 09 08 1 2 3 4 5

To the memory of my mother,
Jane Marie Street, 1932–2007

CONTENTS

Elected officials are only as good or as bad as the forces they feel they must respond to. It's a mistake to expect any more of them than to be vectors of the political pressures they feel working on them.

—ADOLPH REED, JR., FROM "SITTING THIS ONE OUT,"
THE PROGRESSIVE (NOVEMBER 2007)

We who protest the war are not politicians. We are citizens. Whatever politicians may do, let them first feel the full force of citizens who speak for what is right, not for what is winnable. . . . Except for the rare few, our representatives are politicians, and will surrender their integrity, claiming to be "realistic." We are not politicians, but citizens. We have no office to hold on to, only our consciences, which insist on telling the truth. That, history suggests, is the most realistic thing a citizen can do.

—HOWARD ZINN, FROM "ARE WE POLITICIANS OR CITIZENS?"
THE PROGRESSIVE (MAY 2007)

In the election, sensible choices have to be made. But they are secondary to serious political action. The main task is to create a genuinely responsive democratic culture, and that effort goes on before and after electoral extravaganzas, whatever their outcome.

—NOAM CHOMSKY, FROM "THE DISCONNECT IN AMERICAN
DEMOCRACY" (2004), *INTERVENTIONS*

The choice we must make is as important as it is clear. It is a choice between corporate power and the power of democracy. . . . It is caution versus courage. Calculation versus principle. It is the establishment elites versus the American people. . . . Politicians who care more about their careers than their constituents go along to get elected. . . . It's a game that never ends, but every American knows—it's time to end the game.

—JOHN EDWARDS, FROM "TO BUILD ONE AMERICA,"
IN MANCHESTER, NEW HAMPSHIRE, AUGUST 24, 2007

Change doesn't happen from the top down. Change happens from the bottom up.

—BARACK OBAMA, QUOTED IN QUINN CRAUGH'S
"OBAMA GREETS 4,000 AT MONONA TERRACE, CALLS FOR BIG CHANGE,"
UNIVERSITY OF WISCONSIN *DAILY CARDINAL*, OCTOBER 16, 2007

We can't look for saviours on high to get us out of this mess. . . . We have to do it ourselves.

—TARIQ ALI AND ANTHONY ARNOVE, FROM "THE CHALLENGE TO THE
EMPIRE," *SOCIALIST WORKER ONLINE*, OCTOBER 20, 2006

Which side are you on, . . . which side are you on?

—FLORENCE REESE, LYRICS FROM THE 1930s "WHICH SIDE"

PREFACE

EVERY FOUR YEARS, many Americans invest their hopes in an electoral process that does not deserve their trust. These voters hope that a savior can be installed in the White House—someone who will raise wages, roll back war and militarism, provide universal and adequate health care, rebuild the nation's infrastructure, produce high-paying jobs, fix the environmental crisis, reduce inequality, guarantee economic security, and generally make daily life more tolerable.

But the dreams are regularly drowned in the icy waters of historical and political "reality." In the actuality of American politics and policy, the officially "electable" candidates are vetted in advance by what historian and author Laurence Shoup calls "the hidden primary of the ruling class." By prior establishment selection, all of the "viable" presidential contenders are closely tied to corporate and military-imperial power in numerous and interrelated ways. They run safely within the narrow ideological and policy parameters set by those who rule behind the scenes to make sure that the rich and privileged continue to be the leading beneficiaries of the American system.

In its presidential as in its other elections, U.S. "democracy" is "at best" a "guided one; at its worst it is a corrupt farce, amounting to manipulation, with the larger population objects of propaganda in a controlled and trivialized electoral process," Shoup wrote. "It is an illusion," he claimed—correctly in my opinion—"that real change can ever come from electing a different ruling class sponsored candidate."[1]

This is especially true in the corporate-neoliberal era, perhaps, when the Democratic Party has moved ever further away from its declared mission of representing workers, the poor, and minorities—the disadvantaged—in their continuing struggles with plutocracy, inequality, empire, racism, and indifference.[2]

But the deeper and darker truth is that American democracy has always been significantly constrained and compromised by the privileged and the propertied and power elite. Sixty years ago, the historian Richard Hofstader, in his widely read book, *The American Political Tradition,* scrutinized the United States' most significant national leaders, from Jefferson, Hamilton, and Jackson to Lincoln, William Jennings Bryan, Herbert Hoover, and the two Roosevelts—liberals and Democrats as well as conservatives and Republicans. Hofstader found that "the range of vision embraced by the primary contestants in the major parties has always been bounded by the horizons of property and enterprise. . . . They have accepted the economic virtues of capitalist culture as necessary qualities of man. . . . That culture has been intensely nationalistic."[3] We might add that American political culture has also long observed narrow parameters of permissible debate and action surrounding skin color and sex type—barriers that have generally prevented leading politicians and officeholders from seriously attacking underlying structures and patterns of racial and gender disparity.

Through the century in which Hofstader wrote and into the present one, the great radical historian Howard Zinn has noted, "We have seen exactly the same limited vision Hofstader talked about—a capitalist encouragement of enormous fortunes alongside desperate poverty, a nationalistic acceptance of war and preparation for war. Government power swung from Republicans to Democrats and back again, but neither party showed itself capable of going beyond that vision."[4]

* * *

CONTRARY TO THE HOPES AND DREAMS of many nominally "progressive" U.S. voters and activists and others in 2007 and early 2008, this book resists the notion that Barack Obama is some sort of special, magical exception to the cold truths that Shoup, Zinn, and other commentators tell about American politics past and present.[5] The Obama portrayed in this book is very different from the "revolutionary outsider" and "entirely new breed of candidate" he has been portrayed as in dominant corporate media.[6]

Future history remains open and contingent, and there is no denying that "the Obama phenomenon" has reflected and fed mass excitement and citizen engagement on behalf of "change" and the transcendence of "old" patterns in American politics. But an Obama White House, I maintain, could reasonably be expected to walk in the conservative, capitalist, market/corporate-friendly, nationalistic, and imperialistic footsteps laid down by Hofstader's "American political tradition," in accord with Shoup's "hidden primary," unless compelled to do otherwise by an aroused and organized populace. It could also be expected, I argue, ironically enough, to offer little substantive challenge to the stark racial disparities that continue to undermine America's claim to embody the ideals of democracy and equality.

The "Obama phenomenon" to date, this book shows, is richly continuous with previous centrist Democratic presidencies and presidential campaigns as well as with the broader neoliberal drift of the Democratic Party over the past three and a half decades. Obama, I argue, has demonstrated neither the inclination nor the capacity to transcend the sharp restrictions imposed on

Democratic presidential politicians past and present. Hardly unique to the current presidential election cycle, the relevant limiting factors include the business-dominated, winner-take-all, U.S. elections system, the United States' formidable (to say the least) imperial and military commitments, the massive overconcentration of American wealth in the hands of the privileged few, and a highly commodified, trivialized, and narrow political and ideological culture that leads many conservative and centrist positions and candidates to strike many voters and commentators as "progressive," "liberal," and even "left wing."

Contrary to much progressive mythology and wishful thinking, this book shows the junior senator from Illinois repeatedly demonstrating eager willingness to embrace and advance dominant domestic and imperial hierarchies and doctrines. If anything, I argue, the accuracy of Shoup's, Zinn's, and Hofstader's "cynical" take on American politics is highlighted by the remarkable passion, activism, and expectations sparked by Obama's claim to represent a dramatic break with the "tired past" of U.S. politics, policy, and ideology. I find myself in considerable agreement with the following judgment from Temple University urban studies professor Marc Lamont Hill, written as Obama was beginning to pass Hillary Clinton in the race for the Democratic presidential nomination:

> The media has constructed his early success as a David-over-Goliath narrative that proves that ordinary people have the power to slay the beast that is Washington through a radical politics of hope. Unfortunately, the Obama campaign has perverted the concept of hope by wedding it to a dangerous politics of compromise, concession and cunning.
>
> Obama has clung to a rigid centrism that is incompatible with the full-scale social change. In Obama's corporate-sponsored universe of meaning, hope is not the predicate for radical social change, but an empty slogan that allows for a slick repackaging of the status quo. . . .
>
> . . . Unlike [Martin Luther] King . . . Obama does not aim to disrupt the fundamental structure of society. Rather than dismantling the triple threat of global racism, poverty, and militarism that King warned against, Obama has promoted a doctrine of compromise that is self-serving rather than strategic, milque toast rather than pragmatic.[7]

As I hope to show in this book, this harsh verdict is all too well grounded in the reality of Obama's public record, including specific policy positions and proposals and broader statements of historical and ideological worldview—a record that has been all too neglected thanks in part to the tendency of the dominant U.S. media to focus on superficial matters regarding candidates and elections.

* * *

LEST THIS ALL SOUNDS TOO "NEGATIVE" toward a candidate in whom many well-meaning and genuinely progressive Americans have put considerable faith, I want to be very clear from the outset that this book's main moral and political criticism is not directed primarily at Obama himself. My ultimate critical targets are the corporate-dominated and militaristic U.S. elections system and political culture. That system and culture make it next to impossible for Obama or anyone else to become president without steering to the business-friendly, racially neutral, and imperial center and without distancing themselves from elementary truths about U.S. history, society, and policy.

I do not shrink from making critical judgments about the moral cost inherent in Obama's decision to join rather than to fight "the establishment"—to seek to climb higher in the American system rather than to try to change it. But I am more concerned with the historical system and forces that have compromised Barack Obama—along with countless other Democratic politicians and policymakers past, present, and future—than with the individual compromised. The most critical focus here is not on the candidate-in-question's personal characteristics or moral constitution but rather on the restrictive institutional and societal framework within which his candidacy and celebrity have emerged.

Following the counsel of Martin Luther King, Jr., I do not condemn Obama for acting on what King called "the Drum Major Instinct"—the desire to "be important," "the best," and recognized for personal achievement.[8] I criticize rather the captivity of that natural human instinct by the interrelated and mutually reinforcing logics of empire and inequality.[9] Fittingly enough, this book ends with a specific set of actionable policy and activism proposals to encourage the creation of a more genuinely democratic, egalitarian, responsive, and participatory U.S. political culture—one where the recurrently betrayed populist and peace-oriented promises of Democratic presidential candidates might find concrete actualization.

The same confining historical and political context that I examine in regard to Obama would be under scrutiny if I were writing a book about Obama's strong, ideological look-alike Hillary Clinton or the more "populist" John Edwards. Along with numerous Democratic presidential candidates and presidents from the past, both Edwards and Clinton will also receive considerable critical attention in the pages that follow. What has made Obama distinct, it seems to me, has been his sudden emergence and manufacture amid high spectacle and a strongly media-fed commotion, all of which have helped to market him as an especially potent lightning rod of popular excitement and progressive illusion. This distinctiveness is intimately related, I think, to his ethnocultural identity and to his early opposition to the most spectacular failure of the George W. Bush administration—the disastrous (as widely predicted both within and beyond the U.S. foreign policy establishment) invasion of Iraq. The simple facts of skin color and that early "antiwar" position, I argue, have gone a very long way in helping Obama wrap his conservative, establishment-oriented politics and world-view in the "rebel's clothing" of progressive insurgency.[10]

* * *

I ADDED THE FINISHING TOUCHES to the writing of this manuscript in early June of 2008, as Hillary Clinton stepped down from her quest for the Democratic nomination and it became clear that Obama would be running as the Democratic presidential candidate against John McCain in November. Most of the research for this book was conducted between the publication of Obama's book *The Audacity of Hope* (which marked the de facto beginning of his presidential campaign) and late April of 2008. By the time this volume hits the bookshelves, I am aware that its portrayal of Obama as a relatively conservative, capitalism-/corporate-friendly, racially conciliatory, and Empire-friendly "centrist" will strike some readers as counterintuitive. The nation's still-potent, right-wing Republican, attack machine will already be regularly and unreasonably assailing Obama as a "far left" candidate, a "socialist," a "black nationalist," and a dangerous "anti-American" enemy of God, Country, the Family, and Apple Pie! Obama will also be subjected to no small measure of ugly racial bigotry. The racial fears and bias and toxic color prejudice—already evident across the Internet as I draft this preface in early June of 2008[11]—that his presidential candidacy will arouse will sometimes make it seem like the Obama phenomenon represents a real and substantive challenge to racial hierarchy in the U.S.

These unpleasant facts will make it more difficult than it would be otherwise to understand the Left critique of "the Obama phenomenon" that comes in the chapters that follow. They will also compel many of this book's readers and in fact the book's author to defend Obama against ridiculous, reactionary, and racist assaults.[12] I nonetheless stand behind the often unsympathetic portrayal presented here, claiming my right to walk (criticize Obama from a left-democratic perspective) and chew gum (defend him against racial bigotry and outrageous rightist misrepresentation and abuse) at one and the same time.

The timing factor cuts two ways, moreover. One aspect of the tricky relationship between campaign and publication schedules here may well be favorable to the depiction of Obama given in this book. I have constructed a portrait of Obama as a power-conciliating centrist based significantly on his actions and statements during the primary campaign, when Democratic candidates tend if anything to run to the left of their actual commitments (because the voters in primary races are more liberal than the larger group that votes in general elections). We can expect Obama to tack more strongly to the ideological and policy right and center as the general election campaign proceeds,[13] consistent with the longstanding homogenizing incentives created by the American two-party, "winner-take-all" elections system and political culture—a topic to which I shall turn in some detail in Chapter 6.[14] If Obama becomes president, or if he returns instead to the Senate as a base to continue pursuit of his national political career, he will work from the political center rather than the Left. I spend much of this book explaining why.

* * *

NONE OF THE CRITICAL PERSPECTIVE presented in this book is meant to deny the undeniably brilliant and charismatic Obama's real accomplishments. I believe "the Obama phenomenon" deserves respect for generating, motivating, and mobilizing popular excitement, citizen engagement, voter turnout, youth involvement, and more. Even if I am 100 percent correct in portraying Obama as a corporate-triangulationist Democratic politico in the conservative, "third way" Clinton and Democratic Leadership Council (DLC) mode (ironically enough given the epic nastiness that emerged between Obama and the Clintons during the 2008 campaign), Obama may have helped challenge the Democratic Party's centrist and neoliberal ways by encouraging mass political involvement and interest like no U.S. politician in recent memory.

"Change" is a dangerous and many-sided word, and it is possible that the Obama phenomenon could help spark a transformative wave of progressive, peace-oriented, and multicultural peoples' activism in ways that could help carry American politics beyond its limited and conservative parameters.

For what it's worth, since I live in a state where Republicans threaten strongly to win presidential elections (Iowa), it seems likely that I will vote for Obama on the first Tuesday of November 2008. And here I do not want to be misunderstood. The chapters that follow will demonstrate why I otherwise would prefer to be voting for a third party to the Democrats' left (the Green Party, in all likelihood). If I lived in an uncontested state, that is surely what I would do.

I agree with Shoup that "the main issues of our time . . . will not be solved by the ruling class or their preferred candidates unless the people force them to." "It has been argued," Shoup observed, "that another and better New Deal serving people's needs and not corporate profitability is conceivable under a Democratic administration in 2009." But "this only would be possible," he added, "if people's movements, through direct struggle, give the ruling plutocracy no choice but to grant the people's just demands."[15]

As activists, commentators, and scholars on the Left have long argued, big progressive transformation (on the model of the New Deal,[16] for example) does not come from embracing supposed liberal political knights in shining armor like John Kennedy, Bobby Kennedy, Jimmy Carter, Bill Clinton, Barack Obama, Hillary Clinton, or John Edwards. It comes rather from dedicated mass participation in the sorts of grassroots struggles that shake society to its foundations. Examples include the industrial workers' movement in the 1930s, the Civil Rights Movement in the 1950s and 1960s, and the antiwar movement in the 1960s and early 1970s.[17]

The question of who one does or doesn't vote (or work) for in U.S. elections is secondary to the deeper and bigger task of building and expanding alternative centers of truly popular power and resistance and of creating a more responsive and democratic political culture in the United States. The living historical taproot of meaningful progressive change remains, well, unchanged, regardless of who does or does not successfully negotiate the "hidden primary" at the elite level. The essential sources of significant democratic social and political change are still found in the willingness and capacity of ordinary people to unite and fight for a more just, sustainable, peaceful, and egalitarian society beyond and across quadrennial, corporate-crafted election extravaganzas. This is particularly true in a age of bipartisan corporate-"managed democracy." In the brilliant American political scientist Sheldon Wolin's words, the Deomocratic Party's politics "might be described as inauthentic opposition in the era of Superpower. Having fended off its reformist elements and disclaimed the label liberal," Wolin observes in his important and powerful new book *Democracy Incorporated: Managed Democracy and the Specter of Inverted Totalitarianism* (published as I finished this study), "it is trapped by the new rules of the game which dictate that a party exists to win elections rather than to promote a vision of the good society. . . . Should Democrats somehow be elected, corporate sponsors make it politically impossible for the new officeholders to alter significantly the direction of society."[18]

Still, as Noam Chomsky has argued, America's presidential elections should not simply be ignored, especially when one of the two corporate-sponsored parties contending for power (the Republicans) is dedicated to ruling the world by sheer force and to undoing nearly all of the basic public protections and social programs "won by popular struggles over the last century."[19] "Another and better New Deal serving people's needs" would certainly have to be forced from below on an Obama White House, but it could never be attained by any means under a Republican administration. The same could be said in regard to foreign policy: Progress toward a less militaristic and imperial approach to the world is at least imaginable under a Democratic White House but seems inconceivable under a Republican one. At the same time, the space for the emergence and relevance of people's movements would be considerably broader under an Obama White House than it could ever be in the dark shadow of a John McCain administration.

It is possible, finally, that the populist and peace-oriented sentiments and energies simultaneously tapped, exploited, captured, encouraged, and contained by the "deeply conservative"[20] Obama portrayed in this study could move an Obama White House in something like a progressive direction.

My sense is that the space for progress toward economic justice, a decent foreign policy, and popular mobilization will be significantly greater under an Obama administration than it could have been under a third and (perhaps) fourth Clinton presidency.

The Obama phenomenon is not without dialectical complexity and progressive potential. But only the future can tell how much potential and what it will mean for American politics and society in the twenty-first century.

Regardless of whether Obama wins the presidency, finally, he is a relatively young and vibrant officeholder and politician with what seems likely to be a long and significant political future. I have oriented my research and writing here around questions that will affect both his career and the future of American politics more broadly for many years to come.

"A Man for All Seasons?" The Dark Essences of American Politics

The "Age of Obama"

As I completed this introduction in early June of 2008, the black United States Senator Barack Obama's (D-IL) remarkable and "improbable quest" for the United States presidency seemed less of a fantasy. Thanks largely to the uncertain politics of race, Obama's ascendancy to the White House in January of 2009 is by no means guaranteed. John McCain should hardly be counted out as a serious contender for the U.S. presidency. Yet no matter what transpires in coming months, the junior senator has already entered the pages of U.S. political history. As Associated Press correspondent Christopher Wills noted in early February 2008, "Even if he loses, the 46-year-old senator has made himself into a national figure—probably for years to come."[1] One could quibble (this book will) with the phrase "made himself," but Wills was right to note that Obama has likely become a long-term fixture in the national political arena. Describing Obama as "galloping onto the national stage," Obama's biographer and *Chicago Tribune* reporter David Mendell noted last year:

> Obama would become a source of hope and optimism for disillusioned Democrats from California to New Hampshire. Obama's come-from-nowhere ascent would make it starkly evident just how passionately many Americans yearned for an inspirational leader who could mend the various divisions within the country—racial, political, cultural, spiritual. . . . Not since the days of Jack and Bobby Kennedy and their luminous political Camelot had a politician captured so quickly the imagination of such a broad array of Americans. . . . Not since Ronald Reagan had a politician been so adept at sharing his own unwavering optimism with a disheartened electorate. Wherever he went, Obama drew impassioned crowds in the thousands.[2]

Obama's largest campaign speaking engagements in 2007 and early 2008 became giant events with big city and major university sports arenas filled beyond capacity by masses of cheering, starstruck voters chanting "O-ba-ma, O-ba-ma!" and "We Want Change, We Want Change." The Indian journalist K. V. Prasad described a typical scene as Obama's primary campaign peaked in early and mid-February 2008: "Fresh from his weekend victories across four states, Mr. Obama took the stage before a packed house in the 17,500-capacity Comcast Centre auditorium [in College Park, Maryland]. It began filling up as soon as the gates opened, *some four hours before* the Illinois Senator was scheduled to appear."[3]

In early March 2008, *The New Republic* writer John Judis aptly captured the rolling political spectacle that was "the Obama phenomenon":

> When Barack Obama announced a year ago that he was running for president, I scoffed. How could a black man whose middle name is Hussein and who looks like he is 25 years old win the White House? . . . One year later . . . Obama has done more than cobble together a political coalition. He has made himself into a political phenomenon, the likes of which this country has not seen since Ronald Reagan. He fills stadiums. His rallies—where he asks the crowd to "stand up for change" and it responds by shouting, "Yes, we can!"—are like revival meetings. He has inspired thousands of volunteers and dramatically boosted turnout rates, particularly among young voters. Al Gore and John Kerry, the last two Democratic nominees, clearly never attracted this kind of following.[4]

Picking up on the widely noted "quasi-religious dimensions of Obama's presidential run, Chicago attorney and author Tom Levinson observed that Obama's campaign had "the distinct feel" of "a low-grade millennial movement." Obama's quest for the White House "is a new expression," Levinson wrote in the *Chicago Tribune,* "of an age-old millennial vision because it's believed that the 'Change' preached by the candidate has the potential to transform American life—completely and soon."[5] More than a year before, Obama had educed such passionate support from white voters that *Slate's* Timothy Noah set up "The Obama Messiah Watch," a regular link quoting from the flood of "gratuitously adoring" articles on the candidate.[6]

Mendell's characterization of Obama was itself part of a distinguishing characteristic of the Obama phenomenon: the astonishing intensity and breadth of the adulation with which he and his call for "hope" and "change" were received and transmitted by dominant U.S. media. Among the leading media outlets that gave Obama fawning cover-page publicity during his time in the U.S. Senate and on the presidential campaign trail over the past three years were *Time, Newsweek, GQ, Men's Vogue, Marie Claire, Washington Life,* and *Vibe.* "The last time a guy had a build-up like this, he had 12 Apostles around him," joked Chicago political analyst and professor Paul Green in the summer of 2006.[7]

During the 2007–2008 presidential campaign through Super Tuesday, Obama received by far and away the most frequent and favorable media exposure, coverage, and commentary of any candidate. An epitome of this remarkable media approval came after he won the early Iowa caucus, when *Newsweek*'s cover portrayed Obama surrounded by what seemed to be a halo next to a quote from his grandiose Iowa victory speech: "Our Time for Change Has Come."[8] I will give numerous other examples from early 2008 in Chapter 2 of this book.

By the time Obama won Iowa, in fact, America was already nearly into the second half of year four of the significantly media-generated "Obama phenomenon." The "Age of Obama"[9] officially began with a bang during his instantly famous, nationally broadcast keynote address to the 2004 Democratic National Convention. After that spectacularly well-received address, which catapulted Obama onto the national and global stage practically overnight, many political insiders knew that it was just a matter of time until its deliverer made a run at the White House.

Origins: Good Fortune and Powerful Friends

How did Obama happen? Where did he come from? Though there is no denying his special talents, hard work, and grandiose ambition—his academic, professional, and political cohorts all testify to these Obama attributes (a close family friend reports that "he's always wanted to be president")—it should be admitted that Obama has been the beneficiary of remarkable good fortune on the path to national and global prominence. Looking back on his political career, even a skeptic might find it hard not to get a sense of stars repeatedly aligning to enable his ascendancy. As the black left Chicago journalist Salim Muwakill noted in the summer of 2007, "Conditions conspired perfectly to grease Obama's route. . . . Those of us following the 'Obama phenomenon' from its inception were amazed by the magical, dreamlike quality of his ascent. A local astrologer explained it by the notion of a propitious celestial alignment in Obama's chart."[10] Obama's former rival, U.S. Congressman Bobby Rush (D-IL), told the *New York Times* that it was the result of divine intervention.[11] At the same time, another key ingredient in Obama's magical rise to sudden national prominence was preliminary big-money sponsorship, without which Obama would not likely have been able to rocket to stardom as quickly as he did.

Reynolds and Palmer

An early example of the luck factor came in 1995. That was the year that the black South Side Chicago Democratic U.S. congressman Mel Reynolds was sentenced to five years behind bars for sexual misconduct with an underage campaign volunteer. Reynolds's Second Congressional District seat opened up, enticing the popular, respected, and progressive black state senator Alice Palmer to throw her hat into the congressional ring. It was a chance opening for Obama, a young lawyer and political activist (and resident of Palmer's district), eager to enter electoral politics after a celebrated career as a student at Harvard Law. He entered the spring 1996 state legislative Democratic primary with Palmer's initial blessing. With the popular incumbent removed from the race and with the support of Jesse Jackson, Jr. (who defeated Palmer in the special election for the open congressional seat), Obama coasted easily to victory in the Illinois Senate's predominantly black Thirteenth District, a seat he would hold between 1997 and 2004.[12]

Fitzgerald and Braun

In 2003, fortune smiled again on Obama, who was worried about becoming a "lifer in the state legislature" and had long imagined a run for the U.S. presidency.[13] That's when the sitting Republican U.S. senator from Illinois, Peter Fitzgerald, announced that he would not be running for reelection in 2004. It was an unexpected opportunity. Obama had been dreaming of running for the elite U.S. representative body for many years and knew that his chances of winning would be much better if the seat was truly open than if he had to go up against an incumbent Republican.

He would not have attempted a U.S. Senate campaign, however, but for another fortuitous development in December 2002. That's when Carol Moseley Braun, the former possessor of Fitzgerald's U.S. Senate seat, announced her candidacy for the U.S. presidency, ending speculation that she would seek to win it back. By Obama's calculations, he had no chance of winning the Democratic nomination for the 2004 Senate race if Moseley Braun was in the running, since she would have dominated his two critical potential bases of support: African Americans and affluent white liberals.[14]

Axelrod and Hull

Another break on Obama's path to the U.S. Senate took place more than two years before the November 2004 elections. That's when the legendary, Chicago-based, political consultant David Axelrod—the longtime media strategist and image architect of Chicago's powerful mayor, Richard M. Daley—met repeatedly with Blair Hull, a onetime professional Las Vegas gambler who had accumulated remarkable personal wealth trading stocks on Wall Street. Having sold his company to Goldman Sachs for $531 million, Hull was looking to invest part of his fortune in a largely self-financed campaign for the Fitzgerald seat and was prepared to pay Axelrod a giant sum. But Axelrod, concerned that allegations of past abuse from Hull's ex-wife and rumors of a past alcohol problem might undermine Hull's candidacy, declined. If the meetings had gone differently, America and the world might well never have heard of Barack Obama. As Mendell noted,

> The discussions between Axelrod and Hull ultimately pushed Axelrod into the campaign of Obama, rearranging the dynamics of the race and instantly turning the little-known state senator into a serious contender. Without Axelrod as his marketing specialist, it's unclear if Obama would have won the Democratic primary. And if Obama had still managed to pull off victory, there's absolutely no question that he would never have done it in such an astonishing fashion—in a way that propelled him to national stardom even before he hit Washington. Obama possessed the innate talent for success, to be sure. But Axelrod was the coach who harnessed the talent and massaged it into its present form, and then he was the publicity agent who sold Obama to Illinois voters.[15]

Hull's primary campaign imploded in February 2004 on the basis of public revelations regarding his past abusive domestic behavior. He nonetheless stayed on to garner nearly 10 percent of the vote in the Democratic primary and to unintentionally assist Obama in critical ways. His presence helped siphon away white votes from Obama's main competitor after Hull's collapse—popular state comptroller, Dan Hynes. It also helped Obama raise much more money (developing critical relationships with wealthy campaign investors along the way) than would have been possible otherwise. Under the rules of the recently passed McCain-Feingold campaign finance reform law—another stroke of luck for Obama—a candidate was permitted to raise significantly more than the usual limit when running against a wealthy opponent who was financing her or his own campaign. For the 2004 primary, Obama was free to raise $12,000 from each donor instead of $2,000.[16]

How Obama (and Not Jennifer Granholm) Got the Keynote Address

After winning the Democratic primary and developing a remarkably elevated fundraising profile with the help of McCain-Feingold's "millionaire's amendment," Obama fell upon more good fortune. A series of events and considerations led to him getting the nod—a real coup for a mere state senator—for the fateful 2004 keynote address. As *Washington Post* writer

Liza Mundy noted in a 2007 profile entitled "A Series of Fortunate Events," Obama benefited from five basic facts in the Democratic Party's keynote selection process: (1) the party was looking for freshness and youth; (2) it was looking for a midwesterner from a major industrial state to provide geographic counterbalance to the northeastern presidential candidate John Kerry and the southern vice presidential candidate John Edwards; (3) it wanted to increase its power in the U.S. Senate; (4) Obama was running for an open U.S. Senate seat and would benefit in that race from the national prominence typically afforded to keynote speakers; (5) Obama's main rival for the keynote slot, Michigan Governor Jennifer Granholm, was not up for reelection. The last three factors were critical. By Mundy's account, "The decision came down to the fact that Obama, unlike Granholm, was still trying to win an election. . . . The balance in the Senate was 51–48 in favor of Republicans. 'We needed his Senate seat,' says [a Democratic Party] official. So Obama it was."[17]

An Earlier and "Quieter Audition" with "the Moneyed Establishment"

The Obama campaign's narrative about how he attained the pivotal keynote assignment has been less than perfectly truthful in two critical ways. In his bestselling campaign book, *The Audacity of Hope* (2006), Obama claimed it was a complete surprise to him when John Kerry's campaign manager Mary Beth Cahill called and invited him to deliver the 2004 keynote address. "The process by which I was selected as the keynote speaker remains something of a mystery to me," he wrote. But this, Mundy noted, seemed "disingenuous," because the campaign had been told in advance that he was likely to get it; Obama's manager, Axelrod, had in fact been fiercely lobbying for the role.[18]

A bigger problem with the Obama keynote address narrative is the way it neglects what we might call the "political and business class tryout" he received prior to his nationally broadcast introduction to the country and the world. As investigative journalist Ken Silverstein noted in a *Harper's* article in the fall of 2006, "If the speech was his debut to the wider American public, he had already undergone an *equally successful but much quieter audition* with Democratic Party leaders and fund-raisers, *without whose support he would surely never have been chosen for such a prominent role at the convention.*"[19]

A corporate, financial, national and legal vetting of Obama, with an emphasis on the critical money-politics nexus of Washington, D.C., began in October 2003. That's "when Vernon Jordan, the well-known power broker and corporate boardmember who chaired Bill Clinton's presidential transition team after the 1992 election, placed calls to roughly twenty of his friends and invited them to a fund-raiser at his home," according to Silverstein. The fund-raiser "marked his entry into a well-established Washington ritual—the gauntlet of fund-raising parties and meet-and-greets through which potential stars are vetted by fixers, donors, and lobbyists."[20]

Drawing on his undoubted charm, wit, intelligence, and—of no small significance at the level of the political elite—his Harvard credentials, Obama passed this preliminary trial of wealth and power with flying colors. At a series of social meetings and at least one conference with assorted big "players" from the financial, legal, and lobbyist sectors, Obama impressed key establishment figures like Gregory Craig (a longtime leading attorney and former special counsel to the White House), Mike Williams (the legislative director of the Bond Market Association), Tom Quinn (a partner at the leading corporate law firm Venable LLP, who was one of "the leading lobbyists in town" as well as a leading Democratic Party power broker), and Robert Harmala (another Venable partner and "also a big player in Democratic circles," according to Silverstein). Craig liked the fact that Obama was not seen as a racial "polarizer" on the model of past African American leaders like Jesse Jackson and Al Sharpton. Williams was impressed by Obama's reassurances that he was not "anti-business" and became "convinced . . . that the two could work together." "There's a reasonableness about him," Harmala told Silverstein. "I don't see him as being on the liberal fringe."[21]

By Silverstein's account, "word about Obama spread through Washington's blue-chip law firms, lobby shops, and political offices, and this accelerated after his win in the March [2004] Democratic primary." Contributions from elite financial and legal circles and from lobbyists came into the Obama campaign's coffers at an accelerating pace. The good news for Washington and Wall Street insiders was that Obama's "star quality" would not be directed against concentrated wealth or against the elite segments of the business class—the interesting black legislator from the South Side of Chicago was someone the rich and powerful felt they could work with.[22] According to David Mendell,

> Word of Obama's rising star was now rising beyond Illinois, especially through influential Washington political circles like blue chip law firms, party insiders, lobbying houses. They were all hearing about this rare, exciting, charismatic, up-and-coming African American who unbelievably could win votes across color lines. . . . Axelrod, Jim Cauley and Obama's influential Chicago supporters and fund-raisers all vigorously worked their D.C. contacts to help Obama make the rounds with the Democrats' set of power brokers. . . . Obama . . . spent a couple of days and nights shaking hands, making small talk and delivering speeches to liberal groups, national union leaders, lobbyists, fund-raisers and well-heeled money donors. In setting after setting, Obama's Harvard Law resume and his reasonable tone impressed the elite crowd.[23]

"Reasonable tone" was code language with a useful translation for Obama's new elite business-class backers: friendly to capitalism and its opulent masters. Obama now cultivated the support of the privileged few by "advocate[ing] fiscal restraint," "calling for pay-as-you-go government," and "extol[ling] the merits of free trade and charter schools." By Mendell's account, he "moved beyond being an obscure good-government reformer to being a candidate more than palatable to the moneyed and political establishment."[24]

The following chapter will plumb the notable depths of just how "palatable" and "reasonable" Obama has been toward the "moneyed establishment" during his time in public office.

No Viable Republican Opponent

Ironically enough, given the Democratic Party's desire to guarantee a victory in the Senate race, fortune shone on Obama yet again just a few weeks before the Democratic convention when it emerged that his formidable Republican opponent, Jack Ryan, had tried to convince his ex-wife to perform public acts at a sex club. Ryan's campaign was instantly undone and he would eventually withdraw.

To make things yet easier for Obama, the Illinois Republican Party took more than a month to find a replacement for Ryan, and then exhibited the incredibly poor judgment to import the bizarre perennial candidate Alan Keyes from Maryland. Obama would cruise to a 70 percent victory—an almost unimaginably easy triumph. "You could argue," political scientist Ron Walters told Mundy, "that if the Republicans had had a viable candidate, there would be no Barack."[25]

The Novelty Dividend

Once the keynote speech was delivered and his celebrity enshrined, Obama's presidential possibilities and calculations were enhanced and accelerated by further good fortune. According to Pew Research Center president Andrew Kohut, the U.S. populace was "uniquely poised to receive Obama at the precise moment when he materialized." On the eve of the 2004 election the nation had become deeply dissatisfied with the political status quo and the national direction; popular concerns with government and corporate corruption, uneven economic performance, deepening inequality, and the problematic invasion of Iraq were widespread.[26]

"They're looking for political change," Kohut told Mundy in mid-2007, "and he certainly personifies change," adding that a Pew poll showed voters identifying the name "Barack Obama" with the words "new," "young," "charismatic," and "smart." Obama's relative youth, combined with his race and his seemingly (for most Americans) odd-sounding name—and the fact that he had emerged on the national stage seemingly "overnight" and "out of nowhere" to embody the notions of transformation and difference at a time when many were hungry for novelty and qualitative alteration (if not quite revolution), put him into the limelight.[27] I will return to this theme in Chapter 5.

It didn't hurt Obama's presidential possibilities that the stiff, aristocratic, lackluster, and centrist John F. Kerry campaign failed—with no small help from the Republican "Swift-boat" strategy of Karl Rove, to be sure—to dislodge the unpopular Bush-Cheney administration from power. Had Kerry won, it is unlikely that Obama would have been imagining himself in the White House prior to 2017; it is likely that Edwards would have been the logical heir apparent for the 2016 nomination.

It also helped that both of Obama's future leading rivals for the Democratic presidential nomination—John Edwards and Hillary Clinton—committed the significant strategic and (many would argue) moral mistake of voting to authorize Bush's invasion of Iraq in October 2002. Going into the 2008 presidential campaign, Obama enjoyed the supreme advantage of not having been in the U.S. Senate when that fateful "war" authorization vote came up—a vote that, during the 2004 Democratic National Convention, he admitted he might have cast in the affirmative, joining Clinton and Edwards and the majority of both the Senate and the House of Representatives (a topic to which I shall return in Chapter 4). More to his credit, he could also point to a pivotal, fall 2002 speech he gave against the Bush administration's Iraq War plans before an antiwar rally in downtown Chicago.[28]

A status quo gone bad can be a profound advantage to those who seem not to have been part of it. While he was actually not particularly progressive in the sense I use in this book or even in comparison to his leading Democratic presidential rivals, Obama has benefited enormously from what we might call a political candidate's version of a frequently noted economic phenomenon—the "privilege of late development." Along with his considerable talents and impressive ambition, he enjoyed a remarkable novelty dividend not of his own making.

Time magazine commentator Joe Klein gave a compelling example of this special "freshness" bonus in a 2006 piece entitled "The Fresh Face." At one point during a summer 2006 speaking engagement attended by nearly a thousand people in Rockford, Illinois, a middle-aged man stood up to say what seem[ed] to be on everyone's mind, with appropriate passion:

> "Congress hasn't done a damn thing this year. I'm tired of the politicians blaming each other. We should throw them all out and start over."
>
> " Including me?" Obama asked.
>
> A chorus of n-o-o-o-s. "Not you," the man says, "You're brand new."[29]

A Multiculturalism/Race Dividend

The biracial and Hawaiian-born Obama's race and ethnocultural heritage and name—his full name is Barack Hussein Obama—added to his novelty dividend. These critical "identity" factors helped voters see him as "brand new," making it easier for him to advance some very traditional and conservative agendas and beliefs (to be examined in detail in the following chapters) under the guise of originality and progressivism. And this has enhanced his attractiveness to U.S. economic, political, and policy elites and power brokers, who have certainly sensed a need for the United States to seem to be dramatically changing the face of power in the wake of the profound damage that George W. Bush's shockingly regressive, oppressive, and inept presidency has done to American authority at home and abroad. As Meg Hirshberg, an influential New Hampshire political donor, told Mundy, "His election would do more to restore people's faith and belief in the U.S. around the world. Can you imagine them being president and first lady? It knocks me out as far as what we would be saying to ourselves and the world. He's not a descendant of slaves, but [his wife Michelle] is. I think it would be a remarkable moment in history."[30]

She was not the only one to see in Obama the promise of a new era of reconciliation in U.S. foreign relations. Some foreign policy elites hoped that, partly because of the Islamic sound of his name and partly because of his unusual upbringing (he lived in Indonesia for three years as a young boy), he would be uniquely positioned to advance American interests in the Middle East and across the Muslim world—areas of special concern and danger for the United States in a world where extremist Islamo-terrorist threats have been furthered by the provocative, deadly, and prolonged American invasions of Afghanistan and Iraq. By Mundy's account, "it does seem that—in the wake of Abu Ghraib and Guantanamo—part of Obama's appeal is the opportunity to send the world a different message about racial tolerance at a moment when this seems more important than ever."[31]

At the same time, Obama's mixed-race identity and multiculturalism fit very well with what Harvard political scientist Robert Putnam found to be the U.S. populace's "hunger for unity" at a time when "the country feels more fragmented than it is comfortable with." Obama's distinctive biography, Putnam told Mundy, makes him specially qualified to seem to reach out across the great American racial divide. "He's black, but not just black," Putnam told Mundy. "A large number of Americans would like to feel like they're in a country where someone like that could be president."[32] Here perhaps Putnam would have spoken more candidly by saying "black, but not all that black," and by adding that Obama has exhibited a special attraction to a certain kind of white voter—generally on the affluent and highly educated side—who would like to support a certain kind of black candidate: one who reinforces such an individual's sense of not being prejudiced while promising not to impose in any meaningful way on the inherited racial privileges of white voters.[33] This is a topic to which I shall return in greater detail in Chapter 3.

The War Goes Incredibly Bad

From the perspective of Obama's political career, the terrible course of the Iraq War was no small good fortune. As we shall see in greater detail in Chapter 5, as far as his 2002 antiwar speech is concerned he deserves credit for joining a considerable portion of the U.S. foreign policy establishment in foretelling potential strategic disaster for an Iraq invasion. But Obama could by no means have predicted the shocking and distinctly incompetent way in which the Bush administration and the Pentagon would conduct "Operation Iraqi Freedom." The administration's bungling turned what many see as a criminal invasion into possibly the greatest fiasco in the history of U.S. foreign policy.[34] That failure fed the steeply declining popularity of the war among the U.S. populace, making Obama's 2002 speech a critical asset for building his national political profile—and a pivotal campaign asset leading into the 2007–2008 presidential campaign.

"A Man for All Seasons?"

The Feel-Good "Meme of the Moment": "How Can You Vote Against the Future?"

That's how Obama happened and where he came from. But what exactly has his presidential candidacy meant and stood for? During the 2007–2008 campaign, Obama projected "an outside-the-Beltway persona, positioning himself," as *Boston Globe* writer Scott Helman put it, "as the Washington change agent that Americans are pining for."[35] But what sort of "hope" and "change" does the self-described "progressive" Obama represent, precisely? In my experience as a close campaign observer, the answer depended on which Obama admirer you spoke to—and which Obama you encountered.

I heard self-identified leftist activists describe Obama as a peace and justice candidate who wanted to end war and redistribute wealth. I was also told by Republicans that Obama was a Democrat they could imagine voting for, precisely because he wasn't especially left-wing or liberal.

I heard a liberal, public intellectual praise Obama's supposed "Jeffersonian" faith in democracy, and a conservative one recommend his "Hamiltonian" pragmatism.

I heard a trade union member praise Obama for egalitarian "idealism," but I also read the comments of a corporate lobbyist extolling Obama for his "reasonableness" and his rejection of "starry-eyed idealism."

I was told that Obama was the living personification of the struggle for black equality once led by Dr. Martin Luther King, Jr.; I also heard white conservatives praise Obama because "he's not all that black" and for refusing to raise the issue of racism.

I heard Obama hailed as a man of peace but I also heard him applauded as a candidate who could be expected to embrace the United States' awesome capacity (and inclination) to wage war when "required." I heard him held up as a hero by hip-hop artists, and I heard him praised for daring to criticize hip-hop's "destructive" lyrics.

The large and often contradictory number of things Obama was said to represent could often seem ridiculous. Equally preposterous, observers sometimes felt, was the tendency of many of his backers to support him on the basis of what seemed to be no specific policy or ideological position at all. A disturbing number of Obama's enthusiastic backers have appeared to embrace his call for "hope" and "change we can believe in" with only the slightest concept of how or why they thought their candidate could "change America," beyond inspiring the nation to "feel good" by having a handsome, young, charismatic, eloquent, and freshly multicultural "rock star" president in the White House. As the columnist Kathleen Parker (an initial Obama enthusiast) noted after Obama's Iowa triumph,

> Barack Obama is the tipping point man, the meme of the moment, the miracle cure for that chronic American malady: feelin' bad about things.
>
> Obama may be "all that," as they say, but let's be clear: Americans are in thrall not with Obama but with the idea of Obama.
>
> As one who swooned early over Obama—the handsome bi-man of unity—and wrote like a love-drunk teenybopper nearly four years ago, I'm familiar with his spell. He's got It and it's easy to be seduced by a charming idea with a dazzling smile.
>
> . . . Whatever his qualifications for the job, the crowds chanting "O-ba-ma, O-ba-ma, O-ba-ma!" betray an undertow of hysteria. This is not the candidate of reason, but of passion. Of emotion. Sen. Good Vibes.
>
> A handful of voters may have some passing knowledge of Obama's policy positions, but it's a safe bet most couldn't get past the keywords "change" and "hope" and the refrain: "He was always against the war." . . .
>
> . . . Obama isn't just the inevitable dream candidate. He is the self-object of Oprah Nation, love child of the therapeutic generation. What he brings to the table no one quite knows. But what he delivers to the couch is human Prozac.
>
> He may or may not be the right man to fill the Oval Office, but Americans will feel too good to notice.[36]

After reading Parker's essay, I flashed back to the large number of Iowan Obama supporters I canvassed (in my role as a John Edwards volunteer from September 2007 through January 3, 2008) who passionately supported Obama but literally could not give a single policy-specific reason for their allegiance beyond a vague sense that he was "against the war." I also remembered the large number of University of Iowa students I met who had clearly made their presidential decision for Obama based on superficial media images and perceived personal characteristics—candidate A or B is "good-looking" or "strong" or "nice" or "tough" or (fill in the blank)—and not on the basis of issues. This dreadful aspect of the United States' corporate-run and political culture (hardly restricted to young adults or the Obama campaign) is partly to blame for the deep and dangerous chasm—what social scientists and others call a "democracy deficit"—between public opinion and public policy when it comes to the leading issues of the day.[37]

I reflected also on how well the students' decisions matched the Obama campaign's efforts to sell its product as the "fresh-faced" candidate of youth, novelty, and "change" as such. Whether going without a tie on the campaign trail or communicating through a Facebook-like Web page, Obama has consistently attempted to present himself to young adults as a symbol of their passion for novelty. He has repeatedly invoked the need to discard the "tired," "divisive," and "old" politics of their parents and grandparents. "In this election," Obama told a cheering crowd of young political activists at the University of South Carolina in late July 2007, "it's our turn. It's your generation's turn," he added, in a curious comment for somebody born in 1961. "Let's bring a new generation of leadership to America."[38]

By the *Chicago Tribune*'s account in late July 2007, this "generational" angle was working, assisted by Obama's multicultural identity and his relatively recent arrival to the national political culture. "Just as his mixed-race heritage and relative newness on the national political scene signal voters that his candidacy represents change," *Tribune* correspondent Mike Dorning reported, "so does his youth, and that perception is strengthened by a broader following among the young. Enthusiasm from a generation that is just coming of age fits with the message of optimism that Obama seeks to convey."

"He has this message of hopefulness and change," political scientist Ann Crigler told Dorning, "and the attachment of youth to that is very important in signaling 'The new generation is with me, and it's time for a new generation of political leadership.'" Crigler was described as an expert on "the use of emotion in politics."[39]

Seven months later, as Obama swept through ten straight primary victories over "old" Hillary Clinton, he was enrapturing overflow crowds in large sports arenas with victory speeches that repeated the poetic New Age phrases, "WE are the CHANGE that we SEEK. We are the ones we've been waiting for." Heavily youthful audiences followed his lead to chant

"Yes, We Can," the title of a widely viewed Obama music video on YouTube that displayed an attractive group of hip and beautiful young celebrities proclaiming their cool approval of the political and cultural icon. "The video, stark in black and white," noted Joe Klein, "raised an existential question for Democrats: How can you not be moved by this? How can you vote against the future? And yet," Klein worried, with reason:

> There was something just a wee bit creepy about the mass messianism . . . of the Obama campaign. "This time can be different because this campaign for the presidency of the United States of America is different. It's different not because of me. It's different because of you." This is not just maddeningly vague but also disingenuous: the campaign is entirely about Obama and his ability to inspire. Rather than focusing on any specific issue or cause—other than an amorphous desire for change—the message is becoming dangerously self-referential. The Obama campaign is all too often about how wonderful the Obama campaign is.[40]

"For All [Ideological] Seasons" . . . or No Season at All

The candidate likely sensed the "maddening" absurdity and potential "messianism" himself. Obama complained early on that he had become "a blank sheet on which people of vastly different political stripes project their own views." Reflecting on his apparent ability to win approval from people of wildly divergent perspectives, Obama claimed to worry that "everybody's projecting—particularly the way I came in—everybody's projecting their own views onto [me]."[41] The danger, he sensed, was that some of his fans were going to become disappointed when they found out that he did not in fact represent an indefinite spectrum of viewpoints and interests and actually held positions many of them rejected. A related risk was that people would jump off "Senator Good Vibes'" ship of "Hope" once they realized that his real-world version of "change" and "unity" would be compromised by an underlying commitment to existing domestic and global disparities and institutions.

The great dark irony behind Obama's reflection was that he and his media-savvy handlers deliberately and naturally pursued universal appeal in pursuit of victory under America's winner-take-all electoral system, where corporate- and media-crafted candidate image tends to trump substantive policy positions and ideological identifications. As *Rolling Stone* political writer Matt Taibbi noted in a February 2007 article bearing the provocative title "Obama Is the Best BS Artist since Bill Clinton,"

> The Illinois Senator is the ultimate modern media creature. . . . His entire political persona is an ingeniously crafted human cipher, a man without race, ideology, geographic allegiances, or, indeed, sharp edges of any kind. You can't

> run against him on the issues because you can't even find him on the ideological spectrum. Obama's "Man for all seasons" act is so perfect in its particulars that just about *anyone* can find a bit of himself somewhere in the candidate's background, whether in his genes or his upbringing. . . . His strategy seems to be to appear as a sort of ideological Universalist, one who spends a great deal of rhetorical energy showing that he recognizes the validity of all points of view, and conversely emphasizes that when he does take hard positions on issues, he often does so reluctantly. . . . His political ideal is basically a rehash of the Blair-Clinton "third way" deal, an amalgam of Kennedy, Reagan, Clinton and the New Deal; he is aiming for the middle of the middle of the middle.[42]

Acting in accord with what Mendell has called "the timeless dance of politics,"[43] the media-savvy Obama Team cultivated his "blank sheet" appeal by tailoring Obama's message in flexible, chameleon-like style to accord with his own shifting audiences. Claiming to stand above ideology and partisan conflict, Obama bashed Wal-Mart and upheld the right to organize unions when talking to labor audiences but extolled free trade, free markets, and entrepreneurial values when addressing "the business community." He invoked the legacy of the Civil Rights Movement when talking to black audiences but downplayed racial justice when speaking to white farmers and workers. He embraced capitalism's supposed virtues when talking to the rich and powerful but stressed its "drawbacks" when addressing the working class and poor.

The campaign and candidate's conscious pursuit of "universalist" ideological hermaphroditism was strongly displayed in Obama's book *The Audacity of Hope*. Released in the fall of 2006, this bestseller marked the unofficial beginning of his presidential candidacy. In the words of conservative writer Steve Sailer, the book "show[ed] his wordsmith's facility at eloquently restating the views of both his liberal supporters and his conservative opponents, leaving implicit the suggestion that all we require to resolve these wearying Washington disputes is to find a man who understands us—a reasonable man, a man very much like, say, Obama—and turn power over to him."[44]

At the same time, the Obama campaign clearly spent a considerable amount of time, money, and energy cultivating the candidate's pure celebrity. It relished and profited from his emergence as a "BaRockstar"—a mass-cultural as well as mass-political persona certain to absorb the diverse and often confused "hopes and dreams" of a mass constituency containing numerous and often contradictory values and positions.

Pluralist and Pragmatic Illusions and the Kennedy Analogy

Obama's ironic, pseudo-self-critical reflection naturally also omitted mention of the profound structural inequality between and among the multiple actors and interests "project[ing] their own views" on him and on other candidates riding the gray waves between Laurence Shoup's "hidden primary of the ruling class" and the promise of American democracy. Beneath the numerous and often conflicting positions Obama has managed to identify himself with, some structurally entrenched interests and attendant worldviews are far more powerful than others in the United States' corporate, imperial, and white majority democracy. The "corporate community's" twisted and conflated visions of "democracy" and virtuous "free market capitalism" have naturally exercised much greater influence over Obama's sense of "practical" and (a major keyword for his campaign) "pragmatic" policy positions than have the perspectives of the labor movement or of progressive leftists. The white electoral majority's reluctance to acknowledge the continuing power of racism in American life has held significantly more sway over Obama than blacks' accurate sense that racism continues to pose significant barriers to black advancement in the United States, as is clear in his domestic "race" agenda—or lack thereof. (Chapter 3 will address Obama and race.) The nation's imperial foreign policy establishment and military-industrial-academic complex has exercised considerably more influence over Obama's foreign relations approach than have domestic opponents of U.S. militarism.

Along the way, as the Obama campaign has known quite well, the nation's hyper-potent corporate media consistently has had more control over the shaping and transmission of "the Obama phenomenon" than any mere citizens' group of local or national significance has had.

For the masters of the "hidden primary," Obama's outwardly pluralist and universal appeal has been a useful illusion. Also functional for these mostly unseen elites has been the tendency of the media, of Obama, and of other campaigns to elevate the personal image and celebrity of the candidate over difficult and detailed matters of policy, power, and worldview. This has all provided welcome cover for the veiled allegiance to dominant hierarchies and doctrines of class, race, and empire that Obama and the other candidates exhibited.

In this and other ways, the "Obama phenomenon" was in fact richly analogous to the "Camelot" phenomenon of "the first television president," John Fitzgerald Kennedy (JFK). JFK was a handsome, young, ethnically novel, charismatic, and highly telegenic chief executive, but his declared commitment to the idealistic but pragmatic and supposedly nonideological goals of national greatness and unity were deceptive, cloaking a deep and dangerous adherence to dominant domestic and imperial hierarchies and doctrines.

Like the Obama phenomenon today, Kennedy's presidential candidacy and victory were understood to represent a victory of image, "youth," "hopefulness," vaguely defined "change," and personal charisma over substantive matters of policy and worldview. However, Obama—like his fellow centrist Democrat JFK (something of a pragmatic neoliberal before his time)—can in fact, through some basic critical investigation, be found on the ideological spectrum.

Like the Kennedy depicted in Bruce Miroff's remarkable (and forgotten) New Left study *Pragmatic Illusions: The Presidential Politics of John Fitzgerald Kennedy* (1976) and Noam Chomsky's instructive *Rethinking Camelot: JFK, the Vietnam War, and US Political Culture* (1993),[45] Obama is, I believe, a "progressive" of a very particular corporate, imperial, and racially accommodationist type. That is the main part of my answer to Kathleen Parker's implied question of exactly what Obama "brings to the table." Such is the dark historical and political heart of the Obama portrayed in this study, with the time-bound caveat that the ultimate shape, destiny, and meaning of the Obama phenomenon remains contingent and subject to future historical influences, including the rising popular demand for "change" that his candidacy has come to embody, channel, and contain.

"The Essence of American Politics"

From the beginning, Obama has run as the unsullied redeemer and righteous healer from beyond the squalid, divisive, and corrupt culture of Washington. He has postured as a knight in shining armor who has come to restore America's lost promise and power by transcending the intense factional, personal, and ideological conflicts and corrupted loyalties that have soured Americans on their political system. In the place of bitterness, cronyism, and dysfunctional political warfare he promises to restore "hope" with a practical "get things done" approach to policy and a therapeutic sense of "unity" binding Americans in a "common destiny and dream." Repeatedly referring to his early opposition (as a state senator) to the disastrous U.S. invasion of Iraq, he has also promised to restore America's purported onetime positive and functional relationship with the world beyond its borders—a relationship often said to have been egregiously damaged by the ruinous arrogance and unilateral militarism of Dick Cheney and George W. Bush.

That narrative, I shall argue, tells at best very partial truths. At worst, it is a cynically manufactured illusion whose acceptance by many reflects the moral and ideological poverty of a dominant political culture that privileges image over substance. The Obama portrayed in this study follows in the corporate-triangulationist "third way" footsteps of similarly pseudo-progressive politicians like Bill Clinton, who made, in the words of the noted left scholar Edward S. Herman, "populist and peace-stressing promises and gestures that [we]re betrayed instantly on the assumption of power."[46] For all his claims to be a noble reformer "above the fray" of America's imperial plutocracy and ideological politics, the Obama discovered and displayed here is no special exception to—and is in many ways an epitome of—what Christopher Hitchens called (in his 1999 study of the Bill and Hillary Clinton phenomenon) "the essence of American politics." "This essence, when distilled," Hitchens explained, "consists of the manipulation of populism by elitism."[47] Relying heavily on candidates' repeated promises to restore "hope" to a populace disillusioned by corporate control, corruption, and inequality—a standard claim of nonincumbent Democratic presidential candidates—this dark essence of U.S. political culture goes back further than the corporate-neoliberal era in which Obama came of political age. It is arguably as old the Republic itself, always torn by the rift between democratic promise and the authoritarian realities of concentrated wealth and power.[48]

Candidate Qualities over Policies and Ideology

Also less than novel is the Obama campaign's exploitation and occasional pure embodiment of what might be considered a second great dark "essence of American politics." I am referring here to the tendency of candidates, party managers, and their public relations handlers to treat citizens as mere spectators by focusing elections on often trivial questions of candidate character and qualities over substantive matters and issues of policy, power, and ideology. The Obama campaign's effort to "brand" its particular political merchandise as a "new and improved" political package is hardly surprising in a time when U.S. political campaigns have reached new levels of corporate-crafted and candidate-centered commodification. U.S. public opinion on policy issues (often quite progressive) hardly matters when, as Noam Chomsky has said, U.S. "elections are skillfully managed" by professional corporate public relations and media experts "to avoid issues and marginalize the underlying population . . . freeing the elected leadership to serve the substantial people."[49] Chomsky's perceptive observation of the 2004 presidential election holds rich relevance for previous and subsequent "quadrennial electoral extravaganzas" in the United States:

> Bush and Kerry can run because they're funded by similar concentrations of private power. Both candidates understand that the election is supposed to stay away from issues. They are creatures of the public relations industry, which keeps the public out of the election process. Their task is to focus attention on the candidate's "qualities," not policies. Is he a leader? A nice guy? Voters end up endorsing an image, not a platform.
>
> The regular vocation of these industries that sell candidates every few years is to sell commodities. Everyone who has turned on a TV set is aware that business devotes enormous efforts to undermine the market of abstract theory, in which informed consumers make rational choices. An ad does not convey information, as it would in a market system; rather, it relies on deceit and illusions to create uninformed consumers who will make irrational choices. Much the same methods are used to undermine democracy by keeping the electorate uninformed and mired in delusion.[50]

The problem has origins dating prior to the corporate age. "By 1840," the prolific American historian Eric Foner has noted, "the mass democratic politics of the Age of Jackson had absorbed the logic of the marketplace. Selling candidates and their images was as important as the positions for which they stood."[51] The two-party political system that emerged from the U.S. Republic's blueprint does not encourage the development of parties with clear ideological and policy differences or strong relationships between voter choices and citizens' actual positions on key policy issues. It leads rival candidates to blur their policy and ideological distinctions in the quest to win those all-important voters in the middle, focusing on personal qualities rather than hard policy and ideological differences.[52] This harsh reality, combined with and furthered by the corporate takeover of much of the U.S. electoral process in the twentieth century, goes a long way toward explaining why a distinctively large number of American citizens—poor and working-class citizens especially—do not participate in American elections, and why substantive policy issues tend to be badly downplayed in U.S. campaigns. It also explains much of the desperation and myopia that leads many ostensibly progressive voters and activists to back corporate-imperial candidates guaranteed to betray populist and peaceful promises upon the assumption of power.

Limited Novelty on Unity, Practicality, Race, and Empire

There is also nothing especially novel or comforting, I argue, about Obama's claim to represent and personify a spirit of healing and national harmony binding Americans in a shared providence and faith. This has been a standard and highly conservative claim of elite U.S. politicians and policymakers since the nation's earliest days. Equally suspect and timeworn is Obama's claim to represent a realistic, objective, technically proficient and flexible pragmatism that could ease public anxieties by rejecting ideology and elevating a "get things done" practicality above dogma and supposedly harmful partisan conflict. This has been a repeated and dangerously authoritarian theme in the history of corporate-liberal presidents and presidential candidates through much of the previous century and was an especially strong idea in the presidency of Obama's role model, JFK. It is rooted in a centrist American liberal tradition that has long evaded critical reflection on its deep service to dominant domestic and global power structures and (anti-ideological' claims to the contrary) ideologies.[53]

There's also less to celebrate than is often believed, I contend, about the racial and foreign policy promises and meaning of Obama's candidacy. Obama's considerable success in winning approval from whites has been all too contingent, I suggest, on the sense that he has been loath to press the still very important issue of race—more accurately, of racism—in any meaningful or consistent way. At the same time, Obama's rise to national celebrity and "viable" presidential-candidate status has tended to feed white America's exaggerated sense that racism is no longer a problem for black Americans. Like its mass cultural, kissing cousin, "the Oprah phenomenon," the Obama phenomenon has threatened to more strongly entrench the deep institutional racism that lives on beneath the fading and partial victories and memory of the Civil Rights Movement.[54]

To make matters worse, Obama's technical blackness has tended to encourage voters of all races to exaggerate his progressivism, granting him aprioristic and significantly undeserved (I argue) "rebel's clothing" to cloak a deeply conservative commitment to existing interrelated hierarchies of class, race, and empire. Along with his charisma and his early opposition to the invasion of Iraq (a position that he later qualified, as we shall see in Chapter 4), Obama's race has helped him strike untold masses of often naive and/or misinformed voters as more progressive, populist, peace-oriented, and egalitarian than the full record of his expressed opinions and behaviors show him to actually be. People who see Obama as a strong progressive opponent of American plutocracy, racism, and militarism/imperialism are in for a possibly rude awakening in the chapters that follow, which portray the presidential candidate as much closer in worldview to previous presidents and current politicians in both dominant U.S. parties than to Obama's oft-claimed historical role model, Martin Luther King, Jr., when it comes to each of what King called "the triple evils that are interrelated": (1) economic exploitation and poverty; (2) racism (deeply understood); and (3) militarism, war, and imperialism.[55]

It's Systemic

Rather than hold up Obama as some sort of singular "poster boy" for the dark essences of U.S. politics suggested here, I seek in this study to understand him within the broader historical, societal, and institutional framework that has long harshly delimited, conditioned, and defined seriously "electable" U.S. presidential candidates. Obama, I argue, possesses no particular immunity to the historical and sociopolitical forces that have long pushed such candidates and the Democratic Party toward the corporate, imperial, and racially accommodationist "center." The significantly power-friendly, militarist, and neoliberal Obama portrayed in this study is hardly the first—and certainly not the last—conciliatory and conservative Democrat to be produced by the U.S. election system and political culture.

Consistent with this argument, this book contains numerous critical reflections on other leading Democratic politicos, past and present, including Obama's main competitors for the 2008 Democratic presidential nomination.

While I have chosen in this volume to focus above all on the Obama phenomenon (an especially relevant and powerful development in the long history of progressive illusion generated by America's corporate-crafted "winner-take-all" political system), I do not wish to leave the impression that other leading Democrats—and the Democratic Party as a whole—do not deserve searching, radical-democratic criticism along the lines applied to Obama in this study. They do. Obama is, I think, an almost perfect-storm epitome of a deeper problem with U.S. elections, the American political tradition, and late-capitalist political culture: the inherent conflict between the popular democratic promise and authoritarian, corporate-imperial reality. Whether the phenomenon will—against historical odds and its admittedly brief historical record to date—function in any meaningful way on behalf of that promise remains, I am willing to acknowledge, an open question.

What's a "Progressive"?

Some final comments on the terminology used in this study and my qualifications to write it. As any good historian of the United States in the late nineteenth and early twentieth centuries (the Progressive Age) knows, the word "progressive" can elicit numerous, diverse, and often contradictory shades of sociopolitical and ideological meaning, ranging from the corporate liberalism of the onetime National Civic Federation to the middle-class reformism of a Jane Addams and the democratic socialism of leftist presidential candidate Eugene Debs.[56] During my tenure as director of research at a corporate-captive, post–civil rights, social service agency in black Chicago between 2000 and 2005, I periodically received issue briefings through an Obama associate from a think tank affiliated with the Democratic Leadership Council (DLC)—an organization whose historical mission has long been to move the Democratic Party away from its connections to the civil rights, labor, and environmental movements and closer to big business. The name of this think tank is the Progressive Policy Institute.

My own "progressive," moral and ideological heritage hails from a left-libertarian tradition that includes such notable thinkers as Gerrard Winstanley, Karl Marx, Rosa Luxembourg, Rudolph Rocker, George Orwell, and Noam Chomsky. My antiauthoritarian vision of the good and truly democratic society is distinctly unimaginable and "utopian" from the perspective of dominant ideologies today. Its realization would require something along the lines of a revolution in existing political-economic structures and cultural frameworks. At the same time, I have long worked as a real-time progressive, seeking substantive change—"reform"—within the "really existing" U.S. sociopolitical order. By "progressive," I mean a set of values and policies aligned with the following interrelated principles: economic equality and social justice; opposition to socially constructed hierarchies of class, race, gender, ethnicity, nationality, and empire; ecological sustainability; political democracy ("one person, one vote," and equal policymaking influence for all regardless of personal wealth, status, and connections); and the egalitarian and participatory organization of work and schooling. Along with the left-liberal group Progressive Democrats of America (PDA) and much of the U.S. populace, I support the following policy priorities:

- A rapid end to the war in Iraq and the military occupation of that country and a redirection of funds toward social needs at home and humanitarian aid in Iraq.
- Quality health care for all on the basis of a single-payer, government health-insurance system that replaces private insurers, for administrative savings of $300 billion or more.
- Economic justice through progressive taxation, fair trade, increased labor and consumer protections, significantly expanded union organizing and bargaining rights, enhanced government regulation of the financial and corporate sectors, and expanded government spending and investment in the public good.
- Clean, fair, and transparent elections through comprehensive public financing, among other key electoral measures, to reduce the disproportionately high influence of concentrated wealth on the U.S. "dollar democracy."
- Reduced dependence on fossil fuels and increased investment in clean energy and public transportation to reduce greenhouse gases, protect the environment, and stem the tide of global warming.[57]

I would add at least two things to this list:

- A policy of rolling back the extreme budget and culture of U.S. militarism and imperialism and reinvestment of those funds in social justice, the environment, and the like. The Iraq War is but a large and distinctly troubling (indeed criminal) expression of American hyper-militarism and the related dangerous and expensive U.S. quest for global dominance.
- Serious efforts to end persistent and endemic racial and gender bias in the operation and structure of American institutions and policies.

As an anticapitalist left-libertarian, I am skeptical about the extent to which these principles can ever be meaningfully honored under the currently hegemonic, corporate-state profit system. But reform and revolution are not polar opposites. They are dialectically inseparable and mutually reinforcing aspects of a left-democratic political project that permits activists on the left to retain their "big" vision and identity while working on a practical basis with liberals, moderates, and even conservatives for specific, objectively progressive measures like the public financing of political campaigns, enhanced union-organizing rights, and mandatory caps on carbon pollution.

Contrary to one strongly pro-Obama writer's characterization of me,[58] I am capable of making pragmatic and realistic accommodations with "really existing" American politics. During the long period leading up to the pivotal Democratic presidential caucus in Iowa, for example, I (despite being well to the left of Dennis Kucinich) worked as a volunteer for the John Edwards campaign, knocking on hundreds of doors and making thousands of phone calls in and around eastern Iowa in the summer and fall of 2007. This activism was based on three basic and interrelated calculations: (1) that the Republican Party was too dangerously extremist and reactionary for progressives not to try to prevent it from maintaining control of the most powerful single office on earth in November 2008; (2) that the highly imperfect (from a left perspective) Edwards was the most electable of the viable Democratic presidential candidates; (3) that Edwards was the most progressive of the viable Democratic contenders (a judgment that will find some support in Chapters 1 and 3 of this study), especially on domestic policy.[59]

It is not my intention in this book to criticize Obama only or mainly for not being a leftist radical like me. I cannot honestly deny that this criticism is present here, for I think that he and other leading public personalities could contribute more to America and the world by resisting dominant power structures than they presently are by trying to accommodate and climb them. Still, my criticism of Obama focuses mainly on the extent to which he has lived up to his claim to be simply a "progressive" Democratic reformer. I hold no fantastic expectations that Obama could or would ever embrace hard-left ideals.

Whether or not Obama could or would conduct a recognizably half-progressive presidency (leading "another New Deal") if he reaches the White House is not something I would have the audacity to try to foretell. What I will dare to suggest, based on Obama's record and on the deeper history, structure, and culture of U.S. politics, is that an Obama administration would be likely to move in a relatively conservative direction unless and until it was pushed to the left from below by an aroused and organized populace.

Angle of Experience

During the late 1990s I was an urban social policy researcher producing project studies on various Illinois issues that Obama deliberated upon (chiefly campaign finance and welfare reform) in the Illinois state legislature. Through this and related activist involvements, I learned a fair amount about the intersections between race, class, money, politics, and policy in Illinois, where Obama served as a state senator between 1997 and 2004.

Between 2000 and 2005 I was the research director at the Chicago Urban League, a predominantly black civil rights and social service agency located in the historical heart of Chicago's South Side black ghetto. During that time I occasionally worked with black legislators and had some marginal involvement with Obama himself. I organized a fall 2002 conference where he spoke on incarceration issues, referring to a study I did on racially disparate mass imprisonment.[60] I also managed a project study on school technology that he funded through the state of Illinois.

Finally, between August 2007 and January 3, 2008, I was a volunteer for the Edwards campaign and had a great deal of voter contact with mostly white Obama supporters in Iowa City and in Muscatine County in eastern Iowa. I was an Edwards precinct captain on the east side of Iowa City and attended a caucus at a local high school (City High), where "my" candidate (about whom I had few progressive illusions[61]) and Hillary Clinton were rolled over by waves of "Obamania" in a heavily Caucasian, middle-class, and academic constituency—an interesting and exciting thing to behold on January 3 of 2008. I saw Obama and other candidates speak on numerous occasions in Iowa—where the U.S. presidential campaign begins in April of the year before the election—and had repeated contact with Obama campaign staffers in the eastern part of the state. I've been privileged, if that's the right word, to see the Obama phenomenon at its inception, on the ground and from the bottom up, in Chicago and Springfield, Illinois, and in Iowa.

CHAPTER 1

Obama's "Dollar Value"

On condition of anonymity, one Washington lobbyist I spoke with was willing to point out the obvious: that big donors would not be helping out Obama if they didn't see him as a "player." The lobbyist added: "What's the dollar value of a starry-eyed idealist?"

—KEN SILVERSTEIN, *HARPER'S*, NOVEMBER 2006

Mr. Obama is widely portrayed, not least by himself, as a transformational figure who will usher in a new era. But his actual policy proposals, though liberal, tend to be cautious and relatively orthodox.

—PAUL KRUGMAN, *NEW YORK TIMES*, MARCH 28, 2008

In his view of history, in his respect for tradition, in his skepticism that the world can be changed any way but very, very slowly, Obama is deeply conservative.

—LARISSA MACFARQUHAR, FROM *THE NEW YORKER*, MAY 7, 2007

"ONE EVENING IN FEBRUARY 2005, in a four-hour meeting stoked by pepperoni pizza and great ambition," the *Chicago Tribune* reported in the spring of 2007, "Senator Barack Obama and his senior advisors crafted a strategy to fit the Obama 'brand.'" The after-hours session, called by Obama's Senate staff and including Axelrod, took place just weeks after Obama had been sworn into the U.S. Senate. According to *Tribune* Washington Bureau reporters Mike Dorning and Christi Parsons, in an article entitled "Carefully Crafting the Obama Brand,"

> The charismatic celebrity-politician had rocketed from the Illinois state legislature to the U.S. Senate, stirring national interest. The challenge was to

> maintain altitude despite the limited tools available to a freshman senator whose party was in a minority.
>
> Yet even in those early days, Obama and his advisors were thinking ahead. Some called it the "2010–2012–2016" plan: a potential bid for governor or re-election to the Senate in 2010, followed by a bid for the White House as soon as 2012, not 2016. The way to get there, they decided, was by carefully building a record that matched the brand identity: Obama as a unifier and consensus builder, an almost postpolitical leader.
>
> The staffers in that after-hours session, convened by Obama's Senate staff and including Chicago political advisor David Axelrod, planned a low-profile strategy that would emphasize workhorse results over headlines. Obama would invest in the long-term profile by not seeming too eager for the bright lights.[1]

This *Tribune* story is disturbing on numerous levels. It suggests a degree of cynicism, manipulation, and ambition that does not fit very well with the progressive and hopeful image that the Obama campaign has projected. It calls to mind a tension between virtuous public claims and selfish goals behind the scenes. The politician being sold would make sure to seem non-ambitious—"not seeming too eager for the bright lights" and privileging hard work over "headlines"—and respectful toward fellow members of the political class ("establishing good relationships with . . . colleagues"). But, by Dorning and Parsons' account, Obama and his team were actually and quite eagerly all about "the bright lights" and "the headlines" in a "long-term" sense. They were already scheming for the presidency less than a month into his Senate seat. The image of Obama as a humble and hard-working rookie who got along with his colleagues across partisan lines was only part of a marketing strategy to promote him on the path to higher—the highest—office. The great "reformer" Obama may have just become only the third black to sit in the august U.S. Senate since Reconstruction, but for him and his team the Senate was largely a marketing platform for the Next Big Thing—a place to build his reputation as a "unifier" and "consensus builder." They seemed unconcerned about the authoritarian implications of the concept of a "postpolitical leader," a commercialized trademark who would rise above democratic and ideological contestation on the road to power atop the most powerful nation in history.

At the same time, the term "Obama brand" suggested the commodified nature of a political culture that tends to reduce elections to corporate-crafted marketing contests revolving around candidate images and characters packaged and sold by corporate consultants and public relations experts. It implied an officeholder politician for sale and more immersed in the world of money, commerce, and capitalism than in public service.

"A Game Only They Can Afford to Play"

And then, one weekend after announcing his presidential candidacy in Springfield, Illinois, in February 2007, between trips to the critical early primary states of Iowa and New Hampshire, Obama attended an event that put these corporate connections on display. "Amid the whirlwind weekend of campaign speeches and events," *Chicago Tribune* reporters David Jackson and John McCormick noted two months later, "his entourage arrived at the Hyatt Regency Chicago on East Wacker Drive, where eager fans grazed sandwich and fruit platters and offered checks and credit card payments of up to $2,300." The Chicago mayor's brother, former Clinton Commerce Secretary William Daley, was "one of the more prominent faces in a crowd of more than 700 who contributed an estimated $1 million."

The "crowd" came largely from "global Chicago's" heavily corporate-connected legal and financial elite.[2] It stood in interesting contrast to the senator's Springfield claim that he was running to take America back from "the special interests who've turned our government into a game only they can afford to pay." In his candidacy announcement, Obama said, "They write the checks and you get stuck with the bills; they get the access while you get to write a letter; they think they own the government, but we're here to take it back. The time for that politics is over. It's time to turn the page."[3]

Would an Obama presidency really "turn the page" away from big-money influence and melt the icy stranglehold that concentrated wealth has long had on U.S. politics and policy? Without forgetting that campaigns and legislative careers do not completely or always reliably predict presidential policies, I suggest in this chapter that an Obama White House could be expected to tilt toward elite economic interests—its leading inhabitant's onetime populist rhetoric aside—unless and until it was compelled to behave otherwise by an aroused and organized citizenry.

Historical Context: Past Democratic (Party) Betrayals

Like many other Democratic politicians past and present, Obama has throughout his political career walked the thin moral tightrope set up for political candidates under the United States' "dollar democracy." His position between the power of big money and the democratic ideal is hardly unique in the history of the Democratic Party, its presidents, and its presidential candidates. Under the influence of corporate and financial elites, the party's move to the corporate center and away from economic justice on behalf of the poor and the working class—the mission it still purports to uphold with special intensity during campaign seasons—began long before Obama arrived on the political scene. Some review of that history is useful for understanding the nature of the dilemmas faced by those who seek meaningful democratic progress under an Obama (or any other Democratic) presidency.[4]

Jimmy Carter: "Protecting Corporate Wealth and Power"

The Democratic presidency of Jimmy Carter is a case in point. Rising to power on the basis of his promise to recapture and reinvigorate a citizenry disillusioned by the Vietnam War, Watergate, deepening economic insecurity, and growing awareness of environmental deterioration and social disarray, Carter made a populist pitch to American voters. He may have been a millionaire peanut grower, but he put himself forward as an ordinary, plain-speaking farmer moved by simple decency to give ordinary Americans a new sense of hope and change.

Making a special appeal to those who saw themselves as besieged by the rich and powerful, Carter made a heavily publicized speech to the legal profession in which he denounced the use of law to serve and protect the wealthy few. Carter promised to eliminate flagrant tax loopholes for corporations and the rich and proposed to raise the tax on capital gains and reduce rates on individuals. He also promised to introduce major health-care reform providing coverage for millions of uninsured Americans. His personal campaign mission was to restore hope in Washington and America by shrinking the distance between the American people and American politics, and the promise to roll back the power of special corporate interests was a key part of that promise.

Once he attained power, however, Carter "remained," in Howard Zinn's words, "within the historic political boundaries of the American system, protecting corporate wealth and power, maintaining a huge military machine that drained the national wealth." He appointed a strong militarist and nuclear-power advocate as secretary of energy and made numerous other cabinet appointments calculated to win approval from the upper reaches of the "business community." His 1977 tax reform did little to help working-class and poor people, and the tax bill that Congress passed and Carter signed the following year "was perhaps the most regressive measure since the 1920s," according to noted liberal author and journalist William Greider. Renowned economist Robert Lekachman said the bulk of the 1978 tax measure's "benefits accrue[d] to the affluent individuals and corporations." Carter's energy bill benefited oil companies more than consumers, and the health-reform measures he pledged never materialized.[5]

Reflecting his declared neoliberal desire to reduce the size of government and lessen its control over the "free market," Carter supported business-backed legislation that concentrated corporate control and deepened economic insecurity for consumers and workers by deregulating airlines, trucking, natural gas, and banks. He made no effort to expand or renew the antipoverty and social welfare initiatives of his Democratic predecessor, Lyndon B. Johnson, or to strengthen the American labor movement through aggressive enforcement of the National Labor Relations Act. Under Carter, federal funds that might have gone to inner-city schools and health and social services were diverted instead to an expanded military budget even as the press published numerous reports of wasteful "defense" spending and rampant corporate-Pentagon corruption.

By Greider's account, "Carter's aides, like Reagan's, responded mainly to industry complaints, not broad principle."[6] In 1979, as Carter diverted money from social programs and contradicted his aim of shrinking government by approving giant, corporate-friendly Pentagon budgets, the Children's Defense Fund reported that one in every seven American children lacked a known primary health-care source and that one in every three children under the age of seventeen had never seen a dentist.

The confrontation with the plutocratic Reagan administration hardly jolted the Democratic Party out of its rightward drift and back toward the more populist and working-class leanings of the New Deal era. The candidacies of centrist Walter Mondale (1984) and Michael Dukakis (1988) "saw party leaders and pundits massed protectively, standing shoulder to shoulder against the last coherent left populist campaign mounted within the framework of the Democratic Party, by Jesse Jackson and the Rainbow Coalition."[7]

Bill Clinton: "Putting People First"

Things didn't get much better, from a progressive or populist perspective at least, under the Democratic presidency of William Jefferson Clinton. The 1992 Clinton campaign's rhetoric contained a "strong streak of populism," starting with a speech that excoriated the 1980s as "a gilded age of greed."[8] Clinton claimed he would restore hope in America by "putting people first" over and above the big corporate interests and privileged few. Contrasting his plebian origins and passionate concern for ordinary working families with the perceived plutocratic indifference of the arch-aristocratic George H.W. Bush, Clinton promised to strengthen unions, fight poverty, introduce universal health care, and reject the regressive, corporate-globalizationist North American Free Trade Agreement (NAFTA). Clinton was going to usher in a new era of national "unity" that would restore the connection between the American people and U.S. politics by elevating shared goals of democracy and equality above partisan divisions, economic privilege, and special-interest control.

Once in office, however, Clinton "put Wall Street in charge of national economic strategy."[9] His actions most especially reflected not his egalitarian promises but rather his leading role in the rise of the Democratic Leadership Council (DLC). Formed by business-oriented party elites to increase the party's distance from labor, environmentalism, blacks, and civil rights, the DLC's mission was to steer the Democratic Party closer to the corporate, imperial, southern, suburban, and racially accommodationist center. Its goal was to advance postpartisan corporate convergence between Democratic and Republican agendas at the elite level and to impose economically and racially regressive policies underneath the cloak of "progressive" strategy and a "pragmatic," "get-things-done" realism.

Clinton's policies and appointments stayed true to his DLC credentials. They also reflected his captivity to powerful corporate and Wall Street interests that key corporate Clinton advisers—including former Goldman Sachs CEO and Clinton Treasury Secretary Robert Rubin—famously instructed him not to buck. After attaining office on the basis of the Democratic Party's standard egalitarian vows, the president "from Hope" quickly defied mainstream public support for socially democratic policies by conducting the public business in regressive accord with the interrelated neoliberal and racially disparate imperatives of empire and inequality.

Clinton's domestic agenda was first announced as a gigantic jobs-creation program coupled with a determined effort to guarantee health care for all. But, as Howard Zinn has noted, Clinton quickly betrayed these declared campaign priorities by concentrating on reduction of the deficit, which had drastically increased under Reagan and George Bush the First. This emphasis "meant that there would be no bold programs of expenditures for universal health care, education, child care, housing, the environment, the arts, or job creation," wrote Zinn.[10] Clinton's "small gestures" toward social democracy did "not come close to what was needed in a nation where one-fourth of the children lived in poverty; where homeless people lived on the streets in every major city; where women could not look for work for lack of child care; where the air, the water were deteriorating dangerously."[11]

More than being merely inadequate to the needs of America's millions of truly disadvantaged citizens, the Clinton administration with the help of a Newt Gingrich–led Congress actually attacked the disproportionately nonwhite poor in numerous interrelated ways. Clinton signed a punitive neoliberal "welfare-reform" bill that ended the federal government's guarantee of financial help to impoverished families with dependent children. By forcing poor families getting federal cash-assistance (mainly nonwhite, single-parent units) to find employment without establishing concomitant government programs to create or directly provide livable-wage jobs,

Clinton flooded the nation's low- and poverty-wage and no-benefits job market with hundreds of thousands of defenseless new proletarians. He also scored points with the grinders of the poor by taking welfare benefits away from legal as well as illegal immigrants. It was all done in the name of "Personal Responsibility," "Work Opportunity," and "Reconciliation," to use the key Orwellian phrases of the Clinton-Gingrich welfare-elimination program.

Meanwhile, Clinton increased economic insecurity in poor and working-class American communities by signing the investor-rights NAFTA bill without requiring that it contain significant labor and environmental protections for American workers and consumers. NAFTA destroyed tens of thousands of American industrial jobs by tearing down long-established regulatory barriers to the movement of corporate capital and commodities across the U.S.-Mexican border.

Clinton claimed that "the era of big government" was over. He was more than content, however, to sustain funding for the regressive, repressive, and militaristic "right hand of the state." His concern with balanced budgets did not extend to the prison- and military-industrial complexes. As Zinn noted, Clinton's federal government "continued to spend at least $250 billion a year to maintain the military machine" and thereby feed the coffers of the rich and powerful "defense" corporations that had long come to rely on the Pentagon system to feed investors' bottom lines.[12] It was only the left hand of the state, the part that serves the poor and nonaffluent majority, that Clinton targeted in his quest for deficit reduction.

Ironically (or fittingly), given his administration's insistence on throwing poor people on the mercies of the "free" labor market, where most Americans obtain (uniquely among industrialized states) their health insurance, Clinton ended his presidency without making any serious effort to meaningfully deliver on his initial health-insurance promises. He also failed to advance any meaningful initiative to protect the rights of beleaguered workers or to increase the woefully inadequate minimum wage.

Revealingly described as "recognizably progressive" by Obama in 2006, the Clinton campaign and presidency were excellent case studies in the plutocratic dance of populism and elitism that constitutes Hitchens's "essence of American politics." As George Bush the First was showing himself to be hopelessly out of touch with popular concerns, Clinton pitched his White House bid around Jeffersonian promises to the working majority and then proceeded to construct a richly Hamiltonian, corporate-neoliberal administration that tended to serve the rich and powerful and punish the poor. That performance was richly consistent with the Reagan presidency, which demonstrated a special capacity for selling militantly regressive, corporate-plutocratic policy as the politics of the "little guy."[13]

John "Not a Redistribution Democrat" Kerry and "Dropping the Class Language That Once Distinguished Them Sharply from Republicans"

Democratic presidential candidate John F. Kerry's run for the White House offered no progressive departure from the neoliberal Clinton legacy. As veteran radical historian Gabriel Kolko noted on the eve of the 2004 election,

> His statements on domestic policy in favor of fiscal restraint and lower deficits, much less tax breaks for large corporations, are utterly lacking in voter appeal. Kerry is packaging himself as an economic conservative who is also strong on defense spending—a Clinton clone—because that is precisely how he feels. His advisors are the same investment bankers who helped Clinton get the nomination and then raised the funds to get him elected and then defined his economic policy. The most important of them is Robert Rubin, who became Treasury Secretary, and he and his cronies are running the Kerry campaign and will also dictate his economic agenda should he win. . . . Kerry is, to his core, an ambitious patrician educated in elite schools and anything but a populist.[14]

Consistent with his vast personal fortune and related aristocratic bearing, the militantly "centrist" Kerry campaign's socioeconomic radar barely registered anyone beneath the middle class. As he told a wealthy donor audience at a $25,000-a-plate breakfast in Manhattan's 21 Club in April 2004, "I am not a redistribution [of wealth] Democrat." Given the corrosive impact of America's steep socioeconomic disparities—the top 1 percent owned nearly 40 percent of the United States' wealth by the end of the twentieth century—on functioning democracy, this statement raised troubling questions about whether he was any kind of democrat at all. Given the closeness of the 2004 race and the unpopularity of the heavily plutocratic George W. Bush administration by the summer of 2004, it seems possible that Kerry could have won the election if he'd run further to the populist left after achieving the Democratic nomination.[15]

His failure to do so followed in perfect accord with an important and widely read but commonly misunderstood book by historian and cultural critic Thomas Frank on why many working-class Americans vote Republican instead of following their supposed natural "pocketbook" interest in supporting the Democrats. *What's the Matter with Kansas? How Conservatives Won the Heart of America,*[16] released just before Bush defeated Kerry with no small help from working-class whites, has generally been taken to have argued that Democrats lost those heartland voters with excessive liberalism on cultural issues like abortion, gun rights, religion, gay marriage, and gender roles. In this view, the Democrats let the GOP conjure working-class voters away from their real economic interests with diversionary nonmaterial concerns.[17] At the end of his book, however, Frank made it clear that he blamed the DLC-inspired shift of the Democratic Party to the business-friendly right and away from honest discussion of—and opposition to—economic and class inequality for much of whatever success the GOP achieved in winning over white, working-class voters. Frank noted that the DLC had long been advancing the abandonment of blue-collar workers as part of its project of courting white-collar professionals and, above all, corporations. To attract the votes and, most importantly, the money of these elite constituencies, DLC-style "New Democrats" decided, the party should stand solid in support of abortion rights and gun control, but make "endless concessions on economic issues, on welfare, NAFTA, Social Security, labor law, privatization, deregulation. . . . Such Democrats explicitly rule out what they deride as class warfare and take great pains to emphasize their friendliness with business. Like the conservatives," Frank noted, they "take economic issues off the table." They figured that working-class voters would never defect since they had nowhere else to go, and Democrats remained "marginally better on economic issues than Republicans." By Frank's account,

> The problem is not that Democrats are monolithically pro-choice or anti–school prayer; it's that by dropping the class language that once distinguished them sharply from Republicans they have left themselves vulnerable to cultural wedge issues like guns and abortion and the rest whose hallucinatory appeal would ordinarily be overshadowed by material concerns. We are in an environment where Republicans talk constantly about class—in a coded way, to be sure—but where Democrats are afraid to bring it up.[18]

The French-speaking and Ivy-League-aristocrat Kerry's problem wasn't just that workers were diverted from their real economic interests by liberal cultural elitism and smart Republicans who knew how to press cultural issues to get working-class folks to vote against their own pocketbooks. It was also that he followed in the footsteps of previous Democrats by collaborating with Republicans in taking class injustice and the workers' material and (I would add moral) economic issues off the table, thereby encouraging lower-class resentment (which abhors a vacuum) to flow into reactionary channels.[19]

JFK: Technical Expertise "in the Service to Corporate Capitalism"

Lest we conclude that such Democratic presidential departures from the party of Franklin Delano Roosevelt and its declared progressive mission are unique to the neoliberal, post–New Deal era, it's worth noting how President

John F. Kennedy figures into this shift. JFK's frequently declared sympathies for the poor and working class "invariably took a back seat," according to Bruce Miroff, the author of the brilliant study *Pragmatic Illusions: The Presidential Politics of John F. Kennedy*, "to the real determinants of policy: political calculation and economic doctrine." As Miroff noted,

> Political calculation led Kennedy to appease the corporate giants and their allies in government. Economic doctrine told him that the key to the expansion and health of the economy was the health and expansion of those same corporate giants. The architects of Kennedy's "New Economics" liked to portray it as the technically sophisticated and politically neutral management of a modern industrial economy. It is more accurately portrayed as a pragmatic liberalism in the service of corporate capitalism.
>
> . . . His wage guidelines, and other efforts at terminating labor-management conflict over the distribution of income, fit neatly with business's long-standing objective of holding wage costs steady. His liberalization of depreciation allowances furnished business with a tax break which it had sought unsuccessfully from the Eisenhower administration. His proposed reduction in corporate income and personal income taxes in the higher brackets approached tax reductions earlier proposed by the National Association of Manufacturers and the U.S. Chamber of Commerce. Corporate executives may not have had Kennedy's ear, but the functional result was not so different than if they had.[20]

Consistent with that judgment, the Kennedy administration's economic policies conferred significantly greater advantage to the affluent than they did to working-, middle-, and lower-class Americans. Seen against the backdrop of JFK's frequently expressed empathy for America's underdogs, his administration's record on economic equity was less than progressive. The regressive nature of his "New Economics" was cloaked by his recurrent, much-publicized spats with certain members of the business community (the executives of U.S. Steel, above all), his repeated statements of concern for labor and the poor, and his claim to advance a purely technical and pragmatic economic agenda that elevated practical management and administrative expertise, what Kennedy called "some grand warfare of ideologies."[21]

The Selective Skewering of Populist Hypocrisy

Christopher Hitchens's caustic description of the "essence" of the U.S. political game and the Democratic Party is just as relevant today as it was when Reagan or Clinton held power. As I shall argue in greater detail in this book's final chapter, this is largely for structural reasons that have relatively little to do with either the moral character or the personal qualities of Obama, Hillary Clinton, John Edwards, or any other Democratic contender for office at any level past, present, and (no doubt) future. Candidates cannot generally succeed in the highly expensive winner-take-all U.S. electoral process without backing from the stupendous concentrations of private power in America, sources of funding that work to "take the risk out of democracy"[22] by funding campaigns and controlling "public" (corporate) communications and culture in ways that set dangerously narrow and business-friendly parameters of acceptable debate.[23] This harsh reality touched every presidential candidacy in 2007–2008, either by pushing viable campaigns in a more conservative direction in plutocratic ways or by making excessively left (Kucinich), populist (even Edwards), and anti-imperial (Mike Gravel and Ron Paul) contenders inherently unviable.

By early 2007, however, dominant corporate ("mainstream") U.S. media[24] seemed to want voters to believe that populist hypocrisy was a relevant problem only or mainly for John Edwards. When it wasn't ignoring Edwards' strongly pro-labor campaign to portray the Democratic primaries as a two-way contest between Mrs. Clinton and Obama, big U.S. media's treatment of Edwards was inordinately focused on the discrepancy between his individual fortune and his strongly voiced opinions against poverty and economic inequality.

Again and again, voters heard from news broadcasters, political commentators, and comedians (especially Jay Leno) about Edwards's $500 haircut, his opulent new mansion (described in the *New York Times Magazine* by Matt Bai as "the largest home in the county, a 28,000-square-foot mansion with its own indoor basketball and squash courts"), his exorbitant lecture fees, and his presence on the board of a Wall Street hedge fund that invested in "exactly the kind of subprime-mortgage dealers that Edwards has repeatedly castigated for preying on the poor."[25] These and other facts harped on by Leno, Bai, and others (including me) certainly showed that John Edwards lived on the privileged side of the "two Americas" that he talked about so much in his presidential campaign—the rich and the not rich.

Hillary, Inc.

But Edwards was hardly the only leading presidential candidate to belie populist rhetoric with elite and corporate connections and actions. All of the leading Republican candidates followed in Ronald Reagan's footsteps by trying to disguise their party's militantly regressive and plutocratic agenda as the politics of ordinary Americans.

Hillary Clinton tried to sound like a grassroots union or civil rights organizer when talking to labor, minority, and activist audiences about how in her words "everything has been skewed to help the privileged and powerful at the expense of everybody else."[26] But her progressive claims were badly compromised by the fact that she was heavily reliant on large-scale corporate contributions and surrounded herself with advisers "who represent some of the weightiest interests in corporate America," as journalist Ari Berman wrote. "Her chief strategist, Mark Penn," Berman continued, "not only polls for the America's biggest companies but runs one of the world's premier PR agencies."[27] As Berman noted in an article in *The Nation* bearing the title "Hillary Inc." in the spring of 2007,

> A bevy of current and former Hillary advisers, including her communications guru, Howard Wolfson, are linked to a prominent lobbying firm—the Glover Park Group—that has cozied up to the pharmaceutical industry and Rupert Murdoch. Her fundraiser in chief, Terry McAuliffe, has the priciest Rolodex in Washington, luring high-rolling contributors to Clinton's campaign. Her husband, since leaving the presidency, has made millions giving speeches and counsel to investment banks like Goldman Sachs and Citigroup. They house, in addition to other Wall Street firms, the Clintons' closest economic advisers, such as Bob Rubin and Roger Altman, whose DC brain trust, the Hamilton Project, is Clinton's economic team in waiting. . . . "She's got a deeper bench of big money and corporate supporters than her competitors," says Eli Attie, a former speechwriter to Vice President Al Gore. Not only is Hillary more reliant on large donations and corporate money than her Democratic rivals, but advisers in her inner circle are closely affiliated with union-busters, GOP operatives, conservative media and other Democratic Party antagonists.
>
> . . . Her ties to corporate America say as much . . . about what she values and cast doubt on her ability and willingness to fight for the progressive policies she claims to champion. . . .
>
> . . . Courting elements of the Democratic base while signaling to the corporate right that she won't shake up the system is a tricky juggling act.[28]

Obama's Money

How different, if at all, is "the Obama brand" from other recent candidacies? What could and should voters and citizens expect from an Obama White House when it comes to the interrelated questions of corporate power and economic justice? Without discounting the contingency and unpredictability of future events and the possibility that Obama would be more progressive in office than he has been as a presidential candidate and a U.S. senator, I believe his administration would follow the trend of the past half-century of Democratic presidencies. The record captured in this chapter is less than inspiring from a progressive perspective.

"Not Because of Folks Writing Big Checks"

The mainstream U.S. media, while dismissing Edwards' supposedly false populism and portraying Hillary Clinton as the candidate with connections to big money, largely ignored this angle of the Obama story. But in fact, Obama has been engaged in the same "juggling act" as Mrs. Clinton and other candidates during the presidential campaign of 2007 and 2008. After announcing for the presidency, Obama joined Edwards in refusing donations from corporate lobbyists and Political Action Committees (PACs), challenging Clinton to do the same and "casting his decision as a noble departure from the ways of Washington," as *Boston Globe* reporter Scott Helman put it.[29]

"Now" is "the time," Obama told 10,000 listeners in Iowa City in April 2007, echoing key passages from his candidacy announcement, for Americans "to turn the page" on "old" and "cynical" money- and power-dominated "politics."[30] "The people in this stadium," Obama told a Chicago Soldier Field crowd of union members in the summer of 2007, "need to know who we're going to fight for. The reason that I'm running for president is because of you, not because of folks who are writing big checks, and that's a clear message that has to be sent, I think, by every candidate."[31] And in Greenville, South Carolina, he said, "Washington lobbyists haven't funded my campaign, they won't run my White House, and they will not drown out the voices of working Americans when I am president."[32]

In e-mail messages sent in the summer of 2007, Obama told supporters that "candidates typically spend a week like this—right before the critical June 30 financial reporting deadline—on the phone, day and night, begging Washington lobbyists and special interest PACs to write huge checks. Not me. Our campaign has rejected the money-for-influence game and refused to accept funds from registered federal lobbyists and political action committees."[33]

By the time he was employing populist language to denounce big-money influence, however, Obama had become a millionaire. He had recently purchased an opulent Georgian Revival mansion below price at $1.65 million, thanks to some help from a felony-indicted political fund-raiser and longtime friend named Tony Rezko.[34] More importantly, he had raked in impressive campaign largesse from some very rich and powerful interests. His roster of top contributors included Goldman Sachs; Exelon Corporation (a leading midwestern utility and the world's leading nuclear power plant operator); the leading global financial firms JP Morgan Chase, UBS AG, Lehman Brothers, Morgan Stanley, Credit Suisse, and Citadel Investment Groups; leading corporate law and lobbying firms (Kirkland & Ellis and Skadden, Arps, Sidley Austin LLP); and some top Chicago investment firms (Henry Crown and Aerial Capital Management).[35]

The pattern would continue across the primary season. Wall Street veteran Pam Martens examined "Obama's Money Cartel" in late February 2008, after the subprime mortgage lending crisis had burst across the national and international stage, with disastrous implications for millions of American homeowners and the overall U.S. economy. Martens found the same firms—many deeply implicated in the subprime crisis—atop Obama's contributor list, which provided him with more than $100 million well before the end of the primary season:

> Seven of the Obama campaign's top 14 donors consist of officers and employees of the same Wall Street firms charged time and again with looting the public and newly implicated in originating and/or bundling fraudulently made mortgages. These latest frauds have left thousands of children in some of our largest minority communities coming home from school to see eviction notices and foreclosure signs nailed to their front doors. Those scars will last a lifetime.
>
> These seven Wall Street firms are (in order of money given): Goldman Sachs, UBS AG, Lehman Brothers, JP Morgan Chase, Citigroup, Morgan Stanley and Credit Suisse. There is also a large hedge fund, Citadel Investment Group, which is a major source of fee income to Wall Street. There are five large corporate law firms that are also registered lobbyists; and one is a corporate law firm that is no longer a registered lobbyist but does legal work for Wall Street. The cumulative total of these 14 contributors through February 1, 2008, was $2,872,128, and we're still in the primary season.[36]

There was no small deception in Obama's recurrent claim to depend on small donations from ordinary working people. "The Obama campaign prefers the emphasis to be on the army of small donors who are giving—and raising—money for Obama," *Chicago Sun Times* columnist Lynn Sweet noted in April of 2007. "In truth, though, there are two parallel narratives—and the other is that Obama is also heavily reliant on wealthy and well-connected Democrats." Sweet found that a network of more than one hundred wealthy Democratic "bundlers"—"people who solicit their networks for donations and, at the elite giving levels"—was "raising millions of dollars for his White House bid," often with "assistance from campaign fund-raising professionals." Each of Obama's 138 official "bundlers" had promised to raise at least $50,000—a pledge on which most if not all of them delivered. His "bundlers" included Chicago billionaire Penny Pritzker (the Hyatt heiress and his national finance chairwoman), Lou Sussman (Kerry's chief fund-raiser in 2004), personal-injury attorney Bob Clifford, Capri Capital CEO Quintin Primo, Ariel Capital executives John Rogers and Mellody Hobson, Hollywood moguls David Geffen and Jeffrey

Katzenberg, Broadway producer Margo Lion, and Bill Kennard, managing director of the legendary military-industrial Carlyle Group (strongly connected to the Bush family), and "a string of Harvard Law School friends."[37]

Obama's reliance on big money and corporate funders was hardly new to his presidential campaign. According to the *New York Times,* nearly half of the more than $5 million Obama raised for his 2004 Senate primary came from just 300 donors. The charmed circle of 300 included the Pritzker family, founders of the Hyatt Hotel chain. The Pritzkers donated $40,000, and the self-described "centrist"[38] Penny Pritzker became and remained Obama's national finance chairwoman.

Obama's U.S. Senate campaign received a large contribution from the family of James S. Crown, whose investments include a major stake in the military contractor General Dynamics. Crown told the *Times* that his "family members normally avoid taking sides in a primary, in part because it [is] not good for business. But, with Mr. Obama, they made an exception, with ten family members giving a total of $112,500."[39]

"Lawyers" of a Particular (Global and Corporate) Kind

Under the standard procedure for reporting campaign finance data, a widely cited listing of "industry groups" supporting each presidential candidate in the 2008 presidential election compiled by the Center for Responsive Politics (CRP) shows that Barack Obama received $13.2 million from "lawyers and law firms" between January 1, 2007, and January 31, 2008. Lest the untrained observer think that this meant he was supported by local family or personal-injury attorneys, it should be noted that giant multinational corporate law firms made up five of his top twenty campaign contributors. These massive global legal enterprises hardly fit the populist-, labor-, and working family–friendly identity Obama sought to portray on the primary campaign stump. His sixth largest contributor, the law firm Sidley Austin (which gave $252,000 to Obama in the 2008 race), boasted on its Web site in March of 2008 that its "16 offices are strategically located in the major financial and business centers of the world. Our lawyers collaborate, regardless of your business concern, legal issue or geographic location, to offer outstanding service to meet the needs of our clients in this dynamic, global marketplace." Obama's ninth largest contributor, Skadden, Arps et al. (which gave $228,520 to his campaign), claimed twenty-one offices worldwide, including outposts in Beijing, Brussels, Frankfurt, Hong Kong, Moscow, Munich, Paris, Shanghai, Singapore, Sydney, Tokyo, Toronto, and Vienna. Its practice areas include "corporate restructuring," "international trade" and tax, "mass torts and litigation" (that is, class-action lawsuits), "mergers and acquisitions," and "resolving issues that can arise with unions." Hillary Clinton's top twenty campaign backers also included global corporate law firms, and in fact three of them appeared on her list *and* Obama's top-twenty list (Skadden Arps et al., Kirkland & Ellis, and Latham & Watkins).[40]

Although John Edwards had once been a highly successful trial lawyer, his profile of legal campaign finance support was different. Although he was actually the presidential candidate most proportionately reliant on lawyers and law firms, the firms that accounted for all but five of his top twenty contributors were more moderately sized and commonly engaged in trial litigation representing middle- and working-class Americans against corporations and government agencies.[41] During my experience as an Edwards volunteer in 2007, more than a few voters told me that "your candidate gets his money from lawyers." The charge was true enough, but the category "lawyers" is far from monolithic. Some law firms are larger than others, and some are far more linked to global-corporation capitalism than others.

"He Works the Phones Like a Dog"

Obama campaign imagery pretends that his financial backers have simply been drawn in by the humble and earnest idealism of a candidate who eschews reliance on the business elite. The noble Obama did not aggressively pursue them, or so his campaign would like voters to believe. In his 2006 campaign book, *The Audacity of Hope,* Obama portrayed the pursuit of big-money supporters as a distasteful chore that caused him to spend too much time away from the concerns of ordinary voters.[42]

This may well have been a deceptive narrative. "Even as he cultivated an image as an unconventional candidate devoted to the people, not the establishment," *New York Times* reporters Christopher Drew and Mike McIntire noted in April 2007, Obama "systematically built a sophisticated, and in many ways quite conventional, money machine" during and after his race for the U.S. Senate. By Drew and McIntire's account, "He developed a skill at cultivating donors, often with the same disarming directness he uses on the campaign trail. 'I met him on the first hole,' Steven S. Rogers, a former business owner who teaches at the Kellogg School of Management at Northwestern, recalled recently about a golf game in 2001. 'By the sixth hole, he said, "Steve, I want to run for the Senate." And by the ninth hole, he said he needed help to clear up some debts.'"[43] According to Ken Silverstein's account in 2006, Obama moved rapidly and artfully into the money-politics-policy nexus in Washington, D.C.:

> It is . . . startling to see how quickly Obama's senatorship has been woven into the web of institutionalized influence-trading that afflicts official Washington. He quickly established a political machine funded and run by

> a standard Beltway group of lobbyists, P.R. consultants, and hangers-on. For the staff post of policy director he hired Karen Kornbluh, a senior aide to Robert Rubin when the latter, as head of the Treasury Department under Bill Clinton, was a chief advocate for NAFTA and other free-trade policies that decimated the nation's manufacturing sector (and the organized labor wing of the Democratic Party). Obama's top contributors are corporate law and lobbying firms (Kirkland & Ellis and Skadden, Arps, et al. where four attorneys are fund-raisers for Obama as well as donors), Wall Street financial houses (Goldman Sachs and JP Morgan Chase), and big Chicago interests (Henry Crown and Company, an investment firm that has stakes in industries ranging from telecommunications to defense). Obama immediately established a "leadership PAC," a vehicle through which a member of Congress can contribute to other politicians' campaigns—and one that political reform groups generally view as a slush fund through which congressional leaders can evade campaign-finance rules while raising their own political profiles.[44]

Whatever his initial purported inhibitions about seeking sponsorship from the financial aristocracy, Obama overcame reluctance to shake the "moneyed elite's" campaign cash tree during the first quarter of 2007. As Clinton's campaign chairman, Terry McAuliffe, told *Time* magazine in May 2007, regarding the first quarter, Obama "works the phones like a dog. He probably did three to four times the number of [fund-raising] events [Hillary] did." "No matter who I call," McAuliffe reported, "he has already called three or four times."[45]

"Whether Obama was on a book tour in New York or taking a family vacation to Phoenix," *Tribune* reporters Jackson and McCormick noted in April 2007, "his fund-raising machine was almost always in tow for much of 2005 and 2006, just as it is now on the presidential campaign trail."[46]

Obama as Kingpin

National politicians of Obama's stature are givers as well as receivers of campaign largesse. Immediately upon entering the U.S. Senate, Obama set up his own leadership Political Action Committee (PAC). As Silverstein noted, such PACs are mechanisms whereby congresspersons can give to other politicians—organizations that political reformers have long seen as a key way for elected officials to boost their careers while doing an end run around campaign finance regulations.[47]

Obama's PAC, called the Hopefund, doled out tens of thousands of dollars during the 2006 congressional elections. As Alexander Cockburn noted in the spring of 2006, the Hopefund supported fourteen of Obama's colleagues in the U.S. Senate, ten of whom were affiliated with the militantly centrist, business-oriented DLC, making up half the DLC's continuing presence in that body in the spring of 2006.[48]

The Hopefund became especially important in early 2007 as Hillary Clinton and Barack Obama, in a close primary race, did battle for the critical loyalties of the 800 Democratic Party convention "superdelegates." Free to vote as they please in the party's quadrennial conventions, the superdelegates are all leading Democratic officeholders and officials. They were created during the 1970s by party officials to help keep the Democratic Party insulated from what party managers considered to be the potentially unruly and irrational passions of ordinary primary voters. According to a Center for Responsive Politics report issued in mid-February 2008, Obama's Hopefund was giving a remarkably outsized share of money to these authoritarian checks on democratic process within the party. By the CRP's account, Obama had given 77 percent of the total contributions to superdelegates, totaling $698,000.[49]

Obama's PAC itself has received a vast and critical sum of money from other PACs. As the *Boston Globe*'s Scott Helman noted in August 2007, "Obama's own federal PAC, HopeFund, took in $115,000 from 56 PACs in the 2005–06 election cycle out of the $4.4 million the PAC raised. . . . Obama has used these PAC contributions—including thousands from defense contractors, law firms, and the securities and insurance industries—to build strong support for his presidential run by making donations to Democratic Party organizations and candidates around the country."[50]

"Corporate Power—Not Corporate Lobbyists—Should Be in Question"

There are six key difficulties with Obama's remarkably recurrent reference to his refusal to take money from lobbyists as proof of his populist credentials. First, as Helman found, Obama's initial rise to national prominence and presidential viability depended significantly on contributions from lobbyists.[51]

Second, as *Los Angeles Times* reporter Dan Morain discovered in early August 2007, some of the most influential lobbyist players, lawyers and consultants among them, "skirt disclosure requirements by merely advising clients and associates who do actual lobbying, and avoiding regular contact with policymakers. Obama's ban does not cover such individuals." Thus, to give one example, Obama received $33,000 in the first quarter of 2007 from the Atlanta-based law firm Alston & Bird, which maintained a large lobbying division in Washington. The money came bundled from a number of "consultants" employed by the firm.[52]

Third, Obama's "lobbyist ban" does not include state-level lobbyists. Obama took $2,000 from two Springfield, Illinois, lobbyists for Exelon, which spent $500,000 to influence policy in Washington in 2006 and gave $160,000 to Obama in the first three months of his presidential campaign.[53]

Fourth, Obama received large amounts of stealth lobbyist money from corporate law firms that were registered as federal lobbyists, even as he reported them only as "lawyers." "Is it possible," Pam Martens asked, "that Senator Obama does not know that corporate law firms are also frequently registered lobbyists for dozens of corporations? Or is he making a distinction that because these funds are coming from the employees of these firms, he's not really taking money directly from federal lobbyists? That thesis seems disingenuous when many of these individual donors own these law firms as equity partners or shareholders and share in the profits generated from lobbying."[54]

Fifth, as Martens noted, "Far from keeping his distance from lobbyists, Senator Obama and his campaign seems to be brainstorming with them."[55] A Washington-based publication, *The Hill,* reported in December 2007 that Obama's campaign employed three salaried aides who were registered as federal lobbyists for a large number of multinational corporations and that Obama's counsel, Bob Bauer, was employed by a law firm (Perkins, Cole) that was a registered federal lobbyist. Helman determined that Obama was retaining close and lucrative funding relationships with leading Washington-based lobbyists and lobbying firms while claiming to technically avoid direct contributions from those key campaign-finance players.[56]

Sixth, Obama's repeatedly advertised commentary about his "lobbyist ban" overidentified the disproportionate influence of the wealthy few with contributions from lobbyists. Corporations regularly contribute directly to candidates' campaigns (through the bundled contributions of their own top employees) and exercise power over elected officials and candidates in numerous other significant ways. As *In These Times* economic writer David Moberg noted in late March 2008, "Obama provides a distinctly American mix of lofty hopes for the future, as well as nuts-and-bolts pragmatism. The missing ingredient is a coherent analysis of how society works. Rather than attack corporations, he attacks lobbyists. But corporate power—not corporate lobbyists—should be in question." As one activist told Moberg: "We are still at the stage of not quite grappling with the real issue that confronts America, and that issue is the power of the corporations to globalize and drive the political agenda."[57]

"Fooling Voters" on Presidential Financing: "A Parallel Public Financing System"?

One year after Obama announced a presidential candidacy that he claimed would help rescue U.S. politics and government from big-money, special-interest domination, the Center for Responsive Politics reported that he had raised more than $102 million in 2007 (just $13 million less than Hillary Clinton's record-setting pace).[58] An Illinois newspaper reported that his campaign was "bringing in roughly $1 million a day this year"[59] (between January 1 and February 10, 2008). He beat that pace in February, when an Obama finance committee chairman told the *Chicago Tribune* that his candidate's fund-raising total for that month would hit $50 million—a new single-month presidential fund-raising record. Reports from the critical early March primary states of Texas and Ohio indicated that Obama was outspending Clinton on television advertisements by a margin of 2 to 1. In what was almost certainly a false statement from a candidate known to relish the fund-raising game (and excel at it), Obama told the media, "I have no idea how much money we've raised, but I know we've been paying our bills." Meanwhile, Obama campaign officials said they had "passed the 1 million mark in the number of individual donors, many of whom made donations in $25 and $50 increments."[60]

It was against this background of record-setting campaign finance success that Obama refused to reaffirm an earlier commitment he had made one year before. Before he had started raising the prodigious sums he came to enjoy as the campaign advanced, Obama had pledged to accept public financing for the general election if his Republican opponent promised to do the same. In doing so, he swore to accept campaign-spending limits restricting his expenditures to $85 million during the two-month general-election campaign. The commitment was reaffirmed in a response Obama made to a questionnaire sent out in November 2007 by the Midwest Democracy Network, an alliance of public-interest and citizen-action groups. Asked if he would participate in the public-financing system, should he secure the presidential nomination, Obama wrote "yes" and then added the following written statement: "If I am the Democratic nominee, I will aggressively pursue an agreement with the Republican nominee to preserve a publicly financed general election."

The only Republican to take him up on this offer was John McCain. In early February 2008, McCain advisers called for Obama to make good on his promise. "We have a candidate who is quite serious about taking public funds"—and thereby accepting spending limits—"if Mr. Obama does," said a top McCain aide. "It's not a game to McCain," the aide added, noting that Obama "gave his word, and he either places value on that or he's just fooling voters."[61]

Obama's national press secretary, Bill Burton, responded by saying, "We will address that issue in the general election. We're just not entertaining hypotheticals right now." But as longtime leading campaign-finance reform advocate Fred Wertheimer noted, Obama "is now saying public financing is an option. But they made a commitment in 2007 to do this. There were no conditions, no arguments, that 'we'll decide this when we get the nomination.'"

"I think," Wertheimer added, "it's very important for Senator Obama to reaffirm the commitment that he made."[62]

As the New York University Brennan Center's Deborah Goldberg noted, the debate that emerged over whether Obama and McCain had made a deal to accept public funding if they became their party's nominee left out key questions. "What we should be talking about," Goldberg argued, "is why a 'deal' has become necessary and why there is a serious risk that, if it ever existed, it will collapse under the weight of private money flooding the campaigns. We also should be talking about what it means for our country that our leaders are dependent on funds raised from wealthy individuals and special interests to run for office."[63]

It was true, Goldberg acknowledged, that some candidates "are less dependent on deep pockets than others." But for all its talk of a million contributors giving to him in "$25 and $50 increments," the Obama campaign could not claim to rely primarily on small donors, though Obama often seemed to suggest that it did on the campaign trail. An important study released by the Campaign Finance Institute in early February 2008 showed that only Dennis Kucinich, Mike Gravel, Ron Paul, and Tom Tancredo had raised even half their 2007 presidential campaign funds from small donors (those giving $200 or less). Obama received just 32 percent of his campaign funding from such donors, less than Tancredo (81 percent), Kucinich (74 percent), Paul (61 percent), Gravel (61 percent), and Edwards (36 percent), but more than McCain (25 percent), Hillary Clinton (14 percent), Mitt Romney (12 percent), and Rudy Giuliani (8 percent).[64] His top contributors through April 2007 included investment bankers Goldman Sachs (number one at $571,330 for the year 2007), UBS AG (number three at $364,806), Lehman Brothers (number seven at $318,467), and JP Morgan Chase (number four at $362,207); utility (and nuclear) giant Exelon (number fifteen at $236,211); media giants Time Warner (number thirteen at $257,527) and Google (number eight at $309,514); and the giant, multinational, and heavily corporate-globalizationist law firms Skadden, Arps et al. ($294,245), Sidley Austin LLP ($294,245), and Latham & Watkins ($218,615).[65] Obama received a total of $15.8 million from law firms, $7.8 million from securities and investments firms, $5 million from the health-care sector, $4 million from real-estate firms, $3.3 million from corporate media, $3.4 million from business-service firms, $2.9 million from computer and Internet firms, and $1.6 million from commercial banks. He received just $95,000 from American labor unions.[66]

During a Democratic presidential debate in Cleveland in late February 2008, NBC political analyst Tim Russert asked Obama about the contradiction between his earlier public-financing pledge and more recent statements. Obama gave a rambling and indirect answer that included the claim that if he became the nominee he would "sit down with John McCain and make sure we have a system that is fair to both sides." This was an odd comment, given Obama's previous unambiguous promise to work with a willing Republican opponent through an *already existing* and detailed public presidential campaign-finance system (used on numerous previous occasions) allotting equal funding to candidates who honored the spending limits.[67] The notion that he and McCain would or could work up a new "system" was bizarre.

By early April, *Washington Post* reporters Matthew Mosk and Alec MacGillis noted that the Obama campaign had come up with a solution to the conflict between rhetoric and reality in its public-financing position. Obama claimed that his presidential campaign had created "a parallel public financing system" based on what the *Post* called "a wave of modest donations from homemakers and high school teachers": "'Small givers,' he said at a fund-raiser this week, 'will have as much access and influence over the course and direction of our campaign as has traditionally been reserved for the wealthy and powerful.'" This assertion struck Mosk and MacGillis as difficult to fulfill. They noted that people "with wealth and power" had "played a critical role in creating Obama's record-breaking fund-raising machine, and their generosity has earned them a prominent voice in shaping his campaign." Of particular interest, they found that Obama had received support from "seventy-nine 'bundlers,' five of them millionaires," who had "tapped their personal networks to raise at least $200,000 each." "They have helped the campaign recruit more than 27,000 donors," the reporters wrote, "to write checks for $2,300, the maximum allowed."[68]

Investor Results

"What's the Dollar Value of a Starry-Eyed Idealist?"

"It's not always clear what Obama's financial backers want," Ken Silverstein wrote in the fall of 2006, "but it seems safe to conclude that his campaign contributors are not interested merely in clean government and political reform." This seems a reasonable judgment, given well-known facts on the purposes behind election finance at the upper levels.[69]

"On condition of anonymity," Silverstein reported, "one Washington lobbyist I spoke with was willing to point out the obvious: that big donors would not be helping out Obama if they didn't see him as a 'player.' The lobbyist added: 'What's the dollar value of a starry-eyed idealist?'"[70]

Below I examine numerous episodes and examples suggesting the wisdom of Silverstein's judgment and that of his nameless lobbyist source.

"Tort Reform" and Credit-Card Interest Rates

Obama's reliance on wealthy supporters certainly helps explain why he voted for a business-driven federal "tort-reform" law that rolled back the ability of working people to obtain reasonable redress and compensation from misbehaving corporations. The so-called Class Action Fairness Act (CAFA) was a Republican bill backed and signed with great gusto by President Bush on February 18, 2005. Opposed by numerous Democratic U.S. senators, it closed off state courts as a venue to hear many class-action lawsuits. This followed in accord with the observation of many large corporations that such lawsuits often had a much lower chance of surviving corporate legal challenge in the "backlogged Republican-judge dominated federal courts," as Ralph Nader's running mate, Matt Gonzalez, put it. The bill, Gonzalez said, was a "thinly-veiled special interest extravaganza that favored banking, creditors and other corporate interests" over and against workers, consumers, and the public.[71]

"Opposed by most major civil rights and consumer watchdog groups," noted liberal journalist David Sirota, "this Big Business–backed legislation was sold to the public as a way to stop 'frivolous' lawsuits. But everyone in Washington knew the bill's real objective was to protect corporate abusers." And according to Silverstein, "the bill had been long sought by a coalition of business groups and was lobbied for aggressively by financial firms, which constitute Obama's second biggest single bloc of donors." Such firms loathe class-action suits, which can instantly impose massive burdens on industries into which they have often poured untold millions of dollars.

As the CAFA Senate vote approached, senators received an eloquent plea for mercy from more than forty civil rights and labor organizations, including the NAACP, the Lawyers Committee for Civil Rights Under Law, the Human Rights Campaign, the American Civil Liberties Union, the Center for Justice and Democracy, Legal Momentum (formerly NOW Legal Defense and Education Fund), and the Alliance for Justice. "Under the Class Action Fairness Act of 2005," this appeal stated, "citizens are denied the right to use their own state courts to bring class actions against corporations that violate these state wage and hour and state civil rights laws, even where that corporation has hundreds of employees in that state. Moving these state law cases into federal court will delay and likely deny justice for working men and women and victims of discrimination."[72] Obama certainly understood the regressive ramifications. As Pam Martens noted,

> Senator Obama graduated Harvard Law magna cum laude and was the first black president of the *Harvard Law Review*. Given those credentials, one assumes that he understood the ramifications to the poor and middle class in

> this country as he helped to gut one of the few weapons left to seek justice against giant corporations and their legions of giant law firms. The class-action vehicle confers upon each citizen one of the most powerful rights in our society: the ability to function as a private attorney general and seek redress for wrongs inflicted on ourselves as well as for those similarly injured that might not otherwise have a voice.[73]

Obama's vote for big capital and against ordinary working people and consumers in the name of "tort reform" won him praise from Mike Williams, the vice president for legislative affairs at the Bond Market Association. "He's a Democrat, and some people thought he'd do whatever the trial lawyers wanted, but he didn't do that," Williams told Silverstein. "That's a testament to his character."[74]

It was more likely a testament to his well-honed instincts for political calculation, which told him it would not serve his presidential ambitions to snub a critical part of the legislative agenda of his second leading and large-scale investor group.

"Why," asked Matt Gonzalez, "would a civil rights lawyer knowingly make it harder for working-class people to have their day in court, in effect shutting off avenues of redress?" Obama's vote was not even required for CAFA's passage. The Senate majority on its behalf was filibuster-proof. By Cockburn's account in the spring of 2006, "He just wanted the top people to know how safe he was."[75]

The same calculating instincts that likely drove Obama's CAFA vote may help to explain why he opposed an amendment to the Bankruptcy Act that would have capped credit-card interest rates at 30 percent in early 2005. Obama claimed he voted against the amendment because it was "poorly written" and its rate ceiling was "too high." But he advanced no lower rate as an alternative and did not offer an amendment clarifying the language he claimed to find objectionable.[76] Taken together, his positions on these bills suggest that it was his reliance on corporate funding and connections that had led him to serve the interests of financial firms.

"Health Care for Hybrids"

Obama's business-friendly behavior on key policy issues became evident early on, when, as a freshman U.S. senator, he introduced an initiative to pass a "healthcare for hybrids" bill. This legislation would have granted hundreds of millions of federal dollars to the nation's leading auto companies "to relieve them of some of the costs of paying for retirees' healthcare," noted David Sirota. "The companies would produce more fuel-efficient vehicles. The goals are unassailable, but the policy reflects the liberal carrot of appeasing a powerful industry rather than the progressive stick of forcing that industry to shape up by simply mandating higher fuel-efficiency standards." Consistent with the market-oriented language of the corporate-neoliberal era, Obama sought to "incentivize" corporate capital to temper its assault on global ecology at the taxpayers' expense, rather than to compel it to align its behavior with environmental needs in the public interest.[77]

Paying and Playing "the Fool": Taking Up Business-Friendly Right-Wing Talking Points on "the Social Security Crisis"

In the fall of 2007, Obama concerned many progressives by telling an interviewer from *The National Journal* that major government action was required to prevent what he called "the Social Security crisis."[78] Earlier in the same year, Obama had claimed that "everything should be on the table" when it came to "fixing" Social Security, including raising the retirement age. He thereby became linked to the Republican Party's long-standing deceitful propaganda campaign, heavily underwritten and advanced by Wall Street's leading investment houses, to "reform"—meaning dismantle and privatize—Social Security on the spurious pretext that it is approaching a terrible fiscal calamity. The widely accepted notion that a major catastrophe looms in the foreseeable future is a corporate and Republican concoction disseminated through a sophisticated propaganda effort that "compares well," Noam Chomsky noted in 2006, "with . . . the government-media campaign to convince Americans that Saddam Hussein was an immediate threat to their survival."[79]

According to *New York Times* columnist Paul Krugman, Obama "play[ed] along with this new round of scare mongering" because of a foolish "insist[ence] that he can transcend the partisanship of our times" and "find common ground" across angry party lines. "We all wish that American politics weren't so bitter and partisan," Krugman wrote. "But if you try to find common ground where none exists—which is the case for many issues today—you end up being played for a fool. And that's what has just happened to Mr. Obama." By Krugman's account, Obama's naive attachment to the notion of healing party divisions blinded him to the fact that, "on Social Security, as on many other issues, what Washington means by partisanship is mainly that everyone should come together to give conservatives what they want."[80]

Krugman may have been too kind. Obama's highly advertised effort to rise above ideology and find common ground with Republicans might have seemed dysfunctional and ill-advised from Krugman's liberal standpoint. But Obama's "bipartisanship" was functional from the perspective of the elite business actors who vetted the senator and found him to be a "reasonable" and trustworthy "player" beneath his populace-pleasing rhetoric about "changing the system in Washington." After all, conservative policy outcomes are often victories for the very business community Obama sought to win over to his side. And, as I pointed out in a *ZNet Commentary* in early December 2007,

> Obama's "playing" is paying off. Obama has been richly rewarded for playing "the fool" on issues like tort law, Social Security, and national health insurance. According to the Center for Responsive Politics (CRP), the 2008 Obama presidential campaign has received nearly $5 million dollars from securities and investment firms and $866,000 from commercial banks through October of 2007. Obama's top contributor is Goldman Sachs (provider of $369,078 to Obama '08), identified by CRP investigators as "a major proponent of privatizing Social Security as well as legislation that would essentially deregulate the investment banking/securities industry." Of his top twenty election investors, fully eight are securities and investment firms.[81]

Against "Government Mandates"

Obama's reliance on corporate cash and power also likely influenced his opposition in a 2006 interview to the introduction of single-payer national health-insurance. He stated that he opposed the idea on the grounds that such a change would lead to employment difficulties for workers in the private insurance industry and that "voluntary" solutions were "more consonant" with "the American character" than "government mandates."[82] The last comment was revealing. As Chomsky noted in 2006,

> A large majority of the [U.S.] population supports extensive government intervention [in the health-care market], it appears. An NBC–*Wall Street Journal* poll found that "over 2/3s of all Americans thought the government should guarantee 'everyone the best and most advanced health care that technology can supply;' a *Washington Post*–ABC News poll found that 80 percent regard universal health care as "more important than holding down taxes"; polls reported in Business Week found that 67 percent of Americans think it is a good idea to guarantee health care for all U.S. citizens, as Canada and Britain do, with just 27 percent dissenting; the Pew Research Center found that 64 percent of Americans favor the "U.S. government guaranteeing health insurance for all citizens, even if it means raising taxes" (30 percent opposed). By the late 1980s, more than 70 percent of Americans "thought health care should be a constitutional guarantee," while 40 percent "thought it already was."[83]

It is not likely that Obama would have claimed to support the American scourge of racially disparate mass incarceration on the grounds that it provided work for tens of thousands of prison guards, or that the United States should pour nearly half of its federal budget into the Pentagon system because of all the people who find employment in the military-industrial complex.[84] Surely the senator knew of the large number of socially useful and healthy alternatives that exist for the investment of human labor power formerly employed in insurance companies.

In the fall of 2007, Obama's decision to differentiate himself from Hillary Clinton and John Edwards on health care by taking up right-wing talking points against "government mandates" graphically exposed the limits of his proclaimed "progressivism." Sounding like a good Republican discussing socialized medicine, Obama criticized his leading competitors for favoring legislation requiring all adults to be insured even if they didn't want to be. This "mandate" struck Obama as government coercion and as unenforceable short of draconian state penalization. Obama also claimed that his health-care plan put a more efficient, taxpayer-friendly emphasis on cost reduction than his rivals' proposals did. He didn't want to "force" people to buy health insurance when health-care costs were exorbitantly high.

But, as Krugman pointed out, the plans that Edwards and Clinton had proposed included impressive cost-control measures. Difficulties of enforcement, he said, did not mean "we shouldn't have laws." Edwards had proposed a simple and nonpunitive way to make sure that all people were covered: automatic enrollment, without punishment, of all people without proof of insurance when filing income taxes or receiving health care. And Obama's supposed concern with imaginary government oppression hid a reactionary promise to let a few people game the health-care system for their own selfish benefit and at the expense of the common good. As Krugman explained,

> Why have a [health insurance] mandate? The whole point of a universal health insurance system is that everyone pays in, even if they're currently healthy, and in return everyone has insurance coverage if and when they need it.
>
> And it's not just a matter of principle. As a practical matter, letting people opt out if they don't feel like insurance would make insurance substantially more expensive for everyone else.
>
> Here's why: under the Obama plan, as it now stands, healthy people could choose not to buy insurance—then sign up for it if they developed health problems later. Insurance companies couldn't turn them away, because Mr. Obama's plan, like those of his rivals, requires that insurers offer the same policy to everyone.

As a result, people who did the right thing and bought insurance when they were healthy would end up subsidizing those who didn't sign up for insurance until or unless they needed medical care.[85]

Liberal commentator Paul Starr, no left radical, added that

> without an individual mandate for adults . . . other aspects of Obama's [health-care] plan collapse. Insurers cannot be required to ignore pre-existing conditions [a critical promise made by each of the leading Democratic candidates] if people can just wait to buy coverage anytime they're sick. Obama claims to want to bring the costs down first in order to make coverage affordable, but his plan would make insurance more expensive by giving healthy people an incentive not to pay for it until they need it.[86]

Krugman criticized Obama for "giving aid and comfort" to regressive Republicans because of an excessively cautious "reluctance to stake out a clearly partisan position." And again, it is relevant to observe that Obama's business-friendly distance from a progressive Democratic position was consistent with his campaign-funding profile. According to the CRP, Obama's presidential run was assisted by more than $2 million from the health-care sector and nearly $400,000 from the insurance industry through October 2007. He received $708,000 from medical and insurance interests between 2001 and 2006. His wife Michelle, a fellow Harvard Law graduate, was a vice president for community and external affairs at the University of Chicago Hospitals, a position that paid her $273,618 in 2006.[87]

Limiting Patients' Compensation

Obama's strong financial connection to the medical-industrial complex was likely also related to his determination to act against patients' rights to full compensation in lawsuits resulting from medical mistakes. Obama was a sponsor of the National Medical Error Disclosure and Compensation Act of 2005, a bill requiring hospitals to disclose errors to patients. It also, however, rewards doctors and hospitals for such disclosure by limiting patients' economic compensation. "Rather than simply mandating disclosure," Gonzalez noted, "Obama's solution is to trade what should be mandated for something that should never be given away: namely, full recovery for the injured patient."[88]

Opposing a Single-Payer System

Given Obama's repeated claim during the Democratic presidential primaries that he hoped to make health coverage universal by "first making it affordable," it is ironic that he joined all of his party contenders (except Dennis Kucinich and Mike Gravel) in opposing the single-payer option. The supposed "left" and "progressive" Obama rejected HR676, sponsored by Congressmen Kucinich and John Conyers in 2006. Supported by more than seventy-five members of Congress, and by the majority of the populace for decades, single-payer health insurance would slash the administrative costs that make up roughly one-third of every health-care dollar spent by eliminating the duplicative nature of these services.

"The expected $300 billion in annual savings such a system would produce would go," Gonzalez noted, "directly to cover the uninsured and expand coverage to those who already have insurance." Besides leaving millions uninsured in the name of opposing "government mandates," Obama's plan left the health-insurance industry's gigantic and dysfunctional administrative costs in place—a stark and rarely noted (outside "far left" circles) corporate-friendly reality. The popular progressive film director Michael Moore rightly noted this when he observed that "Obama wants the insurance companies to help us develop a new health care plan—the same companies who have created the mess in the first place."[89]

"If Being a Progressive Means Anything"

In early April 2008, nearly two weeks before the Pennsylvania primary, Hillary Clinton was roundly derided both by Republicans and Obama supporters when she got some small facts wrong in telling the story of Trina Bachtel. Bachtel was a young woman from Ohio who died while pregnant after being turned down for medical assistance at a local clinic because of an unpaid balance. But Clinton got the essential circumstances of her story right in trying to make a bigger and valid point about the sorry state of health care in the country. The Obamanists' catcalls elicited a well-deserved criticism from Krugman:

> Look, I know that many progressives have their hearts set on seeing Barack Obama get the Democratic nomination. But politics is supposed to be about more than cheering your team and jeering the other side. It's supposed to be about changing the country for the better.
>
> And if being a progressive means anything, it means believing that we need universal health care, so that terrible stories like those of . . . Trina Bachtel and the thousands of other Americans who die each year from lack of insurance become a thing of the past.[90]

"We Should Explore Nuclear Power"

Also worth reviewing is Obama's role advancing big Illinois energy interests that have bankrolled his campaign. "During debate on the 2005 energy bill,"

Silverstein noted in late 2006, "Obama helped to vote down an amendment that would have killed vast loan guarantees for power-plant operators to develop new energy projects. The loan guarantees were called 'one of the worst provisions in this massive piece of legislation' by Taxpayers for Common Sense and Citizens Against Government Waste; the public will not only pay millions of dollars in loan costs but will risk losing billions of dollars if the companies default."[91]

It is difficult to understand the "reformer" Obama's support for this egregiously wasteful, corporate-welfare provision without noting that the massive power-plant operator Exelon was his sixth largest campaign sponsor, having given him $72,000 between 2001 and 2006.[92]

Exelon's dark shadow also lurked behind Obama's response to an audience questioner who asked the Democratic presidential candidates about their "opinion on nuclear power" during a CNN/YouTube debate in South Carolina in July 2007. Edwards spoke clearly for "wind, solar, [and] cellulose-based biofuels" as "the way we need to go" and against nuclear power on the grounds of cost and safety. "We haven't built a nuclear power plant in decades in this country," he said, because "it is extremely costly . . . it takes an enormous amount of time to get one planned, developed and built." Furthermore, he said, "We still don't have a safe way to dispose of the nuclear waste."

Edwards also stated his opposition to the liquefaction of coal, since "the last thing we need is another carbon-based fuel in America." Obama responded with a rambling answer that called for "putting national interests ahead of special interests," but he led off by saying, "I actually think that we should explore nuclear power as part of the energy mix"—as if nuclear hadn't already been deeply explored for decades and found to be too expensive and unsafe.[93] Edwards likely added his opposition to coal liquefaction because he knew that it was not an especially efficient or ecologically sound use of coal (it's likely to exacerbate global warming) and because he knew that the coal industry had applauded Obama's reintroduction, with Senator Jim Bunning (R-KY), of the Coal-to-Liquid Fuel Promotion Act of 2007, designed to create incentives for coal-liquefaction research and plant construction.

CNN viewers curious about the source of Obama's position on behalf of nuclear power would have done well to visit the CRP's "Open Secrets" site. There they could have learned that Obama's third largest campaign contributor (after Goldman Sachs and Lehman Brothers) at the time was Exelon ($191,000 through the second quarter of 2007), owner and operator of the nation's largest fleet of nuclear energy plants. As for why he backed a law supporting the expanded use of coal, "It seems," wrote *Washington Post* reporter Elizabeth Williamson, "the answer is twofold: his interest in energy independence—and his interest in downstate Illinois, where the senator's green tinge makes the coal industry queasy." Perhaps Obama felt the need to ease the discomfort of Illinois coal operators after he voted against President Bush's Orwellian Clear Skies Initiative in 2005, designed in part to assist the domestic coal industry. Obama felt free to please environmentalists by voting against it only after he determined that, in Silverstein's words, "it would have been more beneficial to western coal producers, not those in Illinois."[94]

Obama's promotion of nuclear power and coal liquefaction was widely understood by environmentalists as a reminder that the "black" Obama was in many ways about "the green"—as in the money, not the earth.

False Posturing on the Braidwood Leak

During the pivotal Iowa campaign, Obama sought to burnish his populist "tinge" by telling a misleading story about his response to an Exelon nuclear accident that outraged Illinois residents in late 2005 and early 2006. On December 1, 2005, Exelon admitted that it had discovered radioactive byproducts of nuclear power in monitoring wells at its Braidwood plant, located in central Illinois. Citizen concerns deepened when radioactive tritium was discovered in a home drinking-well near the plant, and Exelon revealed that this substance came from millions of gallons of water that had leaked from the plant over many years. Exelon had not been required to report the leaks, since the radioactive discharges had not reached the level of what the Nuclear Regulatory Commission called "an emergency."

In November 2007, Obama told a campaign crowd in Iowa that he had introduced a U.S. Senate bill requiring nuclear plant owners to notify local and state authorities immediately when even small leaks had occurred. The bill, he said, was "the only nuclear legislation that I've passed. I just did that last year." His claim, according to Mike McIntire of the *New York Times,* elicited "murmurs of approval."[95]

But, as the *Times* reported in a front-page story two days before Super Tuesday, the truth of what happened after the Braidwood leak was very different from Obama's self-serving version. "While he initially fought to advance" a bill very much like what he claimed, McIntire noted, "Mr. Obama eventually rewrote it to reflect changes sought by Senate Republicans, Exelon, and nuclear regulators. Those revisions propelled the bill through a crucial committee. But contrary to Mr. Obama's comments in Iowa, it ultimately died amid parliamentary wrangling in the full Senate *despite the removal of language mandating prompt reporting.* Instead, the bill simply offered guidance to regulators, whom it charged with addressing the issue of unreported links." As McIntire suggested, this ignominious legislative aftermath contradicted Obama's campaign claim and followed in natural accord with the following facts:

- Obama had received at least $227,000 in campaign cash from Exelon since 2003.
- Exelon had given more support to Obama than it had to other candidates.
- Exelon executives had met repeatedly with Obama's staff to discuss the ultimately diluted and aborted bill.
- Obama's chief political strategist, David Axelrod, had worked as a consultant to Exelon since 2002.[96]

Maytag and Galesburg: "Obama's Fundraising, Rhetoric Collide"

In Barack Obama's stump speech during the long campaign leading up to the Iowa Democratic presidential caucus, the Maytag workers of Galesburg, Illinois, played a central role. Obama repeatedly told the story of how their jobs had been shipped to Mexico, trying to steal John Edwards' pronounced laborite thunder in Iowa by inveighing against mean-spirited corporations that used trade pacts to replace highly paid union workers with cheaper labor abroad. "It is a ready applause line for the Illinois presidential hopeful," *Chicago Tribune* reporter Bob Secter noted in a story appearing four days before the Super Tuesday primaries under the headline "Obama's Fundraising, Rhetoric Collide"—"one that he has been reciting almost verbatim since he was a candidate for the U.S. Senate in 2004, when appliance giant Maytag was in the process of shutting a refrigerator plant [in Galesburg], putting 1,600 people out of work."

Despite Obama's claims of deep concern for Galesburg's proletarian victims, however, Maytag union members told Secter that Obama had done remarkably little to save the Galesburg workers' jobs. Those workers belonged to the International Association of Machinists and Aerospace Workers, whose president noted that "Obama's support for Maytag workers was more show than substance." Current and former Maytag employees were rankled by Obama's inaction because he possessed a special relationship with a leading Maytag decision maker. Between 2003 and 2008, he had received tens of thousands of dollars in campaign contributions from the family of Lester Crown, one of Maytag's directors and largest investors. The Crowns and employees of their family-managed holding company (Henry Crown Investments) gave at least $195,000 to Obama's Senate and presidential campaigns between 2003 and 2008. According to Crown, however, Obama never once raised the fate of Maytag's Galesburg plant with him.

"The high profile treatment given the Maytag situation" by Obama, Secter noted, "is a reminder of the often *awkward intersection of the populist rhetoric, complex issues, and the financial realities of presidential campaigning.*" It often stood in ironic relation to Obama's repeated criticism of his Democratic presidential rivals for "straying from their own populist images," such as when he remarked on Hillary Clinton's tenure many years ago on the board of the antilabor Wal-Mart company.[97]

"None of It Is Particularly Radical": Pseudo-Populist "Campaign Rhetoric" on Trade

When addressing working-class audiences during the 2007 and 2008 primary campaign, Obama repeatedly boasted of his purported opposition to the North American Free Trade Agreement (NAFTA)—widely blamed for job losses by organized labor and many working-class voters, but deemed a boon to the U.S. economy by the corporate interests that provided campaign dollars. "I don't think NAFTA has been good for Americans, and I never have," Obama claimed just before the Ohio Democratic primary, where trade and NAFTA emerged as leading campaign issues.[98]

Obama's record on the corporate-neoliberal "investor rights" bill was considerably less populist than that comment suggested. During his 2004 Senate campaign he argued for "more deals such as NAFTA," claimed that higher, job-protecting tariffs (like those an opponent had called for) would "spark a trade war," and spoke repeatedly of the "enormous benefits" that "accrued to his state from NAFTA."[99]

In late February 2008, *New York Times* business writer David Leonhardt noted that both Obama and Senator Clinton had been "straddling NAFTA and trade issues." After quoting a recent Obama speech telling Youngstown, Ohio, workers they'd seen "job after job disappear because of bad trade deals like NAFTA," Leonhardt noted that Obama's trade agenda was not "particularly radical." "Neither candidate calls for a repeal of NAFTA, or anything close to it. Both instead want to tinker with the bureaucratic innards of the agreement. . . . It's a bit of an odd situation," Leonhardt added. "They call the country's trade policy a disaster, and yet their plan starts with, um, cracking down on Mexican pollution."[100]

Matt Gonzalez noted around the same time that Obama had dropped the populist ball when given an opportunity to protect workers from unfair trade agreements. Obama cast the deciding vote against an amendment to a 2005 commerce appropriations bill that would have "prohibited US trade negotiators from weakening US laws that provide safeguards from unfair foreign trade practices," Gonzalez wrote. The amendment would have been "a vital tool to combat the outsourcing of jobs to foreign workers."[101]

Obama's ambiguous position on "trade" received some especially unwelcome attention in the week before the Ohio and Texas primaries in early March 2008. That's when his campaign was hit by the revelation that a top Obama staff member had made a revealing comment to Michael Wilson, the Canadian ambassador to the United States. As the Canadian Television network (CTV) reported on February 27, 2008, the Obama staffer told Wilson to disregard Obama's populace-pleasing political language on NAFTA and other trade issues. That language was geared toward winning working-class votes in Ohio and should not be taken as a serious threat to the corporate globalization agenda that U.S. and Canadian elites shared, the Obama aide wanted the Canadian government to know.

According to CTV News, "Barack Obama has ratcheted up his attacks on NAFTA, but a senior member of his campaign team told a Canadian official not to take his criticisms seriously, CTV News has learned. . . . The staff member reassured Wilson that the criticism would only be campaign rhetoric and should not be taken at face value." Subsequent inquiry determined that the "staff member" was none other than Obama's top economic adviser, University of Chicago economist Austan Goolsbee, who also happened to be the chief economist of the DLC—an interesting point, given the fact that Obama had once asked (in response to critical questioning by the black left writers Bruce Dixon and Glen Ford) to have his name stricken from a DLC list of rising stars.[102]

This disturbing news item spoke to cynicism and class elitism at the heart of the Obama campaign. It was briefly noted by *Wall Street Journal* reporter Jackie Calmes and senior CNBC Washington correspondent John Harwood on the February 29 edition of *Washington Week* on PBS. Commenting about the superficiality of Hillary Clinton and Barack Obama's apparent abject anti-NAFTA pandering in Ohio, Harwood coolly observed that the two, Democratic presidential candidates were in fact "both avowed free traders."

Centrist "Obamanomics"

Also suggestive of the likelihood that an Obama presidency would tend toward the pro-business right on economic policy was the tepid centrism of the economic stimulus plan Obama rolled out in early 2008. All the leading Democratic candidates advanced "stimulus packages" in mid-January of the election year when reports indicated that the nation's festering housing crisis was pushing the United States into a recession. Following a pattern established in the long run-up to the Iowa caucus, Edwards took the lead with a plan that included significant assistance to unemployed workers, aid to cash-strapped state and local governments, and public investment in alternative energy. Hillary Clinton followed with a similar but larger, equally detailed proposal. Both Edwards and Clinton made provisions for expanded stimulus measures if the crisis worsened.

Obama's proposal was far less detailed and tilted to the right. It emphasized across-the-board tax cuts over aid to the hardest hit workers and families or to local and state governments and offered little in the way of alternative energy proposals. Meanwhile, Goolsbee announced that a long-term tax cut that Obama had proposed months before could prevent the economic downturn from "morphing into a drastic decline in consumer spending." Team Obama seemed more concerned with tax cuts and deficit reduction than with poverty reduction, sounding vaguely Republican in responding to the difficulties faced by working families.[103]

It was all very consistent with the centrist, business-friendly nature of Obama's economic policy team. By early 2008, Obama's top economic advisers were DLC chief economist Goolsbee and Harvard's David Cutler and Jeffrey Liebman. The last two were also developers of "market solutions to social welfare issues." Employed at the University of Chicago—which the veteran progressive economic writer David Moberg rightly called "the Vatican of the free market fundamentalists"—Goolsbee once published a *New York Times* column touting the positive benefits of subprime lending.[104] *New Republic* writer Noam Scheiber once saw Goolsbee approach the right-wing *New York Times* columnist David Brooks (a follower and loving eulogizer of the late arch-neoliberal University of Chicago free-market economist and guru Milton Friedman) in Des Moines and "gush when the quirky conservative agreed to pose for a picture." Brooks had repeatedly praised Obama for tending toward the pro-business "Hamiltonian" center and went out of his way to marginalize and dismiss the excessively (in Brooks's view) populist campaign of Edwards.[105]

By Moberg's account, the scholarly publications of Obama's economic brain trust suggested that he would "rely on marginal tinkering with markets and incentives to try to achieve some progressive ends, such as more equality or opportunity." Obama repeatedly said, for example, that he would "make sure trade works for American workers" by ending tax breaks for companies investing abroad and creating tax incentives for companies to produce good jobs inside the United States. The first proposal was unlikely to alter corporate behavior in any significant way, and the second Moberg deemed "symbolically laudable but ineffective and probably a waste of public funds."[106]

Moberg added that the top economic advisers in an Obama White House would "likely be drawn from the Democratic establishment. Wall Street representatives, such as President Clinton's former Treasury Secretary Robert Rubin, are likely to have a big voice in an Obama administration. They will focus on balanced budgets, a strong dollar, low inflation, a light hand in financial regulation and restraint on spending that might spook traders." This would mean a corporate-neoliberal agenda.

According to AFL-CIO chief economist Ron Blackwell, such an approach would be unlikely to produce sustainable recovery in accord with progressive objectives. For such a recovery to occur, Blackwell argued, the trade deficit and foreign borrowing had to be restrained, since they had "flooded global capital markets with dollars, fueling the housing bubble and recovery driven by consumer debt." The government would also need to more closely regulate financial markets and to increase the bargaining power of workers by restoring the right to organize unions and making full employment as important a national goal as stable prices.[107]

"Obama," Moberg noted, "has not promised anything so ambitious." Obama and his advisers failed to understand that "governments reduce inequality more through spending (say, on health care or free education) than through progressive taxation alone." Moberg agreed that Obama's proposal to roll back George W. Bush's tax cuts for people earning $200,000 and up was a worthy idea, and it was one that all the other Democratic presidential contenders shared; but Moberg concluded that the Obama team was relying too heavily and conservatively "on varied tax cuts (and a few hikes) to bring change."[108]

A "Deeply Conservative" Conciliator

It was all very consistent with what Obama's former University of Chicago colleague Cass Sunstein called Obama's "minimalist" approach—a preference for "modest adjustments in institutions in search of his 'visionary' goals." It was in harmony also with the pronounced absence of any sweeping proposals to confront and overcome the steep disparities of U.S. wealth and power in Obama's *Audacity of Hope* and in his campaign presentations in early 2007. As Larissa MacFarquhar noted in a May 2007 Obama portrait entitled "The Conciliator," the solutions offered in Obama's book, speeches, and town-hall meetings were "small and local rather than deep-reaching and systemic." He preferred to pick and choose in eclectic fashion from whatever ideological tradition seemed convenient.[109]

At the same time, Obama became practically notorious in mid-2007 for addressing deep social problems with no policy at all, preferring to substitute empty political platitudes and soothing bromides of hope and togetherness for concrete policy-action proposals. "When he talks about poverty," MacFarquhar noted, "he tends not to talk about gorging plutocrats and unjust tax breaks: he says that we are our brother's keeper, that caring for the poor is one of our traditions." Such refusal to advance large reform—for example, a single-payer health-insurance program on the Canadian model—reflected what MacFarquhar found to be Obama's "deeply conservative" take on history, society, and politics:

> In his view of history, in his respect for tradition, in his skepticism that the world can be changed any way but very, very slowly, Obama is deeply conservative. There are moments when he sounds almost Burkean. He distrusts abstractions, generalizations, extrapolations, projections. It's not just that he thinks revolutions are unlikely: he values continuity and stability for their own sake, sometimes even more than he values change for the good. Take health care, for example. "If you're starting from scratch," he says, "then a single-payer system"—a government-managed system like Canada's, which disconnects health insurance from employment—"would probably make sense. But we've got all these legacy systems in place, and managing the transition, as well as adjusting the culture to a different system, would be difficult to pull off. So we may need a system that's not so disruptive that people feel like suddenly what they've known for most of their lives is thrown by the wayside."
>
> . . . Asked whether he has changed his mind about anything in the past twenty years, he says, "I'm probably more humble now about the speed with which government programs can solve every problem. For example, I think the impact of parents and communities is at least as significant as the amount of money that's put into education."[110]

MacFarquhar believed Obama's "deep conservatism" was what allowed Republicans to "continue to find him congenial, especially those who opposed the war on much the same conservative grounds that he did." She noted that some of Bush's top fund-raisers were contributing to Obama's campaign and observed that Obama garnered 40 percent of the Republican vote in his 2004 Senate victory.[111]

Consistent with MacFarquhar's portrait, Obama "eschewed the phrase 'war on poverty'" when he spoke to the editorial board of the *Milwaukee Journal-Sentinel* two days prior to the Wisconsin presidential primary in mid-February 2008. The paper's editors may have been advocates of a radical and regressive policy experiment—private school vouchers—but they praised Obama for "preferring instead to describe the task [of ending poverty] as a long-haul effort." "No one should launch a program," they wrote, "fight a battle and declare mission accomplished, he seemed to say. Instead, it will require continuous and unflagging efforts along several fronts—taxation, education, economic development, and yes, personal responsibility—to make progress."[112] Obama spoke to the board in gradualist, safe, "reasonable," and corporate-neoliberal language, making sure to place a proper share of the personal and moral blame for poverty onto the most truly disadvantaged.

Obama's rhetoric on poverty contrasted sharply with that of Edwards, who insistently related poverty at the bottom to wealth at the top and to unjust patterns of inequality, and who spoke—in terms consistent with the rhetoric of the historical left—not of the traditional duty to merely care for "our poor" but of Americans' radical obligation and ability to abolish the obscenity of poverty in the world's richest nation.

"Subprime Obama": Outflanking Hillary on the Right

What about the housing crisis behind the recession, driven by the aggressive marketing of dubious subprime (high-interest and high-risk) loans to disproportionately nonwhite poor and working-class homebuyers? As a liberal writer for *The Nation,* Max Fraser, noted in a February 11, 2008, article entitled "Subprime Obama," both Edwards and Clinton responded to the deepening foreclosure crisis by "pledging substantial federal resources to stabilize the mortgage market on behalf of borrowers." Edwards advanced aggressive and progressive plans, including a mandatory moratorium on foreclosures, a freeze on interest rates for seven years, and significant federal subsidies to help people keep up with mortgage payments and restructure loans. His plan included explicit measures to regulate the financial sector and punish predatory lenders. Clinton's plan had a shorter freeze, fewer regulations, and a voluntary moratorium but still guaranteed $30 billion in federal assistance to shattered homeowners and communities.[113]

Obama's proposal was "tepid by comparison," Fraser said, "short on aggressive government involvement and infused with conservative rhetoric about fiscal responsibility." "As he has done on domestic issues like healthcare, job creation, and energy policy," he wrote, "Obama is staking out a position to the right not only of populist Edwards but Clinton as well." Sounding less like a Democrat—"progressive" or otherwise—than a Republican, Obama did not call for a moratorium on foreclosures or a freeze on mortgage interest rates and remained silent on financial regulations. "And much like his broader economic stimulus package," Fraser added, "Obama's foreclosure plan mostly avoided direct government spending in favor of a tax credit for homeowners," amounting to $500 on average. This mild proposal was accompanied by rhetoric focusing on the moral responsibility of homeowners and tended to ignore the pivotal role played by leading sectors of the financial community.[114]

More than a month later, during the last week of March 2008, all three of the remaining viable presidential candidates came out with major statements on the U.S. mortgage crisis. The presumptive Republican candidate, John McCain, spoke in orthodox, hard-line, right-wing language, rejecting both increased government regulation and government assistance to homeowners. His call for voluntary action on the part of lenders amounted to a call for doing nothing. By sharp and progressive contrast, Hillary Clinton called for an updated version of the Home Owners' Loan Corporation, a New Deal program that took over the mortgages of families whose home values had fallen below their debt burden and then cut payments to a point homeowners could afford.

Obama staked out his usual position in the neoliberal middle, embracing some increased federal regulation but seeking to create "incentives for lenders" to restructure mortgages without giving that job to government. By Krugman's estimation, this comparatively lukewarm plan "followed the cautious pattern of his earlier statements on economic issues." "Mr. Obama is widely portrayed, not least by himself," Krugman added, "as a transformational figure who will usher in a new era. But his actual policy proposals, though liberal, tend to be cautious and relatively orthodox."[115]

"Who Better to Sell This Agenda?"

By Max Fraser's account, Obama's tepid and business-friendly response could be explained largely by "the centrist politics of his three chief economic advisors and his campaign's ties to Wall Street institutions opposed to increased financial regulation."[116] And Pam Martens, a twenty-one-year Wall Street veteran, noted the irony of the nation's potential first black president, a former community organizer who had once worked as a civil rights lawyer, being sponsored to a large extent by financial institutions known to have contributed significantly to a foreclosure wave that was wreaking special and disparate devastation in black and Latino communities: "The very same cast of characters making the Obama hit parade of campaign loot," she wrote, "are the clever creators of the industry solutions to the wave of foreclosures gripping this nation's poor and middle class, effectively putting the solution in the hands of the robbers. The names of these programs (that have failed to make a dent in the problem) have the same vacuous ring: Hope Now; Project Lifeline."[117]

Between February 16 and February 29, 2008, according to Martens, the CEOs of Goldman Sachs and UBS rewarded Obama for his accommodating positions on issues that mattered to their firms by raising $200,000 each for his campaign. A managing director at Citigroup raised the same amount during that period. Noting that the Obama-supported Class Action Fairness Act poses significant corporate-friendly obstacles for "defrauded homeowners of the housing bubble and defrauded investors of the bundled mortgages [who] try to fight back through the class-action vehicle," Martens hypothesized in early March that Wall Street was bankrolling Obama so as to produce a president who could be expected to sweep the corruption under the rug, avoid prosecutions, and "get on with an unprecedented taxpayer bailout of Wall Street." "Who better to sell this agenda to the millions of duped mortgage-holders and foreclosed homeowners in minority communities across America," she asked, "than our first, beloved, black president of hope and change?" Martens's bitter take on the dire implications of Obama's Wall Street support and policy behavior included some good questions for those who insisted (like many of my neighbors in Iowa City) on believing that Obama was a shining true progressive:

> How should we react when we learn that the top contributors to the Obama campaign are the very Wall Street firms whose shady mortgage lenders buried the elderly and the poor and minority under predatory loans? How should we react when we learn that on the big donor list is Citigroup, whose former employee at CitiFinancial testified to the Federal Trade Commission that it was standard practice to target people based on race and educational level, with the sales force winning bonuses called "Rocopoly Money" (like a sick board game), after "blitz" nights of soliciting loans by phone? How should we react when we learn that these very same firms, arm in arm with their corporate lawyers and registered lobbyists, have weakened our ability to fight back with the class-action vehicle?[118]

Here it is perhaps worth noting that the Pritzker family once owned 50 percent of Superior Bank, a subprime lending pioneer that collapsed in 2001. When the bank failed, Moberg noted, federal "regulators" gave the Pritzkers a "sweetheart deal . . . that let [them] off with a profit while many depositors lost money."[119]

"Our Free Market System"

All They Want Is "a Decent Shot at Life": Downsizing Popular Hopes

Consistent with Mendell's "timeless dance" and Hitchens's dark "essence" of American "winner-take-all politics, Obama has tended to downplay populist rhetoric when talking to and writing for more elite audiences. It's one thing to rail against big-money special interests when speaking to steelworkers in Johnstown, Pennsylvania, or autoworkers in Janesveille, Wisconsin. It's another and less advisable thing to speak in such terms to privileged and affluent Wall Street investors, lawyers, accountants, managers, and professors.

In *The Audacity of Hope,* clearly written for members of the U.S. educational and occupational elite, Obama praised ordinary Americans he claimed to have met for harboring "modest hopes" and low expectations regarding state and society. The outer boundaries of popular demands, as far as Obama could tell in *Audacity,* were "that people shouldn't have to file for bankruptcy because they get sick," that "every child" should have "*a decent shot at life,*" and that folks should get "to retire with some dignity and respect . . . when they get old. That [is] about it. It [isn't] much."[120] Americans,

Obama claimed, seek little more from government than a few minimal protections and base supports at the bottom end.

There was nothing in *Audacity* about the need American parents feel for their children to have equal access to the conditions and opportunities that make for good living. There was nothing about the indecent right of some children to receive limitless "shots" at—indeed an inherited guarantee of—luxuriant hyper-affluence while a much larger number of less fortunate others are socially preselected for lifelong poverty and despair, receiving perhaps one or two passing shots at middle-class "decency" if they are lucky.[121] There was nothing, of course, about the critical difference between the mythical bourgeois promise of equal opportunity and the classic left goal of social and economic equality as such.

Yet Obama's book fell short even within its "equal opportunity" framework, failing to acknowledge that the doors to the "decent life" are not even close to being "open to all" and that the United States scores quite poorly in social mobility measures, compared to other industrialized states. In the brand of "progressivism" trumpeted in *Audacity* (where the word "progressive" was used favorably at least ten times), serious and genuinely democratic concern over—and response to—the nation's harsh socioeconomic disparities was consigned to leftist "cranks" and other assorted "unreasonable zealots"—people walking in the "absolutist" and "naively idealistic" footsteps of Marx and (though Obama would never acknowledge this) the democratic socialist Martin Luther King, Jr.[122] One might interpret *Audacity* to imply that modestly hopeful Americans, reasonably rejecting "ideology" and its evil partner, "moral absolutism," know better than to push for actual equality and decent lives for all. They embrace "realistic"—that is, savagely scaled-down—ambitions that are marvelously aligned with the core neoliberal project of shifting government's main functions from the "left" to the "right hand of the state." As such, they approve reducing government's essential roles to serving the needs of the investor class, fighting class wars, punishing/warehousing the poor, and repressing dissent.[123]

"Our Greatest Asset"?

One key question addressed in *Audacity* came straight out of the neoconservative worldview: What makes the United States so exceptionally wonderful? To a remarkable extent, Obama found the answer to this nationally narcissistic question in the wise and benevolent leadership of the nation's great white Founders and subsequent honored policymakers like Franklin Delano Roosevelt, Harry Truman, and JFK. But Obama also grounded the United States' distinctive greatness in its free market capitalist system and "business culture." The American overclass should have been gratified by Obama's paean to the United States' system of (state and corporate) capitalism:

> Calvin Coolidge once said that "the chief business of the American people is business," and indeed, it would be hard to find a country on earth that's been more consistently hospitable to the logic of the marketplace. Our Constitution places the ownership of private property at the very heart of our system of liberty. Our religious traditions celebrate the value of hard work and express the conviction that a virtuous life will result in material rewards. Rather than vilify the rich, we hold them up as role models. . . . As Ted Turner famously said, in America money is how we keep score.
>
> The result of this business culture has been a prosperity that's unmatched in human history. It takes a trip overseas to fully appreciate just how good Americans have it; even our poor take for granted goods and services—electricity, clean water, indoor plumbing, telephones, televisions, and household appliances—that are still unattainable for most of the world. America may have been blessed with some of the planet's best real estate, but clearly it's not just our natural resources that account for our economic success. *Our greatest asset has been our system of social organization, a system that for generations has encouraged constant innovation, individual initiative and efficient allocation of resources . . . our free market system.*[124]

Audacity's paean to American capitalism was consistent with Obama's famous 2004 keynote address to the Democratic National Convention, when he referred to the United States as "a magical place" that served as "a beacon of freedom and opportunity" to those who exhibit "hard work and perseverance." His keynote address also praised the United States for introducing what he called a democratic "miracle"—"that we can say what we think, write what we think, without hearing a sudden knock on the door," and that "we can participate in the political process without fear of retribution, and that our votes will be counted—or at least, most of the time."

These were remarkably conservative reflections. *Audacity* and the keynote speech left it to more radically inclined left progressives—characterized by Obama and many of his elite supporters as insufficiently "realistic" and excessively "moral absolutist" carpers, "cranks," "zealots," and "gadflies" (Obama's insulting description of the revered populist U.S. senator Paul Wellstone[125])—to observe some of the undesirable and less-than-"efficient" outcomes of America's heavily state-protected "free market system" and "business culture." Those outcomes include the climate-warming contributions of a nation that constitutes 5 percent of the world's population but contributes more than a quarter of the planet's carbon emissions. Other notable effects include the generation of poverty for tens of millions of U.S. children, while executives atop "defense" firms like Boeing, Lockheed-Martin, and Raytheon rake in billions of taxpayer dollars for helping the United States maintain the deadly and controversial occupation of Iraq and Afghanistan.[126] It was also left to insufficiently "pragmatic" left thinkers and activists to note the American system's arguably wasteful and destructive allocation of more than a third of the nation's wealth to the top 1 percent of the U.S. population and its systematic subordination of the common good to private profit.

"Unreasonable" radicals were left to observe that business-ruled workplaces and labor markets steal "individual initiative" from millions of American workers subjected to the monotonous repetition of often imbecilic and soul-crushing operations, and that these operations are conducted for such increasingly unbearable stretches of time—at stagnating levels of material reward and security—that working people are often unable to participate meaningfully in the great "democracy" that Obama trumpets as the Founders' great legacy.[127] They were left also to complain about the fact that U.S. social mobility rates are actually quite low in comparison to other leading industrialized states, indicating a relatively fixed class structure in "magical" America,[128] and to observe that Obama's keynote speech advanced a shockingly truncated and negative concept of democracy—one where Americans are supposed to be grateful simply because they don't live under the iron heel of openly authoritarian state dictatorship.

Obama's ode to the absence of state dictatorship in the United States left the profound weakness of substantive positive democracy there unexamined. It evaded the unpleasant fact that much of the freedom of ordinary U.S. citizens to "say," "write," and "think" whatever they wish amounts to the equivalent of the liberty to whisper to one's immediate neighbor in the front row of a crowded movie theater while a blaring soundtrack is playing: The voices are all too commonly drowned out by giant, concentrated corporate media and the special megaphones possessed by private and state power. In a similar vein, as many campaign-finance reformers note, ordinary working Americans—even when counted (as they usually are)—are mere political half-pennies compared to the structurally empowered "moneyed interests" and corporations, which, as if bestowed with super-citizenship, exercise a well-known and disproportionate influence on U.S. "market democracy."[129]

Some "unreasonable" thinkers have darkly noted that the United States' free-speech and civil-libertarian traditions are an invitation to thought-control and propaganda when they exist side by side with the nation's stark socioeconomic inequalities. Precisely because Americans can't be dominated in purely coercive ways, they must be controlled in more subtle and less overtly oppressive fashion. Because they are "free to speak their minds," their minds must be influenced by those who wish to maintain extreme disparities of wealth and power. Thus, there is a huge investment in the United States in what Noam Chomsky and Edward S. Herman have called "manufacturing consent," and what Alex Carey called "Taking the Risk Out of Democracy."[130]

Such are some of the harsh realities of the system of private socioeconomic management that Sunstein lauded Obama for valuing when he offered the following praise in a gigantic commentary (entitled "The Obama I Know"). The piece was granted two-thirds of the *Chicago Tribune*'s opinion-editorial page on March 14, 2008: "He is strongly committed to helping the disadvantaged, but his University of Chicago background shows he appreciates the virtues and power of free markets." Surely knowledgeable that the term "free markets" is code language for untrammeled capitalism, Sunstein did not comment on that system's inherent generation of sharp economic inequality—a crippling challenge to viable democracy (as U.S. Founders like Jefferson and Madison warned)—or on the leftist case for abolishing socially imposed economic "disadvantage" (oppression) rather than merely "helping" its victims.[131]

A Revealing and Selective Comparison

Also richly suggestive of his desire to stay close to the American business elite was Obama's insistence in *Audacity* on "just how good" even "our poor" "have it" compared to their more truly miserable counterparts in Africa and Latin America. Obama omitted considerably less favorable (at least from a progressive standpoint) contrasts of America with Western Europe and Japan, the most relevant comparisons, where dominant norms and existing social policies create considerably slighter levels of poverty and inequality than what is found in the militantly hierarchical United States.

Obama's claim in *Audacity* that Americans need only take a trip overseas to see how good they have it simplifies matters greatly.[132] In reality, it depends on where the "overseas" trip takes the American traveler in search of this reassurance. If it brings the traveler to somewhere else in the industrialized world, it may well be a place where state (so-called "free market") capitalism's inherent tendencies toward wealth inequality and corporate rule are considerably more tempered by social-democratic programs and popular movements than in the United States, and the comparison will be less than flattering to America. The comparison may in fact remind the minimally attentive societal observer that the United States' "unmatched prosperity" is doled out in harshly regressive ways that create relatively high percentages and numbers of poor and uninsured households, drastically long working hours, rampant economic insecurity, and generally inadequate and underfunded public services alongside simply spectacular opulence for the privileged few.[133]

And of course, one does not have to cross the sea to appreciate these distinctions. A trip across the Rio Grande to the proximate "Third World" nation of Mexico will yield many examples consistent with Obama's praise of the United States' grand "prosperity." But a trip to Canada will instead reveal considerably lower poverty rates and broader economic security, partly reflecting the fact that Canada possesses a single-payer health-insurance system that entitles the janitor as well as the company executive to quality health coverage.

Given Obama's desire to raise money and win approval from the top 1 percent that owns half the United States' financial wealth, it makes sense that he prefers to compare the U.S. poor with the desperately impoverished masses of Nairobi, Jakarta, and Bogotá over the relatively well-off lower classes of Oslo, Paris, and Toronto.

Obama's proclaimed role model, Dr. King, by contrast—a true leftist progressive who said in 1956, the year he first emerged on the national stage, "We want no classes and castes"—was struck in the summer of 1966 by the greater poverty that existed in the United States in comparison with other First World states. "Maybe something is wrong with our economic system," King told an interviewer, observing, in David Garrow's words, that "in democratic socialist societies such as Sweden there was no poverty, no unemployment and no slums."[134]

Against Independent Development

In *Audacity* Obama recognized that big U.S. capital's neoliberal economic agenda reaches beyond our shores. In his foreign policy chapter (to be discussed in Chapter 4), he criticized "left-leaning populists" like Hugo Chavez in Venezuela for thinking that developing nations "should resist America's efforts to expand its hegemony" and for daring—imagine!—to *"follow their own path to development."* Such dysfunctional "reject[ion] [of] the ideals of free markets and liberal democracy," along with "American" ideas like "the rule of law" and "democratic elections"—interesting terms for the heavily state-sponsored U.S. effort to impose authoritarian and corporate-state capitalist policy imperatives on subordinate "developing nations"—will only worsen the situation of the global poor, Obama claimed. Obama did not comment on the remarkable respect the United States showed for "democratic elections" and "the rule of law" when it supported an attempted military coup to overthrow the democratically elected Chavez government (because of his opposition to the U.S. neoliberal agenda) in April 2002.[135]

Obama also ignored a preponderance of evidence showing that the imposition of the "free market" corporate-neoliberal "Washington Consensus" has deepened poverty across the world in recent decades. Billions are forced to live in ever more extreme conditions of poverty as Obama audaciously instructs poor and exploited states that "the system of free markets and liberal democracy" is "constantly subject to change and improvement." Those who have the time and energy to examine the overwork-plagued U.S. "homeland" might note the ever-escalating inequality of U.S. society and the related, ever-deepening insecurity experienced by American working people. Such is the ugly reality of life, even in the United States—home to what Obama obsequiously called "a prosperity that's unmatched in history"—under the rule of the neoliberal doctrine that big business upholds.[136]

The Invisible Business Elite

A critical part of Obama's effort to stay inside business-friendly political parameters is a reluctance to identify the nation's largely business-based power elite as a source of the difficulties he claims to address. As the conservative writer Andrew Ferguson noted in a clever reflection on "The Wit & Wisdom of Barack Obama," Obama has often been maddeningly vague on exactly which human agents and social forces are behind the widespread unease and despair for which he claimed to offer solutions. By Ferguson's account in mid-March 2008,

> Obama truly is the unity candidate. There is no white America or black America, as he says; no blue states or red states, in his famous formulation, but only the United States of America. And what unites all these people—what unites us—is our shared status as victims.
>
> Unfortunately, this raises the question of who the victimizer is. It's an uncomfortable question for a candidate who, having drawn such a depressing picture, wants to pivot toward the positive and upbeat and hopeful. Suddenly Obama's gift for the identifying detail leaves him. With unaccustomed vagueness he refers to "lobbyists" and "overpaid CEOs" but never names them. It's a world without human villains, improbably enough. Who are the agents of this despair? By whose hand has the country been brought so low? Whoever they are, they vanish in the fog of sentences like this: "We are up against decades of bitter partisanship that cause politicians to demonize their opponents instead of coming together to make college affordable or energy cleaner." So not even politicians in power are responsible; it's decades of bitter partisanship that has forced them into demonization, and the demonization has in turn prevented them from getting things done.
>
> This is a murky place. Cause and effect are blurred. Bad things happen though nobody does them. Instead we face disembodied entities, ghostly apparitions. "Make no mistake about what we're up against," he will announce, with what sounds, for a moment, like clarity; but then he goes on to say what we're up against: "the belief that it's okay for lobbyists to dominate our government"; "the conventional thinking that says your ability to lead as president comes from longevity in Washington"; "forces that feed the habits that prevent us from being who we are"; "the idea that it's acceptable to do anything to win an election."

> Some agents of despair these turn out to be! A belief, a way of thinking, an idea, forces that feed habits, and decades of partisanship. He won't even bring himself to blame Republicans.[137]

Ferguson's point here was that all of this murky blamelessness was actually a smokescreen for for the fact that a left-learning Obama saw the business class and concentrated wealth as evil culprits. But that argument finds little support in Obama's policy record and broader political and intellectual history. The moral and ideological obfuscation that Ferguson correctly identified was more likely true to Obama's inner worldview, not a reflection of some effort to cloak the senator's underlying populism.

Intentionally or not, Noam Chomsky put his finger on a similar point about Obama and the broader political culture that produced "the Obama phenomenon" during an interview with David Barsamian in January 2007. "There is a lot of talk right now," Chomsky told Barsamian, "about how the United States is a divided country. We have to bring it together, 'red states' and 'blue states.' In fact, it is a divided country, but not in the way that's being discussed. It's divided between the public and the power systems, the government and the corporate system." Chomsky rightly added that "the major fissure [in the United States] is the basic split between the public and the country's real power sectors. Both of the political parties and the business sector are well to the right of the population on a host of major issues."[138]

This is a strictly unmentionable insight in the political discourse of the Obama campaign, which has hitched its claim to power on a munificent pledge to save the Republic from terrible divisions between "red state" (white-patriarchal and more rural, evangelical, and militarist) Republicans and "blue state" (more multicolored, feminist, gay-friendly and urban-cosmopolitan) Democrats. The actual, business-based power elite is invisible in his promise to lead us into a glorious future of countrywide cohesion by transcending the frightening and bitter partisan discord inherited (he claims to think) from the late 1960s and restore the lost Camelot of noble national unity and meaning beyond (supposedly) petty and dysfunctional squabbles over abortion, drugs, race, and guns.

"Outrage Does Not Make Sense"

Consistent with Thomas Frank's observation on the Democrats' DLC-inspired "dropping [of] the class language that once distinguished them sharply from Republicans," Obama's *Audacity of Hope* was devoid of the righteous anger that characterized the short-lived campaigns of Kucinich and Edwards and that has always been associated with populist and progressive critiques of the extreme wealth inequality that is currently prevalent in the United States today. The supposedly nonideological Obama rejects the venerable progressive exercise of cultivating popular indignation by relating working Americans' economic problems to the machinations of powerful elites who gain wealth by exploiting ordinary folks. He seems to hold the opinion that a discourse of anger at injustice is dysfunctional and works against the higher goal of national "unity." "He rarely accuses," MacFarquhar noted, *"preferring to talk about problems in the passive voice, as things that are amiss with us rather than as wrongs that have been perpetrated by them."*[139] He favors an academic or even *medical* approach that deletes elite culpability in the creation of social misery. MacFarquhar usefully captured this supposedly neutral and nonideological tone on the campaign trail:

> In the past couple of months, Obama has hosted health-care forums of his own—in New Hampshire, in Iowa. In these forums, he is tranquil and relaxed, as though on a power-conserve setting. He paces slowly, he revolves, he tilts his head. He comments in a neutral, detached way. He doesn't express sympathy for sickness, or scorn for bureaucracy, or outrage at unfairness. He says that the system is broken and needs to be fixed, but conveys no particular urgency.
>
> This mode of his is often called professorial, and Obama himself likens these forums to the constitutional-law classes that he taught at the University of Chicago. [But] Obama's detachment, his calm, in such small venues, is less professorial than medical—like that of a doctor who, by listening to a patient's story without emotional reaction, reassures the patient that the symptoms are familiar to him. It is also doctorly in the sense that Obama thinks about the body politic as a whole thing. If you are presenting a problem as something that they have perpetrated on us, then whipping up outrage is natural enough; but if you take unity seriously, as Obama does, then outrage does not make sense, any more than it would make sense for a doctor to express outrage that a patient's kidney is causing pain in his back.[140]

Never mind, most good populists would say, that the body politic is deeply poisoned by the plutocratic power and specific agency of the corporate elite and urgently requires the sort of democratic detoxification that still requires popular outrage—however insufficient such anger might be in and of itself. Or that such transformation requires dropping the widespread illusion that ordinary people's problems are about "things that are amiss with us" and looking hard at—and acting against—the wrongs that are regularly perpetrated by the wealthy few.[141] And never mind that tens of millions of Americans are afraid to visit a *real doctor* thanks to the structurally super-empowered U.S. business community's long-standing efforts to prevent the elementarily decent introduction of universal health insurance in the "land of the free."

By MacFarquhar's account of "The Conciliator," Obama's reluctance to speak in the venerable language of class was evident in the contrasting ways that he and Hillary Clinton spoke about preventive health care during a spring 2007 AFL-CIO forum in Las Vegas. Here was Clinton's commentary, emphasizing the perfidious and powerful role of insurance corporations:

> We have to change the way we finance health care, and that's going to mean taking money away from people who make out really well right now, so this is going to be a big political battle. The insurance companies make money by employing a lot of people to try to avoid insuring you and then, if you're insured, to try to avoid paying for the health care you received. . . . A lot of insurance companies will not pay for someone who's pre-diabetic or been diagnosed with diabetes to go to a nutritionist to find out how better to feed themselves, or to go to a podiatrist to have their feet checked. The insurance companies will tell you this: they don't want to pay for preventive health care because that's like lost money because they're not sure that the patient will still be with them. But if they're confronted with the doctor saying we're going to have to amputate the foot they're stuck with it. That is upside down and backwards![142]

Here's what Obama had to say:

> We've got to put more money in prevention. It makes no sense for children to be going to the emergency room for treatable ailments like asthma. Twenty percent of our patients who have chronic illnesses account for eighty percent of the costs, so it's absolutely critical that we invest in managing those with chronic illnesses like diabetes. If we hire a case manager to work with them to ensure that they're taking the proper treatments, then potentially we're not going to have to spend thirty thousand dollars on a leg amputation.[143]

When an audience member asked Obama about health care for minorities, the senator turned the focus away from powerful corporate players and toward the behavior and very immediate circumstances of impoverished black people. "Obesity and diabetes in minority communities are more severe," Obama said, "so I think we need targeted programs, particularly to children in those communities, to make sure that they've got sound nutrition, that they have access to fruits and vegetables and not just [the popular, fried-chicken, fast-food chain] Popeyes, and that they have decent spaces to play in instead of being cooped up in the house all day."[144]

"No One Has Asked You to Play a Part"

Another key expression of Obama's desire not to offend the "country's real power centers" is found in his efforts to appeal, à la Charles Dickens, to their supposed underlying and farsighted benevolence. In the late summer of 2007, Obama made a revealing statement at the end of a speech that purported to lecture Wall Street's leaders on their "Common Stake in America's Prosperity." Speaking at NASDAQ's headquarters, he told the nation's financial elite, "I believe all of you are as open and willing to listen as anyone else in America. I believe you care about this country and the future we are leaving to the next generation. I believe your work to be a part of building a stronger, more vibrant, and more just America. I think the problem is that no one has asked you to play a part in the project of American renewal."[145]

These were strange beliefs to (claim to) hold in light of the actual historical pattern of business behavior that naturally results from the purpose and structure of the system of private profit. An endless army of nonprofit charities and social-service providers, citizens, environmental and community activists, trade union negotiators, and policymakers has spent decades asking (often enough begging) the American corporate and financial capitalist overclass to contribute to the domestic social good. The positive results are generally marginal and fleeting as the "business community" works with structurally super-empowered effectiveness to distribute wealth and power ever more upward and to serve the needs of private investors and capital accumulation over and above any considerations of social and environmental health and the common good at home or abroad. Holding no special allegiance to the American people in an age of corporate globalization, the economic elite is more than willing to significantly abandon the domestic U.S. society and its workers and communities in order to serve the ultimate business purpose: enhancing its bottom line.

As the founder of the Washington-based Economic Policy Institute, Jeff Faux, noted in his 2006 book, *The Global Class War: How America's Bipartisan Elite Lost Our Future and What It Will Take to Win It Back,* America's largely business-based and bipartisan "governing class" holds no particular attachment to the people, communities, health, or even competitiveness of the United States per se. "As early as the 1950s," Faux wrote, "A Ford Motor executive corrected a U.S. senator who referred to the company as 'an American firm.' 'We're an American company when we are in America,' he said, 'and a British company when we are in Britain, and a Brazilian company when we are in Brazil.'" Forty years later, Ford Motor Company chief Alex Trotman told Robert Reich that "Ford isn't even an American company, strictly speaking. We're global. We're investing all over the world. Forty percent of our employees already live and work outside the United States, and that's rising. Our managers are multinational. We teach them to think and act globally."[146]

Prior to the 1970s, Faux observed, the "American" business community invested in foreign countries primarily to produce for their markets. Afterward, however, global competition and technological changes sparked "the restless American corporate class to see the potential of outsourcing production to places where labor costs were cheaper and weak governments could be bribed to keep them cheap. The ability to produce elsewhere and still sell in America would allow them to abandon the irksome twentieth century American social contract. Just to threaten to move would give more bargaining power over workers and government."[147] The results have included an ongoing epidemic of outsourcing, job loss, union-busting, and capital flight—an "abandonment of America" that has led both to dramatically increased inequality within the United States and declining competitiveness in the U.S. economy as a whole. As Faux observed, the ever more globalized "American" business class makes no serious effort to reverse the nation's declining performance and investment in the critical areas of education, research, infrastructure, health, energy efficiency, and the like.

"Today," Faux wrote, "business elites that cared about America's future would be demanding new government investments" in quality education and national research and development and the like. "Instead, they send their lobbyists to demand more tax cuts, now." At the root of this terrible reality is the simple and obvious fact that "American" capital no longer holds any special allegiance to, or interest in, a specifically American community or economy. Writing about why American corporate CEOs seem hopelessly disinterested in the ongoing domestic decline of the United States, the rabid corporate-globalization enthusiast Thomas Friedman admitted that "in today's flatter [more tightly interconnected] world, many key U.S. companies now make most of their profits abroad and can increasingly recruit the best talent in the world without ever hiring another American."[148]

In his important book *The Transnational Capitalist Class,* Leslie Sklair said corporations interact with three sorts of economies. The first is a "national economy" wherein production and distribution occur within national boundaries. The second is an "international economy" in which goods and services are traded across national lines. The third is a "global economy" where investment, production, and sales are conducted freely and regularly across permeable borders. In the first two, corporations can make some credible claim to represent the "national interest" of their home countries. In the third, however, national interest fades to insignificance in relation to the bottom line.[149]

Thanks in no small part to the corporate-globalizationist thrust of U.S. policy in the world system, the commanding heights of corporate "America" are now strongly rooted in the third sort of economy. Until the last third or quarter of the twentieth century, the American corporate elite's pursuit of profit was at least partly consistent with the project of "building a stronger, more vibrant, and more just America." But that elite has since clearly and unequivocally abandoned that project, as is evidenced not merely by its trade, labor, environmental, and investment practices and agenda, but also by its evident willingness to tolerate and even in some cases encourage harebrained, right-wing schemes to ban stem-cell research, purvey creationism in the public schools, privatize Social Security, attack public education, and the like. This abandonment makes Obama look ridiculous and/or cynical when he claims to believe that all that is lacking is for the U.S. citizenry to belatedly "ask" its capitalist ruling class to "play a part in the project of American renewal."[150]

"Who Is Going to Fight for You?"

The lifelong consumer advocate and left-liberal progressive Ralph Nader probably had Obama's NASDAQ comment in mind when he spoke to MSNBC political talk-show host Chris Mathews in mid-December 2007. Mathews claimed that Nader had "excluded Obama from the progressive coalition." "He's excluded himself," Nader said, "by the statements he's made, unfortunately. He's a lot smarter than his public statements, which are extremely conciliatory to concentrated power and big business." Explaining why he was endorsing Edwards in Iowa, Nader noted that "Edwards raises the question of the concentration of wealth and power in a few hands that are working against the majority of people." In Nader's view, "the voters of Iowa and New Hampshire have to ask themselves a question: 'who is going to fight for you?'"[151]

On the same day that Nader spoke with Mathews, leading liberal economist and columnist Paul Krugman argued in the *New York Times* that "there are large differences among the candidates in their beliefs about what it will take to turn a progressive agenda into reality." In Krugman's view, "Anyone who thinks that the next president can achieve real change without bitter confrontation is living in a fantasy world." Krugman's rhetoric mirrored that of Edwards, who had repeatedly referred to Obama's message of conciliation (with big business and the Republicans) as "singing Kumbaya," and to the Illinois senator's desire to work with and through corporations as "a total fantasy."[152] Consistent with Nader and Krugman's praise, Edwards earned the marginalization he received at the hands of wealthy campaign contributors and (as we shall see in the next chapter) corporate media with some rather remarkable populist rhetoric that neither Clinton nor Obama ever approached at their left-most moments during the 2007–2008 primaries.

Hillary Clinton might have savaged the insurance industry (especially when talking to labor and minority audiences) for denying services and overcharging providers and patients. She also made it clear that she intended to leave the insurance companies "in control of the health care system." It's not for nothing that she received nearly five times as much political money from the insurance industry as the more militantly and consistently populist Edwards ($226,450 versus $46,500) during the first quarter of 2007.[153] And Edwards' ability to match her in raising money from insurance and other large corporations hardly improved after he said the following in a Democratic Party candidates' forum in Charleston, South Carolina, in late July 2007:

> How do we bring about big change? I think that's a fundamental threshold question. And the question is: Do you believe that compromise, triangulation will bring about big change? I don't. I think the people who are powerful in Washington—big insurance companies, big drug companies, big oil companies—they are not going to negotiate. They are not going to give away their power. The only way that they are going to give away their power is if we take it away from them. (APPLAUSE) . . . If you want real change, you need somebody who's *taking these people on and beating them*. . . . We can't trade our insiders for their insiders. That doesn't work. What we need is somebody who will take these people on, these big banks, these mortgage companies, big insurance companies, big drug companies.[154]

One month later, Edwards said the following in Manchester, New Hampshire:

> The choice we must make is as important as it is clear. It is a choice between corporate power and the power of democracy. . . . It is caution versus courage. Calculation versus principle. It is the establishment elites versus the American people. . . . Politicians who care more about their careers than their constituents go along to get elected. . . . It's a game that never ends, but every American knows—it's time to end the game.[155]

Along with Edwards' distinctively strong focus on the problems of poverty and class inequality and his curious propensity for upholding the labor movement as the "greatest anti-poverty program in American history," this sort of rhetoric helped explain why Edwards in particular was skewered for populist hypocrisy by corporate media. "Words," as Obama noted in March 2008, using language borrowed from Massachusetts Governor Deval Patrick, "matter." As liberal media critic Jeff Cohen observed, Edwards' real difficulty in 2007 and early 2008 was that his populist rhetoric was unusually substantive and powerful, putting him on the wrong sides of corporate funding and corporate media power, which are interrelated. Both tend to filter out presidential candidates deemed too hostile or too potentially hostile to the policies and ideological imperatives of concentrated wealth. Edwards' real problem with the big money and big media powers-that-be was that, as far as the masters of Laurence Shoup's "hidden primary" were concerned, the "populist label" fit him all too well.[156]

A Stealth "True Progressive" in Waiting?

What about the claim that Obama is a closeted "true progressive" who has been playing the conservative game of U.S. politics in order to reach the White House, but who will spring populist values on America and the world as soon as he takes the oath of office? This argument has been posed to me on more than a few occasions by Obama supporters trying to explain why they support a candidate who "can't win if he lets on how progressive he is." This curious position inverts the usual progressive observation (consistent with Hitchens's "essence of American politics") that Democratic candidates run to the left of their centrist, business-friendly commitments, betraying egalitarian pledges once they gain office. Instead, the reasoning goes, Obama is running to the right of his actually left and social-democratic beliefs.

This seems highly unlikely for at least two reasons. First, very few people in key positions in the "radically centrist"[157] Obama campaign seem remotely predisposed to follow such a path. Second, Obama's career prior to his emergence as a national celebrity and politician does not jibe particularly well with the "stealth progressive" hypothesis. During his seven years in the Illinois Senate between 1997 and 2004, Obama developed a strong reputation for being intensely ambitious politically, for working closely with Republicans, for engaging in "pragmatic" compromise, and for staying close to corporate money—the great hidden secret to success under the rules of American "market democracy."[158] As *Chicago Tribune* reporters Rick Pearson and Ray Long noted, Obama, as state senator, was a regular at "The Committee Meeting"—a Wednesday night poker game attended by "about a dozen lawmakers and lobbyists." The game was held inside the Springfield, Illinois, headquarters of the Illinois Manufacturers Association, the state's leading business lobby.[159] Obama also "studiously took up golf," the well-known game of choice for businessmen and lobbyists, reporting to his friend and former foundation executive Jean Rudd that "an awful lot happens on the golf course."[160]

In Obama's eight years in the Illinois Senate, *Boston Globe* reporter Scott Helman found that nearly two-thirds of the money he raised—$296,000 out of $461,000—came from Political Action Committees, corporations, and unions. Obama "tapped financial services, real estate developers, healthcare providers, and many other corporate interests," Helman wrote. His

2004 Senate campaign received $128,000 from registered lobbyists and $1.3 million from PACs, according to the Center for Responsive Politics.[161]

These elite funding sources appear to have impacted his policy actions in the Illinois General Assembly. According to *Chicago Tribune* reporters David Jackson and John McCormick, Obama used his position on a state pension committee to direct state funds toward a "network of politically active African-American money managers" that he built in the late 1990s. Obama also played a key role in watering down an important state health-care bill in accord with the interests of the kinds of lobbyists and special interests he tended to demonize during the presidential campaign. According to Helman, "lobbyists praised Obama for taking the insurance industry's concerns into consideration" in the process of moving the legislation from implementing universal health care to mandating little more than the establishment of a commission "charged only with studying how to expand healthcare access." Along the way, Obama fought "to give insurers a voice in how the task force developed its plan."[162]

It was all very consistent with a special penchant for career-advancing accommodation and pragmatic compromise with the "powers that be" that Obama exhibited during his years as the editor of the *Harvard Law Review* and as a community organizer on the South Side of Chicago.[163]

Insofar as Obama behaved in accord with "true progressive" values during his time in Springfield, this appears to be largely because he represented a heavily black district in Chicago where majority opinion ran to the left of mainstream U.S. sentiment. Black Americans are the leftmost sector of the U.S. electorate, and there is little risk involved in taking progressive positions in predominantly African American voting areas. Running and legislating as at least a nominal progressive in such a district would be entirely consistent with Obama's higher political ambitions. When he felt his longer political viability for statewide and even national races threatened, however, he was exceedingly cautious.

That's why he voted "present" instead of "no" on seven bills restricting abortion. He has subsequently claimed that these noncommittal "present" votes were part of a progressive political strategy worked out with liberal groups like Planned Parenthood and designed to provide political "cover" for legislators who could not afford to appear to be "pro-abortion." But legislators interviewed by the *Tribune* recalled no such strategy and noted that Obama needed no such cover in his mostly liberal and predominantly black legislative district on the South Side of Chicago. Obama apparently did think he required cover, however, if he was to fulfill his higher ambitions to run in statewide or even national campaigns someday. As his good friend and former state legislator Terry Link (D–Waukeagan, IL) noted, "a 'present' vote helped if you had had aspirations of doing something else in politics. I think Obama looked at it in that regard."[164]

Long-term political calculation is certainly part of why Obama was nowhere to be seen around the great Chicago marches protesting the beginning of the U.S. assault on Iraq on the evenings of March 19 and 20, 2003. It's also why his subsequently famous October 2002 speech against the planned invasion came down from his Web site in 2003. By this time, Obama was pursuing Peter Fitzgerald's soon-to-be open seat in the U.S. Senate—a national office with a statewide voting base. "Operation Iraqi Freedom," and the false pretexts on which it was sold, might have been widely rejected in the black community from the beginning. But opinion was different and more trusting of the Bush administration in the majority white electorate that would have to support Obama if he was to win a statewide race, an open ambition of his from the beginning of his time in the Illinois legislature. As we shall see in Chapter 4, moreover, Obama's 2002 speech was much less "progressive" and "antiwar" than is commonly thought.[165]

Beyond Guns and God: "Wall Street Has Nothing to Fear"

Those who cling to the notion of Obama as a "true progressive"—whose left and democratic orientation has been "squandered" or carefully hidden thanks to his national political ambitions and/or his political handlers[166]—might want to consider an interesting description of the young phenomenon penned by the veteran black political scientist Adolph Reed, Jr., just as Obama's political career was beginning. By Reed's account, Obama came to the political game with an already advanced and highly cultivated bourgeois taste for incremental change, compromise, and accommodation with power. Alternately praised (by moderates) as "pragmatism" and "realism" and reviled (by left progressives and radicals) as "selling out" and "co-optation," his finely honed centrism was a habit of thought that flowed naturally from his elite socialization in a corporate-neoliberal, post–Civil Rights era at privileged private institutions. It was Columbia, Harvard, and the metropolitan foundations on whose boards he sat and in whose circles he moved while he worked as a Chicago lawyer (including the Woods Fund of Chicago and the Joyce Foundation) that had given shape to his position on the ideological spectrum. This is how Reed described the thirty-something Obama in early 1996, shortly after the latter won his first election to the Illinois legislature and more than eight years before the world beyond Springfield and the Chicago and Washington money-politics elite discovered the "Obama phenomenon":

> In Chicago, for instance, we've gotten a foretaste of the new breed of foundation-hatched black communitarian voices: one of them, a smooth Harvard lawyer with impeccable credentials and vacuous-to-repressive neoliberal

> politics, has won a state senate seat on a base mainly in the liberal foundation and development worlds. His fundamentally bootstrap line was softened by a patina of the rhetoric of authentic community, talk about meeting in kitchens, small-scale solutions to social problems, and the predictable elevation of process over program—the point where identity politics converges with old-fashioned middle class reform in favoring form over substance. I suspect that his ilk is the wave of the future in U.S. black politics here, as in Haiti and wherever the International Monetary Fund has sway.[167]

The young Harvard lawyer and state legislator's ideological character aside, the more seasoned Obama, who is currently standing one election away from the presidency, thinks and functions well within the moral, ideological, and policy parameters set by the economic elite. As Alexander Cockburn noted in March 2008, "Wall Street has nothing to fear from Clinton or from Obama, who floats on vast contributions from Wall Street." Leading U.S. Marxist analyst Doug Henwood made a similar point in early April 2008, noting that possessors of "big capital would have no problem with an Obama presidency. They like him because they're socially liberal, up to a point, and probably eager for a little less war, and think he's the man to do their work. They're also confident he wouldn't undertake any renovations to the distribution of wealth."[168]

In late April 2008, Obama's closeness to the corporate sector received special attention from the Pulitzer Prize–winning journalist and author Chris Hedges. Known mainly for his writings on and against the far right, Hedges turned his critical eye to the supposed liberal progressivism of Obama. He noted that Obama's campaign message was "filled with repeated reassurances to the corporate elite" and that Obama's book *The Audacity of Hope* was a "reminder, bolstered by Obama's voting record that corporations would have nothing to fear from an Obama presidency." According to Hedges,

> The corporate state, which is carrying out a coup d'etat in slow motion, believes it will prosper in Obama's hands. If not, he would not be a viable candidate. . . . Obama is an articulate, intelligent, and attractive politician, but he is also a corporate figurehead. A vote for Obama is a vote for the corporate state. Under an Obama administration, the corporations would continue their ruthless drive to disempower the citizens, to protect an entrenched American oligarchy, and to subvert what is left of our faltering democracy.[169]

This was the deeper elitism that "mainstream" (corporate) media coverage generally overlooked when Obama helped provoke charges of cultural snobbery with some revealing comments to an elite gathering of fund-raisers in San Francisco prior to the April 22 Democratic primary—won decisively by

Hillary Clinton with large support from white working-class voters—in Pennsylvania. "You go into these small towns in Pennsylvania and, like a lot of small towns in the Midwest, the jobs have been gone for 25 years and nothing's replaced them. . . . And it's not surprising that they get bitter, they *cling to guns or religion* [emphasis added] or antipathy toward people who aren't like them." Later, in clarifying his comments, Obama said that poor, white, small-town Americans simply "don't vote on economic issues," turning instead to things like guns, gay marriage, abortion, and religion.[170]

This sounded like very much like the official version of the "Thomas Frank Kansas thesis," technically incorrect since working-class whites actually vote more on the basis of economic concerns than affluent whites do.[171] The bigger difficulty was that Obama's explanation side-stepped the deeper Frank argument on how the Democrats lose working-class voters: by clinging to the corporate center on economic issues, taking the workers' material concerns largely "off the table," and running (unlike Edwards in the 2007–2008 campaign) from "the class language that once distinguished them sharply from Republicans."[172]

The deletion is hardly surprising since Obama seems to be in great danger of repeating the 2004 Kerry mistake. Instead of addressing the problem of elite corporate dominance, Obama, like Kerry, may well epitomize the deeper problem that Frank identified in the all-too-forgotten and/or unread conclusion to his provocative 2004 book: excessive Democratic Party ideological and policy closeness to top business sectors.[173]

CHAPTER 2

The Other Hidden Primary

Spectators are not supposed to bother their heads with issues.

—NOAM CHOMSKY, FROM A SPEECH GIVEN IN BOSTON, FEBRUARY 2008

We have come to know Barack Obama, his toughness and his grace. . . . Barack Obama challenges America to rise up, to do what many of us long to do: to summon the "better angels of our nature."

—JANN S. WENNER, FROM *ROLLING STONE*, MARCH 2008

The 2008 Obama presidential run may be the most slickly orchestrated marketing machine in history. . . . Marketing is not even distantly related to democracy or civil empowerment. Marketing is about creating emotional, even irrational bonds between your product and your target audience.

—BRUCE DIXON, FROM *VOICE*, FEBRUARY 15, 2008

CAMPAIGN CONTRIBUTIONS are not the only filter tending to produce plutocratic election and policy outcomes in America's "democratic" (or "post-democratic") process. Also highly relevant and intimately related to the money question is the far-reaching vetting and image-making power of that very special and powerful section of the business community known as corporate media. Big media's role in defining credibility and selecting candidates considered safe to private wealth is another great factor working for the big-money domination of U.S. politics that Obama claimed to deplore as the possibly unprecedented level of positive media attention he received propelled him into overnight celebrity status and provided a critical defining aspect of "the Obama phenomenon."

As Edward S. Herman has noted, the dominant media "are part of the same corporate community as the election investor-funders: their owners are rich, their advertisers have strong pro-business political interests . . . and they work on the basis of establishment ideology." Having internalized the basic concerns and considerations of the corporate world, dominant media managers tend to let "money flows" dominate their coverage of candidates and elections, giving special focus to "the horse race" (who's winning and who's losing) and superficial candidate qualities—"eschewing," as Herman said, "tendencies toward 'populism,' which is generally anathema to the investor community." Candidates who are seen as too dangerously outside the business establishment's narrow spectrum of acceptable thought and policy (Dennis Kucinich, Ralph Nader, and perhaps even, in 2008, John Edwards) are, by comparison, underreported and unfavorably covered.[1]

Mainstream commentators claim that such selective candidate coverage and commentary simply reflect the public's sentiments, since the media-approved candidates who happen to have large campaign finance war chests also happen to enjoy high ratings in the polls. But this attempt at justification overlooks a self-fulfilling prophecy, the catch-22 at the heart of the process through which candidate viability and desirability are defined by the corporate elite. Candidates' ratings in polls are based largely on the heavy and favorable media coverage that dominant media authorities tend to deny to excessively "populist" and antiestablishment candidates—contenders who cannot expect to raise funds on par with those more favored by the broader business community, of which big media is one critical part. Failure to raise campaign dollars on a giant scale becomes a key part of the media's definition of a candidate as "unelectable," regardless of how well his or her policy positions resonate with popular sentiments on issues. As Herman noted, "the non-electables lose poll status for those anxious that their party win, even with a second- or third-best candidate."[2]

"To Change Minds and Change Hearts" in "the Court of Public Opinion" with the "Power of Branding"

The viciously circular plutocracy of media influence goes deeper than just the coverage allotted candidates in the daily news. The exorbitant expense of media advertisements and media consultants and image-makers drive the ever-escalating costs of campaigns to the point where candidates cannot stay viable without raising the enormous sums that wealthy contributors can best provide. A presidential campaign cannot succeed without raising tens of millions of dollars to pay for mass candidate marketing on a giant scale.

The Obama campaign was hardly an exception. "The 2008 Obama presidential run," noted Bruce Dixon in February 2008, "may be the most slickly orchestrated marketing machine in history."[3] According to the campaign's financial report to the Federal Election Commission, Obama had by then spent $52 million on "media, strategy consultants, image-building, marketing research and telemarketing." As Pam Martens noted in early March 2008,

> The money has gone to firms like GMMB, whose website says its "goal is to change minds and change hearts, win in the court of public opinion and win votes" using "the power of branding—with principles rooted in commercial marketing," and Elevation Ltd., which targets the Hispanic population and has "a combined experience of well over 50 years in developing and implementing advertising and marketing solutions for Fortune 500 companies, political candidates, and government agencies." Their client list includes the Department of Homeland Security. There's also the Birmingham, Alabama–based Parker Group which promises: "Valid research results are assured given our extensive experience with testing, scripting, skip logic, question rotation and quota control. . . . In-house list management and maintenance services encompass sophisticated geo-coding, mapping and scrubbing applications." Is it any wonder America's brains are scrambled?[4]

Besides contracting with sophisticated, big-client, corporate-marketing firms like GMMB and the Parker Group, the Obama operation developed its own considerable internal mass-market research and sales capacities for identifying and seducing political consumers (voters) susceptible to "brand Obama." When ABC News anchorman Charles Gibson visited Obama's sprawling Chicago office seven days before the Ohio and Texas primaries, he observed the quiet hum of a corporate sales office. "The tone of the campaign headquarters," Gibson noted, was "strikingly serene." He observed "33,000 square feet of downtown Chicago office space and no one is sure exactly how many staff." "The 20-somethings in the New Media department," Gibson said, "are responsible for everything from designing merchandise sold on the Web site to blogging to uploading videos and managing chat rooms." By Gibson's account, "The money flows through the computers, a steady infusion of cash in $10, $25, and 50 dollars." Obama's legendary media maven David Axelrod told Gibson, "It's strange that a computer terminal can make politics more intimate, but that's what happened."[5]

In Dixon's judgment, however, the Obama campaign's massive investment in selling the candidate was "not a good thing." "Marketing," Dixon noted, "is not even distantly related to democracy or civil empowerment. Marketing is about creating emotional, even irrational bonds between your product and your target audience."[6]

The "Invisible Primary"

One "target audience" appears to have "bonded" quite strongly: top mainstream media personnel. According to a detailed study of the media's campaign coverage by the Pew Center's Project for Excellence in Journalism (PEJ), called *The Invisible Primary Invisible No Longer: A First Look at Coverage of the 2008 Presidential Campaign,* Obama received by far the most favorable coverage of any presidential candidate in the first five months of the presidential primary campaign. Examining 1,742 campaign stories that appeared in U.S. print and electronic media between January 1 and May 31, 2007, the PEJ found that just five of the eighteen candidates—Hillary Clinton, Obama, Rudy Giuliani, John McCain, and Mitt Romney—were the focus of more than half (53 percent) of the coverage. Two Democratic candidates (Clinton and Obama) received more coverage than all the Republicans combined. Clinton technically received more coverage than Obama, but the PEJ determined that her "advantage" was due to the fact that she was mentioned so much on right-wing talk-radio stations. Obama received more coverage in the broader media if such outlets as Rush Limbaugh were not counted.

The former Democratic vice presidential candidate John Edwards was the focus of just 4 percent of the mainstream media coverage. And a large percentage of his coverage came from stories about his wife's cancer diagnosis. Aside from the cancer stories, he would have received less coverage than a Republican who had yet to formally declare his candidacy—Fred Thompson.

Most disturbing of all, perhaps, is that questions of policy accounted for just 15 percent of the stories analyzed by PEJ. Stories about the "horse race"—who was winning, who was losing, who was raising the most money, and who was performing the best on the speaking stump—made up 63 percent of the stories. The candidates' public record was the focus of a tiny 1.4 percent of the stories, but the personal background of the candidates—their families, marriages, personal health, religion, values, and biographies/autobiographies—made up 17 percent of the stories.

Then there was the imbalance in favorability of coverage. Obama was off the charts in terms of the positive tone of the coverage he received. Just less than half (47 percent) of the stories on him were favorable, compared to just 31 percent for Edwards and 27 percent for Clinton. Just 16 percent of the Obama coverage carried a negative tone, compared to 35 percent for Edwards and 38 percent for Clinton.[7]

Consistent with Herman's argument, the top three leaders in total exposure—Clinton, Obama, and Giuliani—were also the top three in terms of money raised at the time. Edwards' exposure, however, fell well behind his fairly impressive fund-raising. This was likely for reasons suggested by Paul Krugman in mid-December 2007:

> There's a strong populist tide running in America right now. For example, a recent Democracy Corps survey of voter discontent found that the most

> commonly chosen phrase explaining what's wrong with the country was that "Big business gets whatever they want in Washington."
>
> And there's every reason to believe that the Democrats can win big next year if they run with that populist tide. The latest evidence came from focus groups run by both Fox News and CNN during last week's Democratic debate: both declared Mr. Edwards the clear winner.
>
> But the news media recoil from populist appeals. *The Des Moines Register,* which endorsed Edwards in 2004, rejected him this time on the grounds that his "harsh, anti-corporate rhetoric would make it difficult for him to work with the business community to forge change."
>
> And while *The Register* endorsed Hillary Clinton, the prime beneficiary of media distaste for populism has clearly been Obama, with his message of conciliation.[8]

For what it's worth, the PEJ's *Invisible Primary*—a chilling and appropriate title—found that my own personal favorite among the major party presidential candidates, the substantively left-progressive congressman Dennis Kucinich, was the focus of exactly 1 of the 1,742 presidential campaign stories it uncovered during the first half of 2007.

Self-Fulfilling Prophecy Coverage

Three months after the PEJ study, the Obama-friendly disparities in the quantity and quality of media coverage were still evident to trained observers. Northwestern University political scientist Kenneth Janda reasonably attributed Obama's success largely to the proclivity among journalists to cover him with special intensity. "Poor John Edwards was pretty much ignored," Janda wrote.[9]

The media's often remarkable affection for Obama reached a new peak after his Iowa victory, when *Newsweek* published its quasi-religious cover story "Our Time for Change Has Come."[10] Edwards' strong second-place showing in Iowa was a non-story there and in other sectors of the corporate media. None of this would have surprised Clarke Hoyt, the public editor of the *New York Times,* who had made this stark admission on November 18 of the previous year:

> For all its rich offerings, the *New York Times* does not level the playing field for candidates. There is less content on Democrats Mike Gravel and Dennis Kucinich and the Republicans Duncan Hunter and Tom Tancredo than there is on the leading candidates. . . .
>
> In Iowa, which launched a little-known Jimmy Carter to his party's nomination in 1976, John Edwards is close behind Clinton in the most recent *Des Moines Register* poll yet *The Times* has given him comparatively scant

> coverage. Clinton and Obama have been profiled twice each on the front page since Labor Day but Edwards not at all this year. Throughout the paper, *The Times* has published 47 articles about Clinton since Labor Day, only 18 about Edwards.[11]

The lack of coverage impacted Edwards' support levels. In polls and focus groups after presidential debates in Iowa, South Carolina, and Nevada, voters observed that Edwards had "performed best," but said they would not be voting (or caucusing) for him because he had less chance of winning. He had less chance of winning, of course, largely because of his remarkably low media profile. The media had put him in their second tier of candidates even as he ran neck and neck with Obama and Clinton to win the first and pivotal primary race—the Iowa Caucus. This put the media in the curious position of claiming to objectively report current history—in this case, Edwards' "failure to win mass support"—when, to no small extent, it was itself making that history.

"We Have Come to Know . . . His Grace"

Six weeks after *Newsweek*'s "Our Time for Change Has Come" issue, *Time* published an interesting campaign photo essay on the Democratic Party's "Great Divide"—the one between Clinton and Obama. The essay contained four gloomy black-and-white photos of Senator Clinton, all full of foreboding shadows, and four photos of Obama in color. One showed his attractive wife leaning over his shoulder while he edited a speech and saying to him (as noted in a caption), "I love you. You are great." Another showed him cheerfully checking his Blackberry messages. A third showed him playfully kicking a soccer ball while waiting to be introduced to a high-school gymnasium crowd. The message couldn't have been more clear: Obama represented a colorful new and optimistic future; Hillary is harsh, dark, old, and depressing.[12]

But nobody in the mainstream media went further in gratuitously expressing their love for Obama than *Rolling Stone* editor and publisher Jann S. Wenner. The cover of the March 20, 2008, issue of Wenner's popular magazine contained a giant, shiny, airbrushed, and quasi-messianic picture of the candidate looking out against the background of a blue sky. Next to Obama's calm but determined face, the cover read: "BARACK OBAMA. A NEW HOPE. . . . *Inside his people-powered revolution . . . The candidate and the call of history.*"

Thirty-four pages into this cultish issue, Wenner lavished praise on the junior senator from Illinois. He likened Obama to Abraham Lincoln, claiming that "there is a sense of dignity, even majesty, about him, and underneath that ease a resolute discipline. It's not just that he is eloquent—with that ability to speak both to you and to speak for you—it's that he has a quality of thinking and intellectual and emotional honesty that is extraordinary." After recalling his own earlier wonderment at the possibility that there might be "some fate by which we could have this man as president of the United States," Wenner wrote that "we have come to know Barack Obama, his toughness and his grace." He extolled Obama for having "run an impressive, nearly flawless campaign," for "renouncing the politics of fear," and for "speaking frankly on the most pressing issues facing the country and sticking to his principles." According to Wenner, "Barack Obama challenges America to rise up, to do what many of us long to do: to summon the 'better angels of our nature.'"[13] The religious motif at the end was appropriate. Wenner wrote like an acolyte, not a tough-minded member of the Fourth Estate. His paean to His Majesty Obama was a statement of undying fealty. Naturally, Wenner made no reference to the numerous examples supplied in Chapter 1 of the powerful influence that concentrated wealth can reasonably be said to have exercised over Obama's career and campaign, quite contrary to the democratic and populist rhetoric Obama has employed.

The same issue of *Rolling Stone* carried another article on "The Machinery of Hope"—the "grass-roots field operation of Barack Obama." But it omitted any mention of the powerful and pivotal role that corporate money, connections, media, public relations firms, and mass marketing had played in the creation of the Obama phenomenon. It praised the Obama campaign for having "merged technology with the grass roots," but said nothing about the campaign's success in merging politics with corporate power and capital. This article included a short interview with the celebrated black Princeton academic Cornel West, who proclaimed his "deep love" for Obama and said Obama's "calling" was "one of progressive governance." West even said, "I don't think Obama is actually inexperienced when it comes to governing as president."[14]

"No Correlation . . . Between the Issues People Think Are Important and the Candidate They Vote For"

The process of selecting elected officials in the United States is largely controlled by those who have the money to fund expensive campaigns. "In this country, with a highly developed and profitable corporate community," Edward Herman noted, that "money comes disproportionately from Wall Street and a broad array of business interests." Those with large private resources to invest in candidates directly and/or indirectly (as when a candidate's spouse is recruited to sit on a corporate board) generally do so with more than mere enthusiasm for elections in mind. Their supposed interest in funding the "democratic process" cloaks their darker and largely successful agenda of undermining democracy and turning it to their own ends both immediate and systemic. Such is the harsh reality of what Herman sardonically labeled "market democracy," where the masters of the capitalist economy produce election and related policy outcomes meant to further their own wealth and power.[15]

The absence of "consumer" democracy, or citizen "sovereignty,"—that is, "real democracy"—in the United States' "money-driven political system"[16] is largely to blame for the tendency of so many U.S. voters in recent decades to boycott or simply ignore an electoral process they have good reason to see as fixed in advance by big-money elites. Along with the long-standing "winner-take all" rules and structure of the process and (hence) of U.S. political culture (a topic to which I shall return in some detail in this book's final chapter), elitism is also a critical factor behind a commonly noted aspect of U.S. elections: the disproportionate focus on candidate image and identity over substantive matters of policy and ideology. This focus became especially pronounced during the long primary contest between Obama and Hillary Clinton.

To a degree that ought to have been shocking, the prolonged Hillary-Obama duel was about the candidates and their perceived "character." As the leading pollster Andrew Kohut, survey director of the Pew Center, told *Wall Street Journal* reporter Gerald Seib early in the Democratic primary season, "There is no correlation in the exit polls between the issues people think are important and the candidate they vote for. It's about the qualities of the person." Quoting Kohut in a *Journal* article entitled "Issues Recede in '08 Contest as Voters Focus on Character," Seib noted that Democratic South Carolina primary voters who identified "the economy" as the most significant policy issue split their ballots between Clinton and Obama to the same degree as those who picked "health care" and "Iraq" as the most relevant issues. In New Hampshire, Democrats favoring a rapid withdrawal from Iraq broke for Clinton despite the fact that Obama seemed to have a more "staunchly antiwar" message.[17] Candidate fortunes rose and fell on campaign marketers' success or failure—and corporate media's messages on which of the two candidates was mean or nice; honest or deceptive; personally ambitious or socially committed; funny or humorless; tough or soft; self-assured or needy; positively connected to his or her spouse or not; likeable or disagreeable; calm or intense; balanced or neurotic; hip or square; and so on.

"Excited about the Concept of a Black Leader"

In noting the role of these factors in voter decisions, Seib was silent on two other factors—sex and skin color. As the three—and then, after Edwards' exit before the Super Tuesday primary, two—viable candidates engaged in occasionally wonky policy discussions during carefully crafted "debates" staged and broadcast by corporate media outposts like ABC, CNN, and

MSNBC, voters' decisions for or against Hillary or Obama often came down to questions of gender and race—to simply who was black and who was white; who was male and who was female.[18] Again and again during the primaries, an attentive monitor of campaign coverage could hear one Democratic voter after another tell interviewers why they supported Hillary or Obama in terms that related in no substantive way to their favorite candidate's declared policy agenda or public record. Instead, these voters indicated in no uncertain terms that the real basis for their choice was their candidate's racial, ethnic, and/or gender identity. According to Shaila Dewan of the *New York Times,* reporting from Orangeburg, South Carolina—an impoverished blue-collar town with a large black population, where economic issues topped the list of voters' concerns—just days before the South Carolina primary:

> In Orangeburg, unemployment has disproportionately affected blacks even though, at more than 60 percent of the population, they hold the balance of political power. In 2006, unemployment among blacks here was pushing 20 percent, while among whites it was 3.3 percent. Thirteen percent of households were below the poverty level, compared with 38 percent of black households.
>
> Such dismal statistics have encouraged some voters to listen closely to the candidates' proposals to give tax rebates, fix the trade imbalance and increase the minimum wage. But *with the Democratic front-runners, Senators Hillary Rodham Clinton and Barack Obama, in general agreement on many of those issues, some say discontent over the persistent racial divide—along with anger among some black voters over criticism of Mr. Obama by former President Clinton—will contribute to race-motivated voting on Saturday.*[19]

Dewan mentioned the example of Townsend Pelzer, a black retired maintenance worker, "who said he was going to vote for Mr. Obama. Asked why, Mr. Pelzer shrugged, smiled, and pointed to his face, saying, 'Color of my skin, I guess.'"

Scott Mattingly, a white economics teacher at a nearly all-white private school in Bowman, South Carolina, told Dewan that many of his fellow volunteers at the local Obama office were "'ignorant of the issues and are far more excited about the concept of a black leader.'"[20]

Citizens as Spectators: "The Irrelevance of the Population"

In my experience, the standard academic response to evidence showing that U.S. voters make their decisions on the basis of candidate image, likeability, the "horse race," and identity instead of "the issues" is to fault the voters for childishness. But this is an elitist exercise in victim-blaming that ignores the critical and authoritarian role of corporate media, moneyed elites, and corporate campaign marketers in pushing superficial, candidate-centered coverage. The "horse race," race-gender identities of the candidates, and soap-opera sagas trump serious policy and ideological substance. It's an old problem. As Noam Chomsky noted in a speech in Boston in early February 2008, the corporate, government, and academic elites who have crafted "modern democracy" since the rise of the American corporate and imperial eras have long believed that "the important work of the world is the domain of the 'responsible men,' who must 'live free of the trampling and the roar of a bewildered herd,' the general public, 'ignorant and meddlesome outsiders' whose 'function' is to be 'spectators,' not 'participants.'"[21] Further, Chomsky wrote:

> And spectators are not supposed to bother their heads with issues. The *Wall Street Journal* came close to the point in a major front-page article on super-Tuesday, under the heading "Issues Recede in '08 Contest As Voters Focus on Character." To put it more accurately, issues recede as candidates, party managers, and their PR agencies focus on character (qualities, etc.). As usual. And for sound reasons. Apart from the irrelevance of the population, they can be dangerous. The participants in action are surely aware that on a host of major issues, both political parties are well to the right of the general population, and that their positions that are quite consistent over time. . . . It is important, then, for the attention of the herd to be diverted elsewhere.[22]

Chomsky's observations here were consistent with those he expressed on a National Public Radio (NPR) story he heard in the early fall of 2006, by which time Obama's candidacy for the presidency was easy to predict:

> When I was driving home the other day and listening to NPR—my masochist streak—they happened to have a long segment on Barack Obama. It was very favorable, really enthusiastic. Here is a new star rising in the political firmament. I was listening to see if the report would say anything about his position on the issues—any issue. Nothing. It was just about his image. I think they may have had a couple words about him being in favor of doing something about the climate. What are his positions? It just doesn't matter. You read the articles. It's the same. He gives hope. He looks right into your eyes when you talk to him. That's what's considered significant. Not "Should we control our own resources? Should we nationalize our resources? Should we have water for people? Should we have health care systems? Should we stop carrying out aggression? No. That's not mentioned. Because our electoral system, our political system, has been driven to such a low level that issues are completely marginalized. You're not supposed to know the information about the candidates.[23]

The long, drawn-out media battle between the Democratic candidates in the first four months of 2008 developed across numerous developing and overlapping media soap-operas that were heavily overlaid with questions of racial, ethnic, and gender identity. The leading episodes—many directly fanned by the dominant media—included melodramas over

- The report that the Edwards campaign had once paid $400 for a haircut the candidate received.
- The illness of Edwards' wife and its alleged impact on his capacity to be president.
- Obama coldly telling Hillary that she was "likeable enough" during a New Hampshire debate.
- Hollywood mogul and campaign financier David Geffen saying that the Clintons were chronic liars, and the Clinton campaign's subsequent call for Obama to return the money to Geffen.
- Obama linking up with mega-celebrity Oprah Winfrey on the campaign trail in Iowa and New Hampshire.
- Hillary "tearing up" and thereby successfully showing something of her hidden female vulnerability just before her New Hampshire victory.
- The Obama campaign's claim that Hillary had been racist when she said that it took the presidential leadership of Lyndon Baines Johnson, not just the inspiring rhetoric of Martin Luther King, to sign the Voting Rights Act into law.
- The Clinton campaign's charge (accurate) that Obama had lifted a number of key campaign phrases from his friend Patrick Deval, governor of Massachusetts.
- Obama adviser Samantha Power's resignation from the campaign after being quoted calling Hillary "a monster" in a Scottish newspaper.
- Clinton's campaign officer Geraldine Ferraro's resignation after claiming that Obama would not have been in a position to win the Democratic nomination if he wasn't a black man.
- Obama's long-standing close personal relationship with the fiery black Chicago pastor Reverend Jeremiah Wright.
- Claims that Hillary had lied when she claimed to have come under sniper fire in the Balkans as First Lady and that she misrepresented the details of the tragic Trina Bachtel case.
- High-profile endorsements of Obama by such political notables as Edward Kennedy, Caroline Kennedy, and Bill Richardson.
- Recurrent reports of dissension within the Clinton campaign.
- Recurrent claims that Bill Clinton was upstaging his wife on the campaign trail.
- Claims that Obama had wanted to be president since he'd been five years old.

- Allegations about Obama's friendship with Tony Rezko.
- Discussion of Obama's admitted youthful use of illegal drugs.
- Hillary's reference (in late May of 2008) to the 1968 assassination of Robert Fitzgerald Kennedy (RFK) while being interviewed by a local newspaper in South Dakota—absurdly taken by some Obama supporters to suggest a threat on their candidate's life.
- Obama's insensitive reference to a female Detroit television (WXYZ-TV) reporter as "sweetie" in May of 2008.
- Conservative anger over Michelle Obama's ill-advised comment to the effect that she had never been proud of her country until a large number of Americans demonstrated their willingness to vote for her husband as U.S. president.
- Obama's decision not to wear, and then to wear, a U.S. flag lapel pin.
- Obama's perpheral relationship with Chicago education professor Bill Ayers, a former 1960s radical who led the Weathermen sect when Obama was in grade school.

This is a highly abbreviated list of the often superficial "issues" that the U.S. corporate media kept American citizen-spectators focused on during the primary campaign.

Twenty-one days after Super Tuesday and the appearance of Seib's article, Obama distanced himself from the label "liberal," claiming that "people don't want to go back to those old categories of what's liberal and what's conservative."[24] This interesting statement, richly loaded with ideological and policy meaning, was voiced in the middle of a mild "debate" with Hillary Clinton in Cleveland, Ohio. It went widely unnoticed as the media-managed Democratic presidential contest deepened its laser-like focus on the really big issues: the candidates' characters, qualities, images, chances, and identities.

It is all very contrary to the wishes of citizenry itself, which would very much prefer a stronger focus on policy issues. As the Pew Research Center for the People and the Press found last March, at the height of the primary season

> As is often the case, voters say they would like to see more coverage of the candidates' positions on the issues and less coverage of which candidate is leading in the latest polls. More than three-quarters of the public (78 percent) would like to see more coverage of the candidates' positions on domestic issues and 74 percent would like to see more coverage of foreign policy positions.

Democrats, Republicans, and Independents are in agreement that the media should focus more on issues—both foreign and domestic—in covering the presidential campaign. Among both Democrats and Republicans, 77 percent would like to see more coverage of foreign policy issues such as the Iraq war, the war on terror, and world poverty; 73 percent of Independents say the same. Similarly, 83 percent of Democrats, 76 percent of Republicans, and 77 percent of Independents would like to see more coverage of domestic issues such as health care, the economy, and taxes.[25]

"Puzzled" That "Race and Sex Are at the Forefront"

After the racialized Ferraro soap opera, but before the more heavily racialized Reverend Wright drama (to be discussed at some length in Chapter 3), Obama told reporters that he was "puzzled at how, after more than a year of campaigning, race and sex are at the forefront as never before."[26] But part of the explanation for that reality was that his own campaign had not staked out substantive policy and ideological positions all that different from those of his fellow centrist Hillary Clinton, a corporate insider and business-friendly Democrat who shared much the same core philosophical, moral, policy, and ideological space and big-money funding base. Neither on domestic nor—as we shall see in Chapter 4—foreign policy did Obama represent any particularly graphic practical or philosophical alternative to Mrs. Clinton. (This may well have been no small part of why the contest between their two campaigns often became almost legendarily nasty.) As Gerald Seib rightly observed on Super Tuesday,

> Democrats and Republicans have reached the biggest primary day in the nation's history with this much in common: No major candidate on either side has yet offered up ideas or policies that amount to a new ideological course for the country. . . . As voting unfolds on this Super Tuesday, the two hottest candidates at the moment—Republican John McCain and Democrat Barack Obama—are most striking for their ability to appeal to independent voters in the middle of the ideological spectrum, and for their willingness to compromise there.[27]

Seib naturally did not mention that the "invisible primaries" of corporate wealth and media worked powerfully to narrow the spectrum in such a business-friendly fashion—an admission that might have undermined his focus on voters as the primary agents of the "focus on character." When the interrelated "hidden primaries" of money, wealth, media, and empire filter out serious candidates with strong issue positions beyond the narrow corporate-imperial spectrum, and the candidates who remain are largely identical on matters of policy and ideology, what else are voters supposed to base their decisions on except matters of personal character, image, and identity?

Of course, another part of the explanation for race's persistent relevance in the campaign was that, as Shaila Dewan's report from Orangeburg suggested, skin color, like gender, still matters a very great deal in American life, despite Obama's best and politically astute, if misleading, efforts to seem to have "transcended race." I shall examine those efforts, and the broader, related, and critical racial dimension of the Obama phenomenon, in the next chapter.

CHAPTER 3

How "Black" Is Obama?

Color, Class, Generation, and the Perverse Racial Politics of the Post–Civil Rights Era

We'd probably like it better if he talked like Jesse Jackson, but ya'll wouldn't.

—DEBRA DICKERSON, *WASHINGTON POST MAGAZINE*, 2007

What ails working- and middle-class blacks is not fundamentally different from what ails their white counterparts. . . . White guilt has largely exhausted itself in America. . . . Even the most fair-minded of whites . . . tend to push back against suggestions of racial victimization and race-based claims based on the history of racial discrimination in this country.

—BARACK OBAMA, *THE AUDACITY OF HOPE* (2006)

There are a number of commentators—particularly, but not exclusively, conservatives—who seek to portray Obama not just as a generation removed from Jesse Jackson, but the antithesis of everything Jackson stood for. To them his success signals both the failure of "black" politics and removal of "black" issues from the political arena. As such, his victory does not reshape our analysis of how race is understood in America; it marks a repudiation of the existence of American racism itself.

—GARY YOUNGE, *THE GUARDIAN*, JANUARY 7, 2008

Mainly, an Obama presidency allows Americans to put a period at the end of a very long sentence. With a black president, the sins of slavery are not forgiven or forgotten, but we can move along. Nothing left to see here. Obama smoothly, strategically and subtly mines the wells of white guilt.

—KATHLEEN PARKER, *CHICAGO TRIBUNE*, JANUARY 11, 2008

Obama attributed much of the anger of Rev. Wright to the past, as if Rev. Wright is stuck in a time warp, rather than the fact that Rev. Wright's anger about the domestic and foreign policies of the USA are well rooted—and documented—in the current reality of the USA.

—BILL FLETCHER, *BLACK COMMENTATOR*, MARCH 20, 2008

Past Democratic Betrayals

"When Affirmative Action Was White"

The Democratic Party's historical record on race and black equality is less than perfect, to say the least. From its antebellum origins through the mid-1960s, the Democratic Party was, among other things, the party of the openly racist white South, where blacks were denied basic voting and other civil rights with certain exceptions of place (in some southern cities and border states) and time (blacks were briefly enfranchised in Deep South states during the Reconstruction period after the Civil War). The minority of black Americans who lived in the North during the 1930s shifted their allegiances from the "party of Lincoln" (the Republicans) to the Democrats with the rise of the New Deal. But the Rooseveltian New Deal and its Fair Deal successor exhibited a less-than-stellar record on racial justice, reflecting the power of the Democratic Party's white southern bosses and the anti-black bias of much of its more blue-collar and white-ethnic northern constituency.

Through uneven application and the discriminatory design and operation of its leading labor, pension, housing, lending, and veterans' programs, the New Deal state pioneered by the Democrats offered far fewer benefits to African Americans than it did to lower- and working-class Caucasians at a time when, in the words of political scientist Ira Katznelson, "Affirmative action was white." By Katznelson's careful account, the social and economic policies enacted by the Democratic Party during and after the Great Depression "not only excluded African Americans from attaining social parity but actually widened the gap between white and black living standards." This hidden history is a critical part of why the average black family still holds less than one-tenth the assets of the average white family more than 140 years after the abolition of slavery and more than 40 years after passage of the Civil Rights Act.[1]

From the Civil Rights to the Neoliberal Era

During the early and mid-1960s, the Democratic presidential administrations of JFK and LBJ offered critical federal (Justice Department) protection to the black struggle for equality. Johnson signed historic civil and voting rights legislation that cemented black voters' identification with the Democratic Party and moved white southerners into the arms of a refashioned, racially regressive Republican Party. But the Kennedy and Johnson administrations had to be pushed into these actions by the Civil Rights Movement (CRM), whose leaders and rank and file forced the hand of reluctant politicians and officials on both a domestic and global stage. The Democratic establishment agreed to guard the CRM and enact elementary racial reforms as much out of concern that domestic racial conflict would make the United States look bad in the Cold War struggle for predominantly nonwhite, Third World "hearts and minds" as out of genuine moral concern for the plight of black Americans. After basic victories over open and especially southern racism were attained, moreover, leading Democrats were mostly unwilling to meaningfully pursue what Dr. King knew to be the deeper and more substantive problems of entrenched black poverty and racialized economic disparity. As the latest wave of "white backlash" set in, and more and more white Americans rejected the notion that white racism was still a relevant problem for blacks, leading Democratic politicians and policymakers became less and less inclined to defend, enforce, and advance core civil rights programs and the increasingly controversial experiments in affirmative action for blacks and other racial minorities.[2]

It didn't help that nonaffluent white income and economic security declined with the onset of regressive corporate deindustrialization, restructuring, and globalization during the early and mid-1970s. The beginning "great U-turn" of American capitalism helped undercut the white majority's never terribly impressive willingness to share space, resources, power, and sentiments with black and brown others. The civil rights victories of the 1960s had been significantly contingent upon the sense that post–World War II American prosperity was so deep and broad that policymakers could meet the needs of the disadvantaged without resorting to "zero-sum" conflicts requiring the redistribution of wealth and income. A "rising tide" of affluence would "lift all boats," admitting everyone—even black Americans, the most distinctively super-exploited and hence most thoroughly stigmatized others in U.S. history—to the American Dream without upsetting underlying and interrelated inequalities of race and class. A receding tide helped spark lingering white anxieties about black advancement, undermining the majority race's sense that blacks could move forward at no great or prohibitive price to ordinary Caucasians.

At the elite level, the end of the postwar "Golden Age of American capitalism" and unchallenged U.S. economic hegemony provided critical background for the onset of a ruling post-corporate-neoliberal doctrine holding that the "free market" was the solution to nearly all social problems, including racial inequality. This neoliberal perspective took hold across the nation's bipartisan political and intellectual elite during the mid- and late 1970s and the 1980s. Henry A. Giroux noted, "The market should be the organizing principle for all political, economic, and social decisions," and that

> collective life is organized around the modalities of privatization, deregulation, and commercialization. . . . Big government is disparaged as either incompetent or threatening to individual freedom. . . . Profit making is touted as the essence of democracy. . . . Citizenship [is defined as] a plunge into consumerism. . . . Human misery is largely defined as a function of personal [bad market] choices. . . . Democracy becomes synonymous with free markets while issues of equality, social justice, and freedom are stripped of any substantive meanings and used to disparage those who suffer systemic deprivation and chronic punishment.[3]

According to the reigning corporate-neoliberal doctrine of the "post–New Deal" and "post–Civil Rights" era, it was now retrograde and nonfunctional for blacks and racial justice advocates to argue for the meaningful enforcement of government programs on behalf of black advancement and equality. Blacks were expected to now look to the supposedly benevolent, liberating, and democratic market for appropriately private solutions to primarily personal and cultural difficulties.

Jimmy Carter: He "Knew the Words to Our Hymns but Not the Numbers on Our Paychecks"

Jimmy Carter's rise and presidency epitomized the post–Civil Rights era and the chasm between Democratic political promise and Democratic policy performance when it came to race. Carter made an especially strong appeal to disillusioned black voters, but he did little of substance for African Americans beyond appointing a large number of blacks to federal judgeships and other posts. According to leading civil rights historian Harvard Sitkoff, Carter

> never sought to make the perpetuation of racial inequality a central concern of Americans, and he proved as ready to beef up defense spending and balance the budget at the expense of school-lunch programs, financial assistance to black students, and health care for the [disproportionately black] poor as the Republicans had been. Carter would not expend his moral or political capital in the national debates raging over affirmative action and busing; and he selected as a head of the Civil Rights Division of the Justice Department a man who hoped publicly that in the fight against segregation "the courts would not overreach." Blacks, moreover, became the chief victims of Carter's unsuccessful battles against inflation and recession. His economic failures resulted in the highest black jobless rates in over a decade, a deterioration of life for the

black poor, and a weakening of the tenuous hold on middle-class status that a slim majority of blacks held. "It is easy to see why many have concluded," Julian Bond commented, that "we voted for a man who knew the words to our hymns, but not the numbers on our paychecks."[4]

Bill Clinton's "New Age Racist Doctrine"

Consistent with the Democratic Leadership Council's conscious effort to distance the Democratic Party from urban minorities and the Civil Rights Movement, the same problem noted by Bond helped define the conservative limits of the presidency of Bill Clinton. Like Carter, Clinton was a southern white governor who rode into the White House partly on the basis of a special appeal to African American voters—an appeal that he quickly betrayed once in office. "At times," Kevin Alexander Gray, a black South Carolina activist and writer, has noted, "Clinton talked the social justice talk, lavishly invoking the name of Martin Luther King."[5] But "the Clinton era began," observed Gray's fellow black writer and activist Elaine Brown, "with the breach of [Bill and Hillary's] pre-election promises to institute a national health care program slated to serve the underserved, particularly poor blacks."[6] Further, Brown wrote:

> For eight years, Clinton vacillated on addressing the failure of school desegregation efforts and the dismantling of affirmative action programs. He hoped that racial discrimination might, in time, resolve itself. For eight years, he repelled requests, even by his black friends, to deliver a presidential apology for slavery, ultimately proclaiming that "the question of race is, in the end, still an affair of the heart." . . . He repudiated even the legitimacy of making any official gesture of atonement to blacks for the crime of slavery and its unrelenting ramifications, arguing that a White House apology would encourage demands for reparations and that time had rendered the question of reparations for blacks for slavery moot: "it's been so long, and we're so many generations removed."[7]

Novelist Toni Morrison may have called Clinton the "first black president," but his racial record during the 1990s included a significant federal contribution to the escalation of racially disparate mass incarceration and a vicious assault on the disproportionately black recipients of public family cash assistance. It also involved the passage of a "trade" (investors' rights) bill (the North American Free Trade Agreement) that exacerbated the disappearance of manufacturing jobs for the disproportionately deindustrialized black working class.

The Clinton White House deepened the ongoing assault on black America with its "Three Strikes" crime bill (part of a prison and drug war) and the enactment of a vicious welfare "reform" that "cut off [black and other poor children's] lifelines to food and medical care" while it kept the "era of big government" subsidy alive for "rich corporations and their executives," Brown wrote. By her account, "Clinton did nothing to elevate the economic status of blacks and other poor people in America." "In fact," Brown said, "the Clinton era was in many ways more detrimental to blacks than the Reagan and Bush years had been."[8]

When Clinton came into office, Gray observed, "just one in four black men were in the toils of the criminal justice system; when he left it was one in three." It didn't help that "he did nothing about mandatory minimum sentences" and "did nothing to change the sentencing disparity between crack and powder cocaine that disproportionately affects African Americans." By Gray's account, "Clinton's policies and attitude on due process, equal protection, and equal treatment or civil rights (rights guaranteed for all) were horrible." Clinton required the nation's predominantly black public-housing residents to surrender their Fourth Amendment privacy rights and summarily evicted them (along with any of their cohabitants) for conviction of a crime.[9]

Adding insult to deep injury, Clinton led the way in the articulation of a post–Civil Rights "New Age Racist doctrine" that "audaciously admonished blacks"—not the persistent underlying structure and cumulative legacy of historical racism—"for creating the deplorable state of black America." During a historic 1993 speech delivered in the same Memphis church where Martin Luther King, Jr., had given his last sermon, Clinton blamed blacks for dishonoring the legacy of King and wasting the "freedom" King had died to give them.

"There in Memphis," Brown bitterly observed,

> Clinton condemned blacks for being unable to overcome the thousand blows dealt during centuries of slavery. In Memphis, Clinton reprimanded blacks for being unable to overcome a post-emancipation America that spawned and nurtured the scourge of the Black Codes, the atrocities of the Ku Klux Klan, the strangulation of Jim Crow, and a long train of racist abuses that sent blacks running from South to North and back again, outnumbered and outgunned in a thousand bloody struggles, including that in which Dr. King himself had been brutally assassinated.[10]

Early in his administration Clinton withdrew the nomination of the African American civil rights lawyer and law professor Lani Guinier for the position of assistant attorney general for civil rights. He rescinded the nomination after right and center critics and newspapers across the country created a political firestorm over past legal writings in which Guinier had dared to argue that racial minorities suffered from underrepresentation in a white majority nation running its elections along "winner-take-all" lines.[11] But Clinton's troubling presidential record on race actually began during the primary season of 1992, with an especially ugly and racially tinged episode—the killing of Ricky Ray Rector. By Christopher Hitchens's chilling account:

> After falling behind in the New Hampshire primary in 1992, and after being caught lying about the affair with Gennifer Flowers to which he later confessed under oath, Clinton left the campaign trail and flew home to Arkansas to give the maximum publicity to his decision to sign a death warrant for Ricky Ray Rector. Rector was a black inmate on death row who had shot himself in the head after committing a double murder and, instead of dying as a result, had achieved the same effect as a lobotomy would have done. He never understood the charge against him or the sentence. After being served his last meal, he left the pecan pie on the side of the tray, as he told the guards who came to take him to the execution chamber, "for later." Several police and prison-officer witnesses expressed extreme queasiness at this execution of a gravely impaired man, and the prison chaplain, Dennis Pigman, later resigned from the prison service.[12]

Like his criticism of the angry black hip-hop artist "Sister Soulja" later in his '92 campaign, Clinton's execution of Rector was designed to exploit racist white "law and order" sentiments on the model of George H.W. Bush's effective use of released black murderer Willie Horton against Democratic presidential candidate Michael Dukakis in 1988.[13]

After Clinton did nothing substantive to counter George W. Bush's blatantly racist theft of the presidential vote in Florida in November and December 2000,[14] the freshly minted U.S. Senator Hillary Clinton, along with Senator John Edwards and numerous other elite Democrats, helped lead the charge for an expensive and arguably racist invasion of Iraq. As it turned out, it was a war that helped to further undermine the domestic social programs upon which blacks were disproportionately reliant because of the cumulative and ongoing record of racial oppression in the United States.

Obama: How Different on Race?

Surely, many progressives might assume, an Obama White House could be expected to break with the depressing history of Democratic civil rights betrayal and black disappointment. Obama is, after all, an African American who has written eloquently about his own past difficulties with racial discrimination. He makes positive references to such past leaders in the struggle for black equality as Frederick Douglass, W. E. B. DuBois, Malcom X, and Martin Luther King, Jr. He was a former community organizer of black poor people on the South Side of Chicago. He came of spiritual age in an

"Afrocentric" black church led by a fiery black minister known to repeatedly denounce the interrelated evils of racism, poverty, inequality, and militarism.[15] Consistent with black opinion, he was the only one of the leading Democratic presidential candidates to have opposed the Iraq occupation at the beginning (albeit on terms very different from those of the peace movement). An administration run by an actually black president wouldn't really follow in the racially accommodationist footsteps of a Carter or a Clinton, channeling Booker T. Washington and Colin Powell as much as DuBois, Douglass, and Dr. King, would it?

Keeping the provisos that the future remains open and contingent and that a President Obama *could* be more progressive than candidate Obama, in this chapter I examine Obama's record to suggest that it probably would. Even as he won large majorities of black votes in the Democratic presidential primaries, Obama has given racial justice advocates a large number of reasons to question how committed he is to racial equality and to suspect that his concept of racial justice tends to abandon nonaffluent and truly disadvantaged blacks in favor of more privileged African Americans who, like himself, have benefited from the past victories of the Civil Rights Movement.

Obama has been noticeably reluctant to explicitly align himself with the historical struggle for black equality or to confront the continuing problems of race and (more to the point) racism in American and global affairs. He has gone to considerable lengths to reassure whites that he will let them feel good about their willingness to vote for a black man and that he will not push defensive white buttons by meaningfully addressing the persistent powerful role white privilege continues to play in the United States. At the same time, this chapter suggests that, ironically, the Obama phenomenon has the potential to do significant damage to the cause of black equality by helping advance the already widespread post–Civil Rights illusion that racism no longer poses significant barriers to black advancement and equality.

This is not, however, to deny that Obama's approach to race reflected a smart strategy on the path to the presidency. Obama is a shrewd politician—a supremely ambitious one at that—as much as he's an advocate for social (including racial) justice. However much it offends radical and race activists, his relatively conservative and accommodating approach to the race question is perfectly pitched to the perverse racial politics of the post–Civil Rights and neoliberal era. It has been masterfully designed to exploit both the willingness of many white voters to proclaim their rejection of old-fashioned race prejudice and the simultaneous unwillingness of most whites to acknowledge the continuing powerful and pervasive role of racism in American life.

Part of the problem, sadly and ironically enough, is precisely that he is African American. This simple fact has combined with white America's pronounced post–Civil Rights racism-denial to compel him—assuming his primary desire is to become president—to exercise particular caution in speaking, acting, and writing about race and, more to the point, about racism.

Meanwhile, as Obama and his advisers certainly know, Obama's black identity has proved enormously important in helping him both as senator and candidate to seem more progressive and change-oriented than he really is. His race has made it considerably easier for the "deeply conservative" Obama to project himself as a progressive, populist, and peace-oriented "agent of change" and to dress up his corporate- and (as we shall see in the next chapter) empire-friendly establishment politics in "rebel's clothing." It has made many voters more reluctant than they might have been otherwise (if Obama was white) to take a deep and honest look at his accommodation with dominant domestic and imperial hierarchies and doctrines. In these and other ways, race has mattered a great deal indeed in the making of the Obama phenomenon and the tone that it took on as the campaign season developed.[16]

Imagining Transcendence

"You can't seriously imagine that racism is still a big problem in the United States," a white reader once wrote me, "when millions of white Americans are ready to vote for Barack Obama, a black man, for president." Consistent with his claim, a *Newsweek* poll conducted in the summer of 2007 found that "race is no longer the barrier it once was to electing a president." Fully 59 percent of the survey's respondents felt that the United States was "ready to elect a black President," up from 37 percent at the beginning of the twenty-first century.[17]

"If Obama gets elected President," a white physicist told me, "it would be a big—probably the biggest since the Emancipation Proclamation—step toward race equality in the U.S. If a half-black man gets elected President," the science professor elaborated, "we could stop focusing so much on race in this country and focus on other things."

These comments were remarkably similar to those sent to a Tennessee Web site by an independent white voter named Joe Lance. Lance supported Obama, he wrote, "because he transcends the old divides between black and white America. . . . It is thrilling to imagine that in electing this person to the highest office, we could see centuries' worth of animosity and despair start to melt."[18]

In a similar vein, a twenty-one-year-old white "antiwar" college student in Iowa City who called himself a "progressive" told me in early March 2008 that "electing Obama to the White House would mean the end of racism in America."

"Do you really believe that?" I asked.

"Absolutely."

A fifth take came to me from the other side of the racial divide. When I published an Internet essay critical of Obama's foreign policy statements, I received an angry response from a black reader who thought I was African American. "How can you betray your race like this?" this individual asked. "Why are you undermining a brother with a shot at the most powerful job in the world?" By this writer's estimation, Obama's black identity was in itself sufficient reason for a responsible black journalist to suspend any and all criticism of the junior senator from Illinois.

The racial meaning of the Obama phenomenon is more complicated than any of these correspondents grasped. Is there anything positive about the fact that droves of whites are willing to embrace a black presidential candidate? Of course there is. Just over forty years ago, as the United States entered the racially turbulent summer of 1967, it would have been impossible for a black politician to become a viable presidential contender. It was the same year the movie *Guess Who's Coming to Dinner* disturbed conventional racial norms by portraying a black doctor (played by Sidney Poitier) dating a white woman (Joanna Drayton), and nothing a black candidate could have said or done could have prevented him from being excluded on the basis of the color of his skin. The fact that this is no longer true is a sign of some (admittedly slow) racial progress more than fifty years after passage of the Civil Rights and Voting Rights acts.

Running from Race/Racism

"I Don't Think of Him as Black"

There are at least three basic reasons not to get overly excited about Obama's cross-racial appeal—a critical part of the Obama phenomenon—from a racial justice perspective. The first difficulty is that part of Obama's appeal to white America has to do with the widespread Caucasian sense that Obama "isn't all that black." Many whites who roll their eyes at the mention of the names of Jesse Jackson or Al Sharpton—former presidential candidates who behave in ways that many whites find too African American—are calmed and "impressed" by the cool, underplayed blackness and ponderous, quasi-academic tone of the half-white, Harvard-educated Obama.

Obama doesn't shout, chant, holler, or drawl. He doesn't rail against injustice, bring the parishioners to their feet, or threaten delicate white suburban and middle-class sensibilities. He stays away from catchy slogans like Jackson's "Keep Hope Alive" and from emotive "truth"-speaking confrontations with power. To use Senator Joe Biden's (D-DE) regrettable terminology, Obama strikes many whites as "clean" and "articulate"—something different from their unfortunately persistent image of blacks as dirty, dangerous, irrational, and unintelligible. "Among the factors contributing to

Obama's rise," Liz Mundy noted in the summer of 2007, was the interesting fact that "his appearance, his voice, and his life story are particularly well suited to attract white votes."[19]

Obama has no moral or political obligation to shed his biracial identity, multicultural background, and elite, private-school education to act more classically and stereotypically black. But whites' racial attitudes are less progressive than might be assumed when their willingness to embrace a black candidate is conditioned by their requirement that his or her "blackness" be qualified. The perceptive mixed-race journalist Don Terry was understandably perturbed when a middle-aged white filmmaker said to him in early 2004: "I love Barack. He's smart. He's handsome. He's charismatic. . . . I don't think of him as black."[20]

Handed to Black America

The perception that Obama is "not all that black" is not restricted to whites, for whom the observation generally holds positive connotations. Some black Americans have voiced the same concern, but with negative undertones, ever since he emerged as a national celebrity. This judgment arises from several facts about Obama's biography and style, including that he is technically half white, that his father was African but not African American (a key cultural distinction), that he spent portions of his childhood in multicultural Hawaii and in Indonesia, that there is a relative absence of southern, black-American accentuation and church-style drama in his voice and oratory, and that he has a history of elite private schooling that put him in regular contact with highly privileged whites.

"It's hard for someone who came out of slavery and Jim Crow," the black scholar Cornel West told Obama in early 2007, "to call [the United States] a magical place."[21] As the black British journalist Gary Younge has noted, Obama seems to have been handed to black America more than he has arisen from within it. He came to black America from Hawaii and Harvard and did not emerge from its racially segregated and disproportionately impoverished neighborhoods, schools, and churches. He arrived from outside and did so, some black Americans point out, with advantages produced by previous struggles launched from within black America—the great civil rights battles and victories of the 1950s and 1960s.[22]

A "Lack of Grievance" and a False Dichotomy between Racial Justice and Social Justice

A second reason, intimately related to the first, not to do racial-justice cartwheels over Obama's popularity with whites is the senator's apparent willingness to deepen his attractiveness to majority-race voters by accommodating white racism-denial in the United States. Expressing what *Newsweek* reporters Richard Wolffe and Darren Briscoe called a "surprising lack of [racial] grievance," the notoriously "mealymouthed"[23] Obama has been less than eager to challenge this reigning white wisdom on the "over"-ness of anti-black racial oppression in post–Civil Rights America. In *The Audacity of Hope,* Obama claimed that his 2004 keynote address had not meant to suggest that "we already live in a color-blind society." He elaborated on the depth and degree of racial disparity in the nation and suggested that it was related to persistent "prejudice" in the United States:

> To say that we are one people is not to suggest that race no longer matters—that the fight for equality has been won or that the problems that minorities face in this country are largely self-inflicted. We know the statistics: On almost every single socioeconomic indicator, from infant mortality to life expectancy to employment to home ownership, black and Latino Americans in particular continue to lag far behind their white counterparts. In corporate boardrooms across America, minorities are grossly underrepresented; in the United States Senate, there are only three Latinos and two Asian members (both from Hawaii), and as I write today I am the chamber's sole African American. To suggest that our racial attitudes play no part in these disparities is to turn a blind eye to both our history and our experience—and to relieve ourselves of the responsibility to make things right.[24]

But in the same chapter, Obama ignored elementary U.S. social reality and a vast body of empirical research by claiming that "what ails working- and middle-class blacks is not fundamentally different from what ails their white counterparts: downsizing, outsourcing, automation, wage stagnation, the dismantling of employer-based health care and pension plans, and schools that fail to teach young people the skills they need to compete in a global economy."

Obama went with the same white-pleasing "class-over-race" theme and purveyed the very "postracial politics" he claimed to reject when the *New York Times* asked him about his last-minute decision not to let Rev. Jeremiah Wright give the invocation before his presidential candidacy announcement. "Reverend Wright is a child of the 60s," Obama told the *New York Times,* "and he often expresses himself in that language of concern with institutional racism and the struggles the African-American community has gone through. He analyzes public events in the context of race." "I tend," Obama said, "to look at them through the context of social justice and inequality."[25]

This was an extremely revealing and—from a racial justice perspective—troubling comment. It unfairly connected the critical empirical and interpretive question of whether or not racism continues to exercise powerful influence in American life to the supposedly discredited and dysfunctional political discourse of the much maligned 1960s. It waffled between two very different terms—"race" and "racism"—in describing the worldview held by Rev. Wright and from which Obama sought to distance himself. And it set up a thoroughly and egregiously false dichotomy (understandable only in terms of Obama's decision to superficially privilege class over race) between (1) racial justice and (2) social justice—a bogus opposition that is frequently (and often disingenuously) brandished by the right (which is no more interested in abolishing class inequality than it is in eradicating racial disparity) in order to attack the notion that racism of any kind continues to pose meaningful barriers to black advancement and equality. That assault has drawn heavily on the ritual bashing of the supposedly excessive and frightening 1960s, a decade Obama has repeatedly showed his willingness to unduly criticize in pursuit of centrist and right-wing votes.

Obama tied his downplaying of race and his related disrespect for the supposedly dysfunctional 1960s into his campaign's "generational" healing meme during a spring 2007 interview with *Newsweek* reporters Richard Wolffe and Darren Briscoe. "I think America is still caught in a little bit of a time warp: the narrative of black politics is still shaped by the '60s and black power," Obama told Wolffe and Briscoe. The real issue, the senator argued, was the daily struggle for economic survival, not racism—that supposedly dysfunctional issue from the "divisive" and crippling Vietnam era. "That is not, I think, how most black voters are thinking. I don't think that's how most white voters are thinking. I think that people are thinking about how to find a job, how to fill up the gas tank, how to send their kids to college. I find that when I talk about those issues, both blacks and whites respond well."[26] Obama's privileging of economics (class and inequality) over race and racism was consistent with his following argument in *Audacity:*

> What would help minority workers are the same things that would help white workers: the opportunity to earn a living wage, the education and training that lead to such jobs, labor laws and tax laws that restore some balance to the distribution of the nation's wealth, and health care, child care, and retirement systems that working people can count on.
>
> This pattern—a rising tide lifting minority boats—has certainly held true in the past. The progress made by the previous generation of Latinos and African Americans occurred primarily because the same ladders of opportunity that built the white middle class were for the first time made available to minorities as well. They benefited, as all people did, from an economy that was growing and a government interested in investing in its people. Not only did tight labor markets, access to capital, and programs like Pell Grants and Perkins Loans benefit blacks directly; growing incomes and a sense of security among whites made them less resistant to minority claims for equality.[27]

But these reflections were sociologically and historically misleading. The leading "class over race" theoretician and black sociologist William Julius Wilson may have been correct to argue that black urban poverty is inextricably bound up with the larger issues and processes of overall socioeconomic organization that generate inequalities of wealth and power independently of race. Racism is not the only significant societal problem or barrier faced by African Americans, who are confronted on numerous levels by issues of class inequality—including the ever-increasing internal socioeconomic polarization of the black community itself. But color-blind capitalism has yet to remotely emerge on the U.S. historical stage.

The evidence of persistent societal bias and discrimination against black Americans—and not just poor blacks—is voluminous. Working- and middle-class blacks continue to face numerous steep and interrelated white-supremacist barriers to equality. Much of what "ails" these poor and ordinary African Americans is in fact "fundamentally different" from what middle- and working-class whites face in the American "opportunity" and class system. A still distinctively black "separate and unequal" experience in the United States results from the continuing operation of a number of objectively race-separatist real-estate and home-lending practices, discriminatory hiring and promotion patterns, the systematic underfunding and under-equipping of schools predominately attended by blacks, the imposition of racially separate and inferior curricula and pedagogies, the disproportionate surveillance, arrest, and incarceration of blacks, and much more. The persistence of these and numerous other related, objectively white-supremacist societal obstacles to black advancement is cataloged in a large social science literature.[28]

While preparing *Audacity,* Obama could have consulted an excellent survey of relevant, persistent forms of societal racism written by political scientist Michael K. Brown and a team of academicians: *Whitewashing Race: The Myth of a Color-Blind Society* (2003).[29] He could also have consulted the conservative Chicago Urban League's comprehensive metropolitan survey, published in the spring of 2005—under the title "Still Separate, Unequal: Race, Place, Policy and the State of Black Chicago" (personal disclosure: I wrote the study)—to examine the latest evidence on various interrelated ways in which social policies and structures in and around his own South Side of Chicago reproduced persistent, systematic, anti-black discrimination and bias in the schooling, feeding, training, hiring, promoting/demoting, healing, insuring, serving, reporting, patrolling, monitoring, arresting, sentencing, incarcerating, transporting, empowering, representing, funding, evaluating, assisting, analyzing, judging, televising, praising, punishing, rewarding, and shaming of the American people. In Obama's Chicago, as across the nation, multidimensional racial discrimination is still rife in post–Civil Rights America.[30] It remains deeply woven into the fabric of the nation's social institutions and draws heavily on the living and unresolved legacy of centuries of not-so-"past" racism. The long centuries of slavery and Jim Crow are still quite historically recent and would continue to exercise a crippling influence on black experience even if the dominant white claim that black "racial victimization" is a "thing of the past" were remotely accurate.[31]

Obama would also have done well to have looked at Ira Katznelson's 2005 book, *When Affirmative Action Was White.* Katznelson showed that racial inequality actually deepened during the long post–World War II U.S. economic expansion—history's ultimate example of a rising economic tide—and thereby provided critical context for the rise of racial violence in urban America during the 1960s.[32]

Just "10 Percent" to Go

Obama has reassured blacks and whites alike that blacks aren't really that far behind whites after all. *The Audacity of Hope* sought to soothe white fears of Obama by claiming that most black Americans had been "pulled into the economic mainstream." During an important speech he gave to a mostly black audience in Selma, Alabama, in early March 2007, Obama claimed that 1950s and 1960s civil rights activists—a group he referred to as "the Moses Generation"—had brought black America "90 percent of the way" to racial equality. It's up to Obama and his fellow "Joshua Generation" members to get past "that 10 percent in order to cross over to the other side."[33]

To buttress the notion that blacks have entered the mainstream, *The Audacity of Hope* cited the example of an extremely wealthy "black friend" who lent him an airplane "one of the first times I needed a corporate jet." Obama mentioned a different black friend "who had been the number one bond salesman at Merrill Lynch" and "decided to start his own investment bank." Another African American, he said, "decided to leave an executive position at General Motors to start his own parking company in partnership with Hyatt," because he wanted "to build something of his own." Obama observed that the first half million dollars he raised for his Senate campaign came from black Chicago professionals and businesses and that "blacks . . . occupy some of the highest management positions in Chicago."[34]

Unfortunately for Obama's arguments in *Audacity* and in Selma, blacks are on the wrong side of a shocking racial wealth gap that keeps their average net worth at *one-eleventh* that of whites. The income structure of black families is starkly and persistently tilted toward poverty. Whites in the United States, considered separately, enjoy the highest quality of life in the world, while black Americans, viewed separately, live at the level of a Third World nation.[35]

Obama could have garnered the following facts from the aforementioned Chicago Urban League study on racial inequality in his own metropolitan backyard:[36]

- Black median household income was just 58 percent of white median household income in the Chicago metropolitan area, according to the 2000 census.
- According to the Economic Policy Institute, the median annual black household income in Chicago in 2000 was more than $6,000 below the amount needed for a "basic family budget"—the no-frills cost of living for a small family of one parent and two children ($35,307).[37] The median white household income in the city exceeded that basic family budget by more than $11,300.
- At the upper end, a fifth of metropolitan-area white households lived on $100,000 or more, compared to just 7.5 percent of blacks. More than half (57 percent) of metropolitan-area white households lived at $50,000 or more, compared to less than a third (32.2 percent) of black households.
- A fourth of the Chicago metropolitan area's black households were officially poor, compared to just 5.6 percent of the white households and 16 percent of the Latino households.
- Sixteen percent of Chicago's blacks lived in what researchers call "deep poverty"—at less than half of the federal government's notoriously low and inadequate poverty level.
- More than a third of the metropolitan area's black children lived in poverty, compared to just 5 percent of the white kids.
- The median income of the average neighborhood inhabited by African Americans in the Chicago metropolitan area ($36,298) was just 59 percent of the median income in the average neighborhood inhabited by whites in the same metropolitan area ($61,952).[38]
- Of the city's fifteen poorest neighborhoods, with poverty measures ranging from 32 to 56 percent, all but one was disproportionately black and eleven were at least 94 percent black.
- Of the city's top fifteen neighborhoods for child poverty, with rates ranging from 55 to 71 percent, ten were disproportionately black and none were disproportionately white, the rest being disproportionately Latino.
- All but one of the fifteen Chicago neighborhoods where more than 25 percent of the kids were growing up in deep poverty had a black population percentage considerably higher than the city average. All but three were at least 94 percent black. There were six predominantly black neighborhoods where more than 40 percent of the children were deeply poor, and in Riverdale it was actually more than half.

- Seventy-two percent of the 107 Chicago public elementary and high schools that reported 97 percent or more of their students as "low income" were 90 percent or more African American. Seventy-one, or two-thirds (66 percent), of those schools were 95 percent or more African American.
- Just 4.4 percent of the officers and directors of large Chicago-area businesses were African American by the late 1990s.
- Only 2.6 percent of corporate officers in large Chicago-area based corporations were African American, and only 7 percent of corporate directors were African American.
- Seventy-five percent of large Chicago-area corporations did not have a single African American corporate officer.
- Forty-six percent of large Chicago-area corporations did not have a single African American on their board of directors.
- African Americans were badly underrepresented among partners of major Chicago law firms. Only 0.7 percent of 2,950 partners in Chicago area law firms were African American.
- Chicago area black-owned businesses are considerably smaller and poorer than their white counterparts.
- Ninety-three percent of Chicago area federal campaign contributions came from zip codes that were *50 percent or more white*. Just *7.2 percent* came from zip codes that were 50 percent or more composed of people of color.

"White Guilt Has Largely Exhausted Itself": Failure to Distinguish between Prejudice and Structural Racism

But so what? Obama argued in *Audacity* that "white guilt has largely exhausted itself in America," as "even the most fair-minded of whites . . . tend to push back against suggestions of racial victimization and race-based claims based on the history of racial discrimination in this country." A slavery-reparations opponent, Obama claimed that this "push back" (also known as denial) is partly due to the bad culture and poor work-ethic of the inner-city black poor, a topic to which I shall return later in this chapter. It is also, he argued, partly due to the fact that whites are no longer materially secure enough to tolerate the granting of surplus resources to disadvantaged minorities.[39]

Given his proclaimed faith in American capitalism, it was interesting to see Obama argue in *The Audacity of Hope* that white Americans are no longer sufficiently economically stable to care about the racial injustice experienced by black Americans. Obama observed in that book that America's "system of social organization" opened the door to black advancement only when it seemed to be "delivering the goods for all whites and there was enough to go around" (during the post–World War II "golden age of American capitalism"). That security is gone today, Obama noted, unintentionally raising questions about just how great an "asset" the United States' "free market system" is to its people. But here Obama's desire to seem to let white America off the hook of racism came into an interesting confrontation with his desire to let the wealthy off the hook of capitalist oppression. It also led him to deny the existence of numerous progressive antiracist whites (including me) who join a large number of black Americans to support black "race-based" claims (including reparations) based on the (living) history of racial discrimination in the United States.

As these antiracist activists and intellectuals know, racial oppression is a persistent social and historical reality in numerous intersecting and overlapping areas of American societal experience, politics, and policy. The notion in mainstream white America that anti-black racial oppression is "a thing of the past" is based on a superficial understanding of racism and on denial of the continuing powerful impact of past racism on contemporary race disparity. That understanding is commonly stuck at the level of conscious and willful prejudice. It fails to understand the effects of a "state-of-being" or structural racism that generates racially disparate results even without racist intent—"state-of-mind" racism—on the part of white actors.[40] It denies the relevance of highly racialized social processes that work in routine and ordinary fashion to sustain racial hierarchy and white supremacy, often and typically without white racist hostility or purpose. It can't or won't deal with critical distinctions such as those made by militant black activist Stokely Carmichael and black political scientist Stanley Hamilton at the beginning of their book, *Black Power:*

> Racism is both overt and covert. It takes two, closely related forms: individual whites acting against individual blacks, and acts by the total white community against the black community. We call these individual racism and institutionalized racism. The first consists of overt acts by individuals, which cause death, injury or the violent destruction of property. This type can be recorded by television cameras; it can frequently be observed in the process of commission. The second type is less overt, far more subtle, less identifiable in terms of specific individuals committing the acts. But it is no less destructive of human life. The second type operates in the operation of established and respected forces in the society, and thus receives far less public condemnation than the first type.[41]

Carmichael and Hamilton illustrated their distinction between overt individual racism and covert institutionalized racism with some compelling historical examples:

> When white terrorists bomb a black church and kill five black children, that is an act of individual racism, widely deplored by most segments of the society. But when in that same city—Birmingham, Alabama—five hundred black babies die each year because of the lack of proper food, shelter and medical facilities, and thousands more are destroyed and maimed physically, emotionally and intellectually because of conditions of poverty and discrimination in the black community, that is a function of institutionalized racism. When a black family moves into a home in a white neighborhood and is stoned, burned or routed out, they are victims of an overt act of individual racism which many people will condemn—at least in words. But it is institutional racism that keeps black people locked in dilapidated slum tenements, subject to the daily prey of exploitative slumlords, merchants, loan sharks and discriminatory real estate agents. The society either pretends it does not know of this latter situation, or is in fact incapable of doing anything meaningful about it.[42]

"The roots of racism are very deep," as Martin Luther King, Jr., told the Southern Christian Leadership Conference (SCLC) in November 1967, reflecting partly on his largely unsuccessful attempt the previous summer to advance the cause of racial equality in Chicago.[43] And today, as in King's day, those "roots" extend far beneath the surface racial sentiments of whites and the outwardly color-blind laws and policies of the nation and its constituent jurisdictions.

At the same time, as the "most fair-minded of whites" know quite well, current racial oppression, partly hidden by the official defeat of overt racism, feeds richly on uncompensated white accumulations from earlier periods when white policy actors and citizens were all too openly and explicitly racist. The problem with ignoring that critical historical dimension—a defining aspect of the "exhausted" white "guilt" that Obama is so willing to accommodate—is that white Americans continue to enjoy and employ a relevant, historically accumulated, and racism-generated surplus of wealth that contributes to the absence of a level, "color-blind" playing field in the United States. The ongoing need for historical acknowledgement and correction, commonly called "reparations," is developed quite well in the following useful analogy advanced by the African American political scientist Roy L. Brooks:

> Two persons—one white and the other black—are playing a game of poker. The game has been in progress for some 300 years. One player—the white one—has been cheating during much of this time, but now announces: "From this day forward, there will be a new game with new players and no more cheating." Hopeful but suspicious, the black player responds, "That's great. I've been waiting to hear you say that for 300 years. Let me ask you, what are you going to do with all those poker chips that you have stacked up on your

> side of the table all these years?" "Well," said the white player, somewhat bewildered by the question, "they are going to stay right here, of course." "That's unfair!" snaps the black player. "The new white player will benefit from your past cheating. Where's the equality in that?" "But you can't realistically expect me to redistribute the poker chips along racial lines when we are trying to move away from considerations of race and when the future offers no guarantees to anyone," insists the white player. "And surely," he continues, "redistributing the poker chips would punish individuals for something they did not do. Punish me, not the innocents!" Emotionally exhausted, the black player answers, "But the innocents will reap a racial windfall."[44]

Seen against the backdrop of Brooks' living "racial windfall," there is something significantly racist about the widespread mainstream white assumption that the broader white majority society owes African Americans nothing in the way of special, ongoing compensation for singular black disadvantages resulting from overt and explicit past racism.[45]

Many white Americans object to the idea that past racial discrimination matters in the present. They are wrong. As anyone who examines capitalism in an honest way knows, what people get from the present and future "free market" is very much about what and how much they bring to that market from the past. "Long ago" racism continues to exact a major toll on current-day black Americans, raising the question of whether unresolved historical inequity is really "past." Slavery and then Jim Crow segregation in the South—and for that matter the open racial terrorism, discrimination, and apartheid imposed on black northerners in places like Chicago and Detroit "long ago"—continue to shape present-day racial inequality.

As Michael K. Brown and his colleagues noted in their study *Whitewashing Race: The Myth of a Color-Blind Society,* racial "inequalities are cumulative, a fact adherents of the new public wisdom on race ignore in their rush to celebrate [racial] progress." Because the "inequalities accumulate over time," the authors argued, the distinction frequently made by "racial conservatives" between "past and present racism" is often inadequate and deceptive."[46] Roy Brooks' surplus poker chips are irrelevant hangovers from "days gone by." They are weapons of racial oppression in the present and future.

It is important to remember that the explicit and overt racism that made it impossible for a black man to seriously consider running for higher office in the not-so-distant past was about more than the sadistic infliction of racial terror in and of itself. That racism served and enforced the economic exploitation and material subordination of black Americans. That long exploitation gave rise to a historically cumulative racial wealth-and-power gap whereby contemporary disparities are deeply fed by past inequalities.[47]

A Hopeful Picture of Cairo, Illinois

Obama is willing to overlook these harsh and important sociological and historical realities to a remarkable extent, peppering his speeches and writings with positive references to the nation's improved racial climate. That climate is seen, he feels, in the willingness of whites to come out and support him even in places like the historically arch-racist town of Cairo, at the far southern tip of Illinois. In *The Audacity of Hope,* he wrote about the progress he observed in U.S. race relations when he visited this former segregationist bastion during his 2004 U.S. Senate campaign. "Turning a corner" in the city's downtown, he saw "a crowd of a couple of hundred" of people who "were milling about": "A quarter of them were black, almost all the rest were white. They were all wearing blue buttons that read OBAMA FOR U.S. SENATE." By the time he left, Obama recalled, "I felt a relationship had been built between me and the people I'd met . . . a quotient of trust had been built" to break down "the hatred and suspicion that [racial] isolation breeds." "To Obama," *Newsweek* reported, "the story of Cairo confirms Martin Luther King Jr.'s observation that the arc of the moral universe bends toward justice."[48]

Obama told a nice story with touching reflections, but it was pitched at the comfortable bourgeois level of individual racism and omitted the messier and less pleasant problem of institutionalized racism. "In the real world," Wolffe and Briscoe noted, "the arc of Cairo has not led so clearly toward racial harmony." "Until recently," they explained, "city politics were deadlocked . . . by a mean-spirited dispute between its white, Republican mayor and the majority black Democrats over patronage and the firing of city workers. Paul Farris (whose terms as mayor ended in May [2007]) blames his opponents for exploiting racial divisions for their own political ends." Meanwhile, the relative underrepresentation of blacks in well-paying city jobs contributes to stark racial disparities in the town that made the technically half-white and thoroughly bourgeois Obama feel personally welcome despite its historical reputation for anti-black prejudice. Black median household income ($14,591) is less than half of white median household income ($32,500) in Cairo, and the black poverty rate (42 percent) is nearly three times the white poverty rate there.[49]

"Conservatives . . . Were Right about Welfare"

To further reinforce conservative whites' sense that Obama harbors no undue "grievance" regarding the officially "over" problem of racism, Obama has spent considerable energy joining neoconservatives in blaming poor blacks for their own poverty. Consistent with his 1997 Illinois Senate vote to impose punitive work requirements on welfare recipients—a measure rejected by most of the state legislature's Black Caucus on the accurate grounds that labor-market opportunities for lesser skilled workers were too slight to justify the command—he agrees with the right that "conservatives and Bill Clinton were right about welfare." The abolished Aid for Families with Dependent Children (AFDC) program, Obama claimed in *Audacity*, "sapped" inner-city blacks of their "initiative" and detached them from the great material and spiritual gains that flow to those who attach themselves to the noble capitalist labor market, including "independence," "income," "order, structure, dignity and opportunity for growth in peoples' lives." He argued that encouraging black girls to finish high school and stop having babies out of wedlock was "the single biggest thing that we could do to reduce inner-city poverty."[50]

Here he ignored the absence of social-scientific evidence for the conservative claim that AFDC destroyed inner-city work ethics or generated intergenerational poverty. Obama also dodged numerous studies showing that the absence of decent, minimally well-paid, and dignified work has always been the single leading cause of black inner-city poverty and "welfare dependency." He disregarded research showing that high black teenage pregnancy rates reflected the absence of meaningful, long-term life and economic opportunities in the nation's hyper-segregated inner-city and suburban-ring ghettos.[51] And he failed to note that the single biggest thing that could be done to reduce inner-city poverty would be to make the simple and elementary moral decision to abolish it through the provision of a decent guaranteed income—something once advocated by Martin Luther King, Jr., and that other dangerous left "moral absolutist" (Obama's description of 1960s New Left peace and justice activists), Richard Nixon. Beneath his repeated claims to be a "progressive," Obama's statements on welfare and other matters have been richly consistent with the left black political scientist Adolph Reed's observation in early April 2008 that "both Democratic presidential candidates qualify their embrace of federal activism and temporize with fealty to market forces and calls to personal responsibility."[52]

"Get Off the Couch," "Get a Job" and "Start a Business"

Welfare aside, Obama has on more than a few occasions exhibited his Bill Cosby side, telling black Americans and anyone else reading or listening that poor blacks' cultural failure and personal irresponsibility create black inner-city poverty. On Father's Day in 2005, Wolffe and Briscoe wrote, Obama "walked into a South Side [Chicago] church to talk about what it means to be a responsible black father": "'There are a lot of folks, a lot of brothers, who are walking around looking like men,' Obama said. 'They've got whiskers, they might even have sired a child, but it's not clear to me that they are full-grown men.'" "The senator urged them not just to get a job," Wolffe and Briscoe observed, "but to start a business; not just to stay at home, but to turn off the TV." In his 2007 Selma speech, Obama called for a caricaturized lazy black female called "cousin Pookie" to "get off the couch," grafting the legacy of the Civil Rights Movement onto a neoliberal, self-help narrative that significantly blamed lower-class blacks for lacking the discipline and fortitude required to rise in the supposed great American land of opportunity.[53]

"Acting Like He's White"

Consistent with his tendency to follow the conventional neoliberal "post–Civil Rights" wisdom that makes poor blacks largely responsible for their own position at the bottom of the nation's overlapping pyramids of class and race, Obama has hardly distinguished himself on the civil rights battlefield during his time in federal office and on the national stage.

He did not support efforts to run a Senate filibuster against the conservative Bush Supreme Court appointee Sam Alito, for example, despite that future justice's well-known opposition to basic civil-rights principles. And in 2005, when liberal bloggers criticized Senator Patrick Leahy (D-VT) for voting in favor of the racially regressive John Roberts' nomination as the chief justice of the Supreme Court, Obama wrote a testy response on the widely read liberal Web site *Daily Kos.* Obama argued that the relatively moderate liberals at places like *Daily Kos* "misread the American people" by valuing confrontation over conciliation in dealing with the deeply reactionary Bush administration.[54]

An exhaustive NAACP report released on February 1, 2008, indicated that there was very little difference between the positions of Obama and Clinton on political issues important to black Americans. Black legal scholar Vernellia Randall reported that Obama had no specific plan for addressing institutionalized and structural racism and that he failed to even acknowledge the issue.[55]

Obama earned Rev. Jesse Jackson's criticism for "acting like he's white" when he failed to meaningfully support the significant mass struggle against the decision in Jena, Louisiana, to charge six African American teenagers with attempted murder for engaging in a school fight with racist white teens who had sought to terrorize black students by placing a noose—symbol of the South's terrible legacy of lynching blacks—on shared high-school grounds. "The Jena 6" case brought tens of thousands of black people and their white, Latino/a, and Asian American allies to the predominantly white town to protest racist criminal-justice practices in early September 2007. "If I were a [presidential] candidate," Jackson said, alluding to the absent

Obama, "I'd be all over Jena. Jena is a defining moment, just like Selma was a defining moment." Some political observers were reminded by this comment of the aftermath of Hurricane Katrina, when Jackson and Obama tangled over the latter's determination to significantly downplay the obvious—indeed overwhelming—role of race (and racism) in the abandonment of black New Orleans residents.[56]

Consistent with an interesting pattern, the comments of presidential candidate John Edwards and his wife Elizabeth on the Jena situation were far more forthright and strident on the persistent problem of racism in the United States. [57]

In late November 2007, just thirty-eight days before the pivotal Democratic caucus in Iowa, Jackson said something remarkable on the opinion-editorial page of the *Chicago Sun Times.* According to Jackson, himself a former presidential candidate who once excited predominantly white voters in Iowa, "The Democratic candidates—with the exception of John Edwards, who opened his campaign in New Orleans and has made addressing poverty central to his campaign—have virtually ignored the plight of African Americans in this country." Jackson might have technically endorsed Obama because of political considerations within Chicago, but this comment was a telling rebuke to his fellow black Chicago South-Sider.[58]

Observing the Democratic presidential campaign leading up to the so-called "black primary" in South Carolina, the left black activist and writer Kevin Alexander Gray found that Obama was very possibly the most objectionable of the top Democratic contenders for the White House. "The Democratic presidential candidates are all attempting to make the right noises," Gray wrote:

> But that's all it is: noise. While Republicans kiss up to one of the most racist white electorates in the country (and that's saying a lot), Democrats make symbolic gestures that do not address the core issues of race-based poverty, redlining, horrific education for Black children, and mass incarceration. Barack Obama is no better than the others in the 'top tier'—maybe worse, because he pretends to be 'one of us' while providing cover for those who blame the victims or prod the victims to blame themselves.[59]

Embracing Ronald Reagan against "the Excesses of the 1960s and 1970s"

Gray's critical perspective was validated by Obama's behavior prior to the mid-January 2008 Democratic presidential caucus in Nevada. Speaking to the conservative white editors of the *Reno Gazette,* Obama gave curious half-praise to a leading historical opponent of racial justice—Ronald Reagan. He told the paper's editors that

> Ronald Reagan changed the trajectory of America in a way that Richard Nixon did not and in a way that Bill Clinton did not. He put us on a fundamentally different path because the country was ready for it. I think they felt like with all the excesses of the 1960s and 1970s and government had grown and grown but there wasn't much sense of accountability in terms of how it was operating. I think people, he just tapped into what people were already feeling, which was we want clarity, we want optimism, we want a return to that sense of dynamism and entrepreneurship that had been missing.[60]

As liberal blogger Matt Stoller noted, Obama

> *agrees* with Reagan's basic frame that the 1960s and 1970s were full of 'excesses' and that government had grown large and unaccountable.
>
> Those excesses, of course, were feminism, the consumer rights movement, the civil rights movement, the environmental movement, and the antiwar movement. The libertarian anti-government ideology of an unaccountable large liberal government was designed by ideological conservatives to take advantage of the backlash against these 'excesses.'
>
> . . . Reagan was not a sunny optimist pushing dynamic entrepreneurship, but a savvy politician using a civil rights backlash to catapult conservatives to power.[61]

To understand the distaste that many blacks and racial-justice supporters felt over the avowedly "progressive" black politician Obama's willingness to embrace the Reagan legacy, it is useful to examine some basic Reagan facts recounted by the liberal historian Gary Gerstle:

> Reagan . . . shared Teddy Roosevelt's discomfort with the presence of African Americans in his nation. He could not describe that discomfort in the same terms TR had used, for the civil rights revolution had banished them from public discourse. But he intended to rid the government of the remedies it had embraced to uproot racism. He wanted to end affirmative action and court-ordered school busing, eliminate bilingual programs, weaken the Voting Rights Act, affirm the right of whites to live in segregated neighborhoods, and allow private universities that excluded blacks and other minorities to maintain federal tax-exempt status. . . . In their election campaigns, Reagan and his successor, George [H.W.] Bush, usually resisted explicit appeals to white racial solidarity. But their campaign committees understood how much could be gained by portraying blacks as lawless, violent, and lazy "others" who threatened the values that "true" Americans held dear.[62]

Gerstle's "'true' Americans" line adds interesting context to Obama's positive identification of Reagan with "patriotism."

It's not for nothing that, as the black political scientist Michael Dawson noted, "Ronald Reagan, the most popular president among white Americans since Franklin D. Roosevelt, was for African Americans the most despised president since early in the [twentieth] century."[63] Such distinctions were naturally lost in Obama's effort to function as a savvy politician using conservative talking-points to win white Republican and Independent votes in the Southwest.

Many progressives were probably more shocked by Obama's Reagan comment than they might have been if they'd followed some of his earlier comments. In *The Audacity of Hope,* Obama praised Reagan for expressing "Americans' longing for order," faith in "personal responsibility," and desire to "rediscover the traditional values" of "hard work, patriotism," and "personal responsibility" after 1960s "excesses" and in response to "the failures of liberal government." And in 2006, Obama told *Time* magazine's Joe Klein that "this country is ready for a transformative politics of the sort that John F. Kennedy, Ronald Reagan and Franklin Roosevelt represented."[64] Obama made no distinction here between the sharp racial regression and backlash that Reagan represented and the relative racial liberalism of Roosevelt and Kennedy.

"People Want to Move Beyond Our [Race] Divisions"

Speaking to a predominantly black audience in the Ebenezer Baptist Church in Atlanta on January 20, 2008, Obama's historical message was different. Obama had a different hero in mind. He praised Dr. Martin Luther King, Jr., who helped lead the movement that provoked the white backlash that Reagan rode to power and who gave many sermons at Ebenezer after 1960. Preaching at Ebenezer one day before the national Martin Luther King, Jr., holiday, Obama had his eyes on the upcoming "black primary" in South Carolina, where more than half of registered Democrats were African American. He offered no praise for Reagan, who remains understandably unpopular in the black community. He gave no criticism of the "excessive" 1960s, when the great social movement King represented ended legal segregation and won black voting rights in the Deep South.

Obama invoked King's memory to advocate focusing on the "common challenges we face—war and poverty; injustice and inequality." He praised Dr. King for leading "by marching and going to jail and suffering threats and being away from his family" and noted that "he led by taking a stand against a war, knowing full well that it would diminish his popularity. He led by challenging our economic structures, understanding that it would cause discomfort." "The changes that are needed," Obama added, "are not just a matter of tinkering at the edges, and they will not come if politicians simply tell us what we want to hear."[65]

Yet even at Ebenezer, Obama displayed politically calculated reluctance to acknowledge something much of white America doesn't "want to hear" about racism—its continuing powerful role in American life. The most he could say on this issue, even to a predominantly black audience, was that "for most of the country's history, we in the African American community have been at the receiving end of man's inhumanity to man. And all of us understand intimately the insidious role that race *still sometimes plays* —on the job, in the schools, in our health care system, and in our criminal justice system."[66] The key words here were "race" and "sometimes." The problem faced by black Americans is more accurately described as the living and powerful legacy and practice of *racism,* and it is experienced by them on a daily, regular, and ubiquitous basis, not just occasionally.

During the Democratic presidential debate that took place the next day in Myrtle Beach, South Carolina, on Dr. King's birthday, race hung heavily in the air. Clinton and Obama had been fighting bitterly over black voters, with the Obama campaign and many of its supporters accusing Hillary (quite unfairly) of racism for a comment she had made on the role that President Lyndon Baines Johnson had played in the passage of the Voting Rights Act of 1965. But during the debate, it was left to Edwards alone to speak with substantive knowledge and respect for King's struggle against racialized economic inequality. Only Edwards acknowledged the depth of racial disparity and the continuing role of cumulative and ongoing historical racism in generating that disparity. Edwards observed:

> If you are an African American in this country today, you are likely to have a net worth of about 10 percent of what white families have.
>
> This is not an accident. I mean, we can go put our heads against the wall and pretend that the past never happened, pretend that we didn't live through decades of slavery, followed by decades of segregation, followed by decades of discrimination, which is still going on today.
>
> (APPLAUSE)
>
> That history and that legacy have consequences. . . .
>
> . . .If you're black, you're much more likely to be poor, you're much less likely to have health care coverage. That community is hurt worse by poverty than any community in America. And it's our responsibility . . . to take on this moral challenge, to try as best we can to walk in the shadow of Dr. King.[67]

By sharp contrast, Obama admonished the media for having "focused a lot on race as we moved down to South Carolina." While "race is a factor in our society," Obama deigned to concede, he was "convinced that white, black, Latino, Asian, people want to move beyond our divisions, and they want to join together . . . in order to create a movement for change in the county."[68]

None of these substantive differences made it into the news or public discussion. The next day in the dominant media coverage, the focus was on the personal conflict that emerged between Hillary and Obama and on Obama's humorous response to a debate moderator's ridiculous query as to whether or not Bill Clinton was (as the black novelist Toni Morrison had once half-jokingly proclaimed) "the nation's first black president." Obama was praised for scoring comedic points by joking that he'd have to research Clinton's "dancing abilities" to determine if the former president was "in fact a brother." Obama was permitted to maintain a positive if superficial connection to "blackness," running to the right of the white southern male Edwards on race. He won South Carolina by a large margin, winning a vast majority of the black vote in that state and effectively ending Edwards' bid to run a viable campaign to the populist left of Senators Clinton and Obama.

"Neoliberal Racism"

In downplaying racism's continuing relevance and the depth and degree of racial inequality and oppression in the United States, Obama is catering to the racial politics of the post–Civil Rights era, wherein the leading architects of policy and opinion have declared that "race" is no longer a barrier to black advancement. It is a time when large numbers of Americans, including many blacks, claim "exhaustion" with race issues. Race- and racism-avoidance have become the orders of the day in an officially "color-blind" neoliberal era, a time when conventional wisdom ascribes people's status and wealth to purely private and personal success or failure in adapting to the permanent, inherently human realities of inequality in a "free market" system of reactionary corporate rule to which "there is no alternative." In the dominant public discourse of this era, the nation's "pervasive racial hierarchies collapse," in the words of Henry Giroux, "into power-evasive strategies such as blaming minorities of class and color for not working hard enough, refusing to exercise individual initiative, or practicing reverse racism." Even as an enveloping, increasingly invisible racism "functions" as "one of the deep and abiding currents in everyday [American] life," this discourse works "to erase the social from the language of public life as to reduce all racial problems to private issues [of] . . . individual character and cultural depravity."

This "neoliberal racism," as Giroux called it, "can imagine public issues only as private concerns." It sees "human agency as simply a matter of individualized choices, the only obstacle to effective citizenship being the lack of principled self-help and moral responsibility" on the part of those most victimized by structural oppression and the amoral agency of those super-empowered actors who stand atop the nation's steep and interrelated hierarchies of class and race. Under its rule, "Human misery is largely defined as a function of personal choices," consistent with "the central neoliberal tenet that all problems are private rather than social in nature."[69]

The technically biracial Obama's campaign and persona are perfectly calibrated for this era of victim-blaming, neoliberal racism. He allows whites to assuage their racial guilt and feel nonracist by liking and perhaps even voting for him, while he reassures them he won't do anything to tackle and redress the steep racial disparities and systemic racial oppression that continue to scar daily American life and institutions. "What . . . me and my country racist?" Obama encourages many white voters to reason. "You can't be serious: we're thinking seriously about voting for a black man as president."

The Deeper Racism Reinforced?

The third reason not to sing racial-justice hosannas over the rise of Obama is that his political success may ironically deepen neoliberal racism's power. The main problem with the conventional white wisdom holding that racism no longer poses relevant barriers to black Americans in the post–Civil Rights era is that it fails to distinguish adequately between overt "state-of-mind" racism and covert institutional, societal, and "state-of-being" racism. The first variety of racism has a long and sordid history. It includes such actions, policies, and practices as the burning of black homes and black churches, the murder of "uppity" blacks and civil rights workers, the public use of derogatory racial slurs and epithets, the open banning of blacks from numerous occupations, the open political disenfranchisement of blacks, and the open segregation of public facilities by race. It is largely defeated, outlawed, and discredited in the "politically correct" environment created partly by the victories of the Civil Rights Movement.

The second variety lives on, with terrible consequences. It involves the more impersonal operation of social, economic, and institutional forces and processes that both reflect and shape the related processes of capitalism in ways that "just happen" but nonetheless serve to reproduce black disadvantage in numerous interrelated key sectors of American life. It includes racial segregation in real-estate and home-lending practices, residential "white flight" from black neighbors, statistical racial discrimination in hiring and promotion, the systematic underfunding and underequipping of schools predominately attended by blacks, the disproportionate surveillance, arrest, and incarceration of blacks, and much more.

Richly enabled by policymakers who declare allegiance to antiracist ideals, this deeper racism has an equally ancient history that has outlived the explicit, open, and public racism of the past and the passage of justly cherished civil rights legislation. It does not necessarily involve individual white bigotry or even subtly prejudiced "ill will" against blacks. Consciously or even unconsciously prejudiced white actors are not necessarily required, and black actors are more than welcome to help enforce the New Age societal racism of the post-King era. This entrenched, enduring, and more concealed societal racism does not depend on racist intent in order to exist as a relevant social and political phenomenon. The racism that matters most today does not require a large portion of the white population to be consciously and willfully prejudiced against blacks or any other racial minority. It needs only to produce racially disparate outcomes through the operation of objectively racialized processes. It critically includes a pivotal failure and/or refusal to acknowledge, address, and reverse the living (present and future) windfall bestowed on sections of the white community by "past" racist structures, policies, and practices that were more willfully and openly discriminatory toward blacks.

"State-of-being" or structural racism generates racially disparate results even without racist intent—"state-of-mind" racism—on the part of white actors. It oppresses blacks with objectively racialized social processes that work in "routine" and "ordinary" fashion to sustain racial hierarchy and white supremacy, often and typically without white racist hostility or purpose.[70]

Sadly, the fact that level-one (overt) racism has been defeated while the deeper level-two racism survives is not just a matter of the social and racial justice glass being half full. It's more darkly complicated than that. This second and deeper level of racial oppression may actually be more firmly entrenched than the first. The victories and achievements of celebrated civil rights victories and related black upward mobility into the middle and upper classes ironically encourage the illusion that racism has disappeared and that the only obstacles left to African American success and equality are internal to individual blacks and their community. In the words of the esteemed black law professor and Civil Rights veteran Derrick Bell, the illusion is that the "the indolence of blacks rather than the injustice of whites explains the socioeconomic gaps separating the races."[71]

"It's hard," communications professor Leonard Steinhorn and Barbara Diggs-Brown have noted, "to blame people" for believing (falsely in Steinhorn and Diggs-Brown's view) that racism is dead in America "when our public life is filled with repeated affirmations of the integration ideal and our ostensible progress towards achieving it." In a similar vein, black Georgetown law professor Sheryl Cashin noted that "there are [now] enough examples of successful middle-class African-Americans to make many whites believe that blacks have reached parity with them. The fact that some blacks now lead powerful mainstream institutions offers evidence to whites that racial barriers have been eliminated; the issue now is individual effort."[72]

And the white-run culture's regular rituals of self-congratulation over the defeat of overt, level-one racism—the Martin Luther King national holiday, the playing of King's "I Have a Dream" speech over school sound systems and on television, the routine reference to integrationist ideals in political speeches, the attainment of elite foreign policy positions by Colin Powell and Condoleezza Rice, and now the presidential viability of the "conservative" Obama, for example,—reinforce the dominant white sentiment that the United States no longer has much of anything to answer for in regard to its treatment of black America and the ubiquitous white American notion that racism is something only from the now relatively irrelevant and distant past. Such is the dark and unpleasant reality behind the white Tennessean Joe Lance's sorely misguided notion that putting Obama in the White House would begin to "melt" "centuries' worth of racial animosity and despair." Substantive and deep societal repair can take place only through a process that includes a serious reckoning with the living past and with the historical present of white supremacy. It cannot be accomplished through a fanciful flight to the future and away from the supposedly ancient history of racial oppression. Melting "racial animosity and despair" must be about something deeper and more radical than changing the technical skin color of some of those who sit atop a disproportionately white-ruled political order.

"Now we can finally forget about race" is the basic dangerous widespread white wish seeking fulfillment in the election of someone like Obama. As one white Obama supporter told the *Washington Post* at a campaign event, he hoped that an Obama presidency would help America "erase all this nonsense about race."[73] How nice to imagine that racial oppression is something so nonsensical and superficial that it could be expunged by the mere act of putting a technically black politician, who has gone out of his way not to threaten white cultural and ideological sensibilities surrounding race, into the Oval Office.

"The Obama Effect": A "Repudiation of the Existence of American Racism Itself"

Such was the basic sentiment of the white Republican physicist who wrote to me in the spring of 2007. His argument was that an Obama presidency would signal the (for him) welcome end of race and racism as problems demanding public discussion, attention, and correction in American life. While telling me candidly that he "hated" Obama, this (in fact openly right-wing and racist) scientist could see a big silver lining in Obama's ascendancy to the White House: It would, he hoped, make black civil rights activists and their white allies shut up once and for all about the long-dead (he felt) problem of racism. He agreed that, as hard right *Washington Post* columnist Charles Krauthammer approvingly claimed in early March 2008, Obama thankfully "transcends race."[74]

A similar and related point was made by the conservative national columnist George Will on the night of Obama's Iowa victory. "The two biggest losers tonight," Will opined, "are probably Jesse Jackson and Al Sharpton, . . . those who have a sort of investment in a traditional and, I believe, utterly exhausted narrative about race relations in the United States." Will subsequently wrote the following in *Newsweek:* "Among the losers in Iowa were Jesse Jackson, Al Sharpton and all the others who still subscribe to a racial narrative of strife and oppression that has remained remarkably unchanged through 50 years of stunning progress, of which Obama's candidacy is powerful evidence." Krauthammer applauded Obama for developing a "post-racial" "vision of America," meaning he could "not run as a candidate of minority grievance."[75]

The national neoconservative scold and former Reagan drug czar William Bennett agreed. He went on CNN to claim that "Obama has taught the black community you don't have to act like Jesse Jackson, you don't have to act like Al Sharpton. You can talk the issues. Great dignity. And this is a breakthrough." Bennett praised Obama because "he never brings race into it. He never plays the race card."[76]

Here is a useful translation for Will, Krauthammer, and Bennett's commentaries: "Excellent! Obama's victory means that black politicians and activists and their misguided white supporters and enablers have shown that the time has come to stop talking about the officially discredited and over problem of racism." The comments of conservative writer Stuart Taylor, Jr., in the *National Journal* required no translation. "Obama embodies and preaches," Taylor wrote last year, "the true and vital message that in today's America, the opportunities available to black people are unlimited if they work hard, play by the rules, and get a good education."[77]

As columnist Kathleen Parker noted after Obama's Iowa victory, "Mainly, an Obama presidency allows Americans to put a period at the end of a very long sentence. With a black president, the sins of slavery are not forgiven or forgotten, but we can move along. Nothing left to see here. Obama smoothly, strategically and subtly mines the wells of white guilt."[78]

The supremely racism-deepening and dangerous point—obvious enough to be acknowledged by a mainstream commentator like Parker yet routinely missed and denied by ostensibly progressive Obama supporters—was not lost on left writers of color. Like others in the "post–Civil Rights cohort," Gary Younge observed on the eve of the Iowa caucus, Obama "represents proof of the nation's unrelenting progress and boundless opportunities."[79] As Younge noted in a perceptive commentary in *The Guardian* four days after Iowa, "There are a number of commentators—particularly, but not exclusively, conservatives—who seek to portray Obama not just as a generation removed from Jackson, but the antithesis of everything Jackson stood for. To them his success signals both the failure of 'black' politics and removal of 'black' issues from the political arena." "As such," Younge worried, "*his victory does not reshape our analysis of how race is understood in America; it marks a repudiation of the existence of American racism itself.*"[80] Even worse, as Younge noted one week earlier in *The Nation*, "The Obama effect . . . does not just make a new chapter in America's racial history; it shreds the entire book and then burns the remains."[81]

Black Agenda Report's Margaret Kimberly added a take on what she called "Obama's Hollow Victory" in Iowa. "A black president who sides against the interests of black people," Kimberly wrote, "will be exponentially worse than a cabinet official or Supreme Court Justice doing the same thing. The sad fact of the matter is that black America will be worse off if Obama becomes president. The handwriting is already on the wall. His success is already used as evidence purporting to prove that racism is in the past, that black people are therefore to blame for their problems, and consequently have no right to make demands on the political system."[82]

In the words of *Black Agenda Report* editor Glen Ford, voiced during an important debate with the black professor and Obama supporter Michael Eric Dyson after Obama's Iowa victory, the Obama campaign was "relentlessly sending out signals to white people that a vote for Barack Obama, an Obama presidency, would signal the beginning of the end of black-specific agitation, that it would take race discourse off of the table." "Barack Obama," Ford explained, "does not carry our burden, in addition to other burdens. He in fact promises to lift white-people-as-a-whole's burden, the burden of having to listen to these very specific and historical black complaints, to deal with the legacies of slavery. That is his promise to them."[83] Urban studies professor Marc Lamont Hill said much the same thing in an important *CounterPunch* critique in early February 2008:

> After Obama's recent success with white voters, particularly his win in Iowa, many have announced America's transition into a post-racial moment. Even Obama himself has claimed that race will no longer prevent the fair-minded citizenry from supporting his bid. In reality, however, an Obama presidency is already being treated as a racial talisman that would instantly heal the scars of a nation wounded by racism.
>
> For whites, an Obama victory would serve as the final piece of evidence that America has reached full racial equality. Such a belief allows them to sidestep mounds of evidence that shows that, despite Obama's claims that "we are 90 percent of the way to equality," black people remain consistently assaulted by the forces of white supremacy. For many black people, Obama's success would provide symbolic value by showing that the black man (not woman!) can make it to the top. Although black faces in high places may provide psychological comfort, they are often incorporated into a Cosbyesque gospel of personal responsibility ("Obama did it, so can you!") that allows dangerous public policies to go unchallenged.[84]

"The Obama Dividend": A "Liberal" Columnist Speaks

Lest we assume that the dangerously conservative uses of Obama were concentrated only in the hands of self-described conservatives, we should stop briefly to consider the curious April 2008 reflections of the avowed "liberal" *Newsweek* columnist Jonathan Alter. In Alter's hands, the post–Civil Rights utility of Barack Obama for American race relations went beyond merely putting an end to supposedly obsolete and dysfunctional complaints about racism as the cause of disproportionate black poverty and misery. In a March 31, 2008, column entitled "The Obama Dividend," Alter voiced the interesting opinion that while "Obama's unique assets," a reference to the senator's blackness and multiculturalism, "have usually been viewed in international terms," the presidential candidate's "most exciting potential for moral leadership could be in the African American community." Alter praised Obama for having lectured a black audience in Texas on how African Americans were producing endemic black childhood obesity by making poor diet decisions and watching too much television. Alter also applauded Obama for telling blacks in Atlanta "that they need to stop being homophobic and anti-Semitic."

"Obviously," Alter pontificated, "not all black adults and children would suddenly start doing exactly what President Obama tells them." Still, he opined, "this is powerful stuff and would make him an important president even if his legislation stalled. . . . Barack Obama knows how to think big, elevate the debate and transport the public to a new place."[85]

There was nothing in Alter's commentary about the way the owners of full-service grocery stores fail to invest in concentrated black communities, leaving their residents over-reliant on small, corner grocery-liquor stores stocked with overpriced foods loaded with salt, starch, and sugar. Alter had nothing to say about the legendary difficulty of finding fresh vegetables and fruits in ghetto neighborhoods or about the relative absence of safe recreational spaces and facilities. He did not comment on the relationship between the savage, racially oppressive absence of economic opportunity and the related high-crime and violent childhood-injury rates in poor and highly segregated black communities—something that makes many black parents understandably reluctant to let their children outdoors. Alter said nothing about Obama's failure and reluctance to speak forcefully against the persistent reality of institutional racism.

He did, however, praise Obama for being a potentially "important president" simply on the grounds that he would tell "black adults and children" to start acting differently. The stark implication was clear as day: The United States is haunted by the terrible specter of dysfunctional black culture. Obama could mishandle U.S. foreign or economic policy, and fail in his tepid efforts to address social problems at home, but he would leave a powerful and important legacy if he could just get "black adults and children"—a category that technically includes every single African American human being—to think and act differently. This was a profoundly racist and—given the fact that blacks make up 12 percent of the U.S. population and are disproportionately removed from key decision-making roles—oddly revealing judgment, to say the least.[85] It was darkly consistent with an argument Alter had made three weeks before in a column that looked forward to an Obama presidency that convinced "the African American community that it must do more to solve its own problems."[86]

Obama, Class, and Generational Conflict within Black America

"A Function of Class, Not Race"

Given his repeated statements privileging class (or economics) over race, it is ironic that a considerable part of Obama's historical difficulty being accepted as a truly "black" candidate by the African American community has been a matter of class. Intimately related to his frequent past identification by many blacks as culturally suspect and overly conciliatory on racial matters has been the sense that Obama was too "bourgeois."

When Obama ran unsuccessfully for the Second Congressional District on Chicago's South Side in 2000, the incumbent black congressman there—former Black Panther Bobby Rush—had little difficulty painting the then state senator as a product of elite institutions. "Class emerged as a subtext in the [2000] Congressional campaign," the *New York Times* noted in September 2007, "along with generational differences that separate Mr. Obama from older black politicians." Obama's Ivy League education and his related establishment connections became an issue. Rush told the weekly *Chicago Reader* that Obama "went to Harvard and became an educated fool. We're not impressed with these folks with these Eastern elite degrees. . . . Barack is a person who read about the civil rights protests and thinks he knows all about it."[87]

Obama was not portrayed as "too white" as much as he was accused of being an elite intellectual who was "not from us, not from the hood."[88] According to media consultant Eric Adelstein, who worked on the 2000 race, "It was 'the Black Panther versus the professor. . . . It was much more a function of class, not race. Nobody said he's 'not black enough.' They said he's a professor, a Harvard elite who lives in Hyde Park."[89] Hyde Park, it should be noted, is one of the nation's few stable, consistently integrated urban neighborhoods across the past five decennial censuses.[90] And issues of "class over race" and internal black class differentiations were not merely a matter of rhetoric: It certainly was not lost on Obama's 2000 opponents that his first campaign for federal office drew heavily on financial support from close friends within the literal black bourgeoisie—what *New York Times* reporter Janny Scott described as a "network of successful, black, Chicago-based entrepreneurs"[91] who would continue to play a pivotal role in bankrolling his career over subsequent bids for office.

Rush subsequently endorsed Obama's presidential campaign, claiming that Obama had been chosen for earthly greatness by no less an authority than God. But the concern that Obama was too "bourgeois" and elite to understand majority black experience and issues "in the hood" would continue to find resonance in black America. Even as black voters lined up strongly, even overwhelmingly, behind the Obama campaign, it remained a commonly heard concern in black neighborhoods and on black talk radio, alongside the fear that Obama's remarkable national stature and potential presidency would put an end to white America's capacity to acknowledge and correct present day historical anti-black racism.

This debate reflected the continuing intimate, inseparable, and mutually reinforcing relationship between class and race inequality in the United States. It drew fuel from Obama's apparent willingness to sign on with elite policy agendas at home and abroad, something that many black activists rightly connect to Obama's reluctance to act or speak forcefully on behalf of those who suffer at the intersection of the nation's harsh and related socioeconomic and racial oppression. For those activists and many others, Obama's perceived excessive "whiteness" is intimately linked to his excessively "bourgeois" identity and values and his deference to the predominantly white masters of capital and empire. They know very well that, as Stephen Steinberg noted in his provocative 1995 book *Turning Back: The Retreat from Racial Justice in American Thought and Policy*, "racism has never been indifferent to class distinctions." As Steinberg explained,

> It may well be that blacks who have acquired the "right" status characteristics are exempted from stereotypes and behaviors that continue to be directed at less privileged blacks. [But] there is nothing new in this phenomenon. Even in the worst days of Jim Crow, there were blacks who owned land, received favored treatment from whites and were held forth as "success stories" to prove that lower-class blacks had only themselves to blame for their destitution. . . . The existence of this black elite did not prove that racism was abating (though illusions to this effect were common even among blacks). On the contrary, the black elite itself was a vital part of the system of [racial] oppression, serving as a buffer between the [ruling white] oppressor and [most truly black] oppressed and furthering the illusion that blacks could surmount their difficulties if only they had the exemplary qualities of the black elite.[92]

The remarkable success of racially respectful, bourgeois, and nonthreatening (to whites), "good" blacks like Obama, Oprah Winfrey, and (once) Colin Powell helps white America believe that most blacks have only themselves to blame for their group's persistently separate and unequal status in the United States. For many whites, loving national media stars like Oprah and Obama is the other side of the coin of fearing inner-city blacks.

Obama is certainly no fool when it comes to the politics of race and class. He has certainly known very well that this is a big part of why so many Caucasians have approved of him—it is a critical and defining aspect of "the Obama phenomenon." Given his primary objective of attaining august federal elective office and the fact that whites continue to hold a large electoral majority in the United States, he's been understandably reluctant to endanger that approval by moving to the forefront of contemporary civil rights struggles. A dedicated electoral realist, Obama has not been eager to complicate his comfortable funding relationships with the likes of Goldman Sachs, Lehman Brothers, Morgan Stanley, Henry Crown, and General Dynamics et al. by substantively criticizing empire and/or inequality at home and abroad. In a similar vein, he hasn't wished to undermine his favorable post–Civil Rights situation with the white electoral majority by making strong public reference to the persistently powerful and pervasive role of anti-black racism in American life. He's been trying, rather, to ride white America's self-serving racial confusion, guilt, arrogance, and denial as far as he can—all the way, he hopes, to the White House.

It has by no means been an easy or simple path. As Cornel West noted to a black audience in Atlanta while Obama announced his run for the White House in February 2007, "He's got large numbers of white brothers and sisters who have fears and anxieties and concerns, and he's got to speak to them in such a way that he holds us at arm's length, so he's walking this tightrope."[93]

A Generational Difference: "Scaring Whites" Versus "Soothing" Them

There's a strong generational component to the strategy. "I'm shocked," Isaac Hunt told *Chicago Tribune* columnist Bill Barnhart in late February 2008, "when I hear Obama speak about how much he loves this country. I say he just hasn't hadn't had the same experiences I have. I could never be that effusive about this country. He's in a different generation than me." Seventy years old at the time, Hunt was the retired African American dean of two law schools and former staff member of the 1968 National Advisory Commission in Civil Disorders which produced the famous report on the 1960s race riots. Known as the Kerner Report, it concluded that white racism was the leading cause of the racial violence that exploded across urban America from 1964 through 1968.[94]

As the British black journalist Gary Younge has noted, there is a significant generational dimension to the intra-black class differences that emerged in relation to Obama's ascendancy. As Jesse Jackson, Al Sharpton, and other black leaders and activists know quite well, Obama is a product of the post–Civil Rights era and owes his rise to prominence to battles fought before and during the 1960s—the supposedly "divisive" and dysfunctional decade from which he has repeatedly tried to distance himself. Along with other upwardly mobile black politicians, such as Massachusetts governor Deval Patrick; Newark mayor Cory Booker; Washington, D.C., mayor Adrian Fenty; and former Tennessee congressman Harold Ford, Jr., he is part of "a new generation in black politics." His generation's experience, Younge noted, "could not be more different" from that of Jackson's cohort. "As the civil rights movement forced open the doors of academe, corporate America, and elite universities," Younge added, "[Obama's] generation strode through."

The disparity in opportunity and the fact the younger generation (the "Joshua generation," to use Obama's Selma terminology) owes much of its selective success to the sacrifices of their elders (the "Moses generation") is a source of no small amount of the distance and conflict between a Jackson and an Obama. But it's not just that the younger generation has benefited from the sacrifices and struggles of the older one. It's also that making sure "that they don't scare white people" in terms of rhetoric, style, and policy is the main commonality among the new wave black leaders. The earlier, heroic cohort of civil rights activists engaged in repeated and profound confrontations of high danger and drama, facing beatings and assassinations in their struggle with white supremacy. As Younge explained,

> However much the [Civil Rights] Movement espoused nonviolence, it most definitely acted to "scare white people" and to tell the dominant racial power structures that the price of not reforming the nation's racial practices and beliefs would be higher than the price of progress. The threat and reality of destabilizing and costly violence and ongoing bitter struggle was a critical asset for the movement—something that came at no small cost to black activists themselves. This too is part of the difference: the earlier generation achieved its success by confronting whites; the current one, whose most prominent figure is now Obama, advances by soothing them. In the process, however, he becomes part of the evisceration of public understanding about the continuing relevance of racism and the shared needs, interests, and struggle of black people.[95]

An Obama aide told the *New York Times* in early February 2008 that "Barack sees himself as an extension of the civil rights movement,"[96] but, as many older black leaders knew, the Obama phenomenon is a distinctly post–Civil Rights development, shaped by very different circumstances that produce a distinctly less confrontational and less forthright confrontation with the white power structure.

The Reverend Wright Affair: The "Tightrope" Sways

Obama's precarious walk along the intertwined "tightropes" of race, class, and generation came to an especially precarious moment in March 2008. That's when ABC News released provocative and decontextualized clips from past speeches by Obama's longtime pastor, the Reverend Jeremiah Wright. Within a matter of days, millions of Americans heard Wright angrily denouncing American racism and American imperialism in scattered clips spliced from videotapes of his many fiery sermons to a predominantly black church on the far South Side of Chicago. One clip showed the Afrocentric black preacher saying on the first Sunday after 9/11: "We have supported state terrorism against the Palestinians and black South Africa, and now we are indignant because the stuff we have done overseas is now brought right back to our own front yards. America's chickens are coming home to roost." In another, he was shown saying that "United States of White America" had been "based upon" racism past and present, and once he even referred to America as "the U.S. of KKK."

On March 14, Obama attempted to contain some of the political damage by posting an essay called "On My Faith and My Church" on the liberal Web site *The Huffington Post.* "I categorically denounce any statement," Obama proclaimed "that disparages our great country or serves to divide us from our allies."[97]

Although many of Wright's disembodied comments struck dispassionate left observers as technically accurate in critical ways, Obama had no choice but to distance himself from them and his "extremist" pastor if he wanted to keep his position on the path to the presidency. Spoken in an angry and recognizably black voice before a predominantly black audience that shared few of the mainstream white political culture's leading assumptions on the purportedly fair and benevolent nature of U.S. society and foreign policy (or at least shared them to a significantly slighter degree), Wright's language was precisely the sort that "scared" rather than "soothed" the racially sensitive white majority. It was outside the dominant but unspoken post–Civil Rights rules governing racial issues that Obama had mastered so well and threatened to knock him off the treacherous racial "high wire" that he was walking in his quest to become the first black to occupy the *White* House. Wright's remarks came at an especially vulnerable moment for Obama, because Clinton had just forcefully challenged his qualifications to be "commander in chief." In response, Obama had assembled a team of retired military commanders to testify to "No Shock Barack's" military readiness.[98]

Still, Obama's stark, reflexive, and sweeping claim to "denounce any statement that disparages our great country" carried rightward and nationalistic implications that ought to have sent a chill down progressive and democratic spines. A democratic political process requires free and open invitation to engage in honest and comprehensive dissent from existing social structures, policies, and practices. It privileges critical scrutiny and candid societal self-examination over blind obedience to flag, blood, and soil. Obama's comment suggested that one indulged in malevolent "anti-Americanism" if one dared to acknowledge and criticize any of Dr. King's "triple evils" (racism, economic inequality/poverty, and militarism/imperialism) in relation to the United States. It left one to wonder if Obama now "categorically denounced" Dr. King's onetime reference to the United States as "the greatest purveyor of violence in the world today"[99]—a description that holds all too much relevance more than forty years after King advanced it, a time when the United States was again embroiled in a remarkably "provocative," deadly, and illegal war—though in Iraq instead of Vietnam.

Equally suspect under Obama's *Huffington Post* formulation, it would seem, were honest and accurate descriptions of the United States as the industrialized world's most unequal and wealth-top-heavy nation in the world[100] or as a globally unmatched mass-incarceration state with a special and pronounced tendency for imprisoning and criminally marking African Americans.[101] Both of these descriptions are accurate—I have personally advanced them in numerous past political and academic writings—but should perhaps not be openly acknowledged as such under the rules of appropriate discourse suggested by Obama's March 14 essay, since they can be easily taken to (and may actually in fact) "disparage" the United States.

Reading his *Huffington Post* essay, I was instantly reminded that the former civil rights lawyer Obama voted in July 2005 to reauthorize the Patriot Act, "easily the worst attack on civil liberties in the last half-century," in the words of Matt Gonzalez. As Gonzalez pointed out, "It allows for wholesale eavesdropping on American citizens under the guise of anti-terrorism efforts."[102]

The Patriot Act was justified and enabled, of course, by the terror attacks that Rev. Wright had accurately but unacceptably linked to U.S. foreign policy, consistent with James Madison's observation that "the fetters imposed on liberty at home have ever been forged out of the weapons provided for defense against real, pretended, or imaginary dangers abroad."[103]

The Speech: "The Anger and the Bitterness of Those Years"

The *Huffington Post* intervention was only the beginning of Obama's attempt to contain the potential injury from the "Wright revelations." His main effort toward this end came on March 18 in Philadelphia, when he gave a major address on race that was immediately and widely hailed—the tributes were quite remarkable—across the dominant media and political spectrum. Addressing how the "discussion of race in this campaign has taken a particularly divisive turn" in recent weeks, Obama rejected "the implication that my candidacy is somehow an exercise in affirmative action; that it's based solely on the desire of wide-eyed liberals to purchase racial reconciliation on the cheap." Here he was reacting also to exit polls showing that many whites were voting against him on the basis of race and to former Democratic vice presidential candidate Geraldine Ferraro's controversial and headline-grabbing statement, issued early in March, claiming that Obama "would not be in the position that he is if he weren't a black male."[104]

Entitled "A More Perfect Union," Obama's speech accused Rev. Wright of "express[ing] a profoundly distorted view of this country—a view that sees white racism as endemic and that elevates what is wrong with America above all that we know is right with America; a view that sees the conflicts in the Middle East as rooted primarily in the actions of stalwart allies like Israel, instead of emanating from the perverse and hateful ideologies of radical Islam." At the same time, Obama gave a sharply *historical* explanation for why many blacks seemed to share his "angry" and now "former" pastor's "divisive," "distorted," "inexcusable" take on America:

> As William Faulkner once wrote, "The past isn't dead and buried. In fact, it isn't even past." We do not need to recite here the history of racial injustice in this country. But we do need to remind ourselves that so many of the disparities that exist in the African American community today can be directly traced to inequalities passed on from an earlier generation that suffered under the brutal legacy of slavery and Jim Crow.
>
> . . . A lack of economic opportunity among black men, and the shame and frustration that came from not being able to provide for one's family, contributed to the erosion of black families—a problem that welfare policies for many years may have worsened. And the lack of basic services in so many urban black neighborhoods—parks for kids to play in, police walking the beat, regular garbage pick-up and building code enforcement—all helped create a cycle of violence, blight and neglect that continue to haunt us.
>
> This is the reality in which Reverend Wright and other African Americans of his generation grew up. They came of age in the late fifties and early sixties, a time when segregation was still the law of the land and opportunity was systematically constricted. What's remarkable is not how many failed in the face of discrimination, but rather how many men and women overcame the odds; how many were able to make a way out of no way for those like me who would come after them.
>
> But for all those who scratched and clawed their way to get a piece of the American Dream, there were many who didn't make it—those who were

> ultimately defeated, in one way or another, by discrimination. That legacy of defeat was passed on to future generations—those young men and increasingly young women who we see standing on street corners or languishing in our prisons, without hope or prospects for the future. Even for those blacks who did make it, questions of race, and racism, continue to define their worldview in fundamental ways. For the men and women of Reverend Wright's generation, the memories of humiliation and doubt and fear have not gone away; nor has the anger and the bitterness of those years.[105]

Later in his speech, Obama proclaimed that "Reverend Wright's comments were not only wrong but divisive, *divisive at a time when we need unity;* racially charged at a time when we need to come together to solve a set of monumental problems—two wars, a terrorist threat, a falling economy, a chronic health care crisis and potentially devastating climate change; problems that are neither black or white or Latino or Asian, but rather problems that confront us all."

Obama claimed, finally, that Wright's "offending speech" had erred in failing to see "change"—that is, progress—in America's troubled racial history. By Obama's account, his own candidacy was proof of that positive transformation: "The profound mistake of Reverend Wright's sermons is not that he spoke about racism in our society. It's that he spoke as if our society was static; as if no progress has been made; as if this country—a country that has made it possible for one of his own members to run for the highest office in the land and build a coalition of white and black; Latino and Asian, rich and poor, young and old—is still irrevocably bound to a tragic past."

Obama's Philadelphia speech won immediate accolades across the "mainstream" U.S. media and political spectrum for contributing to "racial healing." I personally heard the speech effusively praised in profoundly laudatory terms by a number of white self-described progressives and left-liberals.

And yet the oration was flawed in profoundly conservative ways, reflecting the narrow parameters of the dominant, superficially color-blind racial discourse of the post–Civil Rights era. It ignored the fact that structural racism remains *in fact* widespread in the United States, as argued at some length earlier in this chapter. The United States may have stopped being what Wright called—in one of the sound bites from one of his sermons that made it across the U.S. airwaves in March 2008—the "U.S. of KKK." But racism remains deeply entrenched in how the real-estate and labor markets operate, how the education system functions, how home mortgages are marketed, how credit is extended, how the criminal justice system works, how economic development is directed, how health care is structured, and much more.

Obama accurately captured the fact that many—maybe most—white Americans no longer see it as politically correct to be openly race-prejudiced in the United States, and that white America is now much less consciously and intentionally racist than it was in the days of Wright's youth. But he failed to make the important distinction between overt racism (largely defeated) and covert racism (still endemic). He failed to distinguish personal and psychological white racism from (endemic) societal and institutional racism. He did not deal with the crucial difference between "state-of-mind racism" and "state-of-being racism." And he failed to acknowledge that post–Civil Rights America's constant self-congratulation over dropping level-one (overt, deliberate, and conscious) racism (expressed, among other things, in a new white willingness to vote for at least a certain kind of black presidential candidate) can actually further entrench the policies, structures, and practices of (often ostensibly color-blind) institutional racism.

In calling for Americans to put race aside in the quest for unity in pursuit of shared solutions to social and economic problems, Obama did not explain to blacks how they were supposed drop "racially charged sentiments" when the all-too-forgotten reality of institutional racism was still going strong. It was there, beneath the ongoing national celebration about how America is no longer explicitly and openly racist, that covert racism still consigned a grossly disproportionate share of the nation's black populace to the bottom of the nation's steep socioeconomic and institutional hierarchies.

Besides continuing his long-standing avoidance of the deeper racism, Obama's celebrated Philadelphia race speech continued his related tendency to understate racial disparities. This was clear when he said that "race" is "a part of our union that we have yet to perfect." "*Yet to perfect*" was more than a bit mild in a nation where an "astonishing 1-to-11 black-to-white wealth gap now afflicts African American families," where one in three black males possesses a felony record, and where blacks make up 12 percent of the population but nearly half the population of its more than 2 million prisoners.[106]

Obama was certainly correct to note that an exaggerated concern with racial and religious differences can "distract" Americans from educational, health care, and economic issues that matter to people of all colors and creeds. The force of this nominally progressive call for interracial unity was undercut, however, by the fact that his policy agenda on those issues was militantly centrist and business-friendly and therefore inadequate. It stood well to the corporate right of any self-respecting progressive agenda and even to the GOP side of Hillary Clinton's domestic-policy package, not to mention that of the more substantively populist John Edwards.

The most disturbing aspect of Obama's Philadelphia speech was its unmistakable portrayal of the racism that creates black American anger as a function mainly of the past. To be sure, the Faulkner quote was instructive. It was gratifying to see Obama, a reparations opponent, note some of the continuing relevance of cumulative, not-so-"past" racism. But as he delivered his speech there was plenty of living and active racial oppression and discrimination to spark rage among black Americans of all ages, including a large number of younger black males who I have heard denounce Obama as "bourgeois" and "a white man's Negro." As I noted in a *ZNet* commentary that appeared two days after Obama's Philadelphia speech,

> The oppression that angers Wright and other black Americans is more than an overhang from the bad old past. The humiliation and hopelessness felt by millions of those Americans are being reinforced, generated, and expanded anew on a daily basis right now . . . in the *21st century.* Black "anger and bitterness" is being generated within the U.S. by racist policies and practices in *these* "Joshua Generation" years as well as in *"those"* ("Moses Generation") years. New "memories" of racial tyranny are being created *right now* [emphasis added] beneath the national self congratulation over the defeat of level-one racism.[107]

As *Black Commentator*'s Bill Fletcher noted, Obama "attributed much of the anger of Rev. Wright to the past, as if Rev. Wright is stuck in a time warp, *rather than the fact that Rev. Wright's anger about the domestic and foreign policies of the USA are well rooted—and documented—in the current reality of the USA.*"[108]

Another deep flaw in Obama's almost universally heralded Philadelphia oration was that it failed to understand that "change" had also occurred for the worse, not just the better, in U.S. race relations and black American experience. It mentioned none of the ways in which black status and life had actually worsened over recent decades. It acknowledged none of the downsides of the limited and partial civil rights victories or the related problem of increased class inequality within the black community. It naturally did not acknowledge the problematic side of Obama's popularity and candidacy—the way it was being used and understood by many Americans to falsely conclude that racism no longer played a significant role in American life and blinding people to the persistence of a deep institutional racism beneath and beyond the success of selected privileged blacks like Obama.

Regarding "the desire of wide-eyed liberals to purchase racial reconciliation on the cheap," Obama might have wanted to pretend otherwise, but it *was* a critical factor in his coalition. I had numerous conversations with precisely such white liberals—people heavily into Obama's technical blackness for the exact reason Obama mentioned. Affirmative-action hysterics and Geraldine Ferraro's comment aside, moreover, Obama's racial identity was in fact a big part of what made him qualified to win the hidden corporate primaries that permitted him to run a viable campaign for the presidency. His skin color helped to put misleading rebel's clothing around his "deeply conservative" commitment to dominant domestic and (as we shall see in the next chapter) imperial power structures and doctrines.

"To Many of Us . . . the Rev. Jeremiah A. Wright Got It Right"

As was lost in the national salutation over Obama's Philadelphia speech, many of Rev. Wright's harshly critical opinions on U.S. society and policy (both foreign and domestic) are quite widely shared in the black community, whose issue and policy positions stand well to the left of white mainstream opinion in the United States.[109] As Vernon S. Burton noted in a perceptive letter written to the *New York Times* one day after Obama's "beautiful" Race Speech (as the left writer Barbara Ehrenreich described it[110])—a letter that hinted at the hidden issue of reparations:

> As a black man, I have to admit that it was strange to watch and listen to Senator Obama as he tried to assure white folks that he is not a racist and does not intend to hold them accountable for the plight of the black community.
>
> It is ironic that a black man has to convince white people that the blame of the damage that 300 years of slavery, segregation, and oppression has done will not be laid at their door.
>
> Well, Senator Obama is a politician, and we all know that politicians and truth are very often strangers to one another. But to many of us in the black community, the Rev. Jeremiah A. Wright got it right.[111]

As someone who spent many years working as a researcher and social/racial-justice advocate in and around Chicago's South Side black community, I can report that Burton was right. Rev. Wright's highly critical and (often) angry perspective on both domestic U.S. society and U.S. foreign policy is much less controversial and much more common within the black community than most white Americans imagine.

"A Very Dangerous High-Wire Act"

But then, as Michael Dawson noted fourteen years prior to the Wright episode,

> the need to appeal to white voters forces even the most radical of African-American candidates for office to moderate their public stands on racial issues such as economic distribution and black nationalism. The left-wing of African-American politics is far to the left of the Democratic Party of Bill Clinton on issues of economic distribution, foreign policy, and racial policy. . . . The pro–Third World orientation of [Rev. Jesse] Jackson's presidential

campaign has solid roots in the African-American community. This is a foreign policy orientation at odds with that of mainstream America.[112]

The Wright episode was an especially dramatic and treacherous incident demonstrating the problematic nature of Obama's attempt to attain higher office in a white majority nation with a winner-take-all election process. As the black conservative author and Hoover Institution fellow Shelby Steele told Joe Klein two years earlier, "He's working a very dangerous high-wire act. He's got to keep on pleasing white folks without offending black folks and vice versa."[113]

Obama, being "in it to win it," was not about to follow Jesse Jackson's earlier model in pursuing a domestic or foreign policy orientation that violated predominantly white "mainstream" sentiment.

"A Conventionally Opportunistic Politician"

In his automatic condemnation of Wright's foreign policy opinions, Obama was being consistent with his earlier statements and positions. But in his call for Americans to "put race aside" in the name of national unity, he ignored an essential truth: that domestic racial inequality and black poverty are deepened by the imperialist global approach that Obama strongly embraces, beneath peaceful rhetoric to the contrary (as I shall demonstrate in the next chapter).

Consistent with that embrace, Obama's Philadelphia speech honored American "men and women of every color and creed who serve together, and fight together, and bleed together under the same proud flag." Those were revealing words to utter on the eve of the fifth anniversary of the U.S. occupation of Iraq. American troops were coercively united across race, ethnicity, and gender in a monumentally immoral, arch-criminal occupation that Obama promised—as we shall see—to prolong for an indefinite period. The U.S. soldiers' sacrifices were all too real, of course, but they and their commanders have shed a vastly larger quantity of Iraqi and Afghan blood. Sadly, the mere mention of such terrible realities in a heavily exposed public venue inside the United States' narrow-spectrum political and media culture makes one a candidate for reflexive denunciation and mandatory marginalization. This lack of tolerance for alternative views raises disturbing questions about the nation's possible drift into a form of quiet totalitarianism with a democratic face.

The neoconservative *New York Times* columnist William Kristol—no common or natural ally of mine—was on to something when he described the junior senator from Illinois in the following terms in the wake of Obama's early response to the Jeremiah Wright revelations:

> Obama seems to have seen, early in his career, the utility of joining a prominent church that would help him establish political roots in the community in which he lives. Now he sees the utility of distancing himself from that church. The more you learn about him, the more Obama seems to be a conventionally opportunistic politician, impressively smart and disciplined, who has put together a good political career and a terrific presidential campaign. But there's not much audacity of hope there. There's the calculation of ambition, and the construction of artifice, mixed in with a dash of deceit—all covered over with the great conceit that this campaign, and this candidate, is different.[114]

Having It Both Ways on Race

Consistent with the charge of "conventional opportunism," it is worth noting, the Obama campaign has repeatedly contradicted its own claim to "transcend race" during the primary campaign. As the left and black academician Adolph Reed, Jr., noted at the end of April 2008, "Obama supporters have been disposed to cry foul and charge racism at nearly any criticism of him, in steadily more extravagant rhetoric." Examples included the charge that Hillary Clinton was racist when she made the elementary observation that it took President Lyndon Baines Johnson's racial liberalism as well as the inspiring oratory of Dr. King to pass the Voting Rights Act of 1965 and the claim that Clinton was playing to racism when she dared to criticize Obama as "inexperienced." The attempt to portray one's opponent as short on policymaking experience is "standard fare in political campaigns."

Along the way, the Obama campaign has consistently called for voters to support Obama because of the opportunity to "make history." The clear implication is that one would alter the trajectory of history by nominating and then electing a black candidate to the presidency. We might or might not make real history by putting someone who happens to be black in the White House, but advancing the implication that we will is hardly a way of going beyond race.[115]

Postscript: Reverend Wright, Part 2

The research for this chapter was mainly concluded in late March of 2008, prior to a second wave of media Wright obsession that came at the end of April. The second Reverend Wright Affair was deeply troubling to Obama in the wake of his loss to Clinton in Pennsylvania—a defeat that owed much to his continuing failure to win over white, working-class voters. For three days and nights in advance of the North Carolina and Indiana primaries, print media, television, and the blogosphere were afire with new and repeated statements from Wright on race, black liberation theology, U.S. foreign policy, and Obama's motives in distancing himself from his former pastor the previous month. It was a significantly Orwellian episode, deeply suggestive of the persistent powerful toxicity of race as a factor in American political life. Wright was ripped across the dominant media spectrum for saying such supposedly controversial things as that a nation invites terrorist attacks on itself when it practices terrorism abroad and that politicians "say what they say to get elected. I do what pastors do. [Obama] does what politicians do."

The second coming of Reverend Wright included an extended interview with Bill Moyers on the Public Broadcasting System (PBS) and a speech and press conference at the National Press Club. As Glen Ford notes, it led Obama to move from distancing to out and out denunciation in regard to Wright and to shift from "race neutralism" to the white side of the nation's deep racial perception gap on past, present, policy, and politics. Obama now deprecated Rev. Wright as an unbalanced self-"caricature" whose "rants" were "divisive and destructive" and "ended up giving comfort to those who prey on hate. . . . When you start focusing so much on the historically oppressed," Obama actually said, "we lose sight of what we have in common . . . it doesn't describe properly what I believe, in the power of faith to overcome but also to bring together."

He was moving into a more deeply conservative and Caucasian place than he had staked out in Philadelphia, when he had given a speech that was "at root," in the black Left writer Glen Ford's words, "an exercise in moral equivalence that equated white and black grievances in the United States, as if history and gross power discrepancies did not exist." Now Obama branded honest discussion of black oppression and related issues of imperialism and violence in U.S. foreign policy as self-indulgent and hazardously disruptive.[116] By Ford's brilliant analysis,

> Race "neutrality"—an impossibility in the actually existing United States—went out the window as Obama in extremis positioned himself at the political/historical fault line alongside the defenders of the Alamo and American Manifest Destiny. As dictated by the logic of power, Obama furiously maneuvered toward "white space," shamelessly taking cover in a kind of populist white patriotism that has always branded black grievances as selfish, even dangerous distraction from the larger national mission.[117]

Besides engaging in the authoritarian exercise of denouncing as "divisive" and "destructive" what many observers (myself included[118]) saw as a welcome focus on historical (and ongoing) racial oppression, Obama misconstrued Wright's words, which the candidate tellingly dismissed as "rant[ing]." Wright's National Press Club speech included the following widely ignored passage, showing that his focus on "the plight of the historically oppressed" was linked in his view precisely to the goal of reconciliation, not destruction and division:

> The prophetic theology of the black church has always seen and still sees all God's children as sisters and brothers, equals who need reconciliation, who need to be reconciled as equals. . . . Reconciliation means we embrace our individual rich histories, all of them. We retain who we are, as persons of different cultures, while acknowledging that those of other cultures are not superior or inferior to us; they are just different from us. . . . And we recognize . . . that the other who stands before us with a different color of skin, a different texture of hair, different music, different preaching styles, and different dance moves; that other is one of God's children just as we are, no better, no worse, prone to error and in need of forgiveness just as we are. Only then will liberation, transformation, and reconciliation become realities and cease being elusive ideals.[119]

Obama's move into "white space" in late April included telling reporters with a straight face that "if I lose, it would not be because of race" but "because of mistakes I have made on the campaign trail." It also involved issuing the following terse statement in response to a white judge's terrible verdict holding New York City police blameless for killing black American Sean Bell in a senseless fifty-shot attack: "We're a nation of laws and *we respect the verdict that came down* [emphasis added.] Resorting to violence to express displeasure over a verdict is something that is completely unacceptable and is counterproductive." Obama actually got out-flanked on the left by the centrist Hillary Clinton, who issued a carefully worded statement, expressing sympathy for Bell's wife and family and ending with the hope that an ongoing Department of Justice civil rights investigation of the shooting would prevent the occurrence of such tragedies in the future.[120]

Obama's racism-denying rhetoric and behavior was a critical reason that Reed came to see Hillary Clinton as "the lesser evil" in the Democratic race. According to Reed, "Obama's horribly opportunistic approach to the issues bearing on inequality—in which he tosses behaviorist rhetoric to the right and little more than calls to celebrate his success to blacks—stands to pollute debate about racial injustice whether he wins or loses the presidency." Reed shared with this book and other left writers a sense that an Obama presidency *could* be a net negative for the cause of black equality.[121]

That same willingness that Obama demonstrated in the Rev. Wright episodes to stay within narrow limits of acceptable discourse and policy seems to apply to his approach to foreign policy, a subject I take up in the next chapter.

CHAPTER 4

How "Antiwar"?
Obama, Iraq, and the Audacity of Empire

The American people have been extraordinarily resolved. . . . They have seen their sons and daughters killed or wounded in the streets of Fallujah.

—BARACK OBAMA, FROM A SPEECH TO CHICAGO COUNCIL ON GLOBAL AFFAIRS, NOVEMBER 20, 2006

I was always skeptical of the notion we would walk in there and create a Jeffersonian democracy.

—BARACK OBAMA, SPEAKING TO THE EDITORIAL BOARD OF *THE MILWAUKEE JOURNAL-SENTINAL*, FEBRUARY 13, 2008

The American moment is not over, but it must be seized anew.

—BARACK OBAMA, *FOREIGN AFFAIRS*, JULY/AUGUST 2007

I had a hunch this was coming when I watched his speech at the convention four years ago, my wife and I both sat and took it in and looked at each other and said, almost word for word, "He's good, he's very good." The rakish JFK style jabs, the clearly studied rhetorical grace. What better gift to the empire than JFK in sepia? All last year, numerous discussions with people from the old new left who told us, "He'll never get a shot at it because of racist U.S. etc.", to which we maintained, "But what better figure to have out there than one to restore faith in the imperial project, but someone with a black face? They managed to live with Powell and Rice, why not Obama?"

—MICHAEL HUREAUX, *DISSIDENT VOICE*, FEBRUAR1Y 13, 2008

The Bipartisan Imperial Consensus

Reflecting a long nationalist and imperial consensus at the upper reaches of the American political tradition, there has always been considerably more convergence between the "conservative" Republican Party and the "liberal" Democratic Party on matters relating to foreign affairs than in regard to domestic policy. To be sure, since the onset of the Cold War—and particularly since the Vietnam era—arch-militarist sentiment and voters have tended to gravitate more toward the Republican than toward the Democratic wing of the American party system. The Reagan and post-Reagan Republicans have made aggressive and proud chest-pounding nationalist and messianic militarism—brazenly imperialist under George W. Bush and Dick Cheney—core parts of their party's platform and identity. Along with this, they have repeatedly made the charge that Democrats are "soft" on "America's enemies" and on the need to wage and prepare for apparently permanent "war" against evil others abroad and (if necessary) at home.

During the 2008 presidential primaries, the leading Republican candidates Mitt Romney, Rudy Giuliani, and John McCain battled to see which one of them could more strongly identify themselves with support of the Bush-Cheney Iraq occupation; the administration's officially proclaimed, semi-permanent "War on Terror" (which each Republican contender except Ron Paul identified with the Iraq "war"[1]); and with the charge that the Democrats were cowards, "defeatists," and "appeasers" in America's bloody but virtuous struggle with "evil" and "those who would do us harm." The Republican candidate to emerge with the nomination was the most pro-war and militaristic of all in the GOP field—John McCain. He wrapped his general election campaign strongly around his consistent support for Operation Iraqi Freedom, a special appeal to military families and allusion to his "war-hero" past.

Meanwhile, as during and since at least the 1950s, people with progressive peace and non- or even anti-militarist sentiments tend to be registered as Democrats. During the primary season, they exerted pressure on their party's candidates to express commitment to de-escalation, diplomacy, the observance of international law, and the nonviolent and democratic resolution of global conflicts, views that are widely (but almost irrelevantly) favored by most Americans.

Still, for most of the twentieth century, top Democratic and Republican politicians, leaders, and officials maintained general agreement on the essential leading decisions of U.S. foreign policy.[2] The United States entered World Wars I and II under Democratic presidential leadership and conducted both wars with both parties equally and strongly committed to American victory. American imperial Cold War foreign policy was a richly bipartisan affair from Truman through Eisenhower, Kennedy, Johnson, Nixon, Ford, Carter, Reagan, and George H.W. Bush. During the long Cold War era (1945–1991), Republicans and Democrats might have tangled in meaningful ways over domestic policy questions like the minimum wage, occupational health and safety, welfare benefit levels, civil rights, environmental regulation, abortion, and (of course) much more. They were in fundamental agreement, however, when it came to critical foreign policy and "national security" matters: the massive long-term post–World War II escalation of U.S. military spending; the construction of a "permanent U.S. war economy"; nuclear arms development; regular imperial U.S. interventions in a large number of states and regions across the planet (including both direct military action and more covert involvement); the reconstruction of war-ravaged Western Europe and Japan in ways that served U.S. corporate interests and precluded significant autonomous left political developments within those core regions; one-sided support (after 1967) of Israel in its oppression of the Palestinian people and its struggle with surrounding Arab states; the construction of a world economic order calculated and crafted to ensure American global economic hegemony; direct massive U.S. military assaults on Korea and Vietnam; the construction of a global "empire of bases" (Chalmers Johnson's term) that involved setting up hundreds of U.S. military installations scattered across most nations in the world; the sponsorship of pro-U.S. dictatorships and dedicated opposition to popular revolutionary and independent nationalist movements and forces across the "Third World"; the determination that the proper role for "Third World" nations to play in the global economic system was as inferior and impoverished complements to the wealthy, U.S.-led industrial core states, including those of North America (excluding Mexico), Western Europe, and Japan; the false designation of states and movements rejecting that role as "anti-American" partners and agents in supposed Marxist Soviet and Chinese plans for world "communist" domination; and the toleration for Third World "democracy" and independence only insofar as those principles could be reasonably seen to be operating for and within the broader project of U.S. imperial management.

Democrats and Republicans recurrently tussled over certain tactical questions involved in the enactment of this broader imperial agenda. Democratic presidential candidate John F. Kennedy (falsely) claimed that Republican President Dwight D. Eisenhower had permitted the Soviets to develop nuclear missile superiority. Republican presidential candidate Barry Goldwater accused Democratic President Lyndon B. Johnson of being dangerously "soft" on Chinese, Soviet, and Vietnamese "communism." Leading congressional Democrats and Democratic presidential candidate George McGovern criticized Republican President Richard Nixon for provocatively and illegally bombing and invading Cambodia without congressional approval and for bombing and mining North Vietnamese harbors and cities. Republican presidential candidate Ronald Reagan attacked Democratic President Jimmy Carter for allegedly letting U.S. military power unduly wane and for failing to properly manage U.S. client state relations with Iran and the Middle East more broadly. Leading congressional Democrats criticized and investigated the Reagan administration for secretly and illegally selling arms to supposed U.S. enemy Iran in return for that state's promise to free hostages held by radical Islamists in Lebanon, and then using the profits from the sale to help right-wing terrorists buy arms to attack the government of Nicaragua.

But these were primarily disputes over tactics, not doctrine, structure, and worldview. There was no basic argument between the parties over the broader and supposedly noble and progressive role and necessity of American Empire and militarism. There was no serious questioning of the morality of the United States' core and underlying globalism and militarism or its deadly opposition to independence and popular self-determination abroad. Thus, Nixon's mass-murderous bombing of Cambodia went unmentioned in the Articles of Impeachment drawn up by congressional Democrats against Nixon, who was forced out of office for the comparatively minor offense of burgling a Democratic Party campaign office. And, as Howard Zinn noted in regard to the Iran-Contra incident,

> Once the scandal was out in the open, neither the Congressional investigating committees nor the press nor the trial of Colonel Oliver North, who oversaw the contra aid operation, got to the critical questions: What is U.S. foreign policy all about? How are the president and his staff permitted to support a terrorist group in Central America to overthrow a government that, whatever its faults, is welcomed by its own people as a great improvement over the terrible governments the U.S. has supported there for years? What does the scandal tell us about democracy, about freedom of expression, about an open society? . . . The limits of Democratic party criticism of the affair were revealed by a leading Democrat, Senator Sam Nunn of Georgia, who, as the investigation was getting under way, said: "We must, all of us, help the President restore his credibility in foreign affairs."[3]

Such cross-party acquiescence and consensus was hardly surprising in the wake of then U.S. Senator Walter Mondale's foreign policy positions in the last presidential election prior to the congressional Iran-Contra hearings. As Alexander Cockburn has noted,

> As a candidate in 1984 Mondale advanced the schedule of surrender to the period of his doomed candidacy, filing to change his political identity to that of Ronald Reagan by September of that campaign year. Reagan claimed that Nicaragua was exporting revolution to the rest of Latin American and so did Mondale. Reagan said Nicaragua should be "pressured" till it mended its ways, and so did Mondale. Reagan said he would invade Nicaragua if it bought 28-year-old Soviet MIG-21s and so did Mondale. Reagan blamed the missile crisis in Europe on the Russians and so did Mondale. Reagan wanted to hike the military budget and so did Mondale.[4]

"The Essential Continuity in American Foreign Policy"

Democrats were more than simply acquiescent to the U.S. militarism and imperialism of the long Cold War, of course. Americans who insist on strongly identifying the "liberal" Democratic Party with peace, antimilitarism, and anti-imperialism in the last and current century have to ignore a massive record of imperial arrogance and criminality to which Democratic policymakers have richly contributed. The relevant episodes include the following:

- The Franklin D. Roosevelt administration's decision to support Italian and German fascism as reasonable middle-class bulwarks against European social democracy and Soviet "communism"—a decision that was reversed only by the realization that the fascist Axis threatened U.S. imperial power and related global Open Door investment interests.
- The Roosevelt administration's decision to adopt an official position of "neutrality" that translated into support for Spanish fascism and alliance with Stalinist Russia against popular-democratic Spanish forces during the 1930s.
- The Roosevelt administration's decision to restore fascists and monarchists to power in Allied-occupied Italy during and after the great "people's war for democracy" (World War II).
- Harry Truman's decision to demonstrate the mass-murderous power of nuclear weapons by dropping atomic bombs on the densely civilian-populated Japanese cities of Hiroshima and Nagasaki after it was already clear that Japan had been defeated and wished to surrender.
- Truman's decision to back fascist, landlord, and monarchical forces in the brutal suppression of popular democratic rebellion in post–World War II Greece.
- Truman's decision to use that suppression as an opportunity to terrorize the U.S. populace into supporting a massive expansion of the burgeoning U.S. military-industrial complex in the name of countering a mythical Soviet-directed communist conspiracy.
- The liberal Kennedy administration's decision to dramatically escalate the international arms race after campaigning on the monumentally deceptive claim that the United States was on the wrong side of the Soviet-American "missile gap."
- The Kennedy administration's significant escalation of the monumentally illegal and immoral U.S. attack on Vietnam.
- The Kennedy and Johnson administrations' support for numerous Latin American dictatorships in the name of "progress."

- Democratic President Jimmy Carter's support for the repressive, long-standing, U.S-sponsored dictatorships in places like Iran, Saudi Arabia, and Indonesia and his announcement of the "Carter Doctrine," proclaiming the United States' right to employ violence to guarantee its "vital interest" in the uninterrupted extraction of petroleum from the oil-rich Persian Gulf.
- The strong support most congressional Democrats gave to the Reagan administration's funding of U.S.-sponsored counterinsurgency efforts in Central America and George H.W. Bush's military assaults on Panama and Iraq.
- The Clinton administration's decision to enforce mass-murderous "economic sanctions" against the devastated, heavily impoverished nation of Iraq, and to justify the 500,000 resulting deaths of Iraqi children (as of 1996) as "a price worth paying" (as Clinton's secretary of state, Madeleine Albright, put it on national television), which effectively deepened the hold of Saddam Hussein and his brutal regime over the overwhelmed Iraqi populace.
- Clinton's decisions in the summer of 1993 to bomb a suburban Baghdad neighborhood in retaliation for an alleged Iraqi assassination plot against George H.W. Bush, and to attempt to justify that attack in the false name of the United Nations Charter, which permits unilateral military action only in defense against an armed attack and only when there is no opportunity to convene the United Nations Security Council. "None of these factors were present in the Baghdad bombing," Howard Zinn has noted, adding that the evidence for the alleged plot was very weak and that the alleged conspirators never came to trial. The 1993 bombing killed six people, including a prominent Iraqi artist and her husband. The attack showed that Clinton, "facing several foreign policy crises in his two terms in office, would react to them in traditional ways, usually involving military action, claiming humanitarian motives, and often with disastrous results for people abroad as well for the United States."[5]
- The Clinton administration's decision to kill thousands of innocent African civilians by bombing a pharmaceutical factory in the Sudan in loose "retaliation" for terrorist attacks on U.S. embassies in Tanzania and Kenya.
- The Clinton administration's decision (supported by both dominant U.S. political parties) to bomb Serbia to discipline a perceived challenger of U.S. global hegemony in the falsely proclaimed name of humanitarian concern for ethnic Albanians.
- The support of John Edwards, Hillary Clinton, and numerous other Democratic U.S. senators and House representatives for the bombing and invasion of Afghanistan after 9/11 and their October 2002

authorization of George W. Bush's illegal and unnecessary invasion of Iraq, which began in March 2003.

- The willingness of numerous congressional Democrats, including Barack Obama, to fund the illegal and mass-murderous Iraq occupation and to deny the criminal and imperialist, significantly oil-motivated nature of the invasion and accept the notion that the "war" was launched to spread "freedom" and "democracy" to Iraq and the broader Middle East.
- Senator John F. Kerry's decision to run for the presidency on the claim that he would be a more effective manager of U.S. imperial wars in Afghanistan and Iraq than Bush, a message framed with an opening military salute—"this is John Kerry reporting for duty"—and the placement of his Vietnam War patrol-boat "brothers" on the stage of his 2004 Democratic presidential nomination acceptance speech.

As Alexander Cockburn noted prior to the 2004 election, "Kerry offers himself up mainly as a more competent manager of the Bush agenda, a steadier hand on the helm of the Empire. . . . Kerry enthusiastically backed both of Bush's wars, and in June of 2004, at the very moment Bush signaled a desire to retreat, the senator called for 25,000 new troops to be sent to Iraq, with a plan for the US military to remain entrenched there for at least the next four years."[6]

The veteran left historian and brilliant U.S. foreign policy critic Gabriel Kolko elaborated on the standard militarist and imperial continuity theme in John Kerry's "Reporting for Duty" campaign:

> His statements and interviews over the past few months dealing with foreign affairs have mostly been both vague and incoherent, though he is explicitly and ardently pro-Israel and explicitly for regime-change in Venezuela. His policies on the Middle East are identical to Bush's and this alone will prevent the alliance with Europe from being reconstructed. On Iraq, even as violence there escalated and Kerry finally had a crucial issue with which to win the election, his position has been indistinguishable from the President's. "Until" an Iraqi armed force can replace it, Kerry wrote in the April 13 *Washington Post,* the American military has to stay in Iraq—"preferably helped by NATO"; "no matter who is elected President in November, we will persevere in that mission" to build a stable, pluralistic Iraq—which, I must add, has never existed and is unlikely to emerge in the foreseeable future. "It is a matter of national honor and trust." He has promised to leave American troops in Iraq for his entire first term if necessary, but he is vague about their subsequent departure. Not even the scandal over the treatment of Iraqi prisoners evoked Kerry's criticism despite the fact it has profoundly alienated a politically decisive segment of the American public.[7]

Consistent with this unflattering portrayal, Kerry selected as his top national security adviser Randy Beers, a former counterterrorism adviser to President Bush II. Beers was "one of the chief architects of and apologists for the United States' cruel policies in Colombia," according to journalist Sean Donahue, including its disastrous aerial crop fumigation program and its de facto alliance with wealthy landowners and right-wing paramilitaries. The latter, wrote Donahue, "play[ed] a significant role in protecting U.S. economic interests by using massacres to clear off land for oil development, logging, hydro-electric dams, and cattle ranching, and by assassinating union organizers, indigenous leaders, and other critics of the political and economic order in Colombia." As Donahue noted on the eve of the 2004 election, Kerry's appointment of Beers to his national security team belied the illusions of those who naively believed that "Senator Kerry offers a humane alternative to President Bush."[8]

During its many imperial actions, U.S. policymakers of both parties—liberals and conservatives alike—have regularly described U.S. objectives in terms of the advance of "democracy." But the operative U.S. definition of "democracy" is rather different from the dictionary meaning. The United States recognizes only a curious sort of overseas democracy—the kind that supports interrelated U.S. global economic and military-strategic objectives. U.S.-acknowledged "democracies" provide U.S. transnational capital with a favorable investment climate. They accept neoliberal prescriptions that forbid poor states from undertaking commonsense economic-nationalist measures required for them to develop rapidly and independently on the model of the richer states. They agree to serve as neocolonial military vassals of Uncle Sam. Since few world peoples and nations are eager to accept such a curious, absurdly restricted definition of "democracy" (contemporary Iraq is another of many examples), there is a chasm between idealistic liberal ("Wilsonian") rhetoric and authoritarian policy reality in the long and failed history of America's effort to "make the world safe" for both "democracy" and U.S. empire at one and the same time.[9]

The liberal Kennedy epitomized the conditional nature of U.S. "democracy" as a foreign policy objective when he remarked that while the United States would prefer democratic regimes abroad, it would choose "a Trujillo" over "a Castro"—that is, a pro-American dictator over an anti-American one—if those were the only choices. "It is necessary only to add," Chomsky noted in 1991, that Kennedy's "concept of 'a Castro' was very broad, extending to anyone who raises problems for the 'rich men dwelling at peace with their habitations,' who are to rule the world according to [Winston] Churchill's aphorism, while enjoying the benefits of its human and material resources."[10]

"Liberal" former presidential candidate John F. Kerry seems to have applied such reasoning to Venezuela's popular, left-populist, and freely elected president Hugo Chavez. In 2004, Kerry made it clear that he'd like to see the replacement of the left nationalist Chavez by a government that was favorably disposed to granting the United States privileged access to Venezuela's oil wealth.[11]

President Bill Clinton acted upon his proclaimed desire to uphold "the essential continuity in American foreign policy"[12] by maintaining traditional imperial double standards in U.S. global relations. Like American presidents of both parties before and since, he rewarded authoritarian regimes perceived to support U.S. economic and strategic interests while punishing those perceived to threaten U.S. interests. He embraced "humanitarian causes" perceived to work against states and regimes he opposed (for example, in Yugoslavia and Cuba) and ignored or opposed those that worked against states and regimes that the United States supported and/or depended upon, including Saudi Arabia, Suharto's Indonesia before 1999 (when global outrage over Suharto's escalated oppression of East Timor forced the White House to briefly cut off U.S. assistance to the Indonesian military), the "Marxist" forced labor state of China, Boris Yeltsin's Russia, and the U.S.-created dictatorship of Haiti.

Clinton took the lead in opposing international action to stop the greatest human rights crime of the 1990s, the genocide in Rwanda. He continued large-scale arms sales and financial and political support to repressive states like Indonesia and the arch-reactionary, quasi-feudal state of Saudi Arabia. He spoke repeatedly against Iraq's alleged development of "weapons of mass destruction," but said nothing about the well-known nuclear weapons arsenal possessed by Israel, whose illegal and oppressive occupation of Palestine he supported in strict accord with U.S. foreign policy over prior decades. He violated his proclaimed "free trade" principles by maintaining a destructive trade embargo on Cuba and imposing restrictive, deadly economic sanctions on Iraq, even while he assisted the dictatorial Chinese state's entrance into the world trading and investment system, with negative consequences for American workers and economic security.

Also consistent with long-standing imperial practice, Clinton betrayed his 1992 campaign promises to deliver a significant post–Cold War "peace dividend" (the significant transfer of public resources from military to socially useful purposes) by "continu[ing] to spend at least $250 billion a year to maintain the military machine." He "accept[ed] the Republican claim that the nation must be ready to fight 'two regional wars' simultaneously, despite the collapse of the Soviet Union in 1989," wrote Zinn. "At that time," Zinn noted, "[George H. W.] Bush's Secretary of Defense, Dick Cheney, had said, 'The threats have become so remote, so remote that they are difficult to discern.' General Colin Powell spoke similarly . . . 'I'm running out of demons. . . . I'm down to Castro and Kim Il Sung.'"[13]

"The World's Greatest Force for Peace and Freedom"

Intimately related to leading Democrats' eager willingness to join Republicans in the execution of an imperial foreign policy agenda has been their strong acceptance of the notion that the United States is an exceptionally benevolent nation that is uniquely qualified and privileged by God and history to manage the world's affairs. Under Bill Clinton, Secretary of State Madeleine Albright expressed a doctrinal notion held across the bipartisan U.S. governing class when she said that "the United States is good. . . . We try to do our best everywhere." According to Clinton, speaking in 1996 in terms that echoed those of Reagan and JFK (the latter once called the United States the "watchtower on the walls of freedom"), "When I came into office, I was determined that our country would go into the 21st century still the world's greatest force for peace and freedom, for democracy and security and prosperity."[14] Two years later, his top diplomatic official defended his use of cruise missiles against Iraq in stark American exceptionalist terms, telling NBC television's Matt Lauer that "if we have to use force, it is because we are America; we are the indispensable nation. We stand tall and we see . . . into the future."[15] As Zinn noted in *The Progressive* in the spring of 2006,

> Our leaders have taken it for granted, and planted that belief in the minds of many people, that we are entitled, because of our moral superiority, to dominate the world. At the end of World War II, Henry Luce, with an arrogance appropriate to the owner of *Time, Life,* and *Fortune,* pronounced this "the American century," saying that victory in the war gave the United States the right "to exert upon the world the full impact of our influence, for such purposes as we see fit and by such means as we see fit."
>
> Both the Republican and Democratic parties have embraced this notion. George Bush, in his Inaugural Address on January 20, 2005, said that spreading liberty around the world was "the calling of our time." Years before that, in 1993, President Bill Clinton, speaking at a West Point commencement, declared: "The values you learned here . . . will be able to spread throughout this country and throughout the world and give other people the opportunity to live as you have lived, to fulfill your God-given capacities."

Such standard default beliefs inside the U.S. power elite express the intimate, dialectically inseparable relationship between American empire abroad and American inequality and inequality-denying ideology at home.[16] As Zinn asked,

> What is the idea of our moral superiority based on? Surely not on our behavior toward people in other parts of the world. Is it based on how well people

in the United States live? The World Health Organization in 2000 ranked countries in terms of overall health performance, and the United States was thirty-seventh on the list, though it spends more per capita for health care than any other nation. One of five children in this, the richest country in the world, is born in poverty. There are more than forty countries that have better records on infant mortality. Cuba does better. And there is a sure sign of sickness in society when we lead the world in the number of people in prison—more than two million.[17]

"Prevailing Democratic Doctrine Is Not That Different"

As elite Democratic behavior during and since Desert Storm shows, the strongly bipartisan—hardly just "Republican"—nature of U.S. globalism and militarism held fast beyond the end of the Cold War and the collapse of the Soviet Union—and the plausibility of the claim that the "Soviet threat" justified endemic U.S. interventions and involvements around the world. As Tufts University political scientist Tony Smith noted in an important *Washington Post* commentary in the spring of 2007, it is questionable how discontinuous George W. Bush's aggressive and openly imperialist and highly militarized foreign policy was with the neoliberal Clinton administration and with prevailing Democratic foreign relations thinking into the post-9/11 and Iraq War era. "Although they now cast themselves as alternatives to President Bush," Smith wrote, "the fact is that prevailing Democratic doctrine is not that different from the Bush-Cheney doctrine." Smith's analysis merits lengthy quotation:

> Many Democrats, including senators who voted to authorize the war in Iraq, embraced the idea of muscular foreign policy based on American global supremacy and the presumed right to intervene to promote democracy or to defend key U.S. interests long before 9/11, and they have not changed course since. Even those who have shifted against the war have avoided doctrinal questions.
>
> . . . Without a coherent alternative to the Bush doctrine, with its confidence in America's military preeminence and the global appeal of "free market democracy," the Democrats' midterm victory may not be repeated in November 2008. Or, if the Democrats do win in 2008, they could remain staked to a vision of a Pax Americana strikingly reminiscent of Bush's.
>
> Democratic adherents to what might be called the "neoliberal" position are well organized and well positioned. Their credo was enunciated just nine years ago by Madeleine Albright, then President Bill Clinton's secretary of state: "If we have to use force, it is because we are America. We are the indispensable nation. We stand tall and we see further into the future." She was speaking of Bosnia at the time, but her remark had much wider implications.

> Since 1992, the ascendant Democratic faction in foreign policy debates has been the thinkers associated with the Democratic Leadership Council (DLC) and its think tank, the Progressive Policy Institute (PPI). Since 2003, the PPI has issued repeated broadsides damning Bush's handling of the Iraq war, but it has never condemned the invasion. It has criticized Bush's failure to achieve U.S. domination of the Middle East, arguing that Democrats could do it better. . . .
>
> . . . These [Democratic] neoliberals are nearly indistinguishable from the better-known neoconservatives.[18]

"Join the Movement to End the [Iraq] War" by Caucusing for Obama

Contrary to the popular candidate image projected and encouraged by the campaign and media, Obama is no special exception to the broader imperial consensus that has limited what Democratic presidential candidates and presidents have advocated and done in the realm of foreign policy for many decades. The story begins with Iraq and with the predominantly white Iowa Democrats I met in the summer, fall, and winter of 2007.

Of all the Democratic voters I canvassed in eastern Iowa in my role as a volunteer for John Edwards—himself very problematic on foreign policy (from a left perspective[19])—none were more tight-lipped and hostile than Barack Obama's followers. During my many hours as a voter-contact volunteer, I would ask non-Edwards Democrats who they were backing and why, and whether they'd be willing to hear some brief reflections relating to issues and policies and why they might consider my candidate. Obama's folks were not interested and not willing.

If the person I reached by phone or in person supported Bill Richardson, Joe Biden, Dennis Kucinich, or Christopher Dodd, the results were generally quite congenial. A polite and productive conversation would often ensue. When I asked why they were supporting their candidate, they took no offense and typically mentioned two or three policy areas where they felt their candidate had a made a special mark or held special promise. Often I would determine that Edwards was their second choice—a critical thing to know under the rules of the Iowa Caucus system. The results with Clinton supporters were more mixed, but generally they were good-natured.

Most of the "Obamanists" (as I came to call Obama's supporters by mid-December) I encountered seemed offended at the notion that anyone would seek to engage them on candidate differences. On the whole, they did not connect on policy issues. Many of them left me with the impression that they found something highly unpleasant and boorish—crypto-racist, perhaps—about daring to question their Great Leader. This attitude was quite pronounced. One middle-class lady with a poster saying "HOPE—Obama

'08" on her front lawn became positively enraged when I asked her a simple question: "So why are you supporting Obama?"

Wondering if there was something wrong with my own approach to Obama's supporters, I related my experience to other Edwards volunteers. It turned out that my encounters with "Obamanists" were commonplace. A staffer explained it to me in the following terms: "Oh, you can't talk policy and issues with the Obama people. Don't even try. There's no discussion with them. They already know everything. It's a cult." The judgment struck me as a little over-harsh but more accurate than not. It also struck me as ironic, for Obama's supporters were the most highly educated and academic of all the different Democratic candidates' constituents.

This is not to say that I never encountered an open and amiable Iowa "Obamanist" willing to at least explain their candidate allegiance. I found seven of them—four in my Iowa City precinct, one in the small rural town of Wilton, and two in Muscatine (out of at least three hundred Obama supporters I contacted). And while my sample of seven is not exactly a statistically significant survey, it interesting to note that each one of them gave special and pivotal credit to Obama for having "opposed the war on Iraq from the start." Obama struck them as a militantly antiwar candidate who was rejecting the foreign policy of both the Bush administration and the Democratic Party establishment.

Four of them also claimed that Obama's technical nonwhiteness and vaguely Islamic-sounding name (Barack Hussein Obama) would prove highly useful in repairing America's relationship with the rest of the world in the wake of George W. Bush's disastrous policies. They clearly connected their favorite candidates' allegedly antiwar and anti-imperial foreign policy credentials to his black and multicultural identity.

My seven friendly and forthcoming "Obamanists" were emblematic of a broader opinion band in the white middle class. Along with a hope that Obama is a specially charismatic leader with the capacity to "get things done with people across the aisle" and the sense that his technical blackness represents progressive "change," the image of Obama as an antiwar and anti-imperial candidate has been very critical to his support. As Stephen Zunes noted in an important assessment of Obama's positions on the Middle East,

> The strong showings by Senator Barack Obama of Illinois in the early contests for the Democratic presidential nomination don't just mark a repudiation of the Bush administration's Iraq policy and "war on terrorism." They also indicate a rejection of the Democratic Party establishment, much of which supported the invasion of Iraq and other tragic elements of the administration's foreign policy.
>
> There's a lot of evidence to suggest that voters found Senator Obama's opposition to the U.S. invasion of Iraq, in contrast to the strong support for the

> invasion by his principal rivals for the Democratic Party nomination, a major factor contributing to his surprisingly strong challenge to Senator Hillary Clinton (D-NY) in the race for the White House. Indeed, while his current position on Iraq is not significantly different than that of Clinton or the other major challenger, former North Carolina Senator John Edwards, Obama's good judgment not to support the war five years ago has led millions of Democratic and independent voters to find him more trustworthy as a potential commander-in-chief.[20]

The image of Obama as the antiwar candidate was naturally cultivated by his campaign in 2007 and early 2008. Team Obama made their candidate's "opposition to the war from the start" the single leading policy-specific selling point in repeatedly stated contrast to Edwards and Clinton, both of whom rushed in October 2002 to authorize Bush's fateful invasion of Mesopotamia. In speeches, advertisements, and mailings from coast to coast, Obama regularly cited his October 2002 speech against the impending war as an example of his foreign policy superiority over his chief rivals. In appearances across Iowa and New Hampshire, he made sure to refer to the "Iraq mess" as a war that "should have never have been authorized." The statement was a direct shot at Edwards and Clinton. On the very last day before the Iowa Caucus, Obama staffers and volunteers put copies of his October 2002 speech inside the screen doors of tens of thousands of potential caucus-goers.

His campaign even said this in a mass mailing sent across Iowa in the winter of 2007: "From the very beginning, Barack Obama said No to the War in Iraq. Join the movement to end the war and change Washington."[21]

"The movement to end the war": Barack Obama was asking me and my fellow Iowans to equate caucusing for the junior senator from Illinois with joining the antiwar movement.

Five Distinctions

In these ads and mailings, Obama was encouraging us to accept a great delusion. There is in fact a wide gap between image and reality when it comes to Obama's foreign policy record, and many progressives embraced a fantasy when they bought the notion of Obama as some sort of "peace and justice" candidate. I believe that his claim to have consistently and strongly opposed the Iraq War is less than fully honest and accurate.

Progressive peace activists and voters need to keep five key distinctions in their moral and intellectual toolbox as they assess the past and likely future foreign policy performance of Obama: (1) the difference between the Obama campaign and the antiwar movement; (2) the difference between opposing a war in rhetoric and opposing it in reality; (3) the difference between opposing a war consistently and opposing it inconsistently; (4) the difference between opposing a criminal and imperial war because it is a strategic imperial mistake (a "pragmatic" failure) and opposing it because it is immoral, murderous, illegal, and imperial (a moral and legal transgression); (5) the difference between opposing a single imperial war and opposing a broader imperial system that predictably generates war. As we shall see, U.S. Senator and presidential candidate Obama has lined up on the conservative and imperial side of each of these distinctions, raising steep questions about the accuracy of the antiwar and anti-imperial Obama imagery so many American voters were deceived into buying in 2007 and 2008.[22]

"I'm Opposed to Dumb Wars": The Imminent Invasion of Iraq as a Mistake, Not an Imperial Crime

The work of deconstructing Obama's foreign policy mythology begins with taking a closer look at his 2002 speech—an oration I heard live in Chicago's downtown Daley Plaza. It was an impressive performance, given when he could afford to be more reckless and outwardly radical—before he had been tapped to join the national power elite. Obama opposed what he called "the cynical attempt by Richard Perle and Paul Wolfowitz and other armchair, weekend warriors in this administration to shove their own ideological agendas down our throats, irrespective of the costs in lives lost and in hardships borne." He denounced "the attempt by political hacks like Karl Rove to distract us from a rise in the uninsured, a rise in the poverty rate, a drop in the median income, to distract us from corporate scandals and a stock market that has just gone through the worst month since the Great Depression." At the end of his talk, Obama said the following:

> Now let me be clear—I suffer no illusions about Saddam Hussein. He is a brutal man. A ruthless man. A man who butchers his own people to secure his own power. . . . The world, and the Iraqi people, would be better off without him.
>
> But I also know that Saddam poses no imminent and direct threat to the United States, or to his neighbors . . . and that in concert with the international community he can be contained until, in the way of all petty dictators, he falls away into the dustbin of history.
>
> I know that even a successful war against Iraq will require a U.S. occupation of undetermined length, at undetermined cost, with undetermined consequences.
>
> I know that an invasion of Iraq without a clear rationale and without strong international support will only fan the flames of the Middle East, and encourage the worst, rather than best, impulses of the Arab world, and strengthen the recruitment arm of al-Qaeda.

> I am not opposed to all wars. I'm opposed to dumb wars.
>
> So for those of us who seek a more just and secure world for our children, let us send a clear message to the President today.
>
> You want a fight, President Bush? Let's finish the fight with Bin Laden and al-Qaeda, through effective, coordinated intelligence, and a shutting down of the financial networks that support terrorism, and a homeland security program that involves more than color-coded warnings.
>
> You want a fight, President Bush?
>
> Let's fight to make sure that . . . we vigorously enforce a non-proliferation treaty, and that former enemies and current allies like Russia safeguard and ultimately eliminate their stores of nuclear material, and that nations like Pakistan and India never use the terrible weapons already in their possession, and that the arms merchants in our own country stop feeding the countless wars that rage across the globe.
>
> You want a fight, President Bush?
>
> Let's fight to make sure our so-called allies in the Middle East, the Saudis and the Egyptians, stop oppressing their own people, and suppressing dissent, and tolerating corruption and inequality, and mismanaging their economies so that their youth grow up without education, without prospects, without hope, the ready recruits of terrorist cells.
>
> You want a fight, President Bush? Let's fight to wean ourselves off Middle East oil, through an energy policy that doesn't simply serve the interests of Exxon and Mobil.
>
> Those are the battles that we need to fight. Those are the battles that we willingly join. The battles against ignorance and intolerance. Corruption and greed. Poverty and despair.[23]

Obama's speech was accurate and forthright about critical matters. It rightly predicted that invading Iraq would exacerbate Islamic anger and terrorist threats. It correctly observed the politically motivated nature and the potential length and high cost of the planned war. It struck an especially progressive chord when it related the Bush administration's military ambitions to its desire to turn public attention away from pressing domestic problems like poverty and corporate corruption.

But Obama's Daley Plaza oration, subsequently lodged into the screen doors of Iowa City progressives with peace symbols on their porch, was not an especially antiwar message, much less an anti-imperial one, as such. It certainly wasn't a left speech of the sort that people in the actual antiwar movement (including myself) were already making by the fall of 2002. Calling Bush's imminent war "dumb," but not criminal or immoral, it failed to acknowledge the highly illegal and richly petro-imperialist ambitions behind the Iraq invasion being planned in Washington. It said nothing about the racist nature of the administration's determination to conflate Iraq with

9/11 and al Qaeda. It omitted the long and terrible record of imperial U.S. policy that had made 9/11 less than surprising to those (including Obama's own pastor Jeremiah Wright[24]) who paid elementary attention to American global behavior and Middle East politics.

Contrary to the Obama presidential campaign's later effort to reinvent its candidate as an ally of the antiwar movement, his Chicago speech spoke against the planned invasion in much the same terms as George H. W. Bush's former national security adviser, Brent Scowcroft, and much of the rest of the American foreign policy establishment. It argued that invading Iraq would be a foreign policy *mistake*—something that would likely not advance the international status and power of the United States. It did not mention that the unprovoked occupation being worked up by the White House and the Pentagon would be a brazenly illegal and imperial transgression certain to kill untold masses of innocent Iraqis.

The basis for Obama's dissent from Bush and Cheney's plans was not different in any fundamental moral or ideological sense from that of numerous militantly imperial members of the foreign policy establishment. In an August 2007 interview with the *National Journal,* Obama's media consultant David Axelrod said that he "was there in 2002 when [Obama] made his decision to oppose the war and gave what turned out to be an almost chillingly prescient critique of why we shouldn't go."[25] This is true enough, but the reasons Obama gave for not going—economic cost, uncertain outcomes, risks of regional destabilization, and so on (but not immorality, criminality, and the likelihood that many Iraqis would die)—were widely voiced by many top conservative foreign policy thinkers, including Scowcroft.[26]

"U.S. Forces Are Still a Part of the Solution in Iraq": 2005–2006

And yet Obama's sharply qualified and establishment-friendly criticism of the White House's Iraq policy in the fall of 2002 stood to the left of his statements and actions on Iraq over the next four years, as the illegal invasion was launched and then as it turned into a mass-murderous "fiasco."[27] After his successful run for the nation's highest representative body, Obama hardly distinguished himself as an "antiwar" senator.

As the *New York Times* noted in a front-page portrait of Obama during his short Senate career two days after his early March 2008 victory in the Wyoming Democratic primary, he had begun to take a profoundly conservative approach to the invasion that he had so strongly criticized in the fall of 2002. "Determined to be viewed as substantive," *Times* reporters Kate Zernike and Jeff Zeleny noted, "he was cautious—even on the Iraq war, which he had opposed as a Senate candidate. . . . He voted against the withdrawal of troops. He proposed legislation calling for a drawdown after he began running for president." Into 2006, the *Times* noted, Obama "disappointed some Democrats by not taking a more prominent role opposing the war—he voted against a troop withdrawal proposal by Senators John Kerry and Russ Feingold in June 2006, arguing that a firm date for withdrawal would hamstring diplomats and military commanders in the field."[28]

The *Times* could have said much more. Zernike and Zeleny could have gone back to examine a speech Obama gave to the Council on Foreign Relations (CFR) on November 22, 2005. It came at a critical moment. Congressman Jack Murtha (D-PA) had just spoken out courageously against the occupation. This highly decorated military veteran and former chairman of the House Armed Services Committee had said, "I believe we need to turn Iraq over to the Iraqis. The United States [must] immediately redeploy. . . . All of Iraq must know that Iraq is free, free from a United States occupation. And I believe this will send a signal to the Sunnis to join the political process." As Alexander Cockburn noted five months later, "Democrats fled Murtha, few with more transparent calculation than Obama."[29]

In his quest to be "substantive," Obama told the CFR that we should "focus our attention on how to reduce the U.S. military footprint in Iraq. Notice that I say 'reduce,' and not 'fully withdraw.'" Obama's speech included the bland and careful pronouncement that "2006 should be the year that the various Iraqi factions must . . . arrive at a fair political accommodation to defeat the insurgency" and "the Administration must make available to Congress critical information on reality-based benchmarks that will help us succeed in Iraq." As "the war rages on and the insurgency festers—as another father weeps over a flag-draped casket and another wife feeds her husband the dinner he can't fix for himself," Obama said, "it is our duty to ask ourselves hard questions. What do we want to accomplish now that we are in Iraq, and what is it possible to accomplish?" By his account, "U.S. forces are still a part of the solution in Iraq." The tone of his Iraq comments had undergone significant transformation since his 2002 speech.[30]

Continuing with his portrayal of the Iraq invasion as a "blunder" but not a crime, Obama said that "the President could take the politics out of Iraq once and for all if he would simply go on television and say to the American people 'Yes, we made mistakes. Yes, there are things I would have done differently. But now that we're here, I am willing to work with both Republicans and Democrats to find the most responsible way out.'" The speech was titled "Moving Forward in Iraq."[31]

Leading left foreign relations scholar Stephen Zunes offered the following useful summary of Obama's record on Iraq when he was a U.S. senator but not yet running for president:

> Once elected to the U.S. Senate . . . his anti-war voice became muted. Obama supported unconditional funding for the Iraq War in both 2005 and 2006.

> And—despite her false testimonies before Congress and her mismanagement of Iraq policy before, during, and after the U.S. invasion in her role as National Security Advisor—Obama broke with most of his liberal colleagues in the Senate by voting to confirm Condoleezza Rice as secretary of state during his first weeks in office.
>
> Obama didn't even make a floor speech on the war until a full year after his election. In it, he called for a reduction in the number of U.S. troops but no timetable for their withdrawal. In June 2006, he voted against an amendment by Senators Russ Feingold and John Kerry for such a timetable.[32]

The vote for Condoleezza Rice was instructive. As Matt Gonzalez asked, if Obama was an "antiwar" senator, "why would he have voted to make one of the architects of 'Operation Iraqi Liberation' the head of U.S. foreign policy? Curiously, he lacked the courage of 13 of his colleagues who voted against her confirmation."[33]

Equally troubling for antiwar progressives was Obama's decision during the 2006 Democratic congressional primaries to campaign for pro-war incumbents, including his self-chosen Senate mentor, the arch–war hawk Connecticut Senator Joe Lieberman and other conservative Democrats battling antiwar challengers. In Gonzalez's words,

> In March 2006, Obama went out of his way to travel to Connecticut to campaign for Senator Joseph Lieberman who faced a tough challenge by anti-war candidate Ned Lamont. At a Democratic Party dinner attended by Lamont, Obama called Lieberman "his mentor" and urged those in attendance to vote and give financial contributions to him. This is the same Lieberman who Alexander Cockburn [identified as] "Bush's closest Democratic ally on the Iraq War." Why would Obama have done that if he was truly against the war?[34]

Despite the 2006 election results and polls showing that a majority of Americans desired a rapid withdrawal of U.S. forces, Obama gave a conservative war speech entitled "A Way Forward in Iraq" to the Chicago Council of Global Affairs (CCGA).[35] In this speech, Zunes noted, Obama

> acknowledged that U.S. troops may need to stay in that occupied country for an "extended period of time," and that "the U.S. may have no choice but to slog it out in Iraq." Specifically, [Obama] called for U.S. forces to maintain a "reduced but active presence," to "protect logistical supply points" and "American enclaves like the Green Zone" as well as "act as rapid reaction forces to respond to emergencies and go after terrorists." . . . Instead of calling for an end to the increasingly bloody U.S.-led military effort, he instead called for "a pragmatic solution to the real war we're facing in Iraq," with repeated references to the need to defeat the insurgency.[36]

Liberal commentator and Obama supporter Michael Tomasky understated matters in November 2006, when he said Obama "has not been a notable leader on the defining issue of the Bush era."[37]

"He Had Bigger Plans"

Obama actually began "muting" his antiwar voice well before his election to the U.S. Senate. In 2003, the year the criminal invasion was undertaken, Obama removed his Daley Plaza speech from his Web site. Even that speech's relatively tepid (compared to those of antiwar activists) objections to the occupation being planned were seen by him and his handlers as too radical for public consumption as he prepared to make his run for the U.S. Senate. And while Obama may have spoken at a relatively small and elite antiwar rally in the fall of 2002, he was nowhere to be found during the great mass anti-invasion marches (in which I participated) of many thousands that took place in downtown Chicago on the nights of March 19 and March 20, 2003. According to Carl Davidson, a former leading anti–Vietnam War activist who helped organize the Daley Plaza rally, Obama began stepping back from his "antiwar" position after the actual invasion began: "He turned. . . . Now we had to set aside whether it was right or wrong to invade, now we had to find the 'smart' path to victory, not Bush's 'dumb' path. . . . He wasn't listening much to us anymore, but to folks much higher up in the DLC orbit. He had bigger plans."[38]

Obama's heralded Democratic Party convention keynote address in late July 2004 (more than three months prior to his election to the U.S. Senate) steered well clear of any substantive criticism of the invasion and the fraudulent basis on which it was sold to and authorized by Democratic legislators. His main criticism of Bush's criminal invasion was that the United States had gone to war without "enough troops to win." It was all very consistent with the John F. Kerry presidential campaign, which advanced a strongly militarist message and ran on the notion that its standard-bearer would be a more competent and effective administrator of the Iraq occupation than George W. Bush. Kerry was going to conduct the illegal policy in a more efficient way.[39]

"The Difference Is Who's in a Position to Execute?"

But Obama's most telling Iraq War comments during the 2004 Democratic Party convention did not occur during his famous address. One day before he gave his historic speech, Obama told the *New York Times* that he did not know how he would have voted on the 2002 Iraq War resolution had he been serving in the U.S. Senate at the time of the vote. Here is the relevant *Times* passage: "In a recent interview, [Obama] declined to criticize

Senators Kerry and Edwards for voting to authorize the war, although he said he would not have done the same based on the information he had at the time. 'But, I'm not privy to Senate intelligence reports,' Mr. Obama said. 'What would I have done? I don't know.' What I know is that from my vantage point the case was not made.'"[40]

Obama said something just as telling during the convention to *Chicago Tribune* reporters Jeff Zeleny and David Mendell. "There's not that much difference between my position [on Iraq] and George Bush's position at this stage," he told the journalists. "The *difference, in my mind, is who's in a position to execute* [the occupation]." Zeleny and Mendell added that Obama "now believes U.S. forces must remain to stabilize the war-ravaged nation—a position not dissimilar to the current approach of the Bush administration."[41]

Continuing the Occupation beneath "Rhetoric of Withdrawal" (2007–2008)

When Obama became a nearly declared presidential candidate as majority U.S. antiwar sentiment peaked in late 2006, he started for the first time to voice support for "timetables for withdrawal." In the spring of 2007, he began voting against unconditional funding for the war. But this happened only after the bipartisan, Bush-appointed Iraq Study Group, headed by former Secretary of State James Baker and former Congressman Lee Hamilton, called for setting a date to withdraw U.S. combat troops. At the end of March 2007, Obama announced that congressional Democrats would vote to fund the continuing illegal invasion of Iraq into its fifth year if Bush vetoed a bill containing timelines. This, he said, was because "no lawmaker wants to play chicken with the troops"—despite the fact that no proposal to de-fund the war suggested leaving U.S. soldiers defenseless in Iraq. In a critical New Hampshire debate in the fall of 2007, moreover, Obama could not commit to withdrawing all U.S. troops from Iraq before the end of 2013. Neither could Hillary Clinton or John Edwards.[42]

Neither Obama nor any other leading Democrat could acknowledge that Iraq's possession of massive, super-strategic oil resources—and Democratic sensitivity to Republican charges of defeatism and "appeasement" in Iraq—would almost certainly guarantee a continuing U.S. occupation of that country throughout the life of a Democratic White House.[43]

Supporting funding with timetables was hardly a strong anti-occupation position. Antiwar progressives had good reason to be less than impressed with the idea of making funding for the occupation conditional upon the acceptance of some version of the withdrawal (and redeployment) schedules that Obama and other "antiwar" Democrats were embracing by March 2007. In *The Progressive* in April of that year, Zinn put forth an analogy to demonstrate why he disagreed with "timetables" for Iraq: "It's as if, before the Civil War, abolitionists agreed to postpone the emancipation of the slaves for a year, or two years, or five years, and coupled this with an appropriation of funds to enforce the Fugitive Slave Act." "Timetables for withdrawal," Zinn argued,

> are not only morally reprehensible in the case of a brutal occupation (would you give a thug who invaded your house, smashed everything in sight, and terrorized your children a timetable for withdrawal?) but logically nonsensical. If our troops are preventing civil war, helping people, controlling violence, then why withdraw at all? If they are in fact doing the opposite—provoking civil war, hurting people, perpetuating violence—they should withdraw as quickly as ships and planes can carry them home. It is four years since the United States invaded Iraq with a ferocious bombardment, with "shock and awe." That is enough time to decide if the presence of our troops is making the lives of the Iraqis better or worse. The evidence is overwhelming. Since the invasion, hundreds of thousands of Iraqis have died, and, according to the UN High Commissioner for Refugees, about two million Iraqis have left the country, and an almost equal number are internal refugees, forced out of their homes, seeking shelter elsewhere in the country.[44]

And what exactly did Obama and other leading Democrats really mean when they said "withdrawal?" Now that the occupation faced widespread opposition inside the United States, left author and activist Anthony Arnove noted, leaders of both parties were "repackaging it to dampen domestic opposition, cut some of the worst losses and regroup." As Arnove explained in the summer of 2007, the "new approach" of many congressional Republicans and Democrats was "troop reduction, not withdrawal; a greater reliance on air power and 'over the horizon' forces rather than boots on the ground; a retreat to bases and the Green Zone in Baghdad; and a shifting of the blame from the United States and its allies to the Iraqis." "In effect," Arnove noted, "it's a 'blame and hold' strategy. Blame the Iraqis for all the problems we created. Hold onto whatever the U.S. military can salvage in terms of military bases in Iraq—to have some influence over the future of Iraq's massive oil reserves and some ability to continue military operations in Iraq, and to project power against other countries in the region, particularly Iran."[45]

As of late February 2008, Democratic voters commonly believed that Obama was promising a quick and complete withdrawal of all U.S. troops from Iraq. But in actual fact, as his foreign policy adviser Samantha Power told television interviewer Charlie Rose in late February 2008, the most Obama actually pledged was "to try to remove all combat brigades within 16 to 18 months."[46] "Try to" was code language for "probably won't." Reflecting Obama's desire to identify himself with majority peace and (full) withdrawal sentiment, Power neglected to tell Rose that "combat brigades" made up no more than half of the U.S. force structure in Iraq and that strategic global and domestic political considerations would almost certainly guarantee a continuing, large-scale U.S. military presence in Iraq throughout an Obama presidency.[47]

Consistent with that judgment, close examination of Obama's and Hillary Clinton's detailed Iraq plans during the primary campaign showed author and journalist Jeremy Scahill that "both of them intend to keep the Green Zone [the giant American military and diplomatic section of Baghdad] intact. Both of them intend to keep the current US embassy project, which is slated to be the largest embassy in the history of the world. . . . It's 500 CIA operatives alone, a thousand personnel. And they're also going to keep open the Baghdad airport indefinitely. And what that means is that even though the rhetoric of withdrawal is everywhere in the Democratic campaign, we're talking about a pretty substantial level of U.S. forces and personnel remaining in Iraq indefinitely."[48]

In March of 2008, Power casually acknowledged that a President Obama might not bring many troops home at all if new information recommended changes in his Iraq plan. "You can't make a commitment in March 2008 about what circumstances will be like in January of 2009," Power said. "He will, of course, not rely on some plan that he crafted as a presidential candidate or a U.S. senator. He will rely upon a plan—an operational plan that he pulls together in consultation with people on the ground, to whom he doesn't have daily access now as a result of not being president." These comments from a key Obama foreign policy advisor (whose excessive candor helped get her removed from the Obama team later in the spring of 2008) pretty much left the door open for a continuing large-scale occupation of Iraq under an Obama presidency. By "people on the ground," Power meant to refer to top U.S. military commanders in Iraq.[49]

"Obama's Mercenary Position"

Another important thing Scahill discovered was that an Obama presidency would be likely to sustain the occupation through the continued deployment of controversial private security contractors in Iraq. As Scahill noted in an important exposé entitled "Obama's Mercenary Position," published in early March 2008 by *The Nation*, the Obama campaign could not rule out using private military corporations like Blackwater Worldwide, Dyncorp, and Triple Canopy in Iraq. Obama refused to sign on to the Stop Outsourcing Security (SOS) Act proposed by Congresswoman and Obama ally Jan Schakowsky (D-IL), which would have banned the use of such force in U.S. "war zones" by January 2009.[50]

This was no small matter. By early 2008, there were 100,000-plus contractors in Iraq, and some observers wondered if we were "facing what

Democracy Now's Juan Gonzales called "the possibility that a Democratic president would in essence reduce the troops but increase the mercenaries." As Joseph Schmitz, a leading Blackwater executive, said, "There is a scenario where we could as a government, the United States, could pull back the military footprint, and there would be more of a need for private security contractors to go in."[51] Obama appeared ready to sign on to the possibility of such a scenario before any measures could be passed to hold private security firms accountable for crimes against Iraqis like the ones committed in September 2007, when Blackwater killed seventeen civilians in Baghdad's Nisour Square. Thanks to numerous atrocities and regular indignities committed by private security forces since the beginning of the occupation, their presence had become an especially volatile source of "anti-American" sentiment in Iraq. Iraqi government officials have repeatedly demanded the banning of Blackwater and other corporate "security contractors"—hated symbols and agents of the occupation—from Iraq.[52]

Obama, Iraq, and the Doctrine of Good Intentions

"Dreams of Democracy and Hopes for a Perfect Government"

Obama's stealth commitment to the continued occupation of Iraq was intimately related to his dubious official (mis)understanding—shared across the intertwined spectrums of acceptable opinion within dominant U.S. media and the U.S. foreign policy establishment—of the aims behind the occupation. As a state senator in the fall of 2002, he might have escaped the clutches of the initial, brazenly deceptive arguments the Bush administration made for invading Iraq—the false claims about weapons of mass destruction and alleged Iraqi state connections to al Qaeda and 9/11. But Obama has consistently and gullibly endorsed the equally false claim—quickly elevated by the White House once the initial pretexts were shown to be transparently false and (worse) manufactured—that the real reason for the occupation of Iraq was the United States' desire to export democracy and create a truly free and sovereign Iraq. In *The Audacity of Hope,* Obama claimed that the illegal invasion of Iraq had been launched with the "best of [democratic] intentions," including a desire to "export democracy by the barrel of a gun." In his November 2006 speech to the CCGA, he said that Bush occupied Iraq with impractical "dreams of democracy and hopes for a perfect government." Fourteen months later, in February 2008, Obama told the *Milwaukee Journal-Sentinel* that he "was always skeptical of the notion that we would walk in there and create a Jeffersonian democracy."[53]

But the notion that the United States invaded Mesopotamia with such purposes in the minds of its policymakers is and was preposterous. It is flatly contradicted by the fact that the majority of Iraqis have wanted U.S. troops to leave and have seen U.S. troops as occupiers, not liberators, from the beginning. "By 2004," Anthony Arnove noted in 2006, "a survey conducted by USA Today, CNN and the Gallup Organization found that 71 percent of Iraqis considered foreign troops to be occupiers, a number that rises to 81 percent in the autonomous Kurdish region in northern Iraq. A poll released by the Independent Institute for Administration and Civil Society Studies in May 2004 found that 92 percent of Iraqis viewed foreign troops as occupiers, and 2 percent saw them as liberators. In the same poll, only 7 percent of Iraqis expressed confidence in 'coalition forces' led by the United States." A poll commissioned by the British Ministry of Defence in August 2005 found that fully 82 percent of Iraqis were "'strongly opposed' to the presence of foreign troops and that less than 1 percent believed the troops were "responsible for improvement in security."[54] Curiously enough for the Bush administration's claims to be qualified for modeling and even exporting democracy, 72 percent of Americans surveyed by the mainstream Chicago Council on Foreign Relations in the late summer of 2004 said that the United States should remove its military from Iraq if that's what a clear majority of Iraqis wanted.

Also sharply contrary to the democracy-promotion fairy tale that Obama signed on to, one of the first actions of the U.S. occupation authorities was to open up much of Iraq's economy to multinational corporate ownership—an action that would never have been supported by the Iraqi majority and that violated core principles of national independence. The United States was building or expanding a number of permanent military bases in richly oil-strategic Iraq as Obama spoke to the CCGA. It was a close ally and sponsor of the feudal, arch-repressive Saudi Arabian regime along with numerous other authoritarian state and political forces (including the Israeli occupation state) in the region and around the world.

Ignoring Oil

And then there was the matter of Iraq's stupendous oil reserves, widely understood to have been a major precipitating factor behind the invasion and behind the United States' inability to leave Iraq. It is a topic studiously ignored by the highly intelligent Obama, who certainly has known quite well that the notion of the Iraqi state and/or people doing whatever they wish with their own state's massive critical petroleum resources—second or third only to those of Saudi Arabia and Iran—is completely unacceptable to U.S. policymakers in either of the nation's two dominant parties. As James M. Lindsay, a vice president at the Council on Foreign Relations, noted in October 2005, "It was always hard to sustain the argument that if the United States withdrew from Vietnam there would be immense geopolitical consequences. As we look at Iraq, it's a very different issue. It's a country in one of the most volatile parts of the world, which has a very precious resource that modern economies rely on, namely oil."[55]

But the U.S. presence in Iraq in the first place was certainly more than just coincidentally related to the remarkable concentration of that "very precious resource" under its soil. Chomsky summarized harsh but, frankly, *elementary* petro-imperial realities when he observed in January 2006 that "the U.S. invaded Iraq because it has enormous oil resources, mostly untapped, and it's right in the heart of the world's energy system." This reason for the invasion is widely understood—especially, but not exclusively, outside the United States. If the United States succeeds in controlling Iraq, Chomsky noted, "it extends enormously its strategic power, what Zbigniew Brzezinski calls its 'critical leverage' over Europe and Asia. That's a major reason for controlling the oil resources—it gives you strategic power. Even if you're on renewable energy you want to do that. That's the reason for invading Iraq, the fundamental reason"—readily understood, Chomsky added, by anybody who has "three gray cells functioning."[56]

The ongoing and ever-worsening loss of America's onetime supremacy in basic global-capitalist realms of production, trade, international finance, and currency, and the related emergence of the rapidly expanding giant China as a new strategic military (as well as economic) competitor, has made the "critical leverage" more important than ever. As the noted left geographer and world-systems analyst David Harvey has argued, the United States' long decline, reflecting underlying shifts in the spatial patterns of capitalist investment and social infrastructure, gives special urgency to the U.S. project of deepening its control of Middle Eastern oil and using it as a bargaining chip with even more oil-dependent regions like Western Europe and East Asia, homes to the leading challengers to U.S. economic power.[57] That core objective would hardly be attained by bringing about a truly sovereign, democratic, and independent Iraq free to determine its own fortunes. Particularly unimaginable to the architects of U.S. foreign policy is one possible specter that could follow in the wake of serious movement toward independence in majority-Shiite Iraq: a loose Shiite alliance, including Iraqi, Iranian, and Saudi Shiites (who happen to live in direct proximity to most of Saudi Arabia's oil), "controlling most of the world's oil, independent of Washington and probably turning toward the East where China and others are eager to make relationships with them." As Chomsky noted in January 2006, "the U.S. would go to nuclear war before allowing that."[58]

While he may not pay much, if any, attention to writers like Chomsky and Harvey, Obama—no slouch in the "gray cells" department—has certainly been briefed on the strategic imperial factors behind the Iraq invasion by Brzezinski, who signed on as an Obama adviser early in his campaign.[59]

"It's Time to Stop . . . Trying to Put Iraq Back Together"

Obama might have been more vulnerable to significant criticism of his toothless call for "withdrawal" during the presidential primary campaign if Iraq had not been displaced by the economy as the leading campaign issue by the fall and winter of 2007–2008. But then, Obama and other top Democrats and presidential candidates contributed to the displacement. As dominant media helped the Bush administration sell the dubious and deceptive notion that Bush's 2007 "Surge" in Iraq was "working," and as rising prices, growing joblessness, and the home foreclosure crisis moved to the front and center of voters' minds, Obama and other leading Democrats played critical roles in downgrading the bloody Iraq invasion and minimizing its centrality to the presidential contest.

It wasn't just that the relevance of economic concerns increased for voters or that the news about Iraq seemed to be getting more positive. Equally significant was the hidden moral complicity of Obama et al. in accepting and advancing the notion that Iraq had been invaded for noble purposes and in failing to oppose it on ethical and legal grounds. Consistent with the bipartisan imperial consensus underlying the official U.S. foreign policy spectrum for decades, the leading Democratic contenders—opposed to no avail by the inherently marginalized candidates Dennis Kucinich, Mike Gravel, and Ron Paul—had never opposed the invasion on moral grounds. They'd only criticized it on strategic and "pragmatic" grounds, as a policy that wasn't working for American global power. Now, with the widespread dissemination and acceptance of the notion that "the Surge" was *working* (under the wise management of General David Patraeus,) Obama, Hillary Clinton, and Edwards turned their attention to other matters. They couldn't expect to get political traction by continuing to strongly criticize a policy they'd never been willing or able to oppose as a criminal and colonial war of aggression with terrible consequences for Iraqis that dwarfed American casualties.

As Iraq was increasingly pushed to the margins of the Democratic presidential debate (and of mainstream news), the people of that occupied state suffered under the weight of what essentially amounted to a living U.S.-imposed Holocaust. While the media obsessed about a slightly racialized soap-opera conflict between Hillary and Obama, the casualties in Iraq mounted. Left commentator and editor Tom Engelhardt noted the following in mid-January 2008:

> Whether civilian dead between the invasion of 2003 and mid-2006 (before the worst year of civil-war level violence even hit) was in the range of 600,000 as a study in the British medical journal, *The Lancet* reported, or 150,000 as a recent World Health Organization study suggests, whether two million or 2.5 million Iraqis have fled the country, whether 1.1 million or more than two

> million have been displaced internally, whether electricity blackouts and water shortages have marginally increased or decreased, whether the country's health-care system is beyond resuscitation or could still be revived, whether Iraqi oil production has nearly crept back to the low point of the Saddam Hussein-era or not, whether fields of opium poppies are, for the first time, spreading across the country's agricultural lands or still relatively localized, Iraq is a continuing disaster zone on a catastrophic scale hard to match in recent memory.[60]

According to the respected journalist Nir Rosen in the December 2007 edition of the mainstream journal *Current History*, "Iraq has been killed, never to rise again. The American occupation has been more disastrous than that of the Mongols who sacked Baghdad in the thirteenth century. Only fools talk of solutions now. There is no solution. The only hope is that perhaps the damage can be contained."[61]

One wonders what Rosen would have had to say about the following comment offered by Barack Obama to autoworkers assembled at the General Motors plant in Janesville, Wisconsin, on February 13, 2008, just before that state's Democratic primary: "It's time to stop spending billions of dollars a week trying to put Iraq back together and start spending the money putting America back together."[62]

For those who knew the depth and degree of the destruction inflicted on Iraq by two invasions, one ongoing, and more than a decade of deadly economic sanctions (embargo), this statement was nothing short of obscene.

"The Spectrum of Thinkable Thought" and Why Iraq Fell Off "the Radar Screen"

The terrible facts and insights offered by Engelhardt, Rosen, and numerous other investigators and commentators were invisible in the campaign rhetoric of "antiwar" candidates Obama, Clinton, and Edwards both before and after bad economic news crowded out the Iraq War as the top issue in the Democratic presidential primaries. The viable contenders' criticism of the occupation fell firmly within the same narrow "hawk-dove" spectrum that had defined and restricted acceptable power-elite foreign policy debate during the Vietnam era. In both wars, the establishment's "official doves" could only question the practical outcomes (for American power and lives) and implementation of a monumentally mass-murderous and deeply criminal war of aggression they insisted on seeing (or claiming to see) as driven by noble and democratic (never imperialist or racist) goals. The people on the wrong end of Uncle Sam's inherently dignified global guns and policies were beyond the sphere of the "doves'" imaginable concern.

The supposed "antiwar" establishment's critique of the Vietnam War focused on its negative impact on American lives and power, not the U.S. military's role in killing 2 million or more Southeast Asians. "The doves," Chomsky recalled in 1984, "felt that the [Vietnam] war was 'a hopeless cause,' we learn from Anthony Lake, a leading [official] dove [currently an Obama adviser] who resigned from the government in protest against the Cambodia invasion." Everyone across the all-too-narrow elite spectrum—"doves" no less than "hawks"—Chomsky wrote, "agreed that it was a 'failed crusade,' 'noble' but 'illusory' and undertaken with the 'loftiest intentions,' as Stanley Karnow puts it in his best-selling companion volume to [an early 1980s] PBS Series [on the Vietnam War], highly regarded for its critical candor. Those who do not appreciate these self-evident truths, or who maintain the curious view that they should be supported by some evidence, simply demonstrate thereby that they are emotional and irresponsible ideologues, or perhaps outright communists. . . . Their odd views cannot be heard; they are outside the spectrum of thinkable thought."[63]

But "there is a possible position omitted from the fierce debate between hawks and doves," Chomsky noted, "namely, the position of the peace movement, a position in fact shared by the large majority of citizens as recently as 1982: the [Vietnam] war was not merely a 'mistake,' as the official doves allege, but was 'fundamentally wrong and immoral.' To put it plainly: war crimes, including the crime of launching an aggressive war, are wrong, even if they succeed in their 'noble' aims." "This position," Chomsky added, "does not enter the debate, even to be refuted; it is unthinkable within the ideological mainstream." He recalled the comments of the "antiwar" *New York Times* columnist Anthony Lewis, who once described the U.S. assault on Vietnam as "a blundering effort to do good"—consistent with what Chomsky called "the fundamental doctrine that the [U.S.] state is benevolent, governed by the loftiest intentions."[64]

Such, forty years later, was the essential and equally preposterous claims of Obama, Edwards, Hillary Clinton, and other leading Democrats. The notion that the attack on Iraq was criminal and immoral was simply "unthinkable" as far as they were concerned.[65] Stuck within the confining imperial and nationalist boundaries at the ideological heart of the bipartisan imperial consensus, Obama and Clinton were in no position to press the Iraq issue (and likely had little desire to do so) once Bush appeared to have succeeded in advancing the (in fact highly deceptive[66]) notion that the invasion of Iraq had been made functional under the wise direction of General Patraeus. Contrary to the deluded claims of many of his progressive supporters in Iowa, Obama was no special exception and in fact repeated the same tired refrains of what passed for "antiwar" sentiment at the upper reaches of the power elite as the United States prepared for the fifth anniversary of its war of aggression on Iraq. Chomsky, in February 2008, made this harsh judgment of the situation:

> Not very long ago, as you all recall, it was taken for granted that the Iraq war would be the central issue in the 2008 election, as it was in the midterm election two years ago. However, it's virtually disappeared off the radar screen, which has solicited some puzzlement among the punditry.
>
> Actually, the reason is not very obscure. It was cogently explained forty years ago, when the US invasion of South Vietnam was in its fourth year and the surge of that day was about to add another 100,000 troops to the 175,000 already there, while South Vietnam was being bombed to shreds at triple the level of the bombing of the north and the war was expanding to the rest of Indochina. However, *the war was not going very well, so the former hawks were shifting towards doubts*, among them the distinguished historian Arthur Schlesinger, maybe the most distinguished historian of his generation, a Kennedy adviser, who—when he and Kennedy, other Kennedy liberals were beginning to—reluctantly beginning to shift from a dedication to victory to a more dovish position.
>
> And Schlesinger explained the reasons. He explained that—I'll quote him now—"Of course, we all pray that the hawks are right in thinking that the surge . . . will work. And if it does, we may all be saluting the wisdom and statesmanship of the American government in winning a victory in a land that we have turned," he said, "to wreck and ruin. But the surge probably won't work, at an acceptable cost to us, so perhaps strategy should be rethought."
>
> Well, the reasoning and the underlying attitudes carry over with almost no change to the critical commentary on the U.S. invasion of Iraq today. And it is a land of wreck and ruin.[67]

"They Have Seen Their Sons and Daughters Killed . . . in the Streets of Fallujah"

Obama's embrace of the official dove position that America's goals are noble in Iraq and that the United States is making sacrifices there for the good of a nation whose victims must be treated as nearly invisible was hardly new by 2007 and 2008. At one terrible and telling point in his 2006 CCGA speech, the all-but-openly-declared presidential candidate had the cold imperial audacity to say the following in support of his claim that U.S. citizens support "victory" in Iraq: "The American people have been extraordinarily resolved. *They have seen their sons and daughters killed or wounded in the streets of Fallujah.*"[68]

This was a spine-chilling selection of locales. Fallujah was the site of colossal U.S. war atrocities—crimes including the indiscriminate slaughter of civilians, the targeting even of ambulances and hospitals, and the leveling of practically an entire city—in April and November 2004. The town was designated for destruction as an example of the awesome state terror promised to those who dared to resist U.S. power. Not surprisingly, Fallujah became a powerful and instant symbol of American imperialism in the Arab and Muslim worlds. It was a deeply provocative place for Obama to have chosen to highlight American sacrifice and "resolve" in the imperialist occupation of Iraq. In doing so, he hurled insult after injury toward the Iraqis, who are the ones who truly made sacrifices in Fallujah.[69]

Another disturbing moment in Obama's CCGA speech came in its twenty-fourth paragraph, where he said that a "timetable" for "phased withdrawal" of U.S. troops would "send a clear message to the Iraqi factions that *the U.S. is not going to hold together the country indefinitely*—that it will be up to them to form a viable government that can effectively run and secure Iraq." Presaging his Janesville, Wisconsin, comment and consistent with what Arnove would call Obama's "blame and hold strategy," this was a remarkable statement from an ostensibly "antiwar" senator from a military superpower that had spent nearly four years deliberately tearing apart the society and public capacities of what was an already desperately poor and devastated nation (thanks in large measure to U.S. policy actions since at least the first Persian Gulf War).[70]

The vicious and ongoing U.S. assault was naturally missing from Obama's claim to the CCGA that "Iraq is descending into chaos based on ethnic divisions that were around long before American troops arrived." Beyond its belated dating of Iraq's predictable (and predicted) collapse into civil war, this formulation neglected the role of the openly imperial United States in smashing the public institutions that had restricted internal Iraqi "chaos." It naturally deletes the more specific role of the invaders in actively setting Iraqis against each other along ethnic lines.[71]

Also highly problematic from an antiwar perspective was Obama's praise of U.S. occupation soldiers for "performing their duty with bravery, with brilliance, and without question." As an antiwar activist, I had a difficult time determining which aspect of this comment was more disturbing: Obama's blindness (intentional or not) to the important and welcome fact that many troops did in fact question the occupation, or his decision to uphold the unquestioning execution of frankly criminal military orders as a good thing.[72]

The "Mistake" of Telling the Truth on U.S. Torture

Obama and other official doves (including Hillary Clinton and John Edwards) preferred to use "the M word" ("mistake") over "the C word" ("crime") when describing numerous U.S. global transgressions. Obama used "mistake" three times in two sentences in the spring of 2005 in the process of distancing himself from fellow U.S. Senator Dick Durbin (D-IL).

Durbin had gotten in trouble for daring to liken conditions at Guantanamo to those in a Nazi or Stalin-era prison camp. It was one of Durbin's best moments. He read an FBI officer's eyewitness account of the conditions at Guantanamo, describing how he had entered interview rooms "to find a detainee chained hand and foot in a fetal position to the floor, with no chair, food or water. Most times they urinated or defecated on themselves, and had been left there for 18–24 hours or more." "If I read this to you," Durbin told his fellow senators, "and did not tell you that it was an FBI agent describing what Americans had done to prisoners in their control, you would most certainly believe this must have been done by Nazis, Soviets in their gulags, or some mad regime like that of Pol Pot or others that had no concern for human beings. Sadly, that is not the case. This was the action of Americans in the treatment of their prisoners. It is not too late. I hope we will learn from history. I hope we will change course." It was a modest and decent plea based on elementary observation of practices known and documented as widespread in the conduct of the United States' "war on terror."

Republicans and right-wing media representatives went into fits of rage, falsely claiming that Durbin was calling the United States' noble fighting men and women "Nazis" and likening the United States to the Third Reich and Stalinist Russia. Even Chicago's nominally Democratic mayor and key Obama ally Richard M. Daley got into the act. He fumed that Durbin needed to "apologize for comments comparing the actions of American interrogators at Guantanamo Bay to Nazis, Soviet gulags and Khmer Rouge leader Pol Pot. . . . I think it's a disgrace to say that any man or woman in the military acts like that." Daley told reporters that "Durbin was wrong to evoke comparisons to the horrors of the Holocaust or the millions of people killed in Russia under Stalin and in Cambodia under Pol Pot."

But Durbin had never claimed that the United States was conducting a Holocaust à la Hitler or Pol Pot. He did not deny the supreme horror of the Nazi Holocaust, or of Pol Pot's and Stalin's crimes, or—to mention two crimes that never seem to get much attention from Democratic or Republican "politicians on the make"—of the Native American or African American Holocausts. Durbin simply and correctly had observed that American military personnel in Guantanamo behaved in illegal ways that happened to be similar to the practices of state-terrorist actors in other places and times. He was careful to a patriotic fault, denying that such conduct was rooted in specifically "American" traditions. He could have said a lot more regarding the extent of such practices in the American "war on terror" and the culpability of top policymakers. He never called military personnel in Guantanamo "Nazis."

Facing outrageous and heavily militarist criticism that ultimately forced him to issue a teary-eyed apology on the Senate floor, Durbin could have used some support from his fellow Illinois senator and "friend" Barack Obama. It was not forthcoming. Obama said, "We have a tendency to demonize and jump on and make mockery of each other across the aisle and that is particularly pronounced when we make *mistakes.* Each and every one of us is going to make a *mistake* once in a while . . . and what we hope is that our track record of service, the scope of how we've operated and interacted with people, will override whatever particular *mistake* we make [emphases added]."[73]

"We Will Seize the Moment and Begin the World Anew"

Supporting Empire across the Planet

Obama's misleading statements and actions regarding Iraq should not be confused with principled or progressive criticism of either the Iraq War or the broader American Empire Project of which that war is an expression. As left journalist Lance Selfa noted in the spring of 2007, the tepid and highly qualified opposition of many leading Democrats and some Republicans to George W. Bush's "dumb war" by 2005 "represented the American power elite's concern with saving, rather than burying, that project." The bipartisan U.S. foreign policy establishment worried that "failure" in Iraq would drain the strength of the U.S. military overall—a recurrent theme in Obama's foreign policy commentary. It "feared that Bush's unilateralism and clumsiness has wrought a cost in the 'soft power' of the U.S. (its ideological, political, and cultural influence) across the world," Selfa wrote. "So while leading Democrats are bashing Bush's escalation in Iraq . . . they remain hawkish in their criticism of Iran, unshaken in their support of Israel's most outrageous atrocities, and quietly supportive of Defense Secretary Robert Gates' calls to increase the size of the armed forces by almost 100,000."[74] Selfa could have added that they have remained "hawkish" in their support for the continuing morally and legally dubious U.S. invasion of Afghanistan and that they have tended to line up with the Bush administration against the upsurge of social democratic left nationalism and antineoliberalism in Latin America.

Detailed examination of Obama's foreign policy positions regarding regions and nations other than Iraq is beyond the scope of this book. Such investigation shows that Obama has consistently lined up on the side of U.S. globalism and U.S. client states—the occupation and apartheid state Israel and the paramilitary state Colombia, for example—against officially designated U.S. enemies like Palestinian anti-occupation and anti-apartheid fighters and the left nationalist Venezuelan regime of Hugo Chavez. Obama reflexively and unequivocally defended Israel's right to bomb innocent civilians in Lebanon (in the summer of 2006) and to impose a deadly embargo on Gaza (in January 2008). He embraces the United States' supposed right to launch a first (potentially nuclear) strike against Iran on the tenuous pretext that that nation poses a potential nuclear threat to the region, but makes no statements against the U.S.-sponsored nuclear arsenals of Israel and India.[75] He called on one occasion for a possible unilateral U.S. incursion into Pakistan. He has been particularly outspoken in defense of George W. Bush's war on Afghanistan, repeatedly claiming that the "mistaken" Iraq invasion has diverted the United States from its "good" and "proper" war in/on Afghanistan, omitting such accurate terms such as "bloody," "illegal," and "colonial" to describe that invasion.[76]

"The Last, Best Hope on Earth"

Any doubt that Obama's supposed "antiwar" position on Iraq is situated within American global imperialism and militarism and reflects his broader support for those projects should have been silenced by minimally careful attention to a major foreign policy speech he gave to the Chicago Council of Global Affairs on April 23, 2007. Titled "The American Moment," it was a remarkably nationalistic and audaciously world supremacist oration. It proudly embraced U.S. planetary hegemony and the need to not back down (in the wake of the Iraq "mistake") from America's right and duty to aggressively and (where "necessary") unilaterally use the "world's greatest military" to enforce American global dominance.

Proclaiming his nationally narcissistic belief that "the magical place called America" was still "the last, best hope on Earth," Obama "reject[ed] the notion that the American moment had passed." He argued that "the new century" could be "another one . . . where we lead the world in battling immediate evils and promoting the common good." The "world," Obama said, "cannot meet this century . . . without America." This conclusion reflected Obama's openly acknowledged "American exceptionalism"—his brazenly hubristic belief that the United States is a distinctively noble and excellent nation whose leaders are uniquely authorized to manage the world's affairs.[77]

"Our Ability to Put Boots on the Ground"

From this audaciously nationalistic perspective, Obama's CCGA lecture made an interesting statement of what he saw as the leading problem with Bush II's Iraq policy. "The mistakes of the past six years," Obama said, "have made our current task"—leading the world against evil and spreading good—"more difficult. World opinion has turned against us. And after all the [American] lives lost and the billions of dollars spent, many Americans find it tempting to turn inward, and cede our claim of leadership in world affairs. I insist, however, that such an abandonment of our leadership is a mistake we must not make."

By Obama's account, the main difficulty with Operation Iraqi Freedom (OIF) wasn't that it was a brazenly criminal invasion that had killed hundreds of thousands of Iraqis, consistent with the United States' longstanding record (well known beyond U.S. borders) of employing massive force ("because we are America," in Albright's wonderful phrase) in pursuit of imperial ambitions. It wasn't the technically illegal deceptive basis on which the invasion was sold to the U.S populace. The main difficulty for him, rather, was that the occupation had set back America's capacity to "lead"—most of the world's morally and politically cognizant populace would say "rule"—by turning "the world beyond our borders" off to the United States' unmatched moral excellence and by challenging American citizens' willingness to support the costly enforcement of U.S. global dominance.[78]

Obama was especially concerned with the damage the Iraq invasion had done to "the best hope on Earth's" readiness to project military force across the planet. "Two-thirds of the Army," Obama complained, "is now rated 'not ready' for combat. 88 percent of the National Guard is not ready to deploy overseas." Again, he expressed his belief that Cheney and Bush's strategic imperial blunder had not expressed but rather undermined the United States' capacity to exercise global military dominance. One of his specific recommendations was to expand "the ability to put [military] boots on the ground" of other supposedly sovereign nations by "adding 65,000 soldiers to the Army and 27,000 Marines." Former Defense Secretary Donald Rumsfeld came in for special criticism from Obama for saying that "'you go to war with the Army you have, not the one you want.'" "I say," Obama proclaimed, "that if the need arises when I'm president, the Army we have will be the Army we need."[79]

The most remarkable and chilling line in Obama's April 23 speech came about halfway into his oration. Lest any of his elite listeners wondered whether a President Obama's concept of "when the need arises" might include the opportunity to launch a preemptive and unilateral assault on a foreign state, the senator made it clear that he wasn't all that far from Cheney and Bush on such questions. "No president," Obama said, "should ever hesitate to use force—unilaterally if necessary—to protect ourselves and our vital interests when we are attacked or imminently threatened. But when we use force in situations other than self-defense, we should make every effort to garner the clear support and participation of others." The second sentence in this quotation clearly assumed that the United States possesses the right to assault other nations that do not present a threat to "ourselves" or "our vital interests."

There was nothing in Obama's speech about the selective, elitist, and imperial meaning that U.S. foreign policymakers have historically given to the often classically deceptive and misleading phrase "our vital interests"—a term that American elites have used repeatedly to justify foreign policy actions that served privileged Americans while imposing often severe costs on American society as whole. Over the past three decades, the phrase has come to be especially identified with the protection of America's supposedly legitimate right to exercise special imperial control over the Middle East's strategically super-significant petroleum supplies.

Obama's April 23 address praised "our men and women in uniform" for "performing heroically around the world" despite numerous reports that U.S. soldiers had acted on illegal orders to commit egregious war crimes and crimes against humanity in Iraq, Afghanistan, and elsewhere.

"This Is Left-Liberal Foreign Policy?"

The April 23 speech ended with words that ought to have given pause to peace and justice progressives who combined peace symbols and Obama posters on their lawns. "The American moment has not passed," Obama concluded. "The American moment is here. And like generations before us, we will seize that moment and begin the world anew."

Appropriately enough, this speech received strong approval from an interesting source—the arch-militarist, neoconservative *Washington Post* columnist and John McCain foreign policy adviser Robert Kagan. Kagan was a leading early proponent of the Iraq invasion. In a *Post* column entitled "Obama the Interventionist," he gave Obama an enthusiastic thumbs up for "putting an end to the idea that the alleged over-exuberant idealism and America-centric hubris of the past six years is about to give way to a new realism, a more limited and modest view of American interests, capabilities, and responsibilities."

Kagan praised Obama for embracing Cold War language describing the United States as the "leader of the free world" and for advancing an aggressively "interventionist" foreign policy requiring a significant increase in "defense" spending. "When he said, 'We have heard much over the last six years about how America's larger purpose in the world is to promote the spread of freedom,'" Kagan gushed, "you probably expected him to distance himself from this allegedly discredited idealism. Instead, he said, 'I agree.' His critique is not that we've meddled too much but that we haven't meddled enough." Further high praise from Kagan went as follows: "Obama talks about 'rogue nations,' 'hostile dictators,' 'muscular alliances' and maintaining 'a strong nuclear deterrent.' He talks about how we need to 'seize' the 'American moment.' We must 'begin the world anew.' This is realism? This is left-liberal foreign policy? Ask Noam Chomsky next time you see him."[80]

"Beyond Self-Defense"

Obama continued to prove his fierce fealty to the bipartisan imperial consensus in a summer article in the establishment journal *Foreign Affairs.* Containing numerous dubious historical reflections that put a shiny coat of whitewash on various past U.S. crimes abroad, this essay then moved into current events in ways that should have strongly fed suspicions that an Obama presidency could be expected to perpetuate ongoing imperial transgressions and commit new ones. Declaring that "we can be [Kennedy's] America again," he accused the Bush administration of dropping the ball of empire. "The American moment is not over, but it must be seized anew," Obama proclaimed, adding that "we must lead the world by deed and by example" and "must not rule out using military force" in pursuit of "our vital interests."[81]

The last three words harkened back to another Democratic imperialist's agenda for the Middle East, the "Carter Doctrine," which updated the Monroe Doctrine for the global petro-capitalist era to include the Persian Gulf region in the United States' inviolable sphere of special interest and unilateral action. "Our vital interests" is a code phrase for other nations' oil, located primarily in the Middle East.[82] "A strong military," Obama wrote, "is, more than anything, necessary to sustain peace." We must "revitalize our military" to foster "peace," he said, echoing George Orwell, partly by adding 65,000 soldiers to the army and 27,000 Marines.

Obama's rhetoric gave progressives (and anyone else who was listening carefully) reason to expect future unilateral and "preemptive" wars and occupations carried out in the name of the "war on terror" by an Obama White House. "We must retain the capacity to swiftly defeat any conventional threat to our country and our vital interests," he pronounced. "But we must also become better prepared to put boots on the ground in order to take on foes that fight asymmetrical and highly adaptive campaigns on a global scale." Reassuring the more militarist segments of the power elite that he would not be hamstrung by international law and civilized norms when "our vital interests" were "at stake," Obama added that "I will not hesitate to use force unilaterally, if necessary, to protect the American people or our vital interests wherever we are attacked or imminently threatened."

"We must also consider using military force in circumstances beyond self-defense," Obama added, "in order to provide for the common security that underpins global stability—to support friends, participate in stability and reconstruction operations, or confront mass atrocities."[83]

As Glen Ford observed, Obama has gone "out of his way to prove" that he is "no peace candidate."[84] To be more precise, Barack "No Shock" Obama has gone to elaborate lengths to prove his imperial and militarist credentials to the foreign policy establishment while posing as a peace candidate to the predominantly antiwar voting majority.

Obama's False and Revealing Specter of "Isolationism"

The foreign policy opinions embraced by Barack Obama over the period of his ascendancy and national presidential candidacy stand well to the right of majority public opinion. Two years before Obama first voiced his boldly imperial sentiments regarding U.S. foreign policy within and beyond Iraq to the Chicago Council on Global Affairs, the Chicago Council on Foreign Relations released an important survey showing that:[85]

- Fifty-nine percent of Americans thought the United States should remove its military presence from the Middle East if that's what the majority of people there wanted.
- Seventy-two percent of Americans thought the United States should remove its military presence from Iraq if that's what the majority of people there wanted.
- Fifty-eight percent of Americans thought the United States should not have long-term military bases in Iraq.
- Just 20 percent of Americans thought it was the United States' responsibility to function as the world's policeman.

Eleven months later, while the "Obama brand" was making friends in the U.S. Senate and muting his supposed strong "antiwar" sentiments, a *Washington Post*–ABC poll showed that 60 percent of Americans now believed the United States "was wrong to invade Iraq." According to the *Post,* "a clear majority—55 percent—now says the administration deliberately misled the country in making its case for war." A September 2005 CBS–*New York Times* poll showed that the U.S. public's support for an immediate withdrawal stood at 52 percent.[86]

These and other remarkable findings indicating mass U.S. opposition to the occupation went unmentioned in the voluminous speeches and writings of Obama during and since his first two years in the U.S. Senate. Neither his major 2006 foreign policy speech[87] nor his 2006 book, *The Audacity of Hope*, had anything to say about polls showing that most Americans supported what he and other members of the U.S. foreign policy elite called "precipitous withdrawal" from Iraq or that most thought early the U.S. should leave Iraq "if that's what most Iraqis want." *Audacity* also neglected to notice surveys showing that the preponderant majority of Iraqis rejected the invasion and the invaders' claims to be either liberators of stabilizers of Iraq and wanted the United States out immediately. But this is not to say that Obama neglected U.S. public opinion data all together. Both the speech and the book cited survey findings that were meant to illustrate what Obama considered to be the real danger in the wake of the Iraq fiasco: that Americans were leaning dangerously toward "isolationism" and thus turning their backs on the noble superpower's global "responsibilities." "After thousands of lives lost and billions of dollars spent," Obama told the CCGA, "many Americans may be tempted to turn inward and cede our leadership in world affairs. But this," the senator stated, "is a mistake we must not make. America cannot meet the threats of this century alone, and the world cannot meet them without America."[88]

In reality, no serious public opinion research demonstrated that Americans were veering toward "isolationism." Instead, they maintained their long-standing rejection of both aggressive unilateral U.S. imperialism and "isolationism." They continued to support an enlightened and democratic internationalism that honors international law and shows respect for the wishes of others.[89] With their majority repudiation of the Iraq occupation, they rejected the misuse of American power in violation of established global rules and civilized norms—rules and norms that Obama reserved the right to violate and that are violated by an illegal invasion Obama promises to continue.

It was all very consistent with the aggressively globalist foreign policy team Obama assembled in 2007. His top foreign relations advisers included such thoroughly mainstream and eminently respectable Cold War and "war on terror" strategists as former White House national security advisers Zbigniew Brzezinski and Anthony Lake; former Navy Secretary Richard Danzig; former Assistant Secretary of State Susan Rice; and former counterterrorism czar Richard Clarke. His team included Harvard professor Samantha Power, a well-known advocate of American "humanitarian" intervention abroad and a supporter of the U.S. assault on Serbia. Other members were Dennis Ross, a strong defender of Israel's occupation of the Palestinian West Bank; and retired General Merrill McPeak, a supporter of Indonesia's practically genocidal occupation of East Timor.[90]

"What Better Gift to Empire"

The black Seattle-based left poet and activist Michael Hureaux is on solid ground when he says that Obama as president would be about "restor[ing] faith in the imperial project." America, in electing Obama, would be putting an eloquent black leader at its nominal head to function as a "JFK in sepia." As Hureaux observed in the comments section attached to a haunting *Dissident Voice* essay by Juan Santos entitled "Barack Obama and the End of Racism,"

> I'm watching all kinds of people who I'd previously thought had some critical thinking skills cave under this Obamania business. I had a hunch this was coming when I watched his speech at the convention four years ago, my wife and I both sat and took it in and looked at each other and said, almost word

> for word, "He's good, he's very good." The rakish JFK style jabs, the clearly studied rhetorical grace. What better gift to the empire than JFK in sepia? All last year, numerous discussions with people from the old new left who told us, "He'll never get a shot at it because of racist U.S. etc.," to which we maintained, "But what better figure to have out there than one to restore faith in the imperial project, but someone with a black face? They managed to live with Powell and Rice, why not Obama?"[91]

Leading up to the Pennsylvania primary of April 22, 2008, Obama left little doubt that Hureaux was on to something and that he operated within the doctrinal parameters of the bipartisan imperial consensus. Speaking to a town hall event at a local high school gymnasium in Greensburg, Pennsylvania, he said he wanted to return America to the more "traditional" foreign policy of such past presidents as "George Bush's father, or John F. Kennedy," and, "in some respects, Ronald Reagan." He spoke in flattering and favorable terms of the way George H.W. Bush had handled the supposedly virtuous and necessary Persian Gulf War. The Associated Press article reporting this comment was aptly entitled "Obama Aligns Foreign Policy with GOP"[92]—an unintentional rebuke to left-liberal writers who argued that the centrist Obama stood to the progressive side of Hillary Clinton, at least on foreign policy.[93]

Reading this article, I flashed back to an appearance that Obama's foreign policy adviser Samantha Power made on the syndicated "Charlie Rose Show" in late February of 2008. Noting that President Bush had recently been swamped by cries of "O-ba-ma" during a recent state visit to Africa, interviewer Rose asked Power if she was concerned about the "sky-high expectations" much of the world seemed to have for an Obama presidency. There is "a danger" in this, Rose worried. "Yes," Power said, noting that Obama was very concerned about unrealistic hopes and adding that "that's why expectation calibration and expectation management is essential at home and internationally." Behind this disturbing application of openly elitist, manipulative, and technocratic language to the "management" of domestic and global opinion and hopes lay an obvious, if unstated, admission: Obama was as attached to the U.S. imperial project as Bush was, and this would be bound to disappoint hopeful masses at home and abroad. The peoples' naïve faith in change needs to be carefully and downwardly "calibrated."

Before this exchange, Power had just explained to Rose that an Obama presidency would not remove all U.S. troops from Iraq all that quickly. Because of Obama's special concern for "the fate of the Iraqis," Power told Rose, he would actually only "try to get all combat brigades out in sixteen to eighteen months."[94]

More than three months later, the brilliant and prolific left Australian author, journalist, and filmmaker John Pilger provided some useful perspective on the foreign policy prospects of an Obama presidency and the narrow global policy spectrum of the dominant U.S. political culture:

> America's war on Iran has already begun. In December, Bush secretly authorized support for two guerrilla armies inside Iran, one of which, the military arm of Mujahedin-e Khalq, is described by the state department as terrorist. The U.S. is also engaged in attacks or subversion against Somalia, Lebanon, Syria, Afghanistan, India, Pakistan, Bolivia, and Venezuela. A new military command, Africom, is being set up to fight proxy wars for control of Africa's oil and other riches. With U.S. missiles soon to be stationed provocatively on Russia's borders, the Cold War is back. None of these piracies and dangers has raised a whisper in the presidential campaign, not least from its great liberal hope.[95]

Chapter 5

Obama Nation
Sixteen Reasons

> *There is nothing wrong at all in the hopes we have that Obama's rhetoric speaks to. The problem lies in what Herbert Marcuse called "repressive desublimation—a hope, a need, that has been buried and denied by an oppressive system, is allowed some room to breathe, then co-opted and redirected back into a form that ultimately reinforces the oppressive system that denied and suppressed our hopes and needs in the first place.*
>
> —JUAN SANTOS, *DISSIDENT VOICE*, FEBRUARY 13, 2008

"SINCE THE FOUNDING," Barack Obama told Ken Silverstein in the summer of 2006, "the American political tradition has been reformist, not revolutionary. What that means is that for a political leader to get things done, he or she should ideally be ahead of the curve, but not too far ahead."[1]

It would be an understatement to describe the "deeply conservative" Obama as "not too far ahead." He has been behind "the curve" of the U.S. populace on numerous key issues during his time in national politics. Karl Rove and other hard right commentators will continue to reflexively and preposterously call Obama, and for that matter Hillary Clinton and Nancy Pelosi and Harry Reid, etc., members of the "far left." From a different perspective, John F. Kerry can call Obama a "truly transformative" leader who understands that "real change comes only when people form a movement so large that Washington has no choice but to listen." But consistent with Chomsky's observation that "both of the political parties and the business sector are well to the right of the population on a host of major issues," the "neoliberal" (Adolph Reed), "radical centrist"(John Judis), and even "deeply conservative" (Larissa MacFarquhar) Obama stands to the conservative business-and-empire-friendly side of majority U.S. opinion (which is often quite progressive) on key issues like national health insurance, campaign finance, trade, Iraq, and foreign relations in general.[2]

This raises an obvious and uncomfortable question. Why and how has he achieved such remarkable success running as a "progressive" candidate of peace, justice, reform, and democracy? Why did so many primary voters choose Obama over other Democratic presidential candidates, including ones who could legitimately claim to be more progressive than him, like Kucinich and (close to the center) Edwards? And why did the support for Obama among so many voters take on a "millennial" and even "messianic" feeling and aspect, producing an unusually large quantity of gratuitously adoring behavior and commentary, inspirational for some and disturbing for others?

Below I present sixteen mutually reinforcing and overlapping explanations for the often fervent mass constituency behind the "improbable" emergence of an "Obama Nation"[3] in 2007 and 2008. In constructing this list, I have taken the liberty of including some personal and speculative reflections based on my own considerable direct experience with midwestern voters and the presidential campaign in the second half of 2007.

1. The Long-Standing Devaluation of Issues in U.S. Political Culture

It may not matter all that much in terms of election outcomes that Obama's actual issue positions are often to the right of the populace when "issue awareness"—knowledge of and concern for the candidates' actual policy stands—is as remarkably low as it is in the United States. In 2004, roughly one in ten U.S. citizens chose, in an open question, "agendas/ideas/platforms/goals" as a top rationale for their decisions.[4] A much larger number and percentage voted in accord with their sense of candidate "qualities" and "character," including "likeability," "honesty," and "religiosity." In the period covered by this study (July 27, 2004, through mid-April 2008), Obama scored very high among active voters on questions of personal character and attractiveness—questions that seem to have more impact on voters' decisions than policy or ideological "issues" in a candidate- and image-centered elections system and political culture.

That culture is significantly shaped by a corporate media that seems dedicated to the notion that citizens should function as little more than spectators and consumers of history, leaving big and serious questions of policy and ideology to their supposed superiors in the political class. As Chomsky noted in regard to the 2004 presidential election, "news commentary focused on 'style,' 'likability,' 'bonding,' and 'character,' and on such flaws as Bush's occasional 'testiness' or Kerry's getting the name of a football stadium wrong . . . a major triumph of marketing, which permits the leadership to carry out its programs without concern for public opinion."[5] This stark judgment applied all too well to the 2008 Democratic primaries.

The problem, it is worth noting, has origins dating back to the beginning of American mass politics in the antebellum era. "By 1840," historian Eric Foner noted, "the mass democratic politics of the Age of Jackson had absorbed the logic of the marketplace. Selling candidates and their images was as important as the positions for which they stood."[6] As the radical historian Gabriel Kolko noted in his dark classic *Main Currents in American History,*

> With apathy and infantilism two of the main characteristics of American political campaigns . . . concern for the ephemeral rather than the candid fundamentals is . . . a constant in American political dialogue; and it created a nationally underdeveloped politics. . . . Apathy and infantilism aid political hegemony and the stability of machines and hence their utility to politically dominant factions. By linking political issues to the extraneous concerns for race, glamour, religion, or experience, and avoiding central questions of power and purpose in society, the real intellectual and ideological questions of the social order have been wholly obscured and the mass capacity to respond to the problems of that order seriously reduced.[7]

"Presidential elections," Alexander Cockburn noted last March, "are mostly about keeping important issues off the agenda, whether it be U.S. complicity in Israel's atrocious crimes in Gaza or the funds voted by Clinton and Obama for the Iraq War, now arriving at its fifth anniversary, or impeachment of a President destroying constitutional protections."[8]

2. Deception

Elections are also very much about fooling voters on important issues. Consistent with the "timeless dance" of America's "winner-take-all" political culture and party system[9] (a topic to be addressed in more detailed fashion in the next chapter), Obama is by no means unique among other presidential candidates past and present in being a master of flat-out policy and issue deception. His real positions on Iraq, empire (more broadly), health care, energy, and trade might actually be centrist and even in some cases quite conservative, but his rhetoric and image (like those of Hillary Clinton) have been "carefully crafted" to tell progressively inclined primary voters that he is one of them. It's an old game, consistent with Christopher Hitchens's comments on the "essence of American politics." It has been played at one level or another by nearly every major Democratic presidential candidate—Bill Clinton in 1992 was an especially dramatic, textbook example—in recent memory. The Republicans have also long practiced the art of pseudo-populist deception, to no small regressive effect in U.S. political life and policy.

3. Time Poverty and Information Overkill

Time is a severely underestimated "democracy issue" in the United States, home to the people who work the longest hours in the industrialized world. As the founders of the U.S. labor movement observed in the early nineteenth century, the democratic legacy of the American Revolution doesn't mean much to people who lack the time to function as educated and effective citizens.[10] Given the relative absence of serious critical media scrutiny on the considerable conservative content of Obama's (or Hillary Clinton's) public record, discovering the darker, more traditional corporate-imperial and racially accommodationist reality beneath his "fresh" and progressive image and rhetoric is an at times exhausting research project. Most working Americans lack time for such an undertaking.

Another part of the problem is the sheer volume of material that has been put out in the dominant media about and by the Obama campaign. As a veteran researcher and the author of numerous previous books and project studies on complex and detailed matters of policy and history, I have on more than a few occasions gone practically numb trying to wade through the plethora of media commentary and coverage on Obama. One of my hopes for this book is that it will help to fill some of the information gaps for Americans with less time or patience or energy to demystify the Obama phenomenon.

4. Celebrity, Pure and Simple

Two days before Obama spoke at a mass rally in Iowa City in April 2007, I was getting ready to leave an Iowa City coffee shop when a young University of Iowa student sitting nearby announced that she "couldn't wait" to hear him. I asked her if she knew exactly when Obama was going to appear. She gave me an extra flyer.

"So is that who University of Iowa students are going for—Obama?" I asked as I stood to exit.

"Oh totally," the student said. "We love Barack. Everybody in my dorm is going to vote for him."

"Wow," I said, "what's that all about?"

"Oh," the young woman said, "he's just so cool. He's on television all the time and he's just really excellent. Nobody ever heard of him before and then boom—there he is, like . . . I can listen to him all day."

"He's really handsome," another female student chimed in.

"And he's smart. We hate Bush," the second student added.

"Yeah, Bush is an idiot," a third student said.

I asked them what they thought of Ohio Congressman Dennis Kucinich, the leftmost candidate in the Democratic primaries. They'd never heard of him.

"What about John Edwards?" I asked, observing that Edwards actually led the Iowa polls and that his positions were more progressive and detailed than Obama's.

"He's good-looking," the first student said. "And I really admire the way his wife is fighting cancer and all. But I'm with Obama."

"Yeah, and what's up with that haircut?" the second student added, picking up on the corporate media's obsession with the fact that the Edwards campaign had spent $400 on an ill-advised grooming session for the former North Carolina senator.

My "conversation" with the students was nearing its conclusion. "See you at the speech," I said and left. "Way to engage the issues, kids," I muttered to myself on the way out.

"Brand Obama's" pure media-created celebrity-hood has been a major factor in his ascendancy, particularly with regard to younger voters.

5. The Novelty Premium

The 'novelty dividend' mentioned in the Introduction resonates with the deeper "cult of newness" at the heart of American national mythology. It takes on distinctive meaning when the present seems especially oppressive and wrongheaded, as in the spring of 2008, when an astonishing 80 percent of Americans told pollsters that their country was headed in "the wrong direction."[11] Here's how I tried to explain it to an audience of students at the University of Wisconsin–Milwaukee in early March of that year:

> We always crave the new and the fresh in America. But we crave it with special passion in special moments of crisis and despair. The great political and cultural and civil liberties and economic nightmare that is the Bush era is we hope finally coming to an end, and with the imminent demise of proto-fascistic, arch-reactionary Bush-Cheney-ism there's this great and understandable upswell of, well, of hope. It's a wave of euphoria as we realize that finally maybe the Wicked Warlords will soon be dead and we can click our heels and go home again and that maybe the new fresh prince of politics, the great and wonderful wizard of Oz/Obama will point the way back home, where the present is about the future and not the past, as it has always been in the "First New Nation."
>
> Obama and his handlers are riding this wave as much as they are creating it. He is the right candidate in the right place at the right time.
>
> And when it gets bad enough in the present, everything old gets tarred, especially by young people. We become indiscriminate in our rejection of the "old" and our embrace of the new. Hillary gets tarred. John Edwards gets tarred with stink of the past. Heck, middle-aged lefties like me get tarred with the stench of being from the past. You say, "Give us something, someone fresh and brand new."

> There's this great extra special novelty premium when things get as bad as Bush and his crew and the broader imperial plutocracy have been allowed to make them.
>
> And if there's one thing about Barack, it is that he looks new and different: He's black, technically speaking. His father was from Kenya, but his mother was a white lady from Kansas! He grew up in Hawaii and lived three years in Indonesia! And that name!
>
> You get into all of that "newness" and you forget the other more traditional stuff: the ruling class indoctrination at Harvard. The corporate connections and big-money contributions. The connection to the foreign policy establishment and, as I have just shown, to empire. The attachment to class rule I just spoke about. The deception. The traditionalism even or especially on race. It all goes out the window.

"Americans are hungry for a directness and freshness," John Kerry noted last April, "that speaks to the public fatigue with politics as usual."[12] That elementary observation is truer than usual in the wake of the Bush-Cheney experience.

6. *The Intellectual Premium*

As the former editor of the *Harvard Law Review*, a former professor at the University of Chicago Law School, and the author of two serious (and widely read) books, the "refreshingly cerebral" (according to George Will[13]) Obama is a candidate of certified high intelligence. He would perhaps be the most officially intellectual U.S. president since Woodrow Wilson. Displaying a notably "professorial" style in town hall meetings, he has made a point of reaching out to and surrounding himself—on the model of JFK—with numerous intellectual "stars" (professors Austan Goolsbee and Samantha Power, for example) from elite academia.

There is nothing inherently virtuous or progressive about possessing and corralling brain power. High intelligence can be (and often is) marshaled to destructive and regressive causes. At the same time, American political culture has long harbored a special suspicion of "pointy-headed" intellectuals.

Obama has nonetheless benefited from being mentally hyper-competent in the wake of the often highly incompetent Bush administration's "reign of error." After seeing their country and its global reputation seemingly run into the ground by a former C student who has often seemed boorishly out of touch with basic aspects of American policy and experience, citizens are ready, like at no time in recent memory, for a valedictorian chief executive. At the same time, Obama's intellectual and academic credentials and his skill at flattering the intelligentsia have helped him win strong support from the professoriat and other members of the U.S. intellectual and "coordinator" class, for whom professionally certified brain power is all-important.

7. Black Pride

As exit-poll data shows, the two leading and most reliable sections of the Obama coalition during the Democratic primary season were black Americans and affluent, highly educated whites.[14] Racial factors were critical in both cases, as the polls also show. For the huge majority of black voters who have chosen Obama, the decision has been a simple (and understandable) matter of racial pride. Despite lingering reservations about the bourgeois Obama's degree of "blackness," the prospect of electing the nation's "first black president" naturally carries no small weight in the black community.

8. White Psychological Race Wages

With affluent Democrats, the racial calculus has been different and more complex. Two days before the heavily Caucasian Iowa caucus, one unusually forthcoming progressive Iowa City Democrat in a heavily academic and 99 percent white precinct told me something I'd been picking up for some time: "Obama," he reflected, "is a way for highly educated liberal and moderate whites around here to pat themselves on the back and say, 'Hey, I'm not too prejudiced to vote for a black guy.' Look, I hate nuclear power. Your candidate [Edwards] is better on the issues, no doubt about it, but it's not going to mean a hill of beans with these folks around here. This is their big chance to say something on race."

But it was all premised, he agreed, on Obama being a "good," that is, "middle class" and "not-too-fiery" black—one who promised not to offend white sensibilities by confronting white privilege in any meaningful way. Like the racially accommodationist, white-soothing media mogul and mass Obama marketer Oprah Winfrey (who held huge campaign events with Obama in Iowa before that state's critical caucus), Obama could capitalize on many middle- and upper-middle-class whites' repudiation of what I have (in Chapter 3) called "level-one" (state-of-mind) racism, because he reassured them he would honor their reluctance to acknowledge and confront the continuing power of deeper, "level two" (state-of-being) societal and institutional racism in American life.[15]

In my liberal white university town, Obama was something of a Great White Hope. There as elsewhere across the disproportionately white, affluent, educated, and college-town-based white islands of Obama Nation, Kathleen Parker's observation that Obama "smoothly, strategically, and subtly mines the wells of white guilt" is highly relevant.[16] So, sadly, is the following observation from the black conservative Shelby Steele: "It's all about gratitude. White people are just thrilled when a prominent black person comes along and doesn't rub their noses in racial guilt. White people just go crazy over people like that."[17]

Of course, Steele was wrong to generalize about "white people" as a whole. Obama's white support has been disproportionately affluent. Contrary to claims that his campaign transcended race, Obama's primary campaign was heavily plagued by racial bloc voting. While he pulled down more than four in every five black votes in most states, he lost the white working and lower class and rural vote, and he did particularly badly with white voters in the South, reflecting historical tendencies that are well known. A late February 2008 nationwide Pew Research poll showed that white Democrats would be significantly more likely to defect to the Republican presidential nominee John McCain if Obama was the nominee than if Clinton was. Ten percent of the white Democrats surveyed reported they would cross party lines and support McCain if Clinton was the nominee. But twice as many—one in five—said they would choose McCain if Obama was the nominee. Nearly a fourth (24 percent) of white Democrats without college degrees acknowledged that they would defect to the GOP standard-bearer if Obama was the nominee.[18]

It would be comforting (from a progressive standpoint) to think that white working-class voters tended to resist Obama and prefer Hillary Clinton (and to some extent Edwards, who dropped out before Super Tuesday) in the primaries because of the Illinois senator's closeness to capital and empire. I saw some of that dynamic working on the behalf of the surprisingly populist Edwards in union households in Iowa. But Hillary Clinton is just as economically conservative as Obama and if anything closer to the corporate and imperial elite than he is. The "other thing" explaining the reluctance of white working- and lower-class voters to support Obama is that he is black. Perhaps the notion of putting him in the White House works against what W. E. B. DuBois once called the "psychological wage of racism," once usefully summarized by Dr. Martin Luther King, Jr., as "the satisfaction of . . . thinking you are somebody big because you are white."[19] Such "satisfaction" is more commonly sought and "required" by whites in the lower reaches of the United States' steep socioeconomic structure than it is by those in positions of relative wealth, power, and status.

But this does not mean that Iowa City's liberal middle- and upper-middle-class whites were all that much "better" on race and Obama. There are racism- and classism-preserving white psychological "race wages" above as well as within and below the working class. For some whites in more elite occupational and socioeconomic categories, there exists what might be called a "psychological wage of superficial nonracism"—the boosting of one's sense of superiority over less-well-off whites by exhibiting one's rejection of uncouth, lower-class racial bigotry (by voting for a certain kind of safe, technically black politician, for example) while simultaneously resisting any substantive challenge to persistent racial advantages accruing to middle- and upper-class beneficiaries of white-skin privilege. The Obama campaign was perfectly calibrated for that curious mixture of racial pseudo-benevolence and intra-Caucasian class arrogance.[20]

9. Skin Color and the Illusion of Greater Liberalism

At the same time, the fact that Obama is black has helped deepen his appeal to certain white middle class voters by making him seem more liberal and progressive than he really is. According to researchers studying the political psychology of race, voters asked to compare a black and a white candidate with approximately similar political positions will tend to see the black candidate as "more liberal." According to MSNBC's exit polls, Obama was supported by 54 percent of Massachusetts Democratic primary voters who identified themselves as "very liberal," compared to just 36 percent of the state's Democratic primary voters who called themselves "moderates." By clear contrast, Clinton received 42 percent of the state's "very liberal" Democratic vote but 62 percent of its "moderate" Democratic tally. In Illinois, Obama beat Clinton 65 to 34 percent with "very liberal" Democrats and got defeated by her 65 to 34 percent with "moderate" Democrats. Across the country, Obama did much better than Clinton with Democratic primary voters who identified themselves as "very liberal," and Clinton did slightly better with the large number and percentage of Democrats who called themselves "moderates." Since Obama's actual policy agenda was generally no more liberal than Clinton's—and his health care plan was considerably more conservative—it seems likely that many voters were identifying Obama as more liberal at least in part because of his race.[21]

10. Managing Mass Hope and Euphoria from the Top Down

African American voters, starstruck college students, and middle-class professors aside, it is supremely important that key people within the intersecting networks of the corporate, political, military power elite bought into "the Obama phenomenon" from and even before the beginning. As I tried to show in this book's introduction, ordinary voters would never have been in a position to appreciate Obama's virtues (real and perceived) if he had not been approved in advance by some powerful masters of Laurence Shoup's "hidden primary."[22]

For those masters, some writers on the "far left" (John Wilson's term for radical critics of Obama) observe, Obama was nicely suited to stealthily wrap establishment corporate politics and the related American Empire Project in insurgent garb. Once he was properly vetted and found to be "reasonable"—to be someone who would not fundamentally question core underlying power structures and doctrines of class, race, and empire—Obama's multicultural background, race, youth, charisma, and even early opposition to the planned (and ultimately disastrous) Iraq War became useful to corporate and imperial interests in the dark and polarizing wake of the Bush-Cheney regime.

His outwardly revolutionary image and "change" persona promised to divert, capture, and safely control current and coming popular rebellions; to stealthily prick and smoothly drain the alternating boils of mass disgust and mass elation (at the impending passing of the Bush regime); and to simultaneously surf, de-fang, and "manage" the citizenry's hopes for radical structural change—perhaps even revolution. By Los Angeles writer Juan Santos's account in February 2008, Obama is distinctively qualified for the critical task of "repressive desublimation"—an essential system-preserving job, thanks to the vast popular alienation and revulsion that the proto-fascistic Bush administration and Bush era have generated, and to the great popular expectations raised by the ever more imminent passing of the Bush White House.[23] According to Santos,

> There is nothing wrong at all in the hopes we have that Obama's rhetoric speaks to. The problem lies in what Herbert Marcuse called "repressive desublimation—a hope, a need, that has been buried and denied by an oppressive system, is allowed some room to breathe, then co-opted and redirected back into a form that ultimately reinforces the oppressive system that denied and suppressed our hopes and needs in the first place. That's what Obama represents. . . .
>
> The Bush regime was and remains an expression of a conscious plan by the far right . . . to crush everything that came to life in the upheavals of the cultural revolutions of the 60s era. They meant, as they consciously expressed it, to counter the counter culture, the culture of hope, and offer a new "hope" of a "purpose driven life" in the context of the old traditions of oppression. . . .
>
> The regime of Bush the Lesser was the pinnacle of this effort; he carried the agenda as far as it could go, before it began to fracture and collapse under the weight of its own madness. . . . Literally, in terms of time in office, and as a sweeping reactionary social agenda, the Bush regime is coming to an end. With its end, inevitably, comes a wave of hope and euphoria.
>
> This is the wave Obama is riding, the ocean of energy he is trying to steer into an acceptance of the same old deal, the same old wars, the same old systemic racism, packaged as if it were something new. This wave of energy is not something he's inspired, it's something he's riding and that he is uniquely qualified to channel toward his own ends—which are not our ends.[24]

That "channeling" is a key part of what we should understand as the service Obama provides to the moneyed elite when Doug Henwood says that the wealthy see him as "the man to do their work." After noting that Obama is "backed by the biggest Wall Street firms," John Pilger made much the same point in his usual eloquent and deeply informed fashion at the end of May 2008:

> What is Obama's attraction to big business? Precisely the same as Robert Kennedy's [in 1968]. By offering a "new," young, and apparently progressive face of the Democratic Party—with the bonus of being a member of the black elite—he can blunt and divert real opposition. That was Colin Powell's role as Bush's secretary of state. An Obama victory will bring intense pressure on the U.S. antiwar and social justice movements to accept a Democratic administration for all its faults. If that happens, domestic resistance to rapacious America will fall silent.[25]

Unpleasant though it may be to acknowledge, Obama's race is no tiny part of what makes him "uniquely qualified" to perform the task in question. As Aurora Levins Morales noted in a *Z Magazine* reflection written for left progressives, entitled "Thinking Outside the (Ballot) Box," in April 2008,

> We're far more potent as organizers and catalysts than as voters. Our ability to create a world we can thrive on does not depend on who wins this election, it depends on our ability to dismantle profit-based societies in which greed trumps ethics.
>
> This election is about finding a CEO capable of holding domestic constituencies in check as they are further disenfranchised . . . and . . . [to] make them feel that they have a stake in the military aggressiveness that the ruling class believes is necessary. Having a black man and a white woman run helps to obscure the fact that . . . decline of empire is driving the political elite to the right. Both [Obama and Hillary Clinton] represent very reactionary politics. . . . Part of the cleverness of having such candidates is the fact that they will be attacked in ways that make oppressed people feel compelled to protect them.[26]

11. The Emperor's New Clothes? "To Reinvent America's Image Abroad" through "Biography"

As suggested in the introduction to this book, there's a foreign policy dimension to the "work" of the elite. A considerable segment of the U.S. foreign policy establishment certainly thinks that Obama's race, name, experience living in and visiting poor nations, and nominally antiwar history will help them repackage and advance the imperial project in a softer and more politically correct way. John Kerry, who ran for the 2004 presidency largely on the claim that he would be a more effective manager of empire (and the Iraq War) than George W. Bush, is certainly thinking of these critical imperial "soft-power" assets when he praises Obama as someone who could "reinvent America's image abroad."[27] So was Obama himself when he said the following to reporters aboard his campaign plane in the fall of 2007:

> If I am the face of American foreign policy and American power, . . . as long as we are also making prudent strategic decisions, handling emergencies, crises and opportunities in the world in an intelligent and sober way. . . . I think . . . that if you can tell people, "We have a president in the White House who still has a grandmother living in a hut on the shores of Lake Victoria and has a sister who's half-Indonesian, married to a Chinese-Canadian," then they're going to think that he may have a better sense of what's going on in our lives and in our country. And they'd be right.[28]

Obama's distinctive ethnocultural and geographic biography is one of his great attractions to the foreign policy elite in a majority nonwhite world that has been deeply alienated by U.S. behavior in the post-9/11 era (and truthfully before that). Call it "the identity politics of foreign policy." The Empire wants new clothes, and Obama is a good man to wear them.

12. The Power of American Exceptionalism

It is difficult to advance a critique of Obama's toxic nationalism and related imperial militarism when much of the U.S. populace is caught up in the notion of "American exceptionalism." As a long-standing antiwar and political activist, I can report that the nationally narcissistic notion of the United States as an especially benevolent and far-seeing super-state that uses violence only for good and democratic purposes is hardly restricted to the U.S. foreign policy establishment and power elite. Many ordinary Americans have a very difficult time trying to wrap their minds around serious moral and legal criticism of U.S. foreign policy and militarism.

Having witnessed, learned about, and often enough experienced U.S. imperial aggression and oppression over many decades (in the case of Latin America more than a century), the majority of the world's politically and morally cognizant populace knows to respond skeptically to U.S. politicians like Obama (he is hardly unique in this regard) when they say that the United States is "the last, best hope on Earth."[29] Millions of world citizens have been on the wrong end of "noble" America's imperial guns, policies, and "hope" for far too long to share that belief.

But things are very different in the eye of the U.S. imperial hurricane. Few Americans have been encouraged (to say the least) to know or care all that much about "their" nation's remarkable and ongoing record of imperial violence and criminality. When confronted (no matter how politely) with evidence of this record, many Americans find it too morally and ideologically counterintuitive to process. The dark and living record of U.S. foreign policy presented by such fearless historians as William Blum, Noam Chomsky, Howard Zinn, and John Pilger sparks too much painful cognitive dissonance for a populace that has been told again and again, from cradle to grave—at home, in church, at school, in "higher education," on television, at the movies, at the workplace, at the Fourth of July barbecue, from the White House, in video games, on billboards, at the bar, in the grocery store, etc.—that "We Are Good," "We Are Good," "We Are Good."[30]

The faith of "Good Americans" in the essential kindness, integrity, and righteousness of the United States in its dealings with other countries around the world and the related extremely high domestic popularity of the U.S. military[31] is so great and so deeply reinforced by government and media disinformation that people have difficulty grasping the issues at stake. I repeatedly encountered midwestern voters who could formulate opposition to the Iraq War only on the grounds that "we shouldn't be giving our soldiers and money to help the Iraqis when those ungrateful people don't even want our assistance."[32]

Part of this terrible reality is that systematic indoctrination and propaganda are at work—"manufacturing consent."[33] But another part is about the simple human reluctance to admit that one's own country is guilty of deadly and immoral violence and sheer hypocrisy on a monumental scale. Who wants to think that one's tax dollars, allegiances, and more (including, in some cases, one's own child's life or limb and/or sanity and/or eyesight and/or hearing, and so on) have been given to help a "rogue" superpower assault masses of innocent global others while further enriching privileged elites at home, including the leading investors behind such proponents, agents, and beneficiaries of "forward global force projection" (sometimes called "defense") as Lockheed Martin, Raytheon, GE, Boeing, Henry Crown Investments (a leading Obama election investor), Halliburton, and Blackwater Worldwide?[34] For many Americans, it is psychologically preferable to believe that Uncle Sam is a wise and kindly old man who wants nothing but the best for the people at home and abroad and advances that benevolent agenda.[35]

The highly intelligent and ambitious Obama knows all this very well. When he peppers his speeches and comments with references to the United States as a "magical place" with a mission and qualifications to give the world hope and rule world affairs—by force, when and if necessary—he is tapping into a deeply rooted American exceptionalism he hardly invented.

"The level of culture that can be attained in the United States," Chomsky noted in 1966, "is a matter of life and death for large masses of suffering humanity."[36]

13. Media Love Matters

Along with his remarkable campaign finance profile, heavily underwritten by corporate giants, Obama has received abundant and favorable coverage from "mainstream" U.S. media. The media coverage has in fact been a leading expression of the approval Obama has garnered from the corporate and imperial establishment. Once he attained dominant media favor, this coverage became perhaps *the* critical driving force behind "the Obama phenomenon." It permitted news and commentary authorities to report and reflect in superficially objective and detached terms on something they played a critical role in creating. It's all part of that media's remarkable capacity to create celebrity and to shape hearts and minds for or against specific public personalities. Along the way, that media has also rendered special service to Obama in emphasizing candidate image over issues and policy and in suppressing conflicts between his rhetoric and his record.

14. The United States of Amnesia

Another media contribution to Obama has been its failure to subject his claims of "freshness" and originality to sustained and meaningful historical scrutiny. This is a reflection of that media's own amnesiac, market-driven attachment to novelty. The conservative commentator Andrew Ferguson noted and elaborated usefully on the problem in a March 2008 essay that merits lengthy quotation:

> Especially in American politics, policed by a posse of commentators and reporters who crave novelty above all, the past is a blank; every day is Groundhog Day, bringing shocking discoveries of things that have happened over and over again. No politician has benefited from this amnesia as much as Obama. *He is credited with revelatory eloquence for using phrases that have been in circulation for years. . . .*
>
> . . . Timelessness may be the key here: You begin to wonder, listening to Obama's rhetoric, whether anything has changed in 20 years. "This is a defining moment in our history," Obama likes to say; but that's what Elizabeth Dole said when her husband ran for president in 1996. (They're both wrong.) In 1992, Bill Clinton was complaining that "Washington" was a place "people came to just to score political points." Eight years later Bush was complaining that "Washington is obsessed with scoring political points, not solving prob-

> lems." Now, in 2008, "Washington has become a place," Obama says, "where politicians spend too much time trying to score political points."
>
> . . . Obama has had the unbelievable luck to attract listeners who seem to think he's minted it fresh.[37]

Ferguson found that Obama and his speechwriters have recycled numerous words and phrases from past presidential candidates and their speechwriters: "politics is broken" (used by Bill Bradley in 1996 and George W. Bush in 2000); "you need a president who will tell you what you need to know, not what you want to hear" (Geraldine Ferraro, 1984); "this is a defining moment in our history" (Elizabeth Dole, speaking for Bob Dole in 1996); Washington as a place where politicians come to "score political points" (Bill Clinton in 1992 and George W. Bush in 2000); "lifting this country up" instead of dragging or tearing it down (Bob Dole, 1996); "we're going to take this country back" (Howard Dean, 2004); "we can disagree without being disagreeable" (Gerald Ford, 1976); "unity over division" (Jesse Jackson, 1992); "hope over fear" (Bill Clinton, 1992 and John Kerry, 2004); "choose the future over the past" (Al Gore, 1992); overcome our "moral deficit" (Bush and Gore in 2000 and Newt Gingrich, 1994); move "beyond the divisions of race and class" (Bill Clinton, 1992); "the story of our country" (Ross Perot, 1992); "the genius of our country" (Bush, 2000); "the wonder of our country" (George H. W. Bush, 1988); "ordinary people doing extraordinary things" (Perot, 1992; Bush I, 1992; Bush II, 2000; Ronald Reagan, 1984).

15. Little That Seems Viable to His Left

It can be difficult to criticize the Obama phenomenon as insufficiently progressive and excessively centrist when there's little that seems politically or institutionally viable to his left or to the left of the Democratic Party. One of the hallmark characteristics of the distinctively business-friendly electoral and party system of the United States (to be examined in more detail in the next chapter) is the nearly complete absence of genuinely left (socialist or laborite) candidate and party choices on the "electoral market." This terrible shortage explains much of the citizen disengagement and apathy that has long plagued U.S. political culture and elections. It also explains much of the notorious vapidity and "infantilism" (Kolko's term) of U.S. elections and the sometimes desperate willingness of many American progressives to embrace corporate-imperial candidates who are certain to betray "populist and peace-stressing promises and gestures" upon "the assumption of power."[38]

At the same time, the relative weakness, corporate captivity, fragmentation, and tepid, middle-class "leadership" of non- and sub-electoral social movements and organizations in the United States—unions, civil rights groups, environmental justice movements, the antiwar "movement," and the like—make it hard to tell real and ostensibly progressive citizens that electoral politics are neither the most relevant nor the most potent outlet for their passion for change. Mass apathy notwithstanding, moreover, the notion that change is attained through a short trip into the voting booth once every 1,461 days is a venerable, powerful, and widely disseminated idea in the United States.

16. America "Off Center"

And then there's the extreme rightward drift of U.S. politics and policy under the second Bush administration and arguably before that—something that makes even the tepid centrist "progressivism" of Obama seem "truly transformative" to many voters. As Jacob S. Hacker and Paul Pierson show in their important 2005 book *Off Center: The Republican Revolution and the Erosion of American Democracy,* American politics and governance have careened far to the plutocratic and starboard side of the American majority's "moderate" identification. "American politics made a stunning transit to the right even as the American public has not," producing a "stark disconnect between the public and elites," according to Hacker and Pierson.[39]

"The Republicans who have tended to run U.S. government since 2000 have seemingly defied the laws of political gravity," Hacker and Pierson said, transforming the nation's priorities in profoundly regressive, militaristic, and repressive ways even while possessing only the slimmest of majorities. They have repeatedly ignored the sentiments and needs of the majority of Americans and even marginalized and angered many moderate Republicans by siding with the extremely wealthy and the ideological far right. Through various mechanisms and methods, including artful propaganda, bold deception, political gerrymandering, the manipulation of campaign finance laws, and the relentless polarization of the electorate around "moral" issues and "national security" threats, they have seriously "threatened democracy itself" by "attacking the foundation of representative government—the accountability of politicians to ordinary voters."[40]

The success of the hard right and its sponsors in tilting U.S. politics dangerously "off center" creates understandable hunger for a leader like Obama who promises to heal partisan divisions, overcome ideological and cultural "polarization," overcome (right-leaning) "gridlock," and rebuild the moderate "center." It also gives special appeal to Obama's call for "reinventing U.S. politics" and toning down the often vitriolic and bitter climate of the nation's political discourse. The fact that his position and record on numerous key issues aren't particularly populist or progressive—standing to the right of even majority opinion on Iraq, health care, empire, and corporate power—is easily overlooked by many left progressives who would be understandably pleased just to move the center of policy and political gravity closer to the moderate middle and bring the country back from the brink of seemingly permanent hard-right plutocracy, authoritarianism, and messianic militarism. Beggars can't be choosers.

At the same time, Obama's centrism seems to attract a certain number of Republican moderates who have become alienated by the hard right "excesses" of Cheney, Bush, Rove, and Rumsfeld et al. This is no small pragmatic electoral concern for progressives under the rule of the United States' "winner-take-all" elections system—a subject area to be addressed in the next chapter of this book.

CHAPTER 6

Beyond the Narrow Spectrum

Citizens, Politicians, Change, and the Obama Phenomenon

Elected officials are only as good or as bad as the forces they feel they must respond to. It's a mistake to expect any more of them than to be vectors of the political pressures they feel working on them.

—ADOLPH REED, JR., *THE PROGRESSIVE*, NOVEMBER 2007

A huge propaganda campaign is mounted to get people to focus on these personalized quadrennial extravaganzas and to think, "That's politics." But it isn't. It's only a small part of politics.

The urgent task for those who want to shift policy in progressive direction—often in close conformity to majority opinion—is to grow and become strong enough so that they can't be ignored by centers of power. . . .

In the election, sensible choices have to be made. But they are secondary to serious political action. The main task is to create a genuinely responsive democratic culture, and that effort goes on before and after electoral extravaganzas, whatever their outcome.

—NOAM CHOMSKY, FROM *INTERVENTIONS*, 2007

Social motion and movements in America tend to be neither rooted in nor sustained by campaigns for electoral office, no matter how charismatic the leader. . . . Despite the symbolic and cathartic electoral victories of liberal women and people of color, all remain thoroughly shackled by corporate priorities in the economy and in debt-ridden administrations. Under such conditions, the plight of the ill-fed, ill-clad, and ill-housed tends to get worse.

—CORNEL WEST, FROM *THE POLITICS OF LAW*, 1998

We can't look to saviors from on high to get us out of this mess. . . . We have to do it ourselves.

—TARIQ ALI AND ANTHONY ARNOVE, *SOCIALIST WORKER ONLINE,* OCTOBER 20, 2006

Let's remember that even when there is a "better" candidate (yes, better Roosevelt than Hoover, better anyone than George Bush), that difference will not mean anything unless the power of the people asserts itself in ways that the occupant of the White House will find it dangerous to ignore.

—HOWARD ZINN, *THE PROGRESSIVE,* MARCH 2008

IN THE SPRING OF 1967, after he went public with his principled opposition to the Vietnam War, Martin Luther King, Jr., was approached by liberal and left politicos to consider running for the United States presidency. King turned the activists down, saying that he preferred to think of himself "as one trying desperately to be the conscience of all the political parties, rather than being a political candidate." "I've just never thought of myself . . . as a politician," he told them. The minute he threw his hat into the American presidential ring, King knew, he would be encouraged to compromise his increasingly left message[1] against what he called "the triple evils that are interrelated": racism, economic inequality, and militarism.

Reflecting his chastening confrontation with the concentrated black poverty and class oppression in the "liberal" urban North and his shock at the horrors of U.S. policy in Southeast Asia, King had come to radical-democratic conclusions. "For years I have labored with the idea of refining the existing institutions of the society, a little change here, a little change there," he told journalist David Halberstam that spring. "Now I feel quite differently. I think you've got to have a reconstruction of the entire society, a revolution of values." The black freedom movement, King told a crowd at the University of California–Berkeley, had shifted from civil rights to human rights, involving "a struggle for genuine equality" that "demands a radical redistribution of economic and political power."[2] By this time, King had identified the U.S. government as "the greatest purveyor of violence" in the world[3] and denounced U.S. support for U.S.-investment-friendly Third World dictatorships, all part of "the triple evils." As King knew, these were not exactly "winning" ideas in the American political system of his time. They were moral observations with radical implications that led beyond the barriers of existing U.S. politics.

"They Just Have Different Priorities"

As I have tried to demonstrate in the previous chapters of this book, Barack Obama shows little promise of wanting to push past those parameters. To say this is to advance a moral, ideological, and perhaps even spiritual criticism of him, but it is not at all to say that he is a poor politician. Whatever one's standpoint on King's position forty-one years ago, it is naive to expect Obama or any other candidate or elected official to act in accord with King's vision while serving in the U.S. Senate with the hope of retaining his seat and/or making a serious run ("in it to win it") for the U.S. presidency. That's because any comparison of King with Obama is largely one of "apples and oranges." Beyond the obvious generational difference, King was a spiritual and social movement leader who sought to pressure and influence elected officials and politicians, but who came to doubt that significant change in accord with his true and higher ideals could be attained under the prevailing political-economic order. Obama is an elected official and a shrewd politician who would not likely challenge the dominant sociopolitical order in any meaningful way unless compelled to do so by a significant social and political movement.

As Adolph J. Reed, Jr., noted last November in *The Progressive,* in an article entitled "Sitting This One Out," "elected officials are only as good or as bad as the forces they feel they must respond to." "It's a mistake," Reed observed, "to expect any more of them than to be vectors of the political pressures they feel working on them." Reed cited a then recent conflict between the black and historically progressive U.S. House of Representatives judiciary chair, John Conyers (D-MI), and antiwar activists, who accused Conyers of being a "sell out" for failing to aggressively pursue the impeachment of George W. Bush. By Reed's instructive account and analysis:

> [Conyers's] critics accused him of betraying the spirit of Martin Luther King. But that charge only exposes their unrealistic expectations. Conyers isn't a movement leader. He's a Democratic official who wants to get reelected. He's enmeshed in the same web of personal ties, partisan loyalties and obligations, and diverse interest-group commitments as other pols. It was the impeachment activists' naïve error, and I suspect one resting on a partly racial, wrongheaded shorthand, to have expected him to lead an insurgency.[4]

Instead of railing against Conyers's predictable failure to embody King's legacy in the inherently compromised realm of American electoral politics and policy, Reed argued, activists would have served their cause better by trying to organize an effective citizen force for the policy outcome they sought. Underlying the sense of demoralization and defeat that many progressives experience, Reed observed, is a terrible misunderstanding about leading Democratic politicians: "the belief that they just don't know what we want and how important these things are to us." "They know," Reed rightly observed, but "*they just have different priorities.*"[5]

Obama is no special exception to this harsh reality, which does not change, in accord with what Reed calls a "partly racial shorthand," simply because he happens to be African American. The point is often missed on what has passed for the Left in the United States in 2007 and 2008. Many avowedly liberal and progressive voters—even highly sophisticated ones—have often and chronically made precisely the false conflation between self-interested politician and movement activist that Reed rightly disdains. In my experience during the long campaign leading up to the pivotal Iowa Democratic Caucus, the flatly false notion that Obama was some kind of left progressive antiwar populist was held by a considerable number of left-liberals.

Confusion on the difference between Obama and left progressivism can be seen in John Wilson's pro-Obama book *This Improbable Quest* (2007), which criticizes Glen Ford and me (among other "far left" Obama critics) for failing to appreciate Obama's understanding of the Left's need to compromise in order to achieve progressive social-justice goals.[6]

In a similar vein, the highly esteemed left and black historian Manning Marable published an April 2008 *Black Commentator* essay entitled "African-American Peacemakers—Dr. Martin Luther King, Jr., Barack Obama, and the Struggle against Racism, Inequality, and War." Consistent with its title, the essay showed no understanding of Reed's distinction between elected officials and social movement leaders or of Obama's conservative record on issues of empire and inequality at home and abroad. Marable made numerous assertions about "Obama's challenge[s]" in the candidate's supposed mission of following Dr. King's example in the halls of power.[7]

If Reed is correct, and I think he is, then George Lakoff's widely discussed thesis on the Democratic Party's failures is largely beside the point. The well-known liberal linguist and political consultant Lakoff argued that Democratic politicians and party officials have failed to properly articulate and sell their essentially (he thinks) "progressive" paradigm for "framing," explaining, and acting upon the facts of American and global life. To be sure, the necessity of moral and ideological "framing" is very real: it will not suffice simply to discover and state the terrible facts of social disparity to motivate citizen action for social justice; the empirical data has to be explicated in a way that provides a reasonable account of why they exist and compels people toward common action to correct the social practices and policies that generate them. But Lakoff held the dubious belief that Democratic politicians and officials are left-leaning actors possessing at their core egalitarian and socially democratic values, a conviction he has advanced with special emphasis in regard to what he calls the "deeply progressive" Obama.

Many, if not most, of those candidates and officials (I obviously make no special exception for Obama) have likely internalized the authoritarian values of corporation capitalism, socioeconomic inequality, U.S. nationalism, and imperial globalism.[8]

The deeper point, however, is that it might not matter what sort of internal values they may or may not hold, since they are trying to succeed within a political culture and system that tends to militate against progressive commitments. Barack Obama, the nation's leading official "progressive" hope since 2004, could make all the populist-sounding primary-campaign noise he wished in Iowa about Maytag's terrible abandonment of working families in Galesburg. But his concern, real or feigned, for Galesburg's deindustrialized proletarians was not a high enough priority for him to significantly push his elite political investor, Maytag director Henry Crown, to do anything to avert the Galesburg shutdown. Securing his campaign-finance ties to the Crown family took precedence over serving Galesburg workers for the simple reason that one cannot run a viable presidential campaign ("progressive" or otherwise) without the sort of election investments that wealthy and powerful interests like the Crowns provide. Such are the rules of what progressive campaign-finance activists and researchers call "the American Wealth Primary."[9]

We saw that Obama deceptively claimed during his Iowa campaign to have intervened forcefully against the nuclear industry on behalf of public safety after one of Exelon's power plants was shown to have released contaminated water into surrounding communities. That is a troubling bit of campaign history. Still, the cold reality was that the leading reason for that claim was almost certainly that he felt he could not afford to sacrifice the considerable campaign finance support he received from Exelon, one of his top election investors. It was an understandable concern for someone whose top priority is not social justice (à la Dr. King) but winning the White House.

Obama may have wanted to say and do much more than he did regarding the problem of anti-black racism in American life during his presidential campaign. It is a topic he knows well. But the deeper rationality—for a black candidate who is "in it to win it"—of downplaying the sensitive issue of race (already raised by the simple fact of his skin color) is clear under the winner-take-all rules of American elections when majority white post–Civil Rights opinion recoils at the notion that racism still poses significant barriers to black advancement and equality in the United States.

Obama could theoretically and privately share underlying "progressive," peace-oriented values on U.S. foreign policy and foreign relations, values that may have informed his early sympathetic approach (as a state senator) to the Palestinian cause and his 2002 speech against Bush and Cheney's war plans.[10] But how much would it matter if he did? His priority of winning the highest office in the land (and the world) under the existing political order mandates building "credibility" with the foreign policy establishment, which does not confer presidential legitimacy on those who join Obama's former pastor Rev. Wright or Dennis Kucinich in questioning the underlying benevolence of U.S. foreign policy or the American quest for global dominance. The authoritarian comments Obama made to distance himself from Wright may have offended many left activists and commentators—this author included[11]—but they made perfect sense from the perspective of what Obama is trying to accomplish: climbing to the top of the U.S. power structure.

This need to compromise ideals for the sake of the next election, along with biblical injunctions against the pursuit of earthly authority, almost certainly played a role in Dr. King's decision not to pursue being a politician, presidential or otherwise. Obama isn't a social justice movement leader or crusader. He's an extraordinarily ambitious[12] politician trying to be a twenty-first-century JFK, not a twenty-first-century MLK.

The Narrow-Spectrum Two-Party Money-Media Single-Member-Plurality-System-Winner-Take-All-Strong-Executive-Imperial Plutocracy

According to Ralph Nader's 2008 presidential running mate, Matt Gonzalez, "It is shocking how frequently and consistently Obama is willing to subjugate good decision making for his personal and political benefit."[13] Gonzalez's comment came in a well-informed essay detailing the profound conservative and centrist limits of Obama's public record and policy positions—an essay that I cited repeatedly in this book. But is it really "shocking" that Obama would privilege personal and political advancement over what Gonzalez calls "good decision making"? And what constitutes such decision-making, anyway?

It depends on one's goals. Being a strong left and "true" progressive, Gonzalez equates such decision making with consistent action to advance the goals of economic and social justice, peace, antimilitarism, anti-imperialism, civil rights, civil liberties, and true democracy. These are just the sort of goals that the corporate, political, and academic elites who have signed on with the Obama campaign commonly deride as "pie in the sky" utopianism, in contrast to their candidate's "pragmatic," "realistic," "nonideological" approach. The left agenda, alas, is not a policy agenda that serves candidates well under the rules of the current American election system and political culture. The all-too-corporate- and empire-friendly Obama (from a left progressive view)—has been making very *good* decisions from the standpoint of advancing his remarkable political career.

The Corporate Money and Media Filters

Whatever his actual value orientation at the end of the day, Obama's relentless cutting of moral and ideological corners and his tacking to the corporate, imperial, nationalistic, and racially conciliatory center makes sense given the massive barriers to running a feasibly victorious populist, social-democratic, and peace-oriented campaign for the presidency. Those obstacles include, first and foremost, the hidden wealth and media primaries discussed in the first and second chapters of this study. One simply cannot mount a serious run for the presidency without the approval of wealthy election investors from within the top 1 percent of citizens who own more than half the nation's financial wealth and account for more than three-fourths of the significant campaign contributions.[14] People from within that opulent and highly class-conscious category of Americans are quite notoriously and logically hostile to left progressive ideals and movements, which threaten their disproportionate wealth and power.

A candidate also has no chance for the White House if he or she does not gain approval from the powerful people who own and manage national and global corporate media. Besides driving the costs of campaigns so high that backing from the rich and powerful is required for viability, corporate media enjoys practically godlike powers when it comes to shaping the public profile and mass perception of candidates. Dominant media has and exercises the capacity to narrowly restrict the boundaries of acceptable political debate and at the same time to focus public attention away from issues that matter to citizens and toward "spectator"-oriented subjects like candidate "character," "likeability," and "the horse race." Candidates seen by the reigning private communications authorities as too far beyond dominant elite doctrine on empire, inequality, and business rule are efficiently relegated to the media's dunce corners and recycling bins.

The Foreign Policy Filter

Two other key filters against noncentrist presidential candidacies are the foreign-policy vetting process and the American two-party winner-take-all party system. Serious presidential candidates are expected to audition with such august imperial policy-formation bodies as the Council on Foreign Relations (CFR) and to include trusted members of the foreign policy and military-industrial-academic complex on their teams of advisers. These foreign-policy power elites warn party, business, funding, and media authorities of any candidate's lack of safety (ideological, practical, or otherwise) for the imperial project. There is little chance of ultimate success for a candidate who questions the inherent underlying nobility of U.S. global dominance and/or the need to back American hegemony with a stupendous military budget and a fierce readiness to use military force with or (if necessary) without the approval of "the international community."

Winner-Take-All System

What about running with a new party outside the dominant ones that choose candidates who have been carefully vetted and crafted by corporate and imperial interests, and who suck up the lion's share of essential corporate funding and media approval? Beyond the considerable obstacles posed to such a candidacy by the power of money, media, and the foreign policy establishment, the historical American party and elections system we have inherited poses critical stumbling blocks, creating a seemingly permanent "silent spring" for alternative parties. The U.S. "two-party" electoral system predates the rise of the great concentrated corporate and imperial power structures that have worked to filter out substantively populist and peace-oriented presidential candidates since at least the early twentieth century. It is rooted largely in the U.S. Founders' design of an election regime in which congressional representatives, senators, and presidents are selected from single-representative districts in which victory requires just a plurality, not a majority, of popular votes.

This single-member-district plurality system tends to create a narrow-spectrum two-party system that squeezes out meaningful ideological and policy debate in two critical ways. First, it limits the relevant viable party range to just two by producing a series of winner-take-all contests. A vote for a third-, fourth-, or fifth-party candidate of the right, left, or whatever becomes in no small part an effective partial vote for the voter's most disliked candidate. A vote for an alternative candidate matched to one's own ideological and policy orientation plays out as a de facto vote for the candidate and party one fears most. Not wanting to help their "worst enemy" win elections, voters to the left or right (or whatever) of the dominant two parties tend to form the largest possible coalition with the party or candidate they fear least. They dump or bend their core policy and ideological preferences in the interest of not losing more terribly than they might if they voted their "hopes instead of [their] fears."[15]

This harsh, constitutionally mandated reality is no small part of why there have been just two major and relevant political parties for most of U.S. history. The only exceptions are a short-lived one-party era, after the collapse of the Federalists (1814–1828), and a brief period in the 1850s, when the antislavery Republican Party emerged to displace the declining Whigs. During the late 1850s and 1860s, the Republicans essentially supplanted the Whigs as the second major party after the Democrats. Since the collapse of the second (Whigs/Democrats) party system (1830s–1850s), historian

Richard Oestreicher has noted, "no new aspirant in American politics—no party, no politician, no social movement—has gained significant national power except through the Republican or Democratic Party."[16] In the twentieth and twenty-first centuries, third parties have rarely carried on for more than two or three election cycles, and they typically receive no more than 1 or 2 percent of the vote.

This is hardly accidental. Single-member plurality systems have created two-party electoral regimes in 90 percent of the 109 national places and times such systems have been in place. But the homogenizing power of this system is especially strong in the United States because the United States elects a strongly empowered president in the ultimate single-member-district, winner-take all election on a national scale every four years. "Due to the enormous power of the [U.S.] presidency," left sociologist and power analyst G. William Domhoff observed, "the pull toward two parties that exists in any single-member-district system is even greater in the U.S."[17]

To make matters worse for third-party activists and supporters, the winner-take-all Electoral College method of selecting the president compels candidates to focus on winning a plurality in as many states as possible and not only on attaining the largest popular vote count in the nation overall. Such broad geographic reach is generally beyond the resources of small and new parties.

Things are different under the *proportional representation* and parliamentary systems that are commonplace in other industrialized democracies. When 15 percent of the national vote translates into 15 percent of the elected representatives to the national assembly, a third or fourth party can become a relevant electoral and policymaking force, capable of winning and leveraging policy victories that it can take back to constituents with the hope of broadening its base of support. Under electoral systems where a prime minister is elected by a parliament after the national legislative elections, and where the prime minister holds less autonomous power than a U.S. president, moreover, there is much less pressure for voters to shed their core concerns and congeal around just one of two official parties and candidates.[18]

The negative and authoritarian consequences of the American single-member-plurality-winner-take-all-strong-president elections system are quite pronounced. As Domhoff noted,

> A two-party system does not foster parties that articulate clear images and policies, in good part because rival candidates attempt to blur their differences in order to win voters in the middle. It causes candidates to emphasize personal qualities rather than policy preferences. It may even lead to collusion between the two parties to avoid some issues or to avoid competition in some districts. Moreover, there is reason to believe that a two-party system actually

> discourages voting because those in a minority of even 49 percent receive no representation for their efforts. Voting increases considerably in countries where districts have been replaced by proportional representation.[19]

For all these reasons, then, a two-party system leads to the possibility that there may be relatively little relationship between politics and policy. Candidates say one thing to be elected and then do another once in office, which of course gives people with money and information the power to shape legislation. In short, a two-party system creates a set of circumstances in which parties may or may not reflect citizen preferences.

"Politics Is the Shadow Cast on Society by Big Business"

But we should not exaggerate the impact of America's nationally specific electoral institutions and party system on the centrism of Obama and other ambitious and "pragmatic" politicians. As numerous careful political observers since Aristotle have long observed, there is a fundamental contradiction between democracy and economic inequality—a tension that America's Founders sought to resolve by crafting a republican form of government explicitly designed to restrict democracy (reflecting their belief that the "people who own the country should run it"). People with great and concentrated wealth can be counted on to use their superior resources to subvert functioning democracy and thus marginalize genuinely democratic candidates in one way or another, turning "politics," in Progressive era philosopher John Dewey's famous and haunting words, into "the shadow cast on society by big business." As Dewey claimed, American politics will play this "shadow" role as long as power resides in "business for private profit through private control of banking, land, industry, reinforced by command of the press, press agents and other means of publicity and propaganda."[20]

These words from the Progressive Age remain highly relevant today, in a time when the top 1 percent controls 38 percent of total U.S. household wealth, an age of corporate-crafted globalization wherein capital flows and, if dissatisfied, flees from one territory to another with a speed and regularity that earlier corporate masters could never have imagined.[21]

Since inequality and concentration of wealth are inherent in the profit system,[22] we are dealing here with the timeworn conflict between two very different things, falsely conflated in the dominant neoliberal ideology to which Obama subscribes: democracy and capitalism.[23] As Chomsky has argued, "Reforms will not suffice. Fundamental social change is necessary to bring meaningful democracy."[24]

This is especially true in the United States. The corporate community has long been especially strong here because it hasn't had to contend with a feudal (or other kind of precapitalist) aristocracy, strong states, or the hierarchy of an established centralized church, and because the American working class has never succeeded in developing a strong and independent organization. One of the distinctive aspects of American development is that large and powerful corporations emerged in the late nineteenth century, as Dumhoff explained, "well before there was any semblance of a so-called big government at the national level."[25]

What Is to Be Done?

These are harsh realities, but it useful to remember that people "make their own history" to no small degree, and that the inherited circumstances in which they do so are themselves the product of human agency and political contingency. The British historian E. P. Thompson once pointed to "the crucial ambivalence of our own human presence in our own history." Human beings remain "part subjects, part objects, the voluntary agents of their own involuntary determinations."

How can and should liberal, progressive, radical, moderate, and other sorts of citizens and activists respond to the limits and opportunities of "the Obama phenomenon" and the broader political culture and elections system that it reflects? Some of the ten suggestions I give below (borrowing heavily and shamelessly from other progressive writers and activists) are more directed at—and will appeal more to—those who stand with me to the left of the Democratic Party. But I hope that many and perhaps all of them will be relevant to, and merit consideration from, Americans who may identify more toward the liberal and moderate center. Readers will note significant overlap between some of these suggestions, as they are interrelated and mutually reinforcing.

1. Register the Distinction between "Politicians" and "Citizens"

This principle was nicely articulated as follows by Howard Zinn in the spring of 2007:

> We who protest the war are not politicians. We are citizens. Whatever politicians may do, let them first feel the full force of citizens who speak for what is right, not for what is winnable. . . . Except for the rare few . . . our representatives are politicians, and will surrender their integrity, claiming to be "realistic." We are not politicians, but citizens. We have no office to hold on to, only our consciences, which insist on telling the truth. That, history suggests, is the most realistic thing a citizen can do.[26]

As Reed suggested, failure to grasp the citizen-politician difference is a recipe for repeated disillusionment, despair, illusion, and irrelevance.

Democracy's true source lies not in candidates and officeholders but in aroused and organized citizens who promote, push, and punish politicians and government officials. Obama, a militant "realist" and master of the "winnable," is no magical exception and should be given no more freedom from rigorous popular-democratic oversight and pressure than any other politician or elected official.

2. Remember the "Main Task" beyond the Quadrennial "Election Madness"

Given the priorities of politicians and elected officials, Reed argued rightly that progressives should focus less on elections and more on building rank-and-file social movements for democratic change across and between electoral contests and over longer periods of time than just the next election cycle:

> It's a mistake to focus so much on the election cycle; we didn't vote ourselves into this mess, and we're not going to vote ourselves out of it. Electoral politics is an arena for consolidating majorities that have been created on the plane of social movement organizing. It's not an alternative or a shortcut to building those movements, and building them takes time and concerted effort. Not only can that process not be compressed to fit the election cycle; it also doesn't happen through mass actions. It happens through cultivating one-on-one relationships with people who have standing and influence in their neighborhoods, workplaces, schools, families, and organizations. It happens through struggling with people over time for things they're concerned about and linking those concerns to a broader political vision and program. This is how the populist movement grew in the late nineteenth century, the CIO in the 1930s and 1940s, and the civil rights movement after World War II. It is how we've won all our victories. And it is also how the right came to power.[27]

As the left sociologist and noted social critic Charles Derber noted, the leading agents of significant policy change in U.S. history "have not been parties glued to the next election, but social movements that operate on the scale of decades rather than two- and four-year electoral cycles. Political parties have historically become agents of democratic change only when movements infuse the parties with their own long-term vision, moral conviction, and resources." And as current Obama adviser and fan Cornel West observed in 1990, those movements are not generally well served by attachment to "charismatic" and "liberal" candidates and identity politics. "Social motion and movements in America," West wrote, "tend to be neither rooted in nor sustained by campaigns for electoral office, *no matter how charismatic the leader. . . . Despite the symbolic and cathartic electoral victories of liberal women and people of color,* all remain thoroughly shackled by corporate priorities in the economy and in debt-ridden administrations. Under such conditions, the plight of the ill-fed, ill-clad, and ill-housed tends to get worse."[28]

Reed and Derber's point on the need for activists to concentrate first and foremost on building movement capacities is echoed in Noam Chomsky's reflections on the 2004 presidential race and by Howard Zinn's comments on the 2008 contest. By Chomsky's analysis in October 2004,

> The U.S. presidential race, impassioned almost to the point of hysteria, hardly represents healthy democratic impulses.
>
> Americans are encouraged to vote, but not to participate more meaningfully in the political arena. Essentially the election is yet another method of marginalizing the population. A huge propaganda campaign is mounted to get people to focus on these personalized quadrennial extravaganzas and to think, "That's politics." But it isn't. It's only a small part of politics.
>
> The urgent task for those who want to shift policy in progressive direction—often in close conformity to majority opinion—is to grow and become strong enough so that they can't be ignored by centers of power. Forces for change that have come up from the grass roots and shaken the society to its foundations include the labor movement, the civil rights movement, the peace movement, the women's movement and others, cultivated by steady, dedicated work at all levels, everyday, not just once every four years. . . .
>
> So in the election, sensible choices have to be made. But they are secondary to serious political action. The main task is to create a genuinely responsive democratic culture, and that effort goes on before and after electoral extravaganzas, whatever their outcome.[29]

Three and a half years later, during the height of the Obama phenomenon, Zinn made a similar case against the "election madness" he saw "engulfing the entire society, including the left," with special intensity:

> [The election frenzy] seizes the country every four years because we have all been brought up to believe that voting is crucial in determining our destiny, that the most important act a citizen can engage in is to go to the polls and choose one of the two mediocrities who have already been chosen for us. . . .
>
> And sad to say, the Presidential contest has mesmerized liberals and radicals alike. . . .
>
> . . . I'm not taking some ultra-left position that elections are totally insignificant, and that we should refuse to vote to preserve our moral purity. Yes, there are candidates who are somewhat better than others, and at certain times of national crisis (the Thirties, for instance, or right now) where even a slight difference between the two parties may be a matter of life and death.

> I'm talking about a sense of proportion that gets lost in the election madness. Would I support one candidate against another? Yes, for two minutes—the amount of time it takes to pull the lever down in the voting booth.
>
> But before and after those two minutes, our time, our energy, should be spent in educating, agitating, organizing our fellow citizens in the workplace, in the neighborhood, in the schools. Our objective should be to build, painstakingly, patiently but energetically, a movement that, when it reaches a certain critical mass, would shake whoever is in the White House, in Congress, into changing national policy on matters of war and social justice.
>
> Let's remember that even when there is a "better" candidate (yes, better Roosevelt than Hoover, better anyone than George Bush), that difference will not mean anything unless the power of the people asserts itself in ways that the occupant of the White House will find it dangerous to ignore. . . .
>
> Today, we can be sure that the Democratic Party, unless it faces a popular upsurge, will not move off center. The two leading Presidential candidates have made it clear that if elected, they will not bring an immediate end to the Iraq War, or institute a system of free health care for all.
>
> They offer no radical change from the status quo.
>
> They do not propose what the present desperation of people cries out for: a government guarantee of jobs to everyone who needs one, a minimum income for every household, housing relief to everyone who faces eviction or foreclosure.
>
> They do not suggest the deep cuts in the military budget or the radical changes in the tax system that would free billions, even trillions, for social programs to transform the way we live.
>
> None of this should surprise us. The Democratic Party has broken with its historic conservatism, its pandering to the rich, its predilection for war, only when it has encountered rebellion from below, as in the Thirties and the Sixties.[30]

One can bemoan the failure of Obama, Hillary, John Edwards, and other leading Democrats to speak honestly and forcefully in accord with the U.S. populace's demand for a rapid end to the occupation of Iraq. The simple harsh and cold fact of the matter is that the antiwar movement in the United States has not developed the capacity to hold Democratic or other politicians and elected officials' feet to the fire in ways that the party and those officials have to respect in accord with their top priorities of getting elected and staying in office. Peace activists lack structures and active constituencies strong enough to make Democrats accountable. They lack the power and the organized "rebellion from below" to compel leading politicians to reconsider their commitment and captivity to the powerful entrenched interests and broader culture of imperial militarism.

Building rebellions, progressive power, and capacity beneath and beyond the election cycle is a more worthy endeavor than joining an election campaign (as I did in 2007) or picketing the offices of particularly egregious elected Democratic war supporters. It is a more productive progressive project than accusing Democratic officials and politicians of betraying progressive values they may or may not share and that (in any event) do not serve their interests under the existing political system, or (à la Lakoff) of failing to adequately "frame" the progressive issues. The same point can and should be made not just for Iraq but also for numerous other and related issues of special concern to left progressives: women's rights, climate change, economic justice, racial equality, and so on. On these and other issues and on their totality, there is no independent left in the United States worthy of its name.

Here liberal and progressives can learn from the right, which has prefaced its "conservative" (arch-regressive, authoritarian, hyperplutocratic, and messianic-militaristic) takeover of U.S. politics and policy since 1980 with the creation of energetic social movements linked to evangelical religion and corporations and speaking to the working class.[31] "While leftists sit around congratulating themselves on their personal virtue," Thomas Frank rightly observed in 2004, "the right understands the central significance of movement-building, and they have taken on the task with admirable diligence." As Frank wrote,

> Cast your eyes over the vast and complex structure of conservative "movement culture," a phenomenon that has little left-wing counterpart anymore. There are foundations . . . there are think tanks . . . a brigade of lobbyists. A flock of magazines and newspapers. A publishing house or two. And, at the bottom, the committed grassroots organizers . . . going door to door, organizing their neighbors, mortgaging their houses, even, to push the gospel of the [conservative] backlash. And this movement speaks to those at society's bottom, addresses them on a daily basis. From the left they hear nothing, but from the Cons they get an explanation for it all.[32]

3. Rebuilding the Labor Movement

This should be a high priority for moderate and center as well as left progressives. As liberal political scientists Jacob S. Hacker and Paul Pierson argued, "Perhaps no single social change would do more to reverse the off-center tilt of contemporary politics than a revitalization of the American labor movement." Organized labor, whose pronounced decline in the United States is not an "inevitable" result of technical or economic trends (it is largely the result of sheer business hostility and right-wing politics and policy), was the leading institutional mechanism both for checking managerial power in the workplace and for pooling and exercising the social power and capital of working people to counter the regressive business policy agenda on a national scale. It is no mere coincidence that the nation's dangerous and authoritarian shift to a far-right-leaning politics and policy[33] has occurred while union membership has been pushed back toward historic lows.

4. Tactical Voting: "Sensible Choices" Should Be Made" Since It's Coke v. Crack, Not Coke v. Pepsi

My emphasis above on day-to-day movement building (and rebuilding) is hardly an argument for boycotting the ballot box. Contrary to Reed's suggestion that progressives "sit this one"—the 2008 election, that is—"out," Chomsky's argument that "sensible [voting] choices" should be made even within the narrow parameters of the American electoral system still warrants heeding. It is critical to remember that seemingly "small" ideological and policy differences between the two dominant U.S. political parties (typically derided as "Coke v. Pepsi" on the U.S. left), and even between candidates within the same leading party, can matter a great deal.[34] They especially matter to those on the wrong side of American hierarchy and policy—within highly concentrated power systems like the one that exists in the United States—where, as Zinn says, "even a slight difference between the parties may be a matter of life and death."

The need to make "sensible" choices is particularly urgent, Chomsky argues, when "one of the two groups now contending for power happens to be extremist and dangerous, and has already caused plenty of trouble and could cause plenty more." As Chomsky noted on the eve of the 2004 election, "Bush and his administration are publicly committed to dismantling and destroying whatever progressive legislation and social welfare has been won by popular struggles over the past century. Internationally, they are calling for dominating the world by force, including even the 'ownership of space' to expand monitoring and first-strike capabilities.'" That's why Chomsky argued that "if you are in a swing state, you should vote to keep the worst guys [the Republicans] out."[35]

Chomsky's counsel holds true in 2008. The presumptive Republican nominee (as of March 2008) John McCain is committed without ambivalence to the continuation of the Iraq occupation. He falsely conflates that illegal invasion with the U.S. global "war on terror," rejects discussion of timetables for withdrawal, and even suggests the possibility of U.S. troops staying in Iraq for fifty to a hundred years. He proposes to start a new Cold War with Russia and China. He was videotaped singing "Bomb, Bomb, Bomb, Bomb, Bomb, Iran" (to the tune of the Beach Boys' classic pop tune "Barbara Anne") during a 2007 town hall meeting in New Hampshire, and is strongly identified with militarism and Bush's regressive tax cuts for the privileged few. He has advanced blatant falsehoods about the "opposition party's" (the Democrats') policy agenda (absurdly accusing the Democrats of supporting the supposed hideous evil of "socialized medicine") and continues the Republicans' ugly tradition of selling their militantly plutocratic policy goals as the politics of the middle and working classes.

Like all the other leading Republican presidential candidates, McCain can be counted on to defund social programs for the poor, roll back (yet further) government protections for workers and unions, and slash needed regulations on business. He will defy and block the urgent popular demand for universal health insurance.

Again we have the same grim quadrennial reality. The Democratic Party, putting forth a centrist candidate for the White House, may again be what many left progressives rightly consider corporate-neoliberal "Coke." Even the mild (from a left perspective) populism of John Edwards (who could not even join Kucinich in calling for single-payer health insurance)—the party's most genuinely progressive viable candidate—was too much for the elite corporate and financial interests behind the party system's "hidden primary" of wealth and power. But once again the Republicans (who had the common sense to advance their most electable contender) *are worse than mere corporate* "Pepsi." They are more like hyper-reactionary and significantly neoconservative (and arguably even protofascistic) "crack."[36] They continue to pose dangerous and extremist threats to basic democratic principles and institutions and to elementary social programs achieved through decades of popular struggle.

There's more than "a dime's worth of difference" between the Republicans and the Democrats, not because the latter party is particularly left but because the former is so alarmingly far to the right.

The progressive's duty (I think) to not "sit out" the presidential election, to vote to block the GOP's presidential candidate in swing states at least, is about more than reducing harm at home and abroad. It's also and simultaneously about creating a more favorable political and policy environment with more breathing space to advance progressive goals and movement capacities. When progressive activists are constantly fighting rearguard battles against the truly outrageous and extremist policies of an in-power hard right, they have little time or energy to advance their positive objectives and build their strength. At the same time, the Democratic Party is more effectively exposed as captive to corporate and imperial interests when it holds power and has to put the rubber of its real-world agenda and commitments—generally well to the right of its campaign rhetoric (especially its *primary campaign* rhetoric)—on the road of policy. It's harder for the Democrats to pose as a "left" opposition party when they actually hold office.

5. Bring Back Class: Outrage Makes Sense

Thomas Frank (in 2004) and Obama (in April 2008) were wrong to single out white working-class voters as being especially prone to privilege cultural issues (abortion, guns, and gay rights) over material concerns and economic issues. But Frank was correct to note that Democrats have lost white working- and lower-class voters to the GOP and to nonvoting because of an overly business-friendly reluctance to embrace the fighting and populist "class language that once distinguished [the Democrats] sharply from the Republicans."[37] Over numerous recent elections, the Democrats seem to have naively assumed that poor and working-class whites will have nowhere else to go but to the party that "obviously" serves and advances the interests of labor and the poor.

The deeply wrong assumption here is that the Democratic Party can count on white proletarian voters no matter what and is therefore free to abandon populist discourse and commitment and direct its rhetoric and agenda almost entirely toward the more affluent and culturally elite end of the socioeconomic spectrum. No need to get down in the trenches and address the real-life material and moral-economic concerns of the increasingly "outraged" working-class majority, or the intimate relationship between that majority's declining situation and the wealth and power of the privileged few! As Frank noted on the eve of the 2004 debacle of the patrician centrist John Kerry,

> Democratic political strategy simply assumes that people know where their economic interest lies and that they will act on it by instinct. There is no need for any business-bumming class-war rhetoric on the part of candidates or party spokesmen, and there is certainly no need for a liberal to actually get his hands dirty fraternizing with the disgruntled. Let them look at the record and see for themselves: Democrats are slightly more generous with Social Security benefits, slightly stricter on environmental regulations, and do less union-busting than Republicans.[38]

Bad assumption! If Obama gets the nomination, he must be relentlessly reminded that this is a losing as well as a morally vapid approach. He must be pushed to dump his "doctorly" and "professorial" attachment to interclass harmony and start talking and acting more in the "fighting" and "angry" John Edwards mode (who was killed in the primaries by corporate money and media power, not by unpopularity with working-class voters), and he must do this as a defender of working people in their venerable struggle with the rich and powerful.[39] As the old labor tune asks, "Which side are you on?" Obama needs to be made to understand that working-class "outrage" actually *makes* an enormous amount of *sense,* politically as well as morally. Failure to understand this will significantly increase his likelihood of becoming another Dukakis or John "Not a Redistribution Democrat" Kerry—an excessively aristocratic centrist who could not win because he lacked the working-class votes needed to defeat the Republicans.

6. Elevate Issues above Candidates

In late April 2008 a Yahoo–Associated Press poll reported that considerable numbers of Hillary Clinton supporters would vote for John McCain over Obama if their candidate didn't win the nomination. The same was true on the other side of an increasingly bitter and ugly Democratic contest.[40] This was profoundly ironic given the widely noticed fact that Mrs. Clinton and Obama—both centrists—were almost indistinguishable from one another on the moral-ideological and policy spectrums. It was also disturbing in its implications for the future of the nation and the world, if one accepts my judgment that the Republicans are "crack," not "Pepsi," and that it matters in policy terms to block the GOP. Those who share that judgment should find it childishly irresponsible for Democrats to privilege personal candidate likes or dislikes and identity over issues in making their voting decisions this November. No self-respecting Democrat, left or moderate, should be voting for McCain because of a personal dislike for Hillary or Obama, given the existence of relevant "life and death" policy differences—however narrow from a left perspective—between the Democrats and the GOP.

7. Reject Savior-Wish and Race Guilt to Keep the Pressure on a (Possible) Obama Administration

One of the dangers of an Obama administration is that a considerable number of his supporters seem overly attached to Him (the capitalization is intentional), something that may unduly discourage them from acting to keep citizen pressure on the White House. Here it is worth recalling Adolph Reed's dictum that "elected officials are only as good or as bad as the forces they feel they must respond to" and Obama's own repeated observation that real change comes "from the bottom up."

It is one thing to make a tactical decision to support one of the two major party candidates as the least objectionable and most relatively progressive. It's another thing altogether to see the chosen candidate as "the one we have been waiting for"—a quasi-messianic personality whose ascendancy amounts to some sort of millennial moment or revolution in and of itself. With Obama, it's especially important for American voters to remember the wisdom of a comment made by Tariq Ali and Anthony Arnove in regard to the Iraq occupation in 2006: "We can't look to saviors from on high to get us out of this mess. . . . We have to do it ourselves."[41]

A related but different danger is that a considerable portion of the nation's progressive base would feel inhibited about engaging in serious confrontation with an Obama administration because of Obama's status as the nation's first black president and/or by the illusion that he must be especially progressive because he's black. Here it is important to remember both Aurora Levins Morales's point about the power elite's "cleverness" in putting forth candidates (Hillary Clinton and Obama) who "will be attacked in ways that make oppressed people feel compelled to protect them" and John Pilger's warning that an Obama victory will compel American "antiwar and social justice movements to accept a Democratic administration for all its faults" and to thereby silence "domestic resistance" to "rapacious" U.S. policies.[42]

Bearing in mind that a black Democratic president may feel compelled to be more conservative than a white Democratic president, and that an Obama presidency would likely come with real downsides for the cause of racial justice (it would certainly encourage many whites to falsely conclude that anti-black racism had been completely swept into the dustbin of history), citizens and activists should feel just as free to march—for, say, an immediate withdrawal from Iraq, and/or national health insurance—on an Obama White House as they would to protest a John Edwards, Hillary Clinton, or Joe Biden White House. The same point stands for gender and a potential Clinton II administration.

8. Call for Electoral Reform

Reed and Zinn were certainly right to argue that progressives should reject unrealistic expectations about existing electoral politics and organize to force change from below, consistent with the lessons of past social movements. But is there nothing that could be done that would make it possible for an ambitious politico—another future Obama, so to speak—to see where his or her sense of "good" self-interested political "decision making" might be more positively aligned with progressive ideals and agendas? As it happens, there's quite a bit that might be introduced in that regard, proposed by progressive electoral reformers whose interesting ideas have long included the following important proposals:

- Take private money out of public elections through the full mandatory equal and public financing of federal campaigns.
- Introduce proportional representation in the election of state and congressional representatives.
- Provide extra public resources and public access—a form of political-party affirmative action—for third, fourth, and fifth parties that have been discriminated against in the past.

- Introduce a parliamentary system whereby the chief executive is selected by and ultimately subordinated to the representative branch of government.
- If a presidential system remains, introduce "instant run-off" voting—a mechanism permitting third and fourth parties to avoid functioning as "spoilers" by requiring that winners must receive at least 50 percent of the total vote. Let all voters mark their second and third favorite choices, and hold an instant run-off between the top candidates until one candidate secures at least 50 percent plus one.
- Permit "fusion" voting, whereby voters are free to support a major-party candidate in the name of their own favorite third (or fourth, etc.) party.
- Mandate free media advertisements for all candidates.
- Remove candidate debates from private media corporations and hand them over to publicly funded, publicly elected, and publicly overseen citizens committees.
- Activate antitrust laws to break up the current corporate media oligopoly and distribute political news and information across a broader and more diverse range of print and media outlets.
- Require media campaign coverage to spend a designated relevant and disproportionate amount of time on policy and ideological differences between and among candidates and parties.

Introducing the top reforms suggested above, it should be acknowledged, would almost certainly require a constitutional amendment. However they were pursued and implemented, these would be meaningful changes and should be consistently advanced by progressives. All of them are consistent with Obama's recurrent call for Americans to act to change not just policies but also the very process and nature of U.S. politics itself.

Only their enactment could tell us how much democratic difference they could make short of the "fundamental social change" (Chomsky) required to produce a democratic society and politics. Remembering that reform and revolution are not mutually exclusive and that progressives can and must "chew gum and walk at the same time," we must not do one and not the other. One can simultaneously advocate political reform and share King's call for "the radical reconstruction of society itself."[43]

9. Surf the Obama Wave

It is possible to be highly critical of Obama from his left and still find progressive hope in the Obama phenomenon. At the most basic level, there is the simple fact that, as David Moberg noted, "campaigns often fail to foretell presidential policies. Centrist candidate Franklin Roosevelt shifted to the left. Centrist candidate Bill Clinton shifted to the right. . . . An energized constituency could push Obama's centrist economic plan to the left."[44]

That's true enough, but it tells us nothing in particular about the distinctive nature of "the Obama phenomenon." The single most flattering thing that can be said about the Obama experience, by my observation—and this is no small praise, in my opinion—is that it has encouraged an extraordinary amount of new popular engagement in the political process, sparking millions of Americans to overcome their endemic disgust with politics and their sense of powerlessness within the U.S. sociopolitical order. One chant frequently heard at Obama rallies—"Yes, We Can"—is not to be taken lightly. It is a very welcome sentiment to hear, and Obama deserves credit for encouraging it in an often eloquent and inspiring way.

In the previous chapters of this book I have suggested that Obama has ridden, reflected, and raised popular expectations for democratic transformation that an Obama White House would be likely to largely disappoint. But that likelihood need not be a source of dark dismay and depression for those who remain attached to progressive ideals. Such disappointment carries potentially progressive consequences that might help move citizens off what Derber aptly calls "The Election Trap"—the belief that serious progressive change is mainly about voting[45]—and into the significant work (Chomsky's "main task") of building the sorts of grassroots and political movements that have previously "shaken society to its foundations."[46] It could also fuel popular demands for changing the political system in such a way that electoral hopes could become less of a "trap."

As an anonymous "progressive economist" told David Moberg, "the fact that [Obama is] raising hope, that's tremendously important. . . . Bill Clinton's genius was lowering expectations. But revolutions, historian Barrington Moore argued, come when there are rising expectations."[47]

Perhaps nobody has captured my own sentiments on the dialectical sort of hope that can be meaningfully drawn from the prospect of an Obama presidency better than *Left Business Observer* editor and author Doug Henwood. In an April 2008 essay entitled "Would You Like Change with That?" Henwood criticized Obama's subservience to big capital, his militarism, his disingenuous claims to be against the Iraq War, his "empty" slogans, his allegedly vapid "fan club" ("he doesn't really have a movement behind him"), and his denial of the extent of racial inequality in the United States. But then Henwood shifted gears to think more deeply and positively, and in historically informed terms, about the potential upside of the Obama phenomenon:

> Enough critique; the dialectic demands something constructive to induce some forward motion. There's no doubt that Obamalust does embody some phantasmic longing for a better world—more peaceful, egalitarian, and

> humane. He'll deliver little of that—but there's evidence of some admirable popular desires behind the crush. And they will inevitably be disappointed.
>
> . . . There's great political potential in popular disillusionment with Democrats. The phenomenon was first diagnosed by Garry Wills in *Nixon Agonistes*. As Wills explained it, throughout the 1950s, left-liberals intellectuals [*sic*] thought that the national malaise was the fault of Eisenhower, and a Democrat would cure it. Well, they got JFK and everything still pretty much sucked, which is what gave rise to the rebellions of the 1960s (and all that excess that Obama wants to junk any remnant of). You could argue that the movements of the 1990s that culminated in Seattle were a minor rerun of this. The sense of malaise and alienation is probably stronger now than it was 50 years ago, and includes a lot more of the working class, [who are] . . . really pissed off about the cost of living and the way the rich are lording it over the rest of us.
>
> Never did the possibility of disappointment offer so much hope. That's not what the candidate means by that word, but history can be a great ironist.[48]

Personally ambitious corporate- and empire-captive Democrats like Barack Obama (or Hillary Clinton or John F. Kerry or Bill Clinton or Jimmy Carter or Michael Dukakis) are better able to pose as progressive alternatives to corporate-imperial regimes when out of office than when in power. They are more effectively exposed as inadequate tribunes of the people when they hold outward public power and fail to deliver on popular hopes and dreams they've ridden and/or raised on the road to power. Keeping their eyes on the prize of movement-building between and across the "quadrennial extravaganzas," voters of popular and democratic sentiments would do well to block the GOP and get Obama into the White House, and then to push as hard as they can for his administration and the government more broadly to do the sorts of things that should be expected of Democratic officeholders and candidates who call themselves "progressive."

Obama can surf the people, but the inverse is true as well. Perhaps progressive activists and citizens can escape the clutches of Obamanist "repressive de-sublimation"—the containment and exploitation of their hope and anger to re-legitimize dominant oppression structures and ideologies—by riding and steering the Obama wave into places (both within and beyond electoral politics) closer to progressive ideals. Like earlier Democratic presidencies, an Obama White House will almost certainly fail to deliver on progressive, populist, and peaceful-sounding promises made to the populace. There is radical potential in the confrontation between that likely failure and the popular expectations ridden, channelled, aroused, and contained by Obama in his quest for power.[49] The energy and hopes lifted will need new and better, more genuinely egalitarian, liberating, and antiauthoritarian outlets than an Obama candidacy and (perhaps) presidency can provide, consistent with the fact that most Americans actually oppose Dr. King's "triple evils" (and other American "evils," too) in ways that point beyond the limited parameters of existing U.S. political culture.

10. Call for Radical Change

In trying to work creatively with the Obama moment, people engaged in progressive political action should not be afraid of demanding something along the lines of revolution. King's 'radical reconstruction of society itself' and the related drastic reordering of national and global priorities is a matter of increasing urgency and indeed survival for the democratic ideal and for sustainable human existence.[50] "Reforms will not suffice," and capitalism and democracy are two very different and indeed fundamentally opposed beasts.[51] At the same time, reforms—including, I would add, electoral reforms—are necessary. And they are not generally won unless and until governing classes and power elites are convinced that the price of not bending the system is greater than the cost of change.

Obama might talk about the "reformist" and not the revolutionary nature of the "American political tradition," but that tradition was born in revolution, and the leading reforms introduced in modern U.S. history have often come in response to elite fears of audacious rebellion by aroused "citizens, not politicians."[52]

The Obama phenomenon portrayed in this volume is hardly about the introduction of the "radical reconstruction" that is ultimately and (I think) urgently required. Quite to the contrary, it seems to represent a contemporary triumph of corporate-sponsored conservatism on what passes for the "left" on the shockingly narrow party and ideological spectrums that characterize U.S. political culture. Still, this does not mean that the phenomenon in question is without dialectical complexity and radical potential for the future of American politics. What it shall become and produce in subsequent months and years is still an open matter, subject to historical contingency and social contestation, with outcomes I would not pretend to possess the capacity to foretell.

Imagining a Progressive Future

As I penned this Afterword on June 7 of 2008, Barack Obama had just the previous night secured the Democratic nomination for the presidency. The historic nature of his enshrinement as the first black presidential nominee of a major U.S. political party was the leading story in major U.S news media. The nation and indeed the world buzzed with the news that the long Democratic contest was finally over. Obama's "improbable quest" had in less than four years brought him from the backbenches of the Illinois State Assembly to within one election of the highest office atop the most powerful nation in the world. The story of this remarkable occurrence was ubiquitous—along with Obama's visage and video splices from his victory speech before eighteen thousand raucous fans in Saint Paul, Minnesota's Xcel Energy Center—across American television and computer screens. It was an exceptional and, for many, vaguely unreal accomplishment for an individual who had been a virtually unknown state senator just four years earlier. I had expected Obama to be the 2008 Democratic presidential nominee since mid-November of 2004, but this was considered an eccentric prediction before Obama won the Iowa primary on a cold and snowy day in early January of 2008.

"Because He's Black"

Still, Obama's path to the White House seemed in some ways more perilous in early June than it did January and February of 2008. Obama won just six of the thirteen Democratic primaries between March 4 and May 27. He received 6.1 million votes, compared to 6.6 million for Hillary during that period.[1] In the last major matchup poll pitting the two nominees against each other, conducted by the Gallup Poll at the end of April, McCain won by six points, 48 to 42 percent.[2] The "Obama phenomenon" seemed to have lost no small measure of its luster since the heady days of January and February.

The major reason was quite simply the politics of race and class. Exit polls in March, April, and May of 2008 showed Clinton beating Obama with Caucasian voters, particularly whites without college degrees. Clinton garnered 64 percent of the white vote in Ohio and 63 percent in Pennsylvania.[3] She won more than two-thirds of white voters without college degrees in Pennsylvania, North Carolina, and Indiana.

In mid-May of 2008, Clinton won predominantly (94 percent) white West Virginia by a whopping margin of 67 to 26 percent.[4] Obama received support from less than a third of West Virginia Democratic primary voters from homes earning $50,000 or less—a group that made up more than half of the state's households.[5]

Obama's general election prospects didn't get much better on May 20 of 2008. That's when Obama lost predominantly (90 percent) white Kentucky to Clinton by 35 points (65 to 30 percent). Obama received 23 percent of the state's white Democratic vote and was backed by just one in five Kentucky Democratic voters living in rural area and small towns.[6]

The racially polarized results from Ohio, Indiana, Pennsylvania, North Carolina, West Virginia, and Kentucky spoke less to dreams of a "post-racial" future than to the living nightmare of a still heavily racialized past and present.[7] They stood in cruelly ironic relation to the Obama campaign's efforts—covered in some detail in the third chapter of this book—to run a "race-neutral" campaign that went to great lengths to downplay the relevance of racism in American life and politics.

As her chances for the nomination dwindled yet further last May, Mrs. Clinton ruffled politically correct feathers by telling *USA Today* that "I have a much broader base to build a winning coalition on." Clinton cited an Associated Press report "that showed," she said, "how Senator Obama's support among working, hardworking Americans, *white Americans* [emphasis added], is weakening again, and how whites in both states who had not completed college degrees were supporting me. . . . These are the people you have to win," Clinton added, with no small justice, ". . . to actually win the election."[8] Meanwhile, Clinton continued to mimic timeworn Republican "culture war" talking points against Obama by pressing her claim—which was highly ironic given her own strong corporate connections and corporate-neoliberal agenda, along with the fact that she was wealthy enough to lend her own campaign many millions of dollars—that he was too culturally "elitist" to win working-class votes.[9]

The nationally syndicated black *Chicago Tribune* columnist and frequent television commentator Clarence Page was (understandably) offended by the former First Lady's suggestion "that [Obama's] supporters are not hard-working enough, white enough, or undereducated enough." Still, Page admitted that "she has a point . . . she's right to observe that Obama has a challenge ahead in winning white [working-class] swing voters" who wonder "whether a candidate is on their side."[10]

According to Ed Sarpolus, a pollster with the Michigan Education Association, in late April of 2008, Obama lacked a compelling "working-class message." This, and not "race," Sarpolous told the black journalist Ellis Cose, was the main source of the bourgeois Obama's increasingly evident difficulties with working-class whites.[11]

The allegation of bourgeois elitism was at least partly Obama's own doing. It had become especially potent after early March, *Time* magazine reporter Karen Tumulty reminds us, when Obama arrogantly described "bitter" working-class "small town" whites as "narrow-minded, churchgoing, gun nuts" (in Tumulty's words) while speaking "at a private [San Francisco] fundraiser where the rich and powerful gather[ed] for shrimp and special access."[12]

Obama tried to blunt the charge of elitism by telling the story of his supposedly under-privileged upbringing and referring to himself as a "skinny guy with a funny-sounding name from the South Side of Chicago" (his repeated self-description throughout the campaign). This was his version of the "log cabin" mythology that has been part of American presidential political culture since the 1830s.[13]

It isn't very convincing to those with a substantive grasp on his biography. Obama may be thin and possess an "unusual" (for an American) name, but he is not really "*from* the South Side of Chicago"—an urban identification that has long carried a strong working-class feel to it.[14] He is from a highly educated middle-class background in Hawaii, and he passed through a number of elite private schools, including Columbia University and no less august a ruling-class finishing academy than Harvard Law. As leading Republican strategist Karl Rove (a reactionary operative with a keen eye for class factors) noted in a public letter to Obama in early May of 2008: "You argue that the son of a single working mom can't be an elitist. But it's not where you start in life; it's where you end up. After a prestigious prep school, Columbia, and Harvard, you've ended up with the values of Cambridge, San Francisco, and Hyde Park. So you're doing badly in Scranton, Youngstown, and Erie, where ordinary Americans live."[15]

Still, Obama's claim to reporters in April that "if I lose, it would not be because of race"[16] was certainly largely incorrect. If he fails to defeat Republican John McCain despite critical trends favoring a Democratic candidate (economic recession, rising prices, and a failed foreign policy in Iraq, above all), in November 2008 it will be largely and perhaps mainly because of race. As John Judis noted in *The New Republic* at the end of May 2008, the racial voting trends were a real cause for Democratic Party concern:

> Clearly Obama gained some votes in the early primaries from college-educated [white] Democrats who liked the idea of an African American transcending the historic conflict over race. And, if he had not been running against a popular female candidate, he might have won more support among white women. But Obama also lost voters to racial prejudice.
>
> . . . . The percentage of voters who backed Hillary Clinton (or, earlier, John Edwards) while saying that the "race of the candidates" was "important" in deciding their vote is a fair proxy for the percentage of primary voters who were disinclined to support Obama *because he is black* [emphasis added]. That number topped 9 percent in New Jersey; in Ohio and Pennsylvania, two crucial swing states, it was more than 11 percent. And that's among Democratic primary voters, who are, on average, more liberal than the Democrats who vote in general elections.[17]

Taking into account also Obama's considerable difficulties with Asian and Latino as well as white voters, Judis's reading of the latest social science literature on the political psychology of race led him to conclude that the simple fact of being African American would cost Obama the general election votes of 15 to 20 percent of the nation's Democrats and Democrat-leaning Independents.[18]

It didn't help Obama's chances of overcoming white voters' racial biases that the corporate media kept the controversy surrounding the senator's relationship with Rev. Wright alive into early May and, perhaps, beyond. As Clarence Page observed, "concerns about Wright" are "certain to return in attack ads in the fall if Obama becomes the nominee." The lingering Wright affair helped bring Obama's "approval ratings down," Page wrote, "to those of mortal people."[19]

It did this primarily by undermining his effort to appear to have "transcended race." The media-led Wright melodrama linked Obama to the toxic stereotype of the hostile and "unpatriotic" African American, threatening to turn Obama into a "black candidate" like Jesse Jackson, Sr., or Al Sharpton. It damaged his ability to appeal to white liberals, Democrats, and Independents with what Adolph Reed, Jr., called "the 'I'm black in a different way than Jesse' qualifier."[20] The Republicans can be expected to resurrect Reverend Wright and to otherwise play the race card (along with the military, nationalist, "moral values," class, and National Security cards) between now and the first Tuesday in November of 2008.

The historical trends are daunting. The Democratic Party's presidential candidates have not won a majority of white voters for more than thirty years.[21] Race has been a big problem for white Democratic presidential candidates since 1948, raising the disturbing question of how bad a problem it will be for an actually black—however "different than Jesse"—Democratic presidential nominee.[22]

Even if Obama wins the election, we can expect race and racism to challenge an Obama White House's ability to govern effectively and in a progressive, popular, and reform-oriented fashion. "Race," really racism, has long been a critical underlying enforcer of conservatism, popular division, and top-down class rule across the broad sweep of U.S. history.[23]

Imagining a Real "Change" Presidency

But let us turn to happier thoughts, accepting the possibility that enough white U.S. voters have now overcome toxic racial prejudice to permit Obama to win the nation's highest office and to perhaps proceed—with some help from popular pressure—with a progressive agenda. Now that Obama has (barely) fended off the Clinton challenge to stand against the unusually aged candidate of a badly damaged and itself divided Republican Party, an interesting question arises. What would a "truly" and "deeply" progressive Obama administration—one willing to take on the interrelated evils of corporate domination, militarism, authoritarianism, repression, and social injustice—do in accord with democratic and egalitarian ideas that are widely (if somewhat secretly) popular in the United States and to which the Obama campaign gave some superficial voice during the primary campaign?[24]

Forget for a moment the "cynical" account of Obama's conservative, power-conciliating record and trajectory presented in the preceding chapters. Put all that aside briefly and go along with the (I think) naïve thesis that he is a stealth "true" and "deeply progressive" candidate who will spring his hidden and actually populist and left-democratic agenda on America and the world once he enters the halls of executive power. What sorts of policies and ideas would a real "change"-oriented Obama administration seek to advance? Here's my short list,[25] hardly original,[26] of what would be included in such an *imagined* agenda. Even if Obama doesn't win, this list also comprises a (I hope) useful compendium of things that could and should be advanced by any true "change" president of the future:

1. Executive Leadership for the Creation of an "Active Citizens' Network"

Consistent with his claims that progressive, historical change comes from the bottom up and that government should be taken back from wealthy special interests, this President Obama would deliver a speech encouraging the formation of a national Active Citizen's Network (ACN)—a well-funded complex of "all the civil associations, nonprofits, labor unions, nongovernmental organizations (NGOs), and social movements in America to take back control of the country from big money" and "eclipse the corporations as the dominant force in America."[27] The core idea behind this network would be that citizens need to mobilize, organize, and act across elections to achieve real popular control over their work lives, business, schools, health systems, politics (including the Democratic Party), and government.

The ACN's mission would be to restore and/or introduce active and participatory democracy to American political life. It would seek to stave off what the brilliant senior political scientist Sheldon Wolin calls "the specter of inverted totalitarianism." Under the corporate-crafted system and doctrine of what Wolin terms "Democracy, Incorporated,"

> the citizenry, supposedly the source of governmental power and authority as well as a participant, has been replaced by the "electorate," that is, by voters who acquire a political life at election time. During the intervals between elections the political existence of the citizenry is relegated to a shadow-citizenship of virtual participation. Instead of participating in power, the virtual citizen is invited to have "opinions": measurable responses to questions predesigned to elicit them.

The corporate-managed "inverted totalitarianism" that passes for "democracy" in post–9/11 America finds its "culminating moment," Wolin notes, in "national elections when the attention of the nation is required to make a choice of personalities rather than a choice between alternatives." By Wolin's chilling account, "What is absent is the political, the commitment to finding where the common good lies amidst the welter of well-financed, highly organized, single-minded interests rabidly seeking governmental favors and overwhelming the practices of representative government and public administration by a sea of cash." The new corporate-totalitarian system, Wolin writes, would "survive even if the Democrats were the majority in control of both the presidency and the Congress," something that is indicated by "the timidity of current Democratic proposals for reform."[28] A president seriously committed to systemic change and deep reform (and to the notion that democratic progress comes from "the bottom up") would use his or her position to empower an active citizenry around public issues across and between elections.

2. Reconstruct the Corporation's Legal Status and Social Purpose

Consistent with his repeated call for America to embrace a new spirit of unity and togetherness that rises above self-interest and personal enrichment, the "true progressive" President Obama imagined here would use the bully pulpit of the White House to advocate the re-writing of corporate charters to require business to serve the public interest and the common good over and above the their currently legally mandated pathological pursuit of investor profit.[29] This "radical" call for public accountability would rely on curiously conservative precedents, for the leaders of the early American Republic believed that corporations were business created by government to serve the public good, not vice versa. "The earliest corporate charters," Charles Derber notes, "stated that corporations must ensure the public interest and be directly accountable to the citizens' representatives in state legislature." Building on those all-too forgotten precedents, Derber joins other progressives in calling for a new corporate charter that "legally redefine[s] big business as a public entity with three chartered missions: serve the public interest and be accountable to it; return profit to shareholders; protect workers, consumers, and other stakeholders, including the environment and democracy itself."[30] The Obama White House conceived of here would support that call.

It would also call for a Constitutional Amendment that ends the practice of granting corporations legal protections as "persons" under the First, Fourth, Fifth, Sixth, Seventh, and Fourteenth Amendments. As Derber notes, "You can have a constitution that protects real citizens or a constitution that protects corporations, but not both."[31]

As part of his determination to promote a new and true Progressive Era, this President Obama would draft laws and enact executive orders prohibiting private for-profit corporations from owning and running schools, military services, health care facilities, and the mass media. As Derber observes, "democracy and active citizenship require that public services remain public. . . . The business of the people must reside . . . in civil society and the hallowed halls of democratic government. Corporations must be constitutionally prevented from owning and running the sources of information on which democracy depends, especially the media and the educational system."[32]

3. End Big Money and Corporate Domination of U.S. Politics and Policy

Besides the full public financing of elections (practiced in most European states) and other election reforms advocated in this book's last chapter, here are some common sense democratic policy recommendations the President Obama envisioned here would advance in connection with his repeatedly proclaimed campaign desire to wrest control of government back from "the people who write the big checks" and to return it to "we the people":[33]

- Sharply restrict corporate lobbying.
- Restrict the right of corporations to draft laws governing their industries.
- Make it illegal to use shareholder funds for political reasons.

- Forbid former high-level politicians from becoming business lobbyists for ten years or more.
- Forbid current or former high-level corporate officers from sitting on commissions with regulatory power over their industries.
- Make it illegal for corporations to try to influence their employees' votes.
- Repeal "investor rights" clauses in trade agreements, which let foreign and multinational corporations sue a national government for passing environmental, safety (job and consumer), labor, and/or anti-discrimination laws.
- Prohibit the granting of subsidies to companies who do not contribute to social and ecological health.
- Institute penalties for companies that extort concessions from workers, communities, and governments by threatening to leave a city, county, state, or country.
- Break up the powerful corporate media monopoly through the vigorous enforcement of antitrust laws and the introduction of strict limits on what percentage of local and national media can be owned by single firms.
- Significantly expand public media and provide significant new public subsidies and other resources for alternative and grassroots citizens' media.

4. Counter Global Corporate Blackmail and Exit Threats

Anticipating the objection that capital is global and will just relocate to more favorable zones of the world economic system if the above measures are instituted, a "truly" and "deeply progressive" Obama presidency would advance a number of key measures to prevent transnational capital and corporations from terrorizing nations (including the United States) with the threat to leave:[34]

- Institute strong labor, environmental, and human rights protections in all existing and future trade agreements.
- Create powerful and democratic new global trade and financing authorities (replacing the WTO, IMF, and World Bank) to enforce these agreements and to generate sustained and equitable development in poor nations.
- Write and enforce new socially and ecologically responsible and public accountable global corporate charters, simultaneously enforced by the United Nations, regional authorities, and national governments.
- Tax short term speculative investment and provide preferred tax treatment for long-term global investors.

5. Transform the "Moral Values" Conversation and Honor the United Nations Declaration of Human Rights

After almost having been defeated by a Republican Party that employed (yet again) a perverse notion of "moral values"—one that denounces abortion, gun control, and gay marriage but says nothing about grotesque inequalities of wealth, mass poverty, corporate eco-cide, and mass death in immoral U.S. wars[35]—President Obama should deliver a speech that seeks to give historic redefinition to the concept of "moral values" in politics and policy. As Derber notes, meaningful post-Bush II "regime change" requires that "the debate about morality be broadened from issues of abortion and other hot-button items on the Evangelical Christian agenda to the central moral issues of social justice and human rights. Corporate morality is stripping ordinary Americans of medical care, good education, and a living wage, and creating violence and wars that violate our own moral codes and Constitution." Corporate morality is also selling sex and violence on national television, computer, and video screens in ways that are doing much to drive right-wing Evangelical counter-reaction ("backlash").[36]

Reflecting its seriousness about national reconciliation and spiritual uplift, the progressive Obama presidency visualized here would move boldly to change the "moral values" discussion. Obama would give an historic speech linking true progressive morality to the United Nations 1948 Declaration of Human Rights and the Democratic Party's previous New Deal. Obama would honor those earlier examples by concluding his instantly famous True Moral Values Address with a broad policy agenda, including legislation guaranteeing all Americans food, clothing, health care (on a single-payer basis), education, employment, union organizing rights (a "change"-oriented Obama would immediately embrace and advance the popular Employee Free Choice Act[37]), and a living wage.[38]

6. Going Deeper on Race

After establishing his populist credentials and giving his "moral values" speech, a truly and deeply progressive President Obama would give a new and updated speech on race and racism. This new historic Race Speech would abandon the often absurd racism-denying "race neutrality" that shaped his campaign.[39] It would transcend the limits of his famous March 2008 Philadelphia Race Speech critiqued in Chapter 3 of this book. It would acknowledge what other investigators and I have identified as the critical difference between "level one" (overt, conscious, explicit, and "state of mind") racism and the deeper problem of "level two" (covert, institutional, "state-of-being") racism. It would highlight and attack the deep, continuing relevance and evils of societal racism and white supremacy, and the powerful living legacy of so-called past racism. President Obama would reject his previous claim that it is needlessly divisive and destructive to talk honestly about the continuing relevance of racial oppression—deeply understood—in American life. His speech would acknowledge the potentially reactionary racial downsides of his presidency, noting that his political ascendancy might encourage many whites to wrongly conclude that racism no longer provides relevant barriers to black equality and thereby further many white Americans' tendency to over-focus on supposed black "self sabotage" in explaining why black Americans remain disproportionately concentrated at the bottom of the nation's socioeconomic and institutional hierarchies. Building on the previous insights of such great left black thinkers and activists as Frederick Douglass, W.E.B. DuBois, and Martin Luther King, Jr., it would include references to the powerful role that racism has played in dividing ordinary American working people, sustaining the plutocratic rule of the mostly white rich and powerful few, and preventing the enactment of basic social democratic policies required for the social uplift of the broad working-class majority. It would conclude with calls for the vigorous enforcement of existing Civil Rights and affirmative action laws and an ambitious new federal agenda to attack institutional racism.

The chance that such an aggressive, honest, and forthright new Race Speech and Agenda could be advanced without triggering white backlash would be enhanced by the fact that it would be preceded by, and coupled with, ongoing cross-racial initiatives against socioeconomic inequality and undue corporate power.

7. End and Reject the Iraq Occupation on Moral and Legal Grounds, Not Just Pragmatic and Strategic Grounds

Many Americans think that the illegal invasion of Iraq, leading to mass Iraqi deaths and the death and injury of tens of thousands of U.S. soldiers, is a "moral issue."[40] All of the leading Democratic presidential campaigns in 2007 and 2008 advanced "antiwar" positions that were crippled by an exaggerated fear of being attacked by the right as "defeatist" on Iraq. This fear was directly related to their refusal or inability to admit that the invasion and occupation of Iraq was criminal, immoral, imperialist, and significantly racist, not just a "strategic blunder," to use Obama's recurrent phrase. As long as Obama and other leading Democrats absurdly claim that the war was fought for the noble intentions (however "unrealistic") of spreading freedom and democracy, they will remain vulnerable to the Republican "stab-in-the-back" charge that their "defeatism" cost the United States and the Iraqi people a "victory." As a "truly" and "deeply progressive" President Obama would know, part of the way out of this significantly self-made dilemma is to acknowledge, expose, and denounce the occupation as illegal and morally wrong and to drop the imperial assumption that Iraq was "ours" to "lose" in the first place. As long as Obama and other Democrats believe (or claim to believe) that the occupation was initiated and has been enforced with "the best of intentions" and a desire to "help" Iraq and even (to use Obama's own highly disturbing words) "put it back together" (even if the occupation was a "strategic blunder"[41]), they will be (somewhat deserving) targets for the "defeatism" charge. They will also be morally ill-equipped to understand the United States' obligations to Iraq and the world community over future years—something that will reinforce the heightened terrorist risk to Americans in the wake of the U.S. foreign policy "elite's" provocative actions.

8. Renounce Empire and Big Brother

To overcome growing social inequality, rising mass poverty, moral collapse, social insecurity, and ecological crisis at home, the United States needs to stop spending half of its federal budget on a mammoth "defense" budget that maintains more than 720 foreign military bases and accounts for half the world's military spending. This vast and expensive Empire poses a grave threat to the physical and economic security and the political freedom of U.S. citizens by diverting money from social needs, provoking "anti-American" anger and "blowback" around the world and justifying attacks on civil liberties at home as well as abroad. Dr. Martin Luther King Jr. once argued that a nation approaches spiritual death when it spends billions of dollars feeding a cancerous military-industrial complex while millions of even its own children live in poverty. The "sorrows of empire" (Chalmers Johnson) include regular and severe damage to our own justly cherished civil liberties, consistent with James Madison's observation that "the fetters imposed on liberty at home have ever been forged out of the weapons for defense against real, pretended, or imaginary dangers abroad." The Alien and Sedition Acts of Madison's time, the post–World War I Red Scare, the House Un-American Activities Committee, the McCarthy era and the neo-McCarthyite Patriot Act(s) are leading examples.[42]

A "truly" and "deeply progressive" and peace-oriented Obama would do more than simply scale back and redeploy, or even completely remove, U.S. forces from one or two occupied countries (ie, Iraq and Afghanistan). He would abandon longstanding imperial U.S. commitments and doctrine and embrace the United Nations, international law, the International Criminal Court, existing nonproliferation and arms treaties, and genuinely internationalist peacekeeping and disarmament efforts. He would rescind U.S. support for such state-terrorist allies in the so-called U.S. Global War on Terror as Saudi Arabia and Columbia and he would call for the end of Israel's deadly and dangerous occupation of Palestine.[43] He would massively shift resources from the militaristic right hand of the U.S. state to the social-democratic left hand of the state, privileging social uplift, justice, and security over war, colonial occupation, and militarized state capitalism. In renouncing one key aspect of the arch-imperial Bush legacy—the illegal Iraq occupation—a "truly" and "deeply progressive" Obama presidency would go beyond conventional imperial and American Exceptionalist doctrine to oppose the colonial Iraq War on principled moral and legal grounds, not just "pragmatic" and strategic grounds. He would acknowledge that the invasion was brazenly illegal, immoral, and imperial, rescind his earlier comments to the effect that it was launched to promote democracy, and begin the process of paying massive reparations to the people and government of Iraq in partial compensation for the profound devastation the United States has imposed on that country since at least 1991.

The "homeland" benefits of such an historic shift in policy would be remarkable. As Derber notes,

> When we renounce empire, we can massively reduce U.S. spending on nuclear and conventional weapons. We can also withdraw most U.S. forces from Europe and other parts of the world, close U.S. bases abroad, and commit our forces to mainly to international and regional peacekeeping efforts under U.N. authority. By downsizing the military, we can pay down our looming debt and reinvest in social security at home. The conversion from a war economy to a peaceful one. . . will help remedy the economic and moral damage that U.S. warrior politics has caused to the rest of the world and to ourselves.[44]

As the threats of external terror attack decline with America's stand-down from provocative Empire, a "truly progressive" Obama (a former constitutional law professor) would act to repeal the Orwellian Patriot Act and its sequel. He would move aggressively to compel the federal government to stop assaulting domestic U.S. freedoms in the name of the "war on terror" or any other false pretext.

9. Fight Climate Change

A "truly progressive" Obama White House would immediately (there's no time to lose) proclaim it a leading priority for the rich nations to enact detailed plans to reduce greenhouse gas emissions by 90 percent by 2030. Targeting those reductions on the basis of the latest science, Obama's climate change plan would set a steep annual carbon cap to be met through the introduction of national carbon rationing, tough new energy efficiency requirements, new ecological planning, and the significant diversion of public money from weapons development and purchasing to the development of renewable non-nuclear energy sources, including solar, wind, and tidal.[45]

This, I repeat, is the short list.

Beyond Fiction and the Election Trap

Many readers will respond with understandable skepticism to the notion of imagining the Obama portrayed in this book aggressively pursuing any significant portion of this true progressive agenda once he entered the White House. "What is this now," I hear some readers asking, "political science fiction?"

Good question! Such skepticism is well-founded, for reasons that are hopefully less than mysterious at this point in my presentation—reasons that have less to do with Obama's character or values (whatever they may "really" be) than with the broader political culture, elections system, and power and ideological systems—by now potentially totalitarian—he inhabits and reflects.[46] Those systems do not make it terribly likely that Left-progressive intellectuals like Derber, Howard Zinn, and Noam Chomsky are going to rival centrist thinkers and functionaries like Anthony Lake, David Axelrod, and neoliberal economist Austan Goolsbee in influencing the policies of an Obama White House! Like Hillary Clinton, or any other Democrat who might have been nominated for the White House if not for the emergence of "the Obama phenomenon," a President Obama would have to be pushed in a progressive direction by dedicated, aroused, and organized citizens. At the same time, a White House actually pursuing the fantasy progressive agenda outlined above would naturally spark a remarkable corporate-imperial counter-offensive seeking to remove Obama in 2012 if not before. Let's hope the Active Citizens' Network would be up and running by the next election if not sooner!

For what it's worth in our ever-more post-democratic age—the specter of an American species of totalitarianism has never loomed as large as it has in the Bush II era[47]—we should recall that most of the proposals listed above are consistent with majority U.S. public opinion, often quite progressive and to the left of both dominant U.S. political parities on numerous critical issues.[48] This disturbing and yet potentially hopeful fact ought to turn our attention partly away from the colored lights of the next corporate-crafted and candidate-centered "quadrennial election extravaganza" to the "main task" of building alternative popular power centers and building a more genuinely responsive and democratic political culture. That task continues between and across campaign and electoral contests, "whatever their outcomes."[49]

The long-term costs of not pursuing a deeper progressive agenda (however it is politically achieved) and a more substantively democratic political system and culture are greater than the price of losing a presidential election to the significantly and yet all-too slightly less objectionable of the United States' two dominant, business-dominated and militaristic political parties. Those costs include ecological ruin, a deeper descent into corporate authoritarianism and a militarized, possibly even totalitarian politics, endless imperial war, the continuing threat of terrorist attacks, and the final collapse of serious efforts to address racial and economic inequality and poverty at home and abroad. As suggested by the Howard Zinn quote given at the beginning of this book, true progressives are ultimately more concerned with what is right and necessary for a meaningful and worthy human existence, not just what is winnable in the next election cycle. Playing by the rules of "the election trap"[50] is not going to permit us to save our democracy and create a livable planet and truly human existence in the twenty-first century.

ACKNOWLEDGMENTS

Paradigm publisher Dean Birkenkamp made numerous critical suggestions that gave this book a broader audience and deeper perspective than it would have attained without his input. Paradigm's political science editor Jennifer Knerr suggested a more historical approach to the Democratic Party.

Noam Chomsky has exercised a powerful influence over this book. His brilliant, richly informed writings, speeches, and interviews on U.S. policy, society, and political culture have helped shape my interpretation of "the Obama phenomenon."

Henry A. Giroux "discovered" my online political writings and put me into contact with Paradigm Publishers five years ago. His penetrating analysis of the politics of class and race and his warnings about the authoritarian peril in the neoliberal era have influenced my argument and narrative in this and past books.

Glen Ford of *Black Agenda Report* (*BAR*) has modeled tough critiques of Obamamania in relation to each of Dr. Martin Luther King's "triple evils." Both Ford and Bruce Dixon remind us that Obama faces powerful and significant criticism from the black Left, and they have generously opened *BAR*'s pages to my reflections on race, class, empire, and Obama.

Mike Albert, Chris Spannos, and Lydia Sargent of *ZNet* and *Z Magazine* have also provided a marvelous outlet for my writings on the same topics. Many of the ideas presented in this book were first worked out at *Z Communications.*

My brilliant and entertaining son Chris sparked me to make a surprisingly enjoyable and meaningful foray into presidential politics. He has been a regular source of information and analysis on the political scene within and beyond Iowa.

My wife Janet Razbadouski (who regularly reminds me that a bachelor's in engineering trumps a doctorate in history) offered numerous key reflections and let me know when it was time to stop thinking and talking about politics.

I am indebted to the brilliant political historian and social policy researcher Paul Kleppner for introducing me to the intersecting worlds of urban politics, racial politics, and social policy in Chicago and Illinois during the late 1990s.

My debt to the writings of Howard Zinn is apparent in nearly every chapter of this book. My debt to the work of noted Left social critic Charles Derber is obviously very high in the final chapter and Afterword.

The following writers, activists, and/or scholars have influenced my analysis and helped me remember that I am just one of many who think that real progressive change tilts well to the democratic Left of "the Obama phenomenon": John Pilger, Anthony Arnove, Alexander Cockburn, Kevin Alexander Gray, Michael Hureaux, Juan Santos, Matt Gonzales, Doug Henwood, Chris Hedges, Edward S. Herman, Adolph Reed, Jr., Marc Lamont Hill, Ted Glick, Ralph Nader, and Lance Selfa.

Nobody has sent me more supportive ideas and sources than the progressive activist Kelly Gerling.

The left sociologist Kim Scipes and the Chicago-based researcher and fellow *ZNet* writer David Peterson have shared useful reflections and sources on Obama (and related matters) with me on numerous occasions.

The Iowa City, Davenport, and Muscatine staffs and volunteers of the John Edwards Iowa campaign (Chris included) enriched my political experience and widened my angle of vision during the long lead up to the Iowa Caucus.

Copy editor Kathy Streckfus and project editor Lori Hobkirk contributed in very significant ways to the readability of this book.

Thanks to my friend and former colleague Christine Orland for her usual excellent work on the index.

My greatest debt is to Janet, who has been heroically tolerant as I wrote this manuscript under deadline at the end of a difficult year.

APPENDIX A

Americans' Progressive Policy Attitudes

For a useful summary of Americans' progressive majority opinions on key policy issues, see Katherine Adams and Charles Derber, *The New Feminized Majority* (Boulder, CO: Paradigm, 2008), pp. 67–75. As Adams and Derber suggest, a vast amount of polling data contradicts the widespread assumption that the United States is a conservative and imperialist country when it comes to the actual populace, a very different category than the nation's political and policy-making class. Here are some key poll findings mentioned in Adams and Derber's book:

- 69 percent of U.S. voters agree that "government should care for those who cannot care for themselves" (Pew Research, 2007).
- 54 percent of voters agree that "government should help the needy even if it means greater debt" (Pew Research, 2007).
- 58 percent of Americans believe the U.S. government should be doing more for its citizens, not less (National Elections Survey, 2004).
- Twice as many Americans back more government services and spending (even if this means a tax increase) as the number who support fewer services and reduced spending (National Elections Survey, 2004).
- 64 percent of Americans would pay higher taxes to guarantee health care for all U.S. citizens (CNN Opinion Research Poll, May 2007).
- 69 percent of Americans think it is the responsibility of the federal government to provide health coverage to all U.S. citizens (Gallup Poll, 2006).
- 80 percent of Americans support a government-mandated increase in the minimum wage (Associated Press/AOL Poll, December 2006).
- 86 percent of Americans want Congress to pass legislation to raise the federal minimum wage (CNN, August 2006).
- 71 percent of Americans think that taxes on corporations are too low (Gallup Poll, April 2007).
- 66 percent of Americans think taxes on upper-income people are too low (Gallup Poll, April 2007).
- 59 percent of Americans are favorable toward unions, with just 29 percent unfavorable (Gallup Poll, 2006).
- 52 percent of Americans generally side with unions in labor disputes. Just 34 percent side with management (Gallup Poll, 2006).
- 57 percent of Americans want to keep abortion legal in all or most cases (*Washington Post*/ABC News, 2007).

- 78 percent of Americans think "women should have an equal role with men in running business, industry, and government" (National Elections Survey, 2004).
- 57 percent of Americans support programs which "give special preference to qualified women and minorities in hiring" (Pew Poll, 2003).
- A majority of American voters think that the United States' "most urgent moral question" is either "greed and materialism" (33 percent) or "poverty and economic injustice" (31 percent). Just 16 percent identify abortion and 12 percent pick gay marriage as the nation's "most urgent moral question" (Zogby, 2004). Thus, nearly two-thirds (64 percent) of the population think that injustice and inequality are the nation's leading "moral issues."
- 67 percent of Americans think the U.S. should emphasize diplomatic and economic means over military methods in combating terrorism (Public Agenda and Foreign Affairs, 2007).
- Just 15 percent of Americans think the U.S. should play "the leading role in the world" (Gallup Poll. February 2007)—a remarkable rejection of U.S. global hegemony and empire.
- 58 percent of Americans think the U.S. should play "a major role but not the leading role in the world" (Gallup Poll, February 2007).
- 62 percent of Americans in September of 2007 thought the invasion of Iraq was "a mistake" (CBS News, September 2007).
- A majority of Americans want a firm deadline for U.S. withdrawal from Iraq (*Washington Post*/ABC News, February 2007).
- 70 percent of Americans want a multilateral nuclear disarmament treaty (Pew Poll, November 2005).

Here are some other relevant survey findings not reported in Adams and Derber's book:

- "When voters surveyed were asked to list the moral issue that most affected their vote, the Iraq War placed first at 42 percent, while 13 percent named abortion and 9 percent named gay marriage."[1]
- 73 percent of Americans think preventing the spread of nuclear weapons should be a very important goal of U.S. foreign policy, compared to 50 percent who think maintaining a superior military worldwide should be a very important goal (Chicago Council on Foreign Relations [hereafter "CCFR"], "Global Views," October 2004). Survival here trumps hegemony as a top global aim for citizens.
- Just 29 percent of Americans support the expansion of government spending on "defense." By contrast, 79 percent support increased spending on health care, 69 percent support increased spending on education, and 69 percent support increased spending on Social Security (CCFR, "Global Views,"2004).
- 58 percent of Americans in 2004 did not think the U.S. should have long-term military bases in Iraq (CCFR, 2004).
- 59 percent of Americans in 2004 thought the U.S. should remove its military presence form the Middle East if that's what the majority of people there want (CCFR, 2004).

- 72 percent of Americans in 2004 thought the U.S. should remove its military presence form Iraq if that's what the majority of people there want (CCFR, 2004).[2]
- To counter terrorism, 87 percent of Americans think the U.S. should work through the United Nations (UN) to strengthen international law and make sure that the UN enforces that law; 67 percent think the U.S. should work to develop poor economies; 64 percent think the U.S. should make a major effort to be even-handed in the Israel-Palestine conflict. Just 29 percent think the U.S. should use torture to extract information from terrorists. (CCFR, 2004)
- 77 percent of Americans think the U.S. has the unilateral right to go to war only if the U.S. has strong evidence it is in imminent danger of being attacked (53 percent) or (24 percent) if the other country attacks first (CCFR, 2004).
- 89 percent of Americans reject the United States' right to overthrow a government supporting terrorists who might pose a threat to the U.S. without UN approval (CCFR, 2004).
- 79 percent of Americans reject the first use of nuclear weapons and 22 percent reject the use of nuclear weapons ever (CCFR, 2004).
- Two thirds (66 percent) of Americans think the U.S. should be more willing to make international relations decisions within the UN even if this means the U.S. will sometimes have to go along with a policy that is not its first choice (CCFR, 2004).
- 59 percent of Americans favor dropping the veto power granted to the five permanent members of the UN Security Council, including the United States (CCFR, 2004).
- 57 percent of Americans favor general compliance with the decisions of the World Court, not just case-by-case (as under current U.S. policy) compliance (CCFR, 2004).
- 74 percent of Americans favor giving the UN a standing peacekeeping force selected, trained, and commanded by the UN (CCFR, 2004).
- 57 percent of Americans favor giving the UN the right to regulate the international arms trade (CCFR, 2004).
- 76 percent of Americans think the U.S. should participate in the International Criminal Court, with powers to try individual American military and other officials for war crimes even if their own country will not prosecute them of such crimes (CCFR, 2004).
- 71 percent of Americans think the U.S. should participate in the Kyoto Accord on global warming (CCFR, 2004).
- 93 percent of Americans support minimum standards in international trade agreements for working conditions and 91 percent support minimum standards for environmental protection.

APPENDIX B

Barack Obama's "Shift to the Center" in June of 2008 *(Written July 6, 2008)*

CONSISTENT WITH John Pilger's analysis,[1] Obama lurched to the right in June of 2008, well before the formal beginning of the general election campaign. His move was misleadingly reported in mainstream news media as a shift from "the left to the center." As reported by the *Los Angeles Times*, the *Wall Street Journal*, and the *New York Times*,[2] here are the leading facts that indicated his alleged shift from the portside to the "middle" of the political spectrum:

- Obama's apparent embrace of the Supreme Court ruling, invalidating a Washington, DC, ban on personal handguns and claiming that the Second Constitutional Amendment pertains to private citizens, not just organized state "militias."
- His declaration of his belief in the state's right to kill certain criminals, including child rapists.
- His decision to become the first major party presidential candidate to bypass the public presidential financing system and to reject accompanying spending limits. This violated his earlier pledge to work through the public system and accept those limits.
- His support for a refurbished spy bill that would grant retroactive immunity to telephone corporations for collaborating with the White House in the practice of electronic surveillance against American citizens. This violated his earlier pledge to filibuster any surveillance legislation containing such immunity.
- His appointment of the corporate-friendly Wal-Mart apologist and Hamilton Project[3] economist Jason Furman as his economic policy director—something that stood in curious relation to his earlier bashing ("I won't shop there") of Wal-Mart's low-wage practices.
- His increased emphasis on himself as a supporter of "free trade," something that seemed to contradict his campaign-trail criticism of the North American Free Trade Agreement (NAFTA).
- His "tweaking" of his claim that he would meet with Iran's president (he added new and more restrictive conditions)
- His embrace (in a speech to the powerful pro-Israel lobby American Israel Public Affairs Committee—AIPAC) of Bush-McCain rhetoric on the

supposed Iranian nuclear threat and his related promise to do "anything" to protect the military occupation, apartheid, and nuclear state of Israel from Iran (a nation previously attacked by Israel).

- His call (in his AIPAC speech) for an "undivided" Israel-run Jerusalem, despite the fact that no government on the planet (and not even the Bush administration) supports Israeli's right to annex that UN-designated international city.[4]
- His latest statements on "combat troop" withdrawal from Iraq, indicating that an Obama White House would maintain the immoral and illegal U.S. occupation of that country for an indefinite period.

In addition, there were reports that Obama asked Robert Gates, George W. Bush's hawkish, hard right defense secretary, to stay on into an Obama administration.[5] Obama also came out in a major speech on behalf of a major part of the Republican agenda: the granting of public money to private religious organizations to provide basic social services for disadvantaged Americans.[6] And Obama endorsed the conservative white male Blue Dog Democratic Congressman John Barrow (D-GA) over the progressive black female challenger Regina Thomas in a July 15 primary.[7]

There was a problem with the "shift to the center" narrative that characterized dominant media reporting on these rightward moves. Obama was already positioned well to the corporate- and Empire-friendly "middle" well before all of these recent developments. And some of the supposed "shift to the center" moves were directly continuous with earlier parts of his career. He was a defender of the death penalty during his career in the Illinois State Assembly (1997–2004). He had never been a strong gun control advocate and stayed noticeably mute on guns and the gun lobby after the horrific Virginia Tech killings last year and after the terrible Northern Illinois University killings this year. Consistent with his "categorical" March 2008 denunciation of "any statement that disparages our great country," the former "civil rights lawyer" Obama voted in July 2005 to reauthorize the Patriot Act—a notable assault on civil liberties. Obama's "undivided Jerusalem" comment was over the top and had to be partly rescinded, but there was nothing new in his current conservative and imperial positions on Iraq, Iran, or Israel or in his tendency to work with foreign policy "hawks" and interventionists.

Meanwhile, the supposed centrist John McCain pushed further to the extreme starboard side. He moved from center-right to hard-right. He abandoned his one-time opposition to George W. Bush's hyper-plutocratic tax cuts and to offshore oil drilling. Also consistent with his mission of pinning down his party's far-right base, he dropped his previous "liberal" approach to "illegal immigration.[8]

Meanwhile, we know that the actual American citizenry—the purportedly self-governing masters of the United States' allegedly export worthy "democracy" stood well to the social-democratic and anti-imperial left of both parties on numerous key policy issues, foreign and domestic. [9] The near policy and political irrelevance of this progressive U.S. majority opinion was neither new nor surprising. It is standard and sad American political reality given the harsh imbalance between the extreme power of the Few and the marginalization of the Many that is written into the structure and practices of the United States' corporate-managed democracy.[10]

NOTES

Preface

1. Laurence H. Shoup, "The Presidential Election 2008: Ruling Class Conducts Its Hidden Primary," *Z Magazine* (February 2008), p. 31.

2. The words "neoliberal" and "neoliberalism" as used throughout this volume refer to the ruling corporate and political ideology of post–New Deal America (1980 to the present). The classic, bourgeois, "liberal," free-market, political-economic doctrine of the nineteenth century held that the free market and possessive-individualist, economic rationality were the solution to social and even personal problems. By neoliberal dictates, "The market should be allowed to make major social and political decisions; . . . the State should voluntarily reduce its role in the economy, . . . corporations should be given total freedom, . . . trade unions should be curbed and citizens given much less rather than more social protections." I quote from Susan George, "A Short History of Neoliberalism" (Conference on Economic Sovereignty in a Globalising World, March 24–26, 1999. For useful discussions of the origins, nature, and contradictory practice of neoliberalism, see Noam Chomsky, *Profits over People: Neoliberalism and Global Order* (New York: Seven Stories, 1999), pp. 65–120; Henry A. Giroux, *The Terror of Neoliberalism: Authoritarianism and the Eclipse of Democracy* (Boulder: Paradigm), pp. xiii–xviii and passim.

3. Richard Hofstader, *The American Political Tradition and the Men Who Made It* (New York: Vintage, 1989 [1948]), pp. xxxiii–xl.

4. Howard Zinn, *The Twentieth Century: A People's History* (New York: HarperPerennial, 1998), p. 328.

5. I will get into definitions of the contested and many-sided term "progressive" in the Introduction.

6. I am quoting Marc Lamont Hill, who uses these words in a critical way—that is, he shares my sense that they do not accurately apply to Obama. See Hill, "Not My Brand of Hope: Obama's Politics of Cunning, Compromise, and Concession," *CounterPunch,* February 11, 2008 accessed at http://www.counterpunch.org/hill02112008.html.

7. Ibid.

8. Martin Luther King, Jr., "The Drum Major Instinct," *A Testament of Hope: The Essential Writings and Speeches of Martin Luther King, Jr.,* ed. James M. Washington (San Francisco: HarperCollins, 1991), pp. 259–267.

9. Paul Street, *Empire and Inequality: America and the World since 9/11* (Boulder: Paradigm, 2004).

10. I have borrowed the phrase "rebel's clothing" from Laura Flanders, who uses it in regard to gender and Hillary Clinton. It applies as well to race and Barack Obama, in my opinion. See Laura Flanders, "Clinton: Class of '68," pp. 9–45 in Laura Flanders, Richard Goldstein, Dean Kuipers, James Ridgeway, Eli Sanders, and Dan Savage, *The Contenders* (New York: Seven Stories, 2008).

11. For just one small sample of the vile hatred that has been around for some time regarding Obama, see the disturbing utterances of "Juanita Gonzales" at a new

Web site called "Stop Obama.org." Gonzales: "He is Threatening US Over His Bitch!" (May 29, 2008), read at http:/www.stop-obama.org/?p=398. The voluminously hateful content on this and numerous similar sites will in all likelihood multiply and intensify over future weeks and months.

12. As I pen this Preface in the wake of Obama's success in securing a majority of the Democratic Convention delegates, it strikes me that racial prejudice has a real chance of causing Obama defeat in the general election, a topic to which I shall return in the book's Afterword.

13. See Appendix B.

14. As John Pilger noted in an important assessment at the end of May: "As their contest for the White House draws closer, watch how, regardless of the inevitable personal smears, Obama and McCain draw nearer to each other." John Pilger, "After Bobby Kennedy (There Was Barack Obama)," *Common Dreams* (May 31, 2008), read at www.commondreams.org/archive/2008/05/31/9327/.

15. Shoup, "Election 2008."

16. The "New Deal" was a set of substantive labor and social reforms introduced under President Franklin D. Roosevelt with the help of a Democratic Congress during the 1930s. Key reforms included the National Labor Relations Act (which significantly expanded union membership and power), the Social Security Act (which produced a government-managed old-age pension system), and the Fair Labor Standards Act (which set a minimum wage and maintained payment for overtime). The New Deal also introduced a series of other business and banking regulations and a number of public works, employment, utility, and housing programs as well as federal cash assistance for poor families.

17. Noam Chomsky, *Interventions* (San Francisco: City Lights, 2007), p. 99.

18. Sheldon Wolin, *Democracy Incorporated: Managed Democracy and the Specter of Inverted Totalitarianism* (Princeton, NJ: Princeton University Press, 2008), p. 201.

19. Ibid., p. 100.

20. I owe this description to Larissa MacFarquhar, "The Conciliator: Where Is Barack Obama Coming From?" *The New Yorker,* May 7, 2007. According to MacFarquhar, "In his view of history, in his respect for tradition, in his skepticism that the world can be changed any way but very, very slowly, Obama is deeply conservative," www.newyorker.com/reporting/2007/05/07/070507fa_fact_macfarquhar.

Introduction

1. Christopher Wills, "Rookie Obama Survived Campaign Year as Others Faltered," *The Pantagraph* (Bloomington-Normal, Ill.), February, 10, 2008, http://www.pantagraph.com/articles/2008/02/10/news/doc47acdc47b8f13898044716.txt.

2. David Mendell, *Obama: From Promise to Power* (New York: HarperCollins, 2007), pp. 8–9.

3. K. V. Prasad, "Obama Seeks Revamp of U.S. Educational System," *The Hindu,* February 13, 2008, http://www.thehindu.com/2008/02/13/stories/2008021354851200.htm (emphasis added).

4. John B. Judis, "American Adam: Obama and the Cult of the New," *The New Republic,* March 12, 2008, p. 23

5. Tom Levinson, "For Some, Obama's Mission Is a Movement for the Ages," *Chicago Tribune*, March 9, 2008, sec. 2, p. 3

6. Steve Sailer, "Obama?s Identity Crisis," *The American Conservative*, March 26, 2007, http://www.amconmag.com/2007/2007_03_12/feature.html.

7. Quoted by Mike Flannery in CBS–2 Chicago, "Barack Obama on the Cover of *Men's Vogue*," August 11, 2006, http://cbs2chicago.com/politics/local_story_223173106.html.

8. *Newsweek*, January 14, 2008, cover.

9. Phillip Klein, "An Age of Obama?" The *American Spectator*, July/August 2007, pp. 25–31.

10. Salim Muwakill, "The Squandering of Obama," *In These Times*, August 14, 2007.

11. Janny Scott, "In 2000, A Streetwise Veteran Schooled a Bold Young Obama," *New York Times*, September 9, 2008, p. A1.

12. Palmer tried to get her Illinois seat back when she realized that she could not defeat Jackson, but Obama would not agree and even went to the length of having her kicked off the primary ballot by questioning her candidacy petition signatures. See David Jackson and Ray Long, "Obama Knows His Way Around a Ballot," *Chicago Tribune*, April 3, 2007; Liza Mundy, "A Series of Fortunate Events: Barack Obama Needed More Than Talent and Ambition to Rocket From Obscure State Senator to Presidential Contender in Three Years," *Washington Post Magazine* (August 12, 2007) http://www.washingtonpost.com/wpdyn/content/article/2007/08/08/AR2007080802038_pf.html.

13. Mendell, *Obama*, p. 7; Mundy.

14. Mundy; Mendell, *Obama*, pp. 157–162.

15. Mendell, *Obama*, p. 163.

16. Mundy.

17. Ibid.

18. Ibid.

19. Ken Silverstein, "Barack Obama, Inc.: The Birth of a Washington Machine," *Harper's*, November 2006 (emphasis added).

20. Ibid.

21. Ibid.

22. Ibid.

23. Mendell, *Obama*, pp. 247–248.

24. Ibid.

25. Mundy, "A Series."

26. Ibid.

27. Ibid.

28. Ibid.

29. Joe Klein, "The Fresh Face," *Time*, October 15, 2006, http://www.time.com/time/magazine/article/0,9171,1546362,00.html.

30. Mundy.

31. Mundy. See also James Traub, "Is (His) Biography (Our) Destiny?" *New York Times Magazine*, November 4, 2007.

32. Mundy.

33. Paul Street, "Barack Obama's White Appeal and the Perverse Racial Politics of the Post–Civil Rights Era," *Black Agenda Report*, June 20, 2007, http://www.blackagendareport.com/index.php?option=com_content&task=view&id=254&Itemid=34.

34. Thomas E. Ricks, *Fiasco: The American Military Adventure in Iraq* (New York: Penguin, 2006).

35. Scott Helman, "PACs and Lobbyists Aided Obama's Rise: Data Contrast with His Theme," *Boston Globe*, August 9, 2007. http://www.commondreams.org/archive/2007/08/09/3074. The "Mr. Smith Goes to Washington" trope is, of course, an ironically old theme in U.S. candidate imagery. It animated the successful presidential campaigns of Jimmy Carter, Ronald Reagan, and Bill Clinton, to give just three of many possible examples. The same claim to be a new and young voice for hope and change was made by John Fitzgerald Kennedy (a leading historical role model for both Bill Clinton and Obama), Robert F. Kennedy (1968), Eugene McCarthy (1968), George McGovern (1972), Howard Dean (2004), and of course Bill Clinton (1992), whose campaign partied at the 1992 Democratic National Convention to the strains of Fleetwood Mac's "Don't Stop Thinking about Tomorrow." With different levels of success and sincerity, to be sure, all of these past presidential candidates attempted to market themselves (in accord with venerable advertising principles) as agents of the "new" and enemies of the dissatisfactory "old."

36. Kathleen Parker, "Obama Has U.S. Hooked on a Feeling," *Chicago Tribune*, January 11, 2008, sec. 1, p. 21.

37. On the shocking disconnect between often objectively progressive U.S. public opinion and official U.S. politics, see Jacob S. Hacker and Paul Pierson, *Off Center: The Republican Revolution and the Erosion of Democracy* (New Haven, Conn.: Yale University Press, 2005), pp. 25–106; Noam Chomsky, *Hegemony or Survival* (New York: Metropolitan, 2003), pp. 2–8, 138–139; Noam Chomsky, *Failed States: The Abuse of Power and the Assault on Democracy* (New York: Metropolitan, 2006), pp. 214–250; Noam Chomsky, *What We Say Goes: Conversation on U.S. Power in a Changing World* (New York: Metropolitan, 2007), pp. 52–54; Benjamin Page and Marshall Bouton, *The Foreign Policy Disconnect: What Americans Want From Our Leaders But Don't Get* (Chicago: University of Chicago Press, 2006); Steven Hill, *Fixing Elections: The Failure of America's Winner Take All Politics* (New York: Routledge, 2002).

38. A mass Obama e-mail directed at youth contained the image of a small deodorant canister with the brand name "Gen BO." "We must get involved and we must do so in a meaningful and positive way," the electronic mailing said. "Enter June 8th—the date we introduce 'Gen BO' to all of our friends, family and colleagues." See http://blogs.chicagoreader.com/chicagoland/2007/06/07/smells-teen-spirit/.

39. Mike Dorning, "Obama Hones Youthful Image," *Chicago Tribune*, June 30, 2007, sec. 1, p. 3.

40. Joe Klein, "Why It's Not about the Issues," *Time*, February 18, 2008, p. 18.

41. As quoted in Mendell, *Obama*, pp. 12, 310.

42. Matt Taibbi, "Obama Is the Best BS Artist since Bill Clinton," RollingStone.com., posted on AlterNet, February 14, 2007, http://www.alternet.org/story/48051.

43. Mendell, *Obama*, p. 250.

44. Sailer, "Obama's Identity Crisis."

45. Bruce Mirrof, *Pragmatic Illusions: The Presidential Politics of John Fitzgerald Kennedy* (New York: Longman's, 1976); Noam Chomsky, *Rethinking Camelot: JFK, the Vietnam War, and US Political Culture* (Boston: South End, 1993). On the pseudo-pragmatist JFK as proto-neoliberal, see Randall Rothenburg, *The Neo-Liberals: Creating the New American Politics* (New York: Simon and Schuster, 1984), pp. 41, 44, 47, 70–71, 128–129.

46. Edward S. Herman, "Democratic Betrayal," *Z Magazine*, January 2007, http://www.zmag.org/zmag/viewArticle/13812.

47. Christopher Hitchens, *No One Left to Lie To: The Values of the Worst Family* (New York: Verso, 2000), pp. 17–18.

48. Hofstader, pp. 3–56; Herbert Aptheker, *The American Revolution, 1763–1783* (New York: International, 1960); Jennifer Nedelsky, *Private Property and the Limits of American Constitutionalism* (Chicago: University of Chicago Press, 1990); Paul Street, "By All Means, Study the Founders: Notes from the Democratic Left," *Review of Education, Pedagogy, and Cultural Studies* 24, no. 4 (October-December 2003): 281–303; Paul Street, "Day after July 4th Reflections on the Founders," *ZNet Magazine,* July 5, 2004, http://www.zmag.org/content/showarticle.cfm?ItemID=5823.

49. Chomsky, *Failed States*, p. 215; Chomsky, *Interventions*, pp. 97–98. The block quote is from the second source. Chomsky adds that "underlying population" and "substantial people" are the acid terms of Thorstein Veblen.

50. Hofstader.

51. Eric Foner, *Give Me Liberty! An American History*, vol. 1 (New York: W. W. Norton, 2005), p. 377.

52. G. William Domhoff, *Who Rules America? Power, Politics, and Social Change* (New York: McGraw Hill, 2006), p. 139.

53. Mirrof, *Pragmatic Illusions,* pp. 283–288; Louis Hartz, *The Liberal Tradition in America* (New York: Harcourt and Brace, 1955), p. 59.

54. See Paul Street, "The Full Blown Oprah Effect: Reflections on Color, Class and New Age Racism," *Black Commentator,* February 24, 2005, http://www.blackcommentator.com/127/127_oprah.html.

55. King, Jr., "Where Do We Go from Here?" *A Testament of Hope,* pp. 250–251.

56. Glenda Gilmore, ed., *Who Were the Progressives?* (New York: St. Martin's Press, 2002); Richard McCormick and Arthur S. Link, *Progressivism* (Arlington Heights, Ill.: Harlan Davidson, 1983); David Kennedy, "Overview: The Progressive Era," *Historian* 37 (May 1975): 453–468; Daniel T. Rodgers, "In Search of Progressivism," *Reviews in American History,* December 1982, pp. 113–181; Peter Filene, "An Obituary for 'The Progressive Movement,'" *American Quarterly* 22 (1970): 20–34.

57. Progressive Democrats of America, "PDA Priorities," 2008, http://pdamerica.org.

58. John K. Wilson, *Barack Obama: This Improbable Quest* (Boulder: Paradigm, 2007).

59. For some of my "real-time" campaign reflections (by no means completely flattering) on the Edwards campaign, see "Corporate Money on the Democrats: The Bad News," *Z Magazine,* December 2007; "A Very Narrow Spectrum: Even John Edwards Is Too Far Left for the U.S. Plutocracy," *ZNet Sustainer Commentary,* August 29, 2007, http://www.zmag.org/sustainers/content/2007–08/29street.cfm; "John Edwards and Dominant Media's Selective Skewering of Populist Hypocrisy," *ZNet Magazine,* June 29, 2007, http://www.zmag.org/content/showarticle.cfm?ItemID=13177; "Imperial Temptations: John Edwards, Barack Obama, and the Myth of Post–World War II United States Benevolence," *ZNet Magazine,* May 28, 2007, http://www.zmag.org/content/showarticle.cfm?ItemID=12928.

60. Paul Street. "The Vicious Circle: Race, Prison, Jobs, and Community in Chicago, Illinois, and the Nation" (Chicago: Chicago Urban League, 2002), www.cul-chicago.org (click on "Research Reports Available Online").

61. See, for example, Paul Street, "Imperial Temptations: John Edwards, Barack Obama, and the Myth of PostWorld War II United States Benevolence," *ZNet*

Magazine (May 28, 2007), read at http://www.zmag.org/content/showarticle.cfm?ItemID=12928; Paul Street, "A Very Narrow Spectrum: Even John Edwards Is Too Far Left for the U.S. Plutocracy," *ZNet Sustainer Commentary* (August 29, 2007), read at http://www.zmag.org/sustainers/content/2007-08/29street.cfm..

Chapter 1

1. Mike Dorning and Christi Parsons, "Carefully Crafting the Obama Brand," *Chicago Tribune,* June 12, 2007, sec.1. p. 1.

2. David Jackson and John McCormick, "Building Obama's Money Machine," *Chicago Tribune,* April 13, 2007.

3. Barack Obama, "Full Text of Senator Barack Obama's Announcement for President," February 10, 2007, Springfield, Illinois, www.barackobama.com/2007/02/10/remaks_of_senattor_barack_abam_11.php.

4. I have relied on the following sources to construct the historical sketches of past Democratic presidential campaigns and presidencies in this section of the chapter: Howard Zinn, *The Twentieth Century: A People's History* (New York: HarperPerennial, 1998) (on Carter and Clinton and the Democratic Leadership Council); Christopher Hitchens, *No One Left to Lie To: The Values of the Worst Family* (New York: Verso, 2000) (on Clinton); William Greider, *Who Will Tell the People? The Betrayal of American Democracy* (New York: Touchstone, 1993) (on Carter); Robert Pollin, *Contours of Descent: U.S. Economic Fractures and the Landscape of Global Austerity* (New York: Verso, 2003), pp. 3–76 (on Clinton); Elaine Brown, *The Condemnation of Little B* (Boston: Beacon Press, 2002) (on Clinton); Bruce Miroff, *Pragmatic Illusions: The Presidential Politics of John F. Kennedy* (New York: Longman, 1979) (on John Kennedy); Alexander Cockburn and Jeffrey St. Clair, *Dime's Worth of Difference: Beyond the Lesser of Two Evils* (Petrolia and Oakland, Calif.: CounterPunch and AK Press, 2004) (on John F. Kerry); Paul Street, "Kerry's Predictable Failure to Make Bush Pay for Rising US Poverty," *Dissident Voice,* September 8, 2004, www.dissidentvoice.org/Sept04/Street0908.htm.

5. Greider, *Who Will Tell?*, p. 90; Zinn, *The Twentieth Century*, pp. 330–339; Lekachman is quoted in Zinn, pp. 338–339.

6. Greider, *Who Will Tell?*, p. 145.

7. Alexander Cockburn, "Presidential Elections Not as Big a Deal as They Say," in *Dime's Worth,* p. 8.

8. Paul Krugman, "Lessons of 1992," *New York Times,* January 28, 2008.

9. Cockburn, "Presidential Elections," p. 12.

10. Howard Zinn, *A People's History of the United States, 1492–Present* (New York: HarperPerennial, 2003), pp. 661.

11. Zinn, *A People's History*, pp. 661–662; Wen Hao Chen and Miles Corak, "Child Poverty and Changes in Child Poverty in Rich Countries Since 1990," UNICEF Innocenti Research Center Working Paper 2005–02 (January 2005), read online at http://www.unicef-irc.org/publications/pef/iwp_2005_02_final.pdf.

12. Zinn, *Twentieth Century*, p. 422.

13. Barack Obama, *Audacity of Hope* (New York: Crown, 2006), pp. 34–35; Hitchens, *No One Left to Lie To,* pp. 17–18. See also the brilliant study by Pollin, *Contours of Descent,* pp. 3–76. For useful reflections, see Greider, *Who Will Tell the People?;* Godfrey Hodgson, *The World Turned Rightside Up: A History of the Conservative Ascendancy in America* (New York: Houghton Mifflin, 1996); Garry Wills,

Reagan's America: Innocents at Home (Garden City, N.Y.: Doubleday, 1986); Michael Lind, *The Next American Nation* (New York: Free Press, 1995).

14. Gabriel Kolko, "Alliances and the American Empire," pp. 270–271 in Cockburn and St. Clair, *Dime's Worth.*

15. Jodi Wilgoren, "Kerry Plans Effort to Show He's a Centrist," *New York Times,* April 16, 2004; Paul Street, "Not-So Sobering News," *Z Magazine,* October 2004, pp. 4–6; Edward N. Wolff, *Top Heavy: A Study of the Increasing Inequality of Wealth in America* (New York: The New Press, 2002). For useful reflections, see Greider, *Who Will Tell the People?;* Gar Alperovitz, *America beyond Capitalism: Reclaiming Our Wealth, Our Liberty, and Our Democracy* (New York: John Wiley, 2005), pp. 50–53; and Noam Chomsky, *Failed States: The Abuse of Power and the Assault on Democracy* (New York: Metropolitan, 2006), pp. 207–208.

16. Thomas Frank, *What's the Matter with Kansas? How Conservatives Won the Heart of America* (New York: Metropolitan, 2004).

17. For a recent example, see Larry Bartels, "Inequalities," *New York Times Magazine,* April 27, 2008, p. 22. As Bartels pointed out, Frank badly exaggerated white working-class voters' susceptibility to cultural diversion: "In recent presidential elections," he noted, "affluent voters, who tend to be liberal on cultural matters, are about twice as likely as middle-class and poor voters to make their decisions on the basis of their cultural concerns." In other words, working-class white voters don't especially privilege "cultural issues" (God, guns, gays, gender, and abortion) over pocketbook concerns and actually do that less than wealthier voters.

18. Frank, *What's the Matter with Kansas?* pp. 242–243, 245.

19. For early reflections, see Paul Street, "Frank Discussion: Moral-Economic Abandonment, Race, Security, and Psychological Wages," *ZNet Magazine,* November 6, 2004, http://www.zmag.org/content/showarticle.cfm?SectionID=72&ItemID=6592%20.

20. Miroff, *Pragmatic Illusions,* p. 168, 201.

21. Ibid., pp. 182–183, 217–218. It was for doctrinal as well as for emotional and calculated political reasons that many of the early proponents of what later came to be known as the Democratic neoliberals (for example, Senators Gary Hart and Bill Bradley; Governors Bruce Babbitt, James Hunt, Richard Lamm, and Bill Clinton; Congressmen Al Gore and Timothy Wirth) made JFK their inspiring role model. See Randall Rothenburg, *The Neoliberals: Creating the New American Politics* (New York: Simon and Schuster, 1984).

22. Alex Carey, *Taking the Risk Out of Democracy: Corporate Propaganda versus Freedom and Liberty* (Urbana: University of Illinois Press, 1997).

23. Edward S. Herman, "How Market-Democracy Keeps the Public and 'Populism' at Bay," *ZNet Sustainer Commentary*, August 13, 2007, available online at http://wwwzmag.org/sustainers/content/2007-08/13herman.cfm.; Thomas Ferguson, *Golden Rule: The Investment Theory of Party Competition and Logic of Money-Driven Political Systems* (Chicago: University of Chicago Press, 1995); Elizabeth Drew, *The Corruption of American Politics: What Went Wrong and Why* (Secaucus, N.J.: Birch Lane Press, 1999); Center for Responsive Politics, *A Brief History of Money in Politics* (Washington, D.C.: Center for Responsive Politics, 1995); Jamin Raskin and John Bonifaz, "The Constitutional Imperative and Practical Imperative of Democratically Financed Elections," *Columbia Law Review* 94, no. 4 (1994): 1160–1203; Charles Lewis, *The Buying of the President* (New York: Avon, 1996),

pp. 1–20; Robert W. McChesney, *Rich Media, Poor Democracy: Communication Politics in Dubious Times* (Urbana: University of Illinois Press, 1999); Paul Street, "Capitalism and Democracy 'Don't Mix Very Well': Reflections on Globalization," *Z Magazine,* February 2000, pp. 20–24; Paul Street, "More Than Entertainment: Neal Gabler and the Illusions of Post-Ideological Society," *Monthly Review,* February 2000, pp. 58–62; and Edward S. Herman and Noam Chomsky, *Manufacturing Consent* (New York: Pantheon, 1988).

24. The mainstream media itself is a leading institutional filter tending to eliminate candidates deemed excessively unfriendly to concentrated wealth—a topic to be addressed in more detail in the next chapter.

25. Matt Bai, "The Poverty Platform," *New York Times Magazine,* June 19, 2007. For me, the biggest tip-off that Edwards was less than a full-blown left populist was his repeated claim that his great aim is to "help people have a chance to be as successful as I have been." This was Edwards's way of saying that he bought into the standard bourgeois American claim that the only acceptable form of equality to be pursued is *equality of opportunity,* not *equality of condition.* This is the same position that Obama takes, which I have criticized.

26. Hillary Clinton, speaking to hundreds of civil rights activists and labor leaders at the National Action Network conference in New York City in the spring of 2007, quoted in Ari Berman, "Hillary, Inc.," *The Nation,* June 4, 2007.

27. Berman, "Hillary, Inc."

28. Ibid., pp. 11–18.

29. Scott Helman, "PACs and Lobbyists Aided Obama's Rise: Data Contrast with His Theme," *Boston Globe,* August 9, 2007. According to one of Obama's Iowa television ads in the summer of 2007: "He's leading by example, refusing contributions from PACs and Washington lobbyists who have too much power today."

30. Paul Street, "Sitting Out the Obama Dance in Iowa City," *ZNet Magazine,* April 28, 2007, http://www.zmag.org/content/showarticle.cfm?SectionID=72&ItemID=12687.

31. Obama, quoted in Helman, "PACs and Lobbyists Aided Obama's Rise."

32. Quoted in Pam Martens, "Obama's Money Cartel," *CounterPunch,* February 23, 2008, http://zcommunications.org/znet/viewArticle/16601.

33. Helman, "PACs and Lobbyists," Martens, "Obama's Money Cartel."

34. "U.S. Senator Obama Gets $1.9 Million Book Deal," CTV (AP), December 18, 2004; David McKinney and Chris Fusco, "Obama on Rezko Deal: It Was a Mistake," *Chicago Sun Times,* November 5, 2006, http://www.suntimes.com/news/124171,CST-NWS-obama05.article.

35. Center for Responsive Politics, "Obama's Leading Contributors, 2001–2006," www.opensecrets.org/politicians/contrib.asp?CID =N00009638&cycle=2006.

36. Martens, "Obama's Money Cartel."

37. Lynn Sweet, "Obama Touts Small Donor Networks But Also Relies on High End 'Bundlers' for Millions," *Chicago Sun Times,* April 16, 2007, http://blogs.suntimes.com/sweet/2007/04/sweet_column_obama_touts_small.html.

38. See Jackson and McCormick, "Building Obama's Money Machine"; David Mendell, *Obama: From Promise to Power* (New York: HarperCollins, 2007), p. 155.

39. Christopher Drew and Mike McIntire, "Obama Built Donor Network from Roots Up," *New York Times,* April 3, 2007.

40. "Barack Obama, Top Industries," http://www.opensecrets.org/pres08/indus.asp?id=N00009638&cycle=2008; Center for Responsive Politics (CRP), "Barack Obama's Top Contributors," http://www.opensecrets.org/pres08/contrib.asp?id=N00009638&cycle=2008; CRP, "Hillary Clinton's Top Contributors," http://www.opensecrets.org/pres08/contrib.asp?id=N00000019&cycle=2008; CRP, "John Edwards' Top Contributors," http://www.opensecrets.org/pres08/summary.asp?id=N00002283&cycle=2008. On the Web sites of Skadden, Arps et al. and Sidley Austin LLP, see http://www.skadden.com/Index.cfm?contentID=5; http://www.sidley.com/ourfirm/.

41. Center for Responsive Politics, "John Edwards, Top Industries," http://www.opensecrets.org/pres08/indus.asp?id=N00002283&cycle=2008. For one example among many, see the Web site of Edwards' fourth largest contributor, Coughlin, Stoia et al., at http://www.csgrr.com/csgrr-cgi-bin/mil?templ=featured/txu&case=.

42. Obama, *Audacity of Hope,* pp. 109–111.

43. Drew and McIntire, "Obama Built Donor Network."

44. Ken Silverstein, "Barack Obama, Inc.: The Birth of a Washington Machine," *Harper's,* November 2006," p. 33.

45. Karen Tumulty and James Carney, "Hillary Pushes Back," *Time,* May 7, 2007, p. 42.

46. Jackson and McCormick, "Building Obama's Money Machine."

47. Silverstein, "Barack Obama, Inc."

48. Alexander Cockburn, "Obama's Game," *CounterPunch,* April 24, 2006, www.counterpunch.org/cockburn04242006.html.

49. Lindsey Rennick Mayer, "Seeking Superdelegates," *Capital Eye,* February 14, 2008, www.capitaleye.org/inside.asp?id=336&format=print.

50. Helman, "PACs and Lobbyists."

51. Ibid. See also Jackson and McCormick, "Building Obama's Money Machine."

52. Dan Morain, "Obama Walks a Thin Green Line," *Los Angeles Times,* August 2, 2007.

53. Ibid. Dan Morain, "Obama's Refusal of Lobbyists/ Money Had Limits," *Los Angeles Times*, April 22, 2007.

54. Martens, "Obama's Money Cartel."

55. Ibid.

56. Helman, "PACs and Lobbyists." See also Jackson and McCormick, "Building Obama's Money Machine."

57. David Moberg, "Obamanomics," *In These Times,* April 2008, p. 35.

58. Center for Responsive Politics, "Presidential Candidate Barack Obama," 2007 campaign finance data, http://www.opensecrets.org/pres08/summary.asp?id=N00009638&cycle=2008.

59. Christopher Wills, "Rookie Obama Survived Campaign Year as Others Faltered," *The Pantagraph* (Bloomington-Normal, IL), February 10, 2008.

60. Christi Parsons and Rick Pearson, "The $50 Million Man," *Chicago Tribune,* February 29, 2008, sec. 1, pp. 1, 6.

61. Elizabeth Bumiller, "McCain and Obama Skirmish on Financing," *New York Times,* February 15, 2008.

62. Ibid.

63. Deborah Goldberg, "The Real Deal," Brennan Center for Justice Web site, February 15, 2007, http://www.brennancenter.org/blog/archives/the_real_deal/.

64. Campaign Finance Institute, "Presidential Fundraising in 2007 Doubles 2003," February 11, 2008, www.cfinst.org.

65. Center for Responsive Politics, "Barack Obama: Top Contributors," http://www.opensecrets.org/pres08/contrib.asp?id=N00009638&cycle=2008.

66. Center for Responsive Politics (CRP), "Barack Obama: Top Industries," http://www.opensecrets.org/pres08/indus.asp?id=N00009638&cycle=2008; CRP, "Barack Obama: By Sector," http://www.opensecrets.org/pres08/sector.asp?id=N00009638&cycle=2008.

67. MSNBC broadcast of Democratic presidential candidates, Cleveland, Ohio, February 26, 2008, http://www.msnbc.msn.com/id/21134540/vp/23361919#23361919. One week earlier, Obama's contorted position on presidential financing evoked a rare critical comment from one of his leading admirers in the establishment media—the right-wing *New York Times* columnist David Brooks: "Barack Obama vowed to abide by the public finance campaign-spending rule in the general election if his opponent did. But now he's waffling on his promise. Why does he need to check with his campaign staff when deciding whether to keep his word? Obama says he is practicing a new kind of politics, but why has his PAC sloshed $698,000 to the campaigns of the superdelegates, according to the Center for Responsive Politics? Is giving Robert Byrd's campaign $10,000 the kind of change we can believe in?" David Brooks, "When the Magic Fades," *New York Times,* February 19, 2008.

68. Matthew Mosk and Alec MacGillis, "Big Donors Among Obama's Grass Roots," *Washington Post,* April 11, 2008, p. A1.

69. Silverstein, "Barack Obama, Inc.," p. 37; Ferguson, *Golden Rule.*

70. Silverstein, "Barack Obama, Inc.," p. 40.

71. David Sirota, "Mr. Obama Goes to Washington," *The Nation,* June 26, 2006; Matt Gonzalez, "The Obama Craze: Count Me Out," *BeyondChron: San Francisco's Online Daily,* February 28, 2008, www.beyondchron.org/articles/index.php?itemid=5413#more; Martens, "Obama's Money Cartel."

72. Sirota, "Mr. Obama"; Silverstein, "Barack Obama, Inc."; Gonzalez, "The Obama Craze."

73. Marten, "Obama's Money Cartel."

74. Silverstein, "Barack Obama, Inc.," p. 37; Sirota, "Mr. Obama." Liberal Obama supporter and political commentator Michael Tomasky strained credulity in the summer of 2006 when he argued that Obama voted for the "tort reform" because "he wanted, even if only to prove to himself that he could do it, to show at least one Democratic interest group that he could say no, and chose the trial lawyers. . . . I feel certain that he just wanted to see how it felt." Tomasky here advanced one of the more bizarre claims I have ever encountered in the world of political journalism, liberal or otherwise. See Tomasky, "The Phenomenon," *New York Review of Books,* November 30, 2006.

75. Ibid.; Cockburn, "Obama's Game,"

76. Sirota, "Mr. Obama"; Silverstein, "Barack Obama, Inc.," p. 37; Gonzalez, "The Obama Craze."

77. Sirota, "Mr. Obama."

78. Transcript of interview of Barack Obama by Linda Douglas, *The National Journal,* November 7, 2007, http://nationaljournal.com/onair/transcripts/071108_obama_barack.htm.

79. Jayson Clayworth, "Clinton Sidesteps Social Security Issue, Obama Says in Des Moines," *Des Moines Register,* October 28, 2007, http://www.desmoines

register.com/apps/pbcs.dll/article?AID=/20071028/NEWS09/710280335/–1/caucus; Paul Krugman, "Played for a Sucker," *New York Times*, November 16, 2007; Dean Baker and Mark Weisbrot, *Social Security: The Phony Crisis* (Chicago: University of Chicago Press, 2001); Chomsky, *Failed States*, p. 248. For background, see Baker and Weisbrot, *Social Security*.

80. Krugman, "Played for a Sucker."

81. Paul Street, "The Obama Disease: Business Rule, 'Common Ground,' and 'P[l]aying the Fool,'" *ZNet Magazine*, December 4, 2007, http://www.zmag.org/znet/viewArticle/15748. For campaign finance data, see Center for Responsive Politics, "Presidential Candidate Barack Obama," www.opensecrets.org/pres08/summary.asp?id=N00009638&cycle=2008.

82. Sirota, "Mr. Obama"; Joe Klein, "The Fresh Face," *Time*, October 17, 2006.

83. Chomsky, *Failed States*, p. 225.

84. See Tera Herivel and Paul Wright, eds., *Prison Nation: The Warehousing of America's Poor* (London: Routledge, 2002).

85. Paul Krugman, "Mandates and Mudslinging," *New York Times*, November 30, 2007.

86. Paul Starr, "The Democrats' Strategic Challenge," *American Prospect*, January-February 2008, p. 14.

87. Paul Krugman, "Mandates and Mudslinging"; Center for Responsive Politics, "Presidential Candidate Barack Obama"; Center for Responsive Politics, "Obama's Leading Contributors by Industry," www.opensecrets.org/politicians/allindus.asp?CID=N00009638; Lynn Sweet, "Barack and Michelle Obama Earned $991,296 in 2006," *Chicago Sun Times*, April 16, 2007, http://blogs.suntimes.com/sweet/2007/04/sweet_blog_extra_barack_and_mi.html#more.

88. Gonzalez, "The Obama Craze."

89. Ibid.

90. Paul Krugman, "Health Care Horror Stories," *New York Times*, April 11, 2008, p. A23.

91. Silverstein, "Barack Obama, Inc.," p. 37.

92. Center for Responsive Politics, "Obama's Top Contributors 2001–2006."

93. Transcript, CNN/YouTube Democratic Presidential Debate (part 2), http://www.cnn.com/2007/POLITICS/07/23/debate.transcript.part2/index.html.

94. Center for Responsive Politics, "Barack Obama's Top Contributors"; Exelon Press Release, "Exelon Nuclear Sets All Time Generation Record," January 17, 2006, http://www.exeloncorp.com/NR/exeres/2E545C20–7421–41E9–88CE-C91236BADD04.htm; Elizabeth Williamson, "The Green Gripe with Obama: Liquified Coal is Still . . . Coal," *Washington Post*, January 10, 2007, p. A11; Silverstein, "Barack Obama, Inc.," p. 35.

95. Mike McIntire, "Nuclear Leaks and Response Tested Obama," *New York Times*, February 3, 2008, sec. 1, p. 1.

96. Ibid. (emphasis added).

97. Bob Secter, "Obama's Fundraising, Rhetoric Collide," *Chicago Tribune*, February 2008, sec. 1, p. 7 (emphasis added).

98. Public Broadcasting System, *PBS News Hour*, "Free Trade Agreement Is Issue for Ohio Voters," March 3, 2008, http://www.pbs.org/newshour/extra/features/us/jan-june08/nafta_3–03.html.

99. For a useful and powerful analysis of NAFTA, see Jeff Faux, *The Global Class War: How America's Bipartisan Elite Lost Our Future and What It Will Take to Win It*

Back (New York: Wiley, 2006), pp. 9–37, 45–47, 126–54; Associated Press, February 28, 2008.

100. David Leonhardt, "The Politics of Trade in Ohio," *New York Times,* February 27, 2008.

101. Matt Gonzalez, "The Obama Craze."

102. CTV.ca News Staff, "Obama Staffer Gave Warning of FANFTA Rhetoric," www.ctv.ca/servlet/ArticleNews/story/CTVNews/20080227/dems_nafta_080227/20080227?; Doug Henwood, "Would You Like Change with That?" *Left Business Observer,* no. 117 (March 2008).

103. Paul Krugman, "Responding to Recession," *New York Times,* January 14, 2008.

104. Moberg, "Obamanomics"; Max Fraser, "Subprime Obama," *The Nation,* February 11, 2008.

105. Noam Scheiber, "The Audacity of Data: Barack Obama's Surprisingly Non-Ideological Policy Shop," *The New Republic,* March 12, 2008, p. 28; David Brooks, "Run, Barack, Run," *New York Times,* October 18, 2006; David Brooks, "The Smile of Reason," *New York Times,* November 19, 2006.

106. Moberg, "Obamanomics."

107. Ibid.

108. Ibid. It should be noted, however, that this assessment was penned before severe financial shocks appeared suggesting the possible emergence of an economic crisis and slowdown on a scale likely to force leading federal elected officials and candidates to think well outside the normal "free market" and neoliberal or "libertarian" box.

109. Larissa MacFarquhar, "The Conciliator: Where Is Barack Obama Coming From?" *The New Yorker,* May 7, 2007. Sunstein is quoted in Moberg, "Obamanomics." For a detailed review of *The Audacity of Hope*, see Paul Street, "Obama's Audacious Deference to Power," *Black Agenda Report* (January 31, 2007), read at www.blackagendareport.com/index.php?option=comcontent&task=view&id=61.

110. MacFarquhar, "The Conciliator."

111. Ibid. MacFarquhar's portrait of Obama's "Burekean" worldview is consistent with what Cass Sunstein, Obama's colleague at the University of Chicago Law School, identified as Obama's "minimalist" approach to law and politics"—a preference for "modest adjustments in institutions in search of his 'visionary' goals." Sunstein is quoted in Moberg, "Obamanomics." In Chapter 4 I will give some basis in support of MacFarquhar's interesting statement that Obama opposed the invasion of Iraq "on conservative grounds."

112. Editorial Board, "Obama: Change for the Good," *Milwaukee Journal Sentinel,* February 16, 2008.

113. Fraser, "Subprime Obama."

114. Ibid.

115. Paul Krugman, "Loans and Leadership," *New York Times,* March 28, 2008, p. A23.

116. Fraser, "Subprime Obama."

117. Ibid.; Martens, "Obama's Money Cartel."

118. Pam Martens, "The Obama Bubble: Why Wall Street Needs a Presidential Brand," *Black Agenda Report,* March 5, 2008.

119. Moberg, "Obamanomics," p. 35.

120. Obama, *Audacity,* p. 7 (emphasis added).

121. For some useful reflections, see Jason DeParle, *American Dream: Three Women, Ten Kids, and a Nation's Drive to End Welfare* (New York: Penguin, 2004); David Shipler, *The Working Poor: Invisible in America* (New York: Alfred A. Knopf, 2004); Jonathan Kozol, *Shame of the Nation: The Restoration of Apartheid Schooling in America* (New York: Three Rivers, 2005); Paul Street, *Segregated Schools: Educational Apartheid in Post-Civil Rights America* (New York: Routledge, 2005); Ruth Sidel, *Keeping Women and Children Last* (New York: Penguin, 1998); Paul Street, *Racial Oppression in the Global Metropolis: A Living Black Chicago History* (New York: Rowman and Littlefield, 2007), pp. 131–284; Brown, *Condemnation;* Pollin, *Contours of Descent.*

122. For an interesting portrait of King as a democratic socialist, see Michael Eric Dyson, *I May Not Get There with You: The True Martin Luther King, Jr.* (New York: Touchstone, 2000), pp. 78–100. For more sources, see Paul Street, "' Until We Get a New Social Order': Reflections on the Radicalism of Martin Luther King, Jr." *ZNet Magazine,* January 16, 2007, http://www.zmag.org/content/showarticle.cfm?ItemID=11871; "The Pale Reflection: Barack Obama, Martin Luther King, Jr., and the Meaning of the Black Revolution," *ZNet Magazine,* March 16, 2007, http://www.zmag.org/content/showarticle.cfm?ItemID=12336.

123. Obama, *Audacity,* pp. 7, 97. For reflections on the regressive corporate-neoliberal project, see Adolph Reed, Jr., "Undone by Neoliberalism: New Orleans Was Decimated by an Ideological Program, Not a Storm," *The Nation,* September 18, 2006, pp. 26–30; Pierre Bourdieu, *Acts of Resistance* (New York: Free Press, 1998), pp. 2, 24–44; John Pilger, *The New Rulers of the World* (London: Verso, 2002), pp. 5, 116; Henry A. Giroux, *The Abandoned Generation: Democracy beyond the Culture of Fear* (New York: Palgrave-MacMillan, 2003), pp. 1–70; Henry A. Giroux, *The Terror of Neoliberalism: Authoritarianism and the Eclipse of Democracy* (Boulder: Paradigm, 2004), pp. 1–53; Street, *Racial Oppression,* pp. 25, 37–38, 40, 148, 162, 285–295.

124. Obama, *Audacity,* pp. 149–150.

125. Sirota, "Mr. Obama."

126. Paul Street, "Profit Surge," *ZNet Magazine,* February 10, 2007, http://www.zmag.org/content/showarticle.cfm?ItemID=12089.

127. For sources and a sample of such unbalanced reflections, see Paul Street, *Empire and Inequality: America and the World since 9/11* (Boulder: Paradigm, 2004), pp. 143–184 and passim. See also Robert Howard, *Brave New Workplace* (New York: Viking, 1985); Edward N. Wolff, *Top Heavy: A Study of the Increasing Inequality of Wealth in America* (New York: The New Press, 2002); Joel Bakan, *The Corporation: The Pathological Pursuit of Profit and Power* (New York: Free Press, 2004); Juliet Schor, *The Overworked America: The Unexpected Decline of Leisure* (New York: Basic, 1992); Godfrey Hodgson, *More Equal Than Others: America from Nixon to the New Century* (New York: Century Foundation, 2004); David Gordon, *Fat and Mean: The Corporate Squeeze of Working Americans and the Myth of Managerial Downsizing* (New York: Free Press, 1996); Paul Street, "Labor Day Reflections: Time as a Democracy Issue," *ZNet Daily Commentaries,* September 3, 2002, www.zmag.org/sustainers/content/ 2002–08/01street.cfm; Barbara Ehrenreich, *Nickel and Dimed: On (Not) Getting By in America* (New York: Metropolitan, 2001); Barbara Ehrenreich, *Bait and Switch: The (Futile) Pursuit of the American Dream* (New York: Henry Holt, 2005). For Obama on the Founders' legacy of democracy, see Obama, *Audacity,* pp. 87–88.

128. For background data, see Janny Scott and David Leonhardt, "Shadowy Lines That Still Divide," *New York Times,* May 15, 2005; Lawrence Mishel, Jared Bernstein, and Heather Boushey, *The State of Working America, 2002–2003* (Ithaca, N.Y.: Economic Policy Institute and Cornell University Press, 2003), pp. 414–422.

129. One term used by some left analysts to describe really existing U.S. "democracy" is "polyarchy," what left sociologist William I. Robinson called "a system in which a small group actually rules and mass participation in decision making is confined to leadership choices carefully managed by competing [business and business-sanctioned] elites." "The polyarchic concept of democracy," noted Robinson, "is an effective arrangement for legitimating and sustaining inequalities within and between nations (deepening in a global economy) far more effectively than authoritarian solutions." William I. Robinson, *Promoting Polyarchy—Globalization, US Intervention, and Hegemony* (Cambridge: Cambridge University Press, 1996), p. 385.

130. Carey, *Taking the Risk,* pp. 11–86, 133–139. The invitation to corporate propaganda and thought control (quite advanced in the United States) arises from two things. First, ordinary Americans are human beings endowed with a basic sense of moral decency. Since we are not born with some sort of masochistic, self-hating impulse that causes us to like the nation's remarkable economic disparities and the perversion of our democracy by the privileged few, the majority of us (not privileged) have to be ruled. Second, thanks to the British, American, and French revolutions and the living legacy of the Enlightenment, we are free to say that we don't like it. It's not generally legitimate to shoot us if and when we voice displeasure with the consequences and—in some cases even the existence—of empire and inequality. It makes sense, then, that, as an American academic named Norman Meier noted in 1950, "Americans are the most propagandized people of any nation." That's what you'd expect in a nation that combines stark class inequality (the United States is by far the most unequal and wealth top-heavy nation in the industrialized world), concentrated (corporate and state) power, and remarkable private/corporate communications capacity (organizational and technological) with the world's strongest free-speech and related civil-libertarian traditions and protections.

131. Cass R. Sunstein, "The Obama I Know: Terrific Listener Goes Wherever Reason Takes Him," *Chicago Tribune,* March 14, 2008, sec. 1, p. 13. The reference to Obama's "University of Chicago background" was perhaps a bit odd insofar as Obama was with that institution's admittedly conservative law school and not with its famous, notorious (in left circles), and much-celebrated/-vilified Economics Department, the leading intellectual stronghold of neoliberal "free market" doctrine since at least the late 1970s; Street, "Democracy and Capitalism 'Don't Mix'"; Paul Street, "By All Means, Study the Founders: Notes from the Democratic Left," *Review of Education, Pedagogy, and Cultural Studies* Volume 24, Number 4 (October-December 2003): 281-303.

132. Obama, *Audacity,* p. 150.

133. Mishel et al., *The State of Working America,* pp. 395–432.

134. Mendell, *Obama,* p. 74; Garrow, *Bearing the Cross: Martin Luther King, Jr., and the Southern Christian Leadership Conference* (New York: HarperCollins, 1986), pp. 71, 568; Street, "Pale Reflection."

135. Obama, *Audacity,* p. 315; Chomsky, *Failed States,* p. 136; Testimony of Mark Weisbrot, Codirector, Center for Economic and Policy Research, on the State of Democracy in Venezuela, before the Senate Committee on Foreign Relations,

Subcommittee on Western Hemisphere, Peace Corps and Narcotics Affairs, June 24, 2004, www.senate.gov/~foreign/testimony/2004/WeisbrotTestimony04624.pdf.

136. Pollin, *Contours of Descent,* pp. 3–172; Mark Weisbrot, "The Mirage of Progress"; Amartya Sen, "How to Judge Globalism"; Mark Alan Healey and Ernesto Seman, "The Costs of Orthodoxy"; and Joseph E. Stiglitz, "Globalization's Discontents," all in *American Prospect,* January 1, 2002; also Schor, *The Overworked American;* Paul Street, "Labor Day Reflections;" Mike Davis, *Planet of Slums* (New York: Verso, 2006).

137. Andrew Ferguson, "The Wit & Wisdom of Barack Obama," *Weekly Standard,* March 24, 2008.

138. Noam Chomsky, *What We Say Goes* (New York: Metropolitan, 2007), p. 95.

139. MacFarquhar, "The Conciliator" (emphasis added).

140. Ibid.

141. Greider, *Who Will Tell the People?;* Lawrence Goodwyn, *The Populist Moment: A Short History of the Agrarian Revolt in America* (New York: Oxford University Press, 1978).

142. Clinton is quoted in MacFarquhar, "The Conciliator."

143. Ibid.

144. Ibid.

145. Obama, "Our Common Stake in America's Prosperity," New York, September 17, 2007.

146. Faux, *The Global Class War,* pp. 87, 168.

147. Ibid., pp. 87–88.

148. Ibid., pp. 187–190; Thomas Friedman, "C.E.O.'s M.I.A," *New York Times,* May 25, 2005, p. A25, quoted in Faux, *The Global Class War,* pp. 189–190.

149. Leslie Sklair, *The Transnational Capitalist Class* (Malden, Mass.: Blackwell, 2000).

150. Faux, *The Global Class War,* pp. 179–2000.

151. MSNBC, "Hardball," December 17, 2007.

152. Paul Krugman, "Big Table Fantasies," *New York Times,* December 17, 2007. Krugman's December 17 column went on my Edwards' campaign clipboard, along with the following note, crafted by me: "Compromise and harmony are wonderful goals in daily life, but serious Democratic politics is not about finding *'common ground'* with Republicans and corporations. This is especially true when most Americans already support core elements of the progressive agenda (blocked by Republican and corporate power) and strongly agree with the basic 'populist' notion that large corporations exercise excessive influence on American politics and government. The popular *consensus* for progressive change *already exists.*"

153. Kip Peterson, "Democrats Debate Universal Coverage," *Z Magazine,* May 2007, http://zmagsite.zmag.org/May2007/sullivan0507.html; Center for Responsive Politics, "Race for the White House," http://www.opensecrets.org/pres08/index.asp?cycle=2008.

154. Transcript of CNN/YouTube Debate, Democratic Presidential Candidates, Charleston, South Carolina, July 24, 2007, http://edition.cnn.com/2007/POLITICS/07/23/debate.transcript/index.html.

155. John Edwards, "To Build One America," Manchester, New Hampshire, August 24, 2007, http://www.addisonindependent.com/?q=node/659.

156. Paul Street, "John Edwards and Dominant Media's Selective Skewering of Populist Hypocrisy," *ZNet Magazine,* June 29, 2007, http://www.zmag.org/content

/showarticle.cfm?SectionID=21&ItemID=13177; Jeff Cohen, "Are Media Out to Get Edwards?" ZNet, June 3, 2007, http://www.zmag.org/content/showarticle.cfm?SectionID=21&ItemID=12981.

157. Judis, "American Adam."

158. In this brief portrait of Obama's earlier career I have relied on the following sources: Janny Scott, "In 2000, a Streetwise Veteran Schooled a Bold Young Obama," *New York Times,* September 9, 2007, pp. A1, A20; Liza Mundy, "A Series of Fortunate Events: Barack Obama Needed More Than Talent and Ambition to Rocket from Obscure State Senator to Presidential Contender in Three Years," *Washington Post Magazine,* August 12, 2007; Janny Scott, "At State Level, Obama Proved to Be Pragmatic and Practical," *New York Times,* July 30, 2007, p. A1; Rick Pearson and Ray Long, "Careful Steps, Looking Ahead," *Chicago Tribune,* May 3, 2007; Mendell, *Obama;* Scott Helman, "In Illinois, Obama Dealt with Lobbyists," *Boston Globe,* September 23, 2007; Bob Secter and John McCormick, "Portrait of a Pragmatist," *Chicago Tribune,* March 30, 2007; David Jackson and John McCormick, "Building Obama's Money Machine," *Chicago Tribune,* April 13, 2007.

159. Pearson and Long, "Careful Steps."

160. Scott, "At the State Level."

161. Helman, "PACs and Lobbyists."

162. Jackson and McCormick, "Building Obama's Money Machine"; Helman, "In Illinois."

163. MacFarquhar, "The Conciliator"; Mundy, "A Series"; Secter and McCormick, "Portrait of a Pragmatist"; Ryan Lizza, "The Agitator: The Unlikely Political Education of Barack Obama," *The New Republic,* March 19, 2007.

164. For useful background and reflections, see Michael C. Dawson, *Behind the Mule: Race and Class in African-American Politics* (Princeton, N.J.: Princeton University Press, 1994); Pearson and Long, "Careful Steps."

165. Ibid.; The speech would be rediscovered and highlighted by his presidential campaign, reflecting the Obama team's accurate calculation that it had become a political asset at a time when most Americans rejected the occupation of Iraq.

166. Salim Muwakill, "The Squandering of Obama," *In These Times,* August 14, 2007.

167. Adolph Reed, Jr., "The Curse of Community," *Village Voice,* January 16, 1996, reproduced in Reed, *Class Notes: Posing as Politics and Other Thoughts on the American Scene* (New York: New Press, 2000).

168. Alexander Cockburn, "The Spitzer Sting," *The Nation,* March 31, 2008, p. 13; Henwood, "Would You Like Change?"

169. Chris Hedges, "Corporate America Hearts Obama," *Truthdig* (April 30, 2008).

170. Mayhill Fowler, "Obama: No Surprise that Hard Pressed Pennsylvanians Bitter" (with audio link to Obama's comments at the San Francisco fund-raiser), *The Huffington Post* (April 11, 2008), read at http://www.huffingtonpost.com/mayhill-fowler/obama-no-surprise-that-ha_b_96188.html; Paul Krugman, "Clinging to a Stereotype," *New York Times*, April 18, 2008, p. A23.

171. Bartels, "Inequalities." Another problem with Frank's book was that it badly underestimated the roles of race, white working-class racism, militarism, and "national security" in explaining how the Republicans' have won white working-class votes. For an early critique (and appreciation) of Frank along these lines, see Street, "Frank Discussion."

172. Frank, *What's the Matter With Kansas?*, p. 245.
173. Ibid. As Krugman has repeatedly suggested, most recently in Krugman, "Clinging to a Stereotype."

Chapter 2

1. Herman, "How Market-Democracy Keeps the Public and 'Populism' at Bay."
2. Ibid. Voter focus groups would often say that the highly proficient Edwards (an extremely skilled debater) had performed the best during the Democratic primary debates of 2007 and early 2008 (Edwards ended his candidacy after his resounding defeat in South Carolina), but they would also report that they would not be voting for him, since he did not seem electable.
3. Bruce Dixon, "Holding Barack Obama Accountable," *Dissident Voice,* February 15, 2008, www.dissidentvoice.org/2008/02/holding-barack-obama-accountable/.
4. Pam Martens, "The Obama Bubble: Why Wall Street Needs a Presidential Brand," *Black Agenda Report,* March 5, 2008.
5. ABC News, "Backstage at Barack Obama's Headquarters," February 28, 2008.
6. Dixon, "Holding Barack Obama Accountable."
7. Pew Research Center, Project for Excellence in Journalism, *The Invisible Primary Invisible No Longer: A First Look at Coverage of the 2008 Presidential Campaign,* October 29, 2007, http://www.journalism.org/node/8191.
8. Paul Krugman, "Big Table Fantasies," *New York Times,* December 17, 2007. p. A29.
9. Quoted in Christopher Wills, "Rookie Obama Survived Campaign Year as Others Faltered," *The Pantagraph* (Bloomington-Normal, IL), February 10, 2008.
10. *Newsweek* (cover), January 14, 2008.
11. Clarke Hoyt, "The Campaign and the Horse Race," *New York Times,* November 18, 2007.
12. "The Great Divide," photographs for *Time* magazine by Diana Walker and Callie Shell, *Time* (February 18, 2008), pp. 20–27.
13. Jann S. Wenner, "A New Hope," *Rolling Stone,* March 20, 2008.
14. Tim Dickinson, "The Machinery of Hope," *Rolling Stone,* March 20, 2008, pp. 36–42.
15. Herman, "Market-Democracy."
16. Thomas Ferguson, *Golden Rule: The Investment Theory of Party Competition and Logic of Money-Driven Political Systems* (Chicago: University of Chicago Press, 1995).
17. Gerald Seib, "Issues Recede in '08 Contest as Voters Focus on Character," *Wall Street Journal,* February 5, 2008, p. A1.
18. Calvin Woodward, "Old Polarities of Race and Gender Persist in Democratic Race," Associated Press, March 15, 2008.
19. Shaila Dewan, "Where Issues Carry Dollar Signs," *New York Times,* January 26, 2008, p. A12 (emphasis added).
20. Ibid.
21. Here Comsky is quoting Walter Lippman.
22. Noam Chomsky, "'Good News,' Iraq and Beyond," *ZNet,* February 16, 2008, http://www.zcommunications.org/znet/viewArticle/16522.
23. Noam Chomsky, *What We Say Goes: Conversations on U.S. Power in a Changing World* (New York: Metropolitan, 2007), p. 54. See also Paul Street, "Bush, Kerry, and 'Body Language' v. 'Message': Notes on Race, Gender, Empire and Mass Infantilization," *ZNet Magazine,* October 12, 2004.

24. Council on Foreign Relations, "Democratic Debate Transcript, Cleveland, Ohio," February 26, 2008, www.cfr.org/publication/15604/.

25. Pew Research Center for the People and the Press, "Public Sees Fair Fight," March 6, 2008, read at www.pewresearch.org/pubs/757/public-sees-fair-fight. Thanks to Noam Chomsky for bringing this source to my attention.

26. Patrick Healy and Jeff Zeleny, "Racial Issue Bubbles Up Again for Democrats," *New York Times,* March 13, 2008, p. A1.

27. Seib, "Issues Recede in '08 Contest."

Chapter 3

1. Ira Katznelson, *When Affirmative Action Was White: An Untold History of Racial Inequality in Twentieth Century America* (New York: W. W. Norton, 2005); Melvin Oliver and Thomas Shapiro, *Black Wealth/White Wealth: A New Approach to Racial Inequality* (New York: Routledge, 1997).

2. This section relies on the following sources: Harvard Sitkoff, *The Struggle for Black Equality, 1954–1980* (New York: Hill and Wang, 1981); Howard Zinn, *The Twentieth Century: A People's History* (New York: HarperPerennial, 1998); Paul Street, *Segregated Schools: Educational Apartheid in the Post–Civil Rights Era* (New York: Routledge, 2005), pp. 40–48; Paul Street, *Racial Oppression in the Global Metropolis: A Living Black Chicago History* (New York: Rowman and Littlefield, 2007), pp. 37–38, 131–151.

3. Henry A. Giroux, *The Terror of Neoliberalism: Authoritarianism and the Eclipse of Democracy* (Boulder: Paradigm, 2004), pp. xiii–xvi.

4. Harvard Sitkoff, *The Struggle for Black Equality, 1954–1980* (New York: Hill and Wang, 1981), p. 226.

5. Kevin Alexander Gray, "Clinton and Black Americans," in Alexander Cockburn and Jeffrey St. Clair, *Dime's Worth of Difference: Beyond the Lesser of Two Evils* (Petrolia and Oakland, Calif.: CounterPunch and AK Press, 2004), p. 97.

6. Elaine Brown, *The Condemnation of Little B* (Boston: Beacon Press, 2002), p. 178.

7. Ibid., pp. 175–176.

8. Ibid., pp. 173–206.

9. Gray, "Clinton and Black Americans," pp. 98–99.

10. Brown, *Condemnation,* p. 178.

11. See Lani Guinier, *The Tyranny of the Majority: Fundamental Fairness in Representative Democracy* (New York: Free Press, 1994).

12. Christopher Hitchens, "Fool Me Thrice: It Should Be No Surprise the Clintons Are Playing the Race Card," *Slate,* January 28, 2008, http://www.slate.com/id/2182938.

13. Christopher Hitchens, *No One Left to Lie To: The Values of the Worst Family* (New York: Verso, 2000), pp. 33–37.

14. Greg Palast, *The Best Democracy Money Can Buy* (London: Pluto Press, 2002), pp. 6–43.

15. Jodi Kantor, "A Candidate, His Minister and the Search for Faith," *New York Times,* April 30, 2007, p. A1.

16. In my experience during the pivotal Iowa Caucus campaign of 2007–2008, the mere fact of Obama's blackness was a significant barrier to communicating with liberal and progressive white caucus-goers about the more sincerely and substan-

tively progressive and populist nature of the John Edwards campaign, which ran to the democratic left of both Hillary Clinton and Barack Obama.

17. Richard Wolffe and Darren Briscoe, "Across the Divide: Barack Obama's Road to Racial Reconstruction," *Newsweek,* July 16, 2007.

18. John B. Judis, "American Adam: Obama and the Cult of the New," *The New Republic,* March 12, 2008.

19. Liza Mundy, "A Series of Fortunate Events: Barack Obama Needed More Than Talent and Ambition to Rocket from Obscure State Senator to Presidential Contender in Three Years," *Washington Post Magazine,* August 12, 2007.

20. Quoted in Don Terry, "The Skin Game: Do White Voters Like Barack Obama Because 'He's Not Really Black'?" *Chicago Tribune Magazine,* October 24, 2004, p. 16.

21. Wolffe and Briscoe, "Across the Divide," pp. 22–23. The depth of West's concern should not be exaggerated. According to *Newsweek* reporters Wolffe and Briscoe, "a few weeks later, the two men met in a downtown Washington, D.C., hotel to chat about Obama's campaign staff. . . . West endorsed Obama and signed up as an unpaid adviser."

22. Gary Younge, "Is Obama Black Enough?" *The Guardian,* March 1, 2007; Gary Younge, "The Obama Effect," *The Nation,* December 31, 2007; Paul Street, "Audacity of Deception," *ZNet,* December 6, 2007, http://www.zcommunications.org/znet/viewArticle/15765.

23. Elaine Brown uses the term "mealymouthing" to wonderful effect in her discussion of how the black president of the National Council of Negro Women played along with the vicious and racist Clinton-Gingrich assault on poor people's public family cash assistance during the 1990s. See Brown, *Condemnation,* p. 249. For a similar usage from a black left critic characterizing Obama's position on the U.S. occupation of Iraq, see Glen Ford and Peter Gamble, "Obama Mouths Mush on War," *Black Commentator,* December 1, 2005, http://www.blackcommentator.com/161/161_cover_obama_iraq.html.

24. Obama, *Audacity,* pp. 232–233.

25. Kantor, "A Candidate, a Minister, and the Search for Faith."

26. Wolffe and Briscoe, "Across the Divide," pp. 22–23.

27. Obama, *Audacity*, pp. 245–246.

28. I would go beyond Wilson in arguing that American capitalism continues its venerable tradition of sowing steep racial divisions and racial hatred within the majority working population and that full black equality will never be accomplished within the framework of capitalism. For my broader thought on race and class, see Street, *Racial Oppression,* pp. 18, 41, 63, 70, 123, 141–146, 182, 261–263; Paul Street, "'Class, Color, and the Hidden Injuries of Race," *Z Magazine,* June 2002, 39–42.

29. Michael Brown, Martin Carnoy, Elliott Currie, and Troy Duster, *Whitewashing Race: The Myth of a Color-Blind Society* (Berkeley: University of California Press, 2003).

30. For an updated and more historically and theoretically ambitious treatment of the data collected an earlier Chicago Urban League study, see my book *Racial Oppression.* The most recent data on racial segregation and inequality is found in Chapters 6 and 7. On societal racism as the cause of persistent racial separatism and inequality, see Chapter 8, entitled "What's Racism Got to Do with It?" For a detailed historical and sociological criticism of the Wilson "class over race" thesis, see pp. 261–263.

31. See Joe Feagin, *Racist America: Roots, Current Realities, and Future Reparations* (New York: Routledge, 2000); Brown et al., *Whitewashing Race.*

32. Katznelson, *When Affirmative Action Was White.*

33. Obama, *Audacity,* pp. 248–249; Barack Obama, "Selma Voting Rights Commemoration," March 4, 2007, http://www.barackobama.com/2007/03/04/selma_voting_rights_march_comm.php.

34. Obama, *Audacity of Hope,* pp. 240–241.

35. James Loewen, *Sundown Towns: A Hidden Dimension of American Racism* (New York: Touchstone, 2005), p. 130; Thomas Shapiro, "Running in Reverse," Center for American Progress (October 22, 2004), read at www.americanprogressaction.org/issues/2004/shapiro_recession.html; Brown, *Condemnation,* pp. 78–79.

36. Chicago Urban League, "Still Separate, Unequal: Race, Place, Policy and the State of Black Chicago" (Chicago: Chicago Urban League, 2005), pp. 30–37, 48–52; U.S. Census Bureau, *Census 2000, SF–1 and SF–3 Sample Data* (Washington, D.C.: Government Printing Office, 2000); Economic Policy Institute, *Hardships in America: The Real Story of Working Families* (Washington, D.C.: Economic Policy Institute, 2001), pp. 1–43, Table A4.2.; Illinois Department of Labor, *The Progress of Women and Minorities in the Illinois Labor Force, Annual Report for FY 2003* (Springfield: Illinois Department of Labor, 2003).

37. This budget takes into account housing, food, child care, transportation, and health care, plus other necessities and taxes.

38. Economic Policy Institute, *Hardships in America,* pp. 1–43, Table A4.2.

39. Obama, *Audacity of Hope,* p. 245, 247, 254–256.

40. For powerful antiracist reflections that have influenced my analysis here, see Feagin, *Racist America*; Brown et al., *Whitewashing Race.*

41. Stokely Carmichael and Charles Hamilton, *Black Power: The Politics of Liberation in America* (New York: Vintage, 1967), p. 4, quoted in Stephen Steinberg, *Turning Back: The Retreat from Racial Justice in American Thought and Policy* (Boston: Beacon Press, 1995), pp. 75–76.

42. Ibid.

43. David Garrow, *Bearing the Cross: Martin Luther King, Jr., and the Southern Christian Leadership Conference* (New York: HarperCollins, 1986), p. 537.

44. Roy Brooks, *Integration or Separation: A Strategy for Racial Equality* (Cambridge: Harvard University Press, 1996), p. ix.

45. The common white reaction to the notion that whites should pay through programs like affirmative action, that mandatory school integration (or equalization) plans should be implemented, or even that the government should pay reparations for slavery and discrimination that took place before they were born is that we must "let bygones be bygones." Many whites believe that "the unjust enrichment gained by whites over centuries should be forgotten," even though, as sociologist Joel Feagin noted, "Some black Americans are [still] only a couple of generations removed from their enslaved ancestors" and "The near slavery of legal segregation only came to an end in the 1960s, well within the lifetimes of many Americans alive today." In Brooks' and Feagin's view, even if the contemporary socioeconomic system became free of racial discrimination and bias in its current operation, compensatory programs, including reparations, would be required to undo the racially disparate historical "windfall" whites received and thereby generate actual equality of opportunity for African Americans. Feagin, *Racist America,* p. 261.

46. Brown et al. *Whitewashing Race,* pp. 24–25.

47. Paul Street, "Prosecuting Jim Crow's Ghosts: The Racist Past Lives On," *TINABANTU: Journal of African National Affairs* 3, no. 1 (2007): 7–12.

48. Obama, *Audacity,* pp. 237–238.

49. Wolffe and Briscoe, "Across the Divide"; U.S. Census Bureau, *American Fact Finder,* community data, http:/factfinder.census.gov/servlet/ACSSAFFacts (search for "Cairo, Illinois").

50. Janny Scott, "At State Level, Obama Proved to Be Pragmatic and Practical," *New York Times,* July 30, 2007, p. A1; Rick Pearson and Ray Long, "Careful Steps, Looking Ahead," *Chicago Tribune,* May 3, 2007; Paul Street, "The Poverty of Workfare: Dubious Claims, Dark Clouds, and a Silver Lining," *Dissent,* Fall 1998, pp. 53–60; Paul Street, *"Find a Job": The Recent History and Future of Welfare "Reform" in the Midwest* (De Kalb: Office for Social Policy Research, Northern Illinois University, 1998); Obama, *Audacity,* p. 256.

51. For details and sources (voluminous) see Street, *Racial Oppression,* pp. 263–269.

52. Adolph Reed, "Race and the New Deal Coalition," *The Nation,* April 7, 2008, p. 24.

53. Wolffe and Briscoe, *Across the Divide*; Obama, "Selma Voting Rights Commemoration."

54. Barack Obama, "Tone, Truth, and the Democratic Party," *Daily Kos,* September 30, 2005, www.dailykos/com/story/2005/9/30/102745/165.

55. NAACP 2008 Presidential Candidate Civil Rights Questionnaire, February 1, 2008, http://www.naacp.org/news/press/2008–02–01/RESPONSES; Vernellia Randall, "Obama's Plan on Eliminating Racial Inequality," February 1, 2008, http://academic.udayton.edu/race/2008ElectionandRacism/Obama/Obama00.htm #INSTITUTIONAL/.

56. CNN, "Jesse Jackson: Obama Needs to Bring Attention to Jena 6," CNNPolitics.com, September 19, 2007, www,cnn.com/2007/POLITICS/09/19/ Jackson.jena6/index.html; Greg Simmons, "'Acting White' Comment Is No Political Time Bomb for Jackson," FoxNews.com, September 24, 2007.

57. Alex McGillis, "The Trail: A Daily Diary of Campaign 2008," September 19, 2007, http:/blog.washingtonpost.com/the-trail/2007/09/19/post_81.html.

58. Jesse Jackson, "Most Democratic Candidates Are Ignoring African Americans," *Chicago Sun Times,* November 27, 2007.

59. Kevin Alexander Gray, "South Carolina: The Black Primary," *Black Agenda Report,* July 25, 2007, http://www.blackagendareport.com/index.php?option=com_content&task=view&id=292&Itemid=34.

60. Transcribed at Matt Stoller, "Obama's Admiration of Reagan," *Open Left,* January 16, 2008, http://www.openleft.com/showDiary.do?diaryId=3263. This site also includes a video clip of Obama saying this.

61. Ibid. (emphasis in original). For the accuracy of Stoller's judgment, see (among many possible citations) Michael Lind, *Up from Conservatism: Why the Right Is Wrong for America* (New York: Free Press, 1996), pp. 192–193.

62. Gary Gerstle, *American Crucible: Race and Nation in the Twentieth Century* (Princeton, N.J.: Princeton University Press, 2001), p. 358.

63. Michael C. Dawson, *Behind the Mule: Race and Class in African-American Politics* (Princeton, N.J.: Princeton University Press, 1994), p. 206.

64. See Obama, *Audacity,* p. 31, where he praises Reagan for expressing America's "longing for order" after the excesses of the 1960s and 1970s; Joe Klein, "The Fresh Face," *Time,* October 17, 2006.

65. Barack Obama, "The Great Need of the Hour," Atlanta, Georgia, January 20, 2008, http://www.barackobama.com/2008/01/20/remarks_of_senator_barack_obam_40.php.

66. Ibid. (emphasis added).

67. Transcript of Democratic Presidential Candidates' Debate, Myrtle Beach, South Carolina, January 21, 2008, www.cnn.com/2008/POLITICS/01/21/debate.transcript/index.html.

68. Ibid.

69. Henry A. Giroux, *The Abandoned Generation: Democracy beyond the Culture of Fear* (New York: Palgrave-MacMillan, 2003), pp. 1–70; Giroux, *The Terror of Neoliberalism,* pp. 1–53.

70. For earlier statements of this argument, see Street, *Racial Oppression,* pp. 229–230; Paul Street, "A Lott Missing: Rituals of Purification and Deep Racism Denial," *Black Commentator,* December 22, 2002, www.blackcommentator.com and http://www. nationinstitute.org/tomdispatch/index.mhtml?pid=258; Street, "Prosecuting Jim Crow's Ghosts."

71. Derrick Bell, *Silent Covenants: Brown V. Board of Education and the Unfulfilled Hopes for Racial Reform* (New York, NY: Oxford University Press 2004), pp. 77–78.

72. Sheryl Cashin, *The Failures of Integration* (New York: PublicAffairs, 2004), pp. xi–xii. See also Leonard Steinhorn and Carbara Diggs-Brown, *By the Color of Our Skin* (New York: Penguin, 2000), p. 7; Stanley Aronowitz, "Race: The Continental Divide," *The Nation,* March 12, 2001; Street, "A Lott Missing."

73. Quoted in Judis, "American Adam," p. 24.

74. Charles Krauthammer, "What We Don't Know about Obama Hurts Him," *Chicago Tribune,* March 10, 2008, sec. 1,.p. 13.

75. Will is quoted in Younge, "An Obama Victory Would Symbolise a Great Deal"; George Will, "The GOP—Grand Old Pulpit," *Newsweek,* January 14, 2008, http://www.newsweek.com/id/84534; Krauthammer, "What We Don't Know about Obama."

76. Media Matters, "CNN's Bennett: Barack Hussein Obama Has Taught the Black Community You Don't Have to Act Like Jesse Jackson," http://mediamatters.org/items/200801040004.

77. Taylor is quoted in Younge, "The Obama Effect."

78. Parker, "Obama Has U.S. Hooked on a Feeling."

79. Younge, "The Obama Effect."

80. Younge, "An Obama Victory Would Symbolize a Great Deal" (emphasis added).

81. Younge, "The Obama Effect."

82. Margaret Kimberly, "Obama's Hollow Victory," *Black Agenda Report,* January 9, 2008, http://www.blackagendareport.com/index.php?option=com_content&task=view&id=485&Itemid=1.

83. Democracy Now, "Barack Obama and the African American Community: A Debate with Michael Eric Dyson and Glen Ford," January 9, 2008.

84. Hill, "Not My Brand of Hope."

85. Jonathan Alter, "The Obama Dividend," *Newsweek,* March 31, 2008, p. 37.

86. Jonathan Alter, "How Much Change Is Change?" *Newsweek,* March 10, 2008, p. 39.

87. Janny Scott, "In 2000, a Streetwise Veteran Schooled a Bold Young Obama," *New York Times,* September 9, 2007; Ted Kleine, "Is Bobby Rush in Trouble?" *Chicago Reader* (March 17, 2000).

88. According to Jerry Morrison, a consultant with the 2000 Rush campaign who is quoted in Scott, "Streetwise Veteran."

89. Scott, "In 2000, a Streetwise Veteran,", pp. A1, A20.

90. Hyde Park is less internally integrated than often assumed, however. See Street, *Racial Oppression,* p. 172. I myself grew up in Hyde Park during the 1960s and can personally attest to its long-standing, relatively integrated nature.

91. Scott, "Streetwise Veteran," p. A20.

92. Stephen Steinberg, *Turning Back: The Retreat from Racial Justice in American Thought and Policy* (Boston: Beacon Press, 1995), pp. 149–150.

93. Wolffe and Briscoe, "Across the Divide."

94. Quoted in Bill Barnhart, "When Rage Bursts: The Lessons of the Kerner Report," *Chicago Tribune,* March 2, 2008, sec. 2, p. 4.

95. Younge, "The Obama Effect."

96. Ginger Thompson, "Seeking Unity, Obama Feels Pull of Racial Divide on Campaign Trail," *New York Times,* February 12, 2008, pp. A1, A16.

97. Barack Obama, "On My Faith and My Church," *The Huffington Post,* March 14, 2008, http://www.huffingtonpost.com/barack-obama/on-my-faith-and-my-church_b_91623.html.

98. John McCormick, "Obama Enlists Ex-Commanders," *Chicago Tribune,* March 13, 2008.

99. Martin Luther King, Jr., "A Time to Break the Silence," April 4, 1967, p. 231, in *A Testament of Hope: The Essential Writings and Speeches of Martin Luther King, Jr.,* ed. James M. Washington (San Francisco: HarperCollins, 1991).

100. Edward Wolffe, *Top Heavy: The Increasing Inequality of Wealth in America and What Can Be Done About It* (New York: New Press, 2002); Janny Scott and David Leonhardt, "Shadowy Lines That Still Divide," *New York Times*, May 15, 2005; Lawrence Mishel, Jared Bernstein, and Heather Boushey, *The State of Working America 2002–2003* (Ithaca, NY: Economic Policy Institute and Cornell University Press, 2003); Paul Street, *Empire and Inequality: America and the World since 9/11* (Boulder: Paradigm, 2004); Kevin Phillips, *Boiling Point: Democrats, Republicans, and the Decline of Middle-Class Prosperity* (New York: HarperPerrenial, 1993); Economic Policy Institute, *State of Working America*; Steve Brouwer, *Sharing the Pie: A Citizen's Guide to Wealth and Power in America* (New York: Henry Holt, 1998).

101. Paul Street, *The Vicious Circle: Race, Prison, Jobs, and Community in Chicago, Illinois, and the Nation* (Chicago: Chicago Urban League, 2002); Paul Street "Color Bind: Prisons and the New American Racism," in Tera Herivel and Paul Wright, eds., *Prison Nation: The Warehousing of America's Poor* (London: Routledge, 2002), pp. 30–40; Christian Parenti, *Lockdown America: Police and Prisons in the Age of Crisis* (London: Verso, 2000). In late October 2002, Obama read and spoke favorably on the first source (a Chicago Urban League project study funded by a foundation on whose board he once sat) cited in this note.

102. Matt Gonzalez, "The Obama Craze: Count Me Out," *BeyondChron: San Francisco's Online Daily,* February 28, 2008, www.beyondchron.org/articles/index.php?itemid=5413#more.

103. Street, *Empire and Inequality,* pp. 46 and passim; James Madison, "Political Reflections," February 23, 1799, quoted in John Samples, "James Madison's Vision of Liberty," *CATO Policy Report,* March/April 2001, p. 12.

104. Jennifer Parker, "Ferraro: Obama Where He Is Because He's Black," ABC News (March 11, 2008), read at http://abcnews.go.com/Politics/Vote2008/story?id=4428719&page=1.

105. Barack Obama, "'A More Perfect Union,'" Philadelphia, PA. March 18, 2008, http://www.barackobama.com/2008/03/18/remarks_of_senator_barrack_obam_53.php.

106. James Loewen, *Sundown Towns: A Hidden Dimension of American Racism* (New York: Touchstone, 2005), p. 130; Street, "Color Bind"; Street, *Vicious Circle.*

107. Street, "Obama's Latest 'Beautiful Speech.'"

108. Bill Fletcher, "Obama Race Speech Analysis," *Black Commentator,* March 20, 2008, http://www.blackcommentator.com/269/269_cover_obama_race_speech_analysis_ed_bd.html (emphasis added).

109. Dawson, *Behind the Mule.*

110. Barbara Ehrenreich, blog-posting at http://ehrenreich.blogs.com/barbaras_blog/2008/03/hillarys-nasty.html.

111. Vernon S. Burton, Letter to the Editor, *New York Times,* March 19, 2008.

112. Dawson, *Behind the Mule,* pp. 206–207.

113. Klein, "The Fresh Face."

114. William Kristol, "Generation Obama? Perhaps Not," *New York Times,* March 17, 2008, p. A23.

115. Adolph Reed, "Obama No," *The Progressive* (May 2007).

116. *Chicago Tribune,* "Transcript: Rev. Jeremiah Wright's Speech to the National Press Club," April 28, 2008), read at http://www.chicagotribune.com/news/nationworld/chi-wrighttranscript-04282008,0,5339764,full.story; FOX News (April 29, 2008), read at http://elections.foxnews.com/2008/04/29/transcript-obama-press-conference-on-jeremiah-wright; Glen Ford, "Obama Stumbles on His Own Contradictions: Pop Goes the Race-Neutral Campaign!," *Black Agenda Report* (April 30, 2008).

117. Ford, "Obama Stumbles."

118. See Street, *Racial Oppression in the Globl Metropolis.*

119. Quoted in Glick, "Obama and Wright: Different Worldviews," *ZNet* (May 4, 2008).

120. Glen Ford, "Obama Stumbles on His Own Contradictions: Pop Goes the Race-Neutral Campaign!," *Black Agenda Report* (April 30, 2008).

121. Reed, "Obama No."

Chapter 4

1. I will dispense with quotation marks regarding the Iraq War for the rest of this chapter but include them here to suggest the morally problematic nature of the routine reference by Obama (and other candidates, elected officials, media representatives, and citizens) to the United States as "a nation at war." Like many other antiwar progressives, I view the Iraq War as one-sided imperial violence and wish to underscore the fact that it is a war of a very specific kind: colonial and imperial aggression on a small and weak nation by the greatest superpower in history.

2. The historical sketch presented here and in the next section is based on numerous sources, including the following: Gar Alperovitz, *The Decision to Use the*

Atomic Bomb (New York: Vintage, 1995); Richard J. Barnet, *Intervention and Revolution* (New York: Meridian, 1972); William Blum, *Rogue State: A Guide to the World's Only Superpower* (Monroe, Maine: Common Courage, 2005); Noam Chomsky, *American Power and the New Mandarins* (New York: New Press, 2002 [1967]); Noam Chomsky, *For Reasons of State* (New York: New Press, 2003 [1970]); Noam Chomsky, *Deterring Democracy* (New York: Hill and Wang, 1991); Noam Chomsky, *Rethinking Camelot: JFK, the Vietnam War, and US Political Culture* (Boston: South End Press, 1993); Noam Chomsky, *Hegemony over Survival: America's Quest for Global Dominance* (New York: Metropolitan, 2003); Noam Chomsky, *World Orders, Old and New* (New York: Columbia University Press, 1994); Noam Chomsky, *Year 501: The Conquest Continues* (Boston: South End, 1993); Noam Chomsky, *On Power and Ideology: The Managua Lectures* (Boston: South End, 1987); Noam Chomsky, *The New Military Humanism: Lessons from Kosovo* (Monroe, Maine: Common Courage, 1999); Noam Chomsky and Gilbert Achcar, *Perilous Power: The Middle East and U.S. Foreign Policy* (Boulder: Paradigm, 2007); Noam Chomsky, *What Uncle Sam Really Wants* (Boston: Odonian Press, 1992); Noam Chomsky, *Understanding Power* (New York: New Press, 2002); Melvyn Dubofsky and Athan Theoharis, *Imperial Democracy: The United States since 1945* (Englewood Cliffs, N.J.: Prentice-Hall, 1988); David Harvey, *The New Imperialism* (New York: Oxford University Press, 2003); Alexander Cockburn, *Corruptions of Empire* (New York: Verso, 1987); Christopher Hitchens, *The Trial of Henry Kissinger* (New York: Verso, 2001); Chalmers Johnson, *Blowback: The Costs and Consequences of American Empire* (New York: Holt and Holt, 2004); Chalmers Johnson, *The Sorrows of Empire: Militarism, Secrecy and the End of the Republic* (New York: Metropolitan, 2004); Frank Kofsky, *Harry S. Truman and the War Scare of 1948* (New York: St. Martin's Press, 1993); Gabriel Kolko, *Main Currents in American History* (New York: Pantheon, 1976), pp. 348–398; Sidney Lens, *The Forging of the American Empire,* 2d ed. (Chicago: Haymarket Books, 2004); Rajul Mahajan, *The New Crusade: America's War on Terrorism* (New York: Monthly Review, 2002); Thomas McCormick, America's *Half Century: United States Foreign Policy in the Cold War* (Baltimore: Johns Hopkins University Press, 1989); Bruce Miroff, *Pragmatic Illusions: The Presidential Politics of John F. Kennedy* (New York: Longman, 1979); John Pilger, *Hidden Agendas* (New York: New Press, 1998); Howard Zinn, *Postwar America: 1945–1971* (Indianapolis: Bobbs-Merrill, 1973), pp. 1–88; Howard Zinn, *A People's History of the United States, 1492-Present* (New York: HarperPerennial, 2003); Howard Zinn, *Terrorism and War* (New York: Seven Stories, 2002); Howard Zinn, *Declarations of Independence: Cross-Examining American Ideology* (New York: HarperPerennial, 1990).

3. Zinn, *The Twentieth Century*, pp. 357–358.

4. Alexander Cockburn, "Presidential Elections: Not as Big a Deal as They Say," in Alexander Cockburn and Jeffrey St. Clair, *Dime's Worth of Difference: Beyond the Lesser of Two Evils* (Petrolia and Oakland, Calif.: CounterPunch and AK Press, 2004), p. 12.

5. Zinn, *A People's History*, pp. 653–654.

6. Cockburn, pp. 11–12.

7. Gabriel Kolko, "Alliances and the American Empire," *Dime's Worth*, p. 270. See also Paul Street, "Time to Scrape the Kerry Sticker Off: On Democrats, Values, and the Lakoff Thesis," *ZNet Sustainer Commentary,* June 17, 2005, http://www.zmag.org/Sustainers/Content/2005–06/17street.cfm; Paul Street, "Kerry Is Coke,

Bush Is Crack," *ZNet Magazine,* March 24, 2004, http://www.zmag.org/content/showarticle.cfm?SectionID=33&ItemID=5204.

8. Sean Donahue, "Randy Beers and Colombia," *Dime's Worth*, pp. 251–255.

9. William I. Robinson, *Promoting Polyarchy—Globalization, US Intervention, and Hegemony* (Cambridge: Cambridge University Press, 1996); Noam Chomsky, *Profit over People: Neoliberalism and Global Order* (Boston: South End, 1999); Paul Street, "Capitalism and Democracy 'Don't Mix Very Well': Reflections on Globalization," *Z Magazine,* February 2000, pp. 20–24; Paul Street, "'People Profit from Trade,'" *ZNet Magazine,* March 9, 2003, http://www.zmag.org/content/showarticle.cfm?SectionID=13&ItemID=3210.

10. Chomsky, *Deterring Democracy,* p. 45.

11. Kolko, "Alliances and the American Empire," p. 270.

12. Zinn, *A People's History,* p. 651.

13. Ibid., pp. 651–652. It is important to add that Cheney's comments were disingenuous. As Chomsky notes (personal communication, June 19, 2008): "It's often ignored that with the collapse of the Berlin wall, the clouds lifted, and the threats were readily and explicitly discerned, in the 1990 budget and National Security strategy, which were quite clear about why we had to keep the Pentagon system as before: because of third world 'radical' nationalism and the need to sustain the domestic high-tech economy. They were pretty frank." For substantiation, see Chomsky *Failed States*, pp. 125–129; Chomsky, *Deterring Democracy*, pp. 9–68, 139–177 and passim.

14. Albright (1999) and Clinton (1996) are quoted in Blum, *Rogue State,* front matter.

15. Interview of U.S. Secretary of State Madeleine Albright on the NBC *Today Show,* February 19, 1998, http://www.fas.org/news/iraq/1998/02/19/98021907_tpo.html.

16. Street, *Empire and Inequality*, pp. xii, 141–171.

17. Howard Zinn, "America's Blinders," *The Progressive,* April 2006.

18. Tony Smith, "It's Uphill for the Democrats: They Need a Global Strategy, Not Just Tactics for Iraq," *Washington Post,* March 11, 2007, p. B01, http://www.washingtonpost.com/wp-dyn/content/article/ 2007/03/09/AR2007030901884_pf.html.

19. See Paul Street, "Imperial Temptations: John Edwards, Barack Obama, and the Myth of Post–World War II United States Benevolence," *ZNet Magazine,* May 28, 2007, http://www.zmag.org/content/showarticle.cfm?ItemID=12928; Paul Street, "'We've Done More Than Talk,'" *Empire and Inequality Report,* no. 7, January 19, 2009, http://www.zmag.org/content/showarticle.cfm?ItemID=11895.

20. Stephen Zunes, "Barack Obama on the Middle East," *Foreign Policy in Focus,* January 10, 2008, http://www.fpif.org/fpiftxt/4886.

21. Flyer from "Obama for America" (Des Moines, Iowa, November 2007).

22. For what it's worth, I think that much the same argument could be reasonably constructed in opposition to the Edwards and (of course) Clinton campaigns, both of which sadly shared Obama's underlying strong attachment to the American Empire Project and the false "American exceptionalist" belief that the United States is an inherently benevolent force in the world. I worked for Edwards primarily for reasons of domestic policy and never held any illusion that he was any less committed to the American Empire Project than Obama.

23. Barack Obama, "Against Going to War with Iraq," speech delivered in Chicago, Illinois, October 2, 2002, www.commondreams.org/archive/2008/02/28/7343/.

24. Jodi Kantor, "A Candidate, His Minister and the Search for Faith," *New York Times,* April 30, 2007, p. A1. On U.S. foreign policy as context for terror attacks on the United States, see Johnson, *Blowback.*

25. "The Obama Strategist," *National Journal,* August 3, 2007.

26. Carl Kaysen, Steven E. Miller, Martin B. Malin, Wlliam D. Nordhaus, and John D. Steinbruner, *War with Iraq: Costs, Consequences, and Alternatives* (Cambridge, Mass.: Committee on International Security Studies of the American Academy of Arts and Sciences, 2002); Street, *Empire and Inequality,* pp. 57–63.

27. Thomas E. Ricks, *Fiasco: The American Military Adventure in Iraq* (New York: Penguin, 2006).

28. Kate Zernike and Jeff Zeleny, "Obama in Senate: Star Power, Minor Role," *New York Times,* March 9, 2008, sec. 1, pp. 1, 18.

29. The quote is reproduced in Alexander Cockburn, "Obama's Game," *CounterPunch,* April 24, 2006, www.counterpunch.org/cockburn04242006.html.

30. Barack Obama, "Moving Forward in Iraq," Speech to Chicago Council on Foreign Relations" (November 22, 2005), http://obama.senate.gov/speech/051122-moving_forward/.

31. The U.S. invasion of Iraq was profoundly illegal, violating the United Nations Charter's ban on aggressive and unprovoked warfare. By some estimates as of this writing (in mid-April 2008), it has caused the deaths of more than 1 million Iraqis and led to the exodus and displacement of millions more. Barack Obama, "Moving Forward in Iraq."

32. Zunes, "Barack Obama on the Middle East."

33. Matt Gonzalez, "The Obama Craze: Count Me Out," *BeyondChron: San Francisco's Online Daily,* February 28, 2008, www.beyondchron.org/articles/index.php?itemid=5413#more.

34. Ibid.

35. Barack Obama, "A Way Forward in Iraq," speech to Chicago Council on Global Affairs, Chicago, November 20, 2006, http://obama.senate.gov/speech/061120-a_way_forward _in_iraq/index.html; Zunes, "Barack Obama on the Middle East." See also my articles "Neanderthal Continuities of a Bipartisan Nature," *ZNet Magazine,* November 20, 2006; "Victory without Vision," *ZNet Magazine,* November 11, 2006; "Blaming the Iraqis: What Took So Long?" *ZNet Magazine,* December 5, 2007; "The Whole World Is Watching," *ZNet Magazine,* December 2, 2006; "'You Just Don't Like George,'" *ZNet Magazine,* November 30, 2006; "'Nobody's Leaving': Never Mind Democracy and Imperial Democracy," *ZNet Magazine,* December 10, 2006; "Vilsacking Iraq," *ZNet Magazine,* December 22, 2006.

36. Zunes, "Barack Obama on the Middle East."

37. Michael Tomasky, "The Phenomenon," *New York Review of Books,* November 30, 2006.

38. Davidson is quoted in Adam Turl, "Is Obama Different?" *Socialist Worker Online,* February 2, 2007. Davidson's comment should not be taken to mean that Obama ever questioned whether the Iraq invasion was *morally and/or legally* "wrong." Obama never questioned the invasion publicly with regard to that sort of definition of "wrong."

39. Street, "Kerry Is Coke, Bush Is Crack."

40. Monica Davey, "The Speaker: A Surprise Senate Contender Reaches Biggest Stage Yet," *New York Times,* July 26, 2004.

41. David Mendell and Jeff Zeleny, "Obama Says War Will Decide Election," *Chicago Tribune,* July 27, 2004 (emphasis added).

42. "Congress Will Fund War if Bush Uses Veto," *USA Today,* April 1, 2007; Stephen Zunes, "The Foreign Policy Agenda of the Democratic Front-Runners: Comparisons on Some Key Issues," *Common Dreams,* January 25, 2008.

43. Chomsky and Achcar, *Perilous Power,* pp. 56–57; Paul Street, "'Nobody's Leaving"; Jeremy Brecher and Brendan Smith, "The Stab in the Back Trap," *Common Dreams,* April 26, 2007, http://www.commondreams.org/archive/2007/04/26/766/.

44. Howard Zinn, "Are We Politicians or Citizens?" *The Progressive,* April 2007, reproduced on ZNet (March 27, 2007) at http://www.zmag.org/content/showarticle.cfm?SectionID=51&ItemID=12413.

45. Anthony Arnove, "Why Bush Won't Admit Failure in Iraq," *Socialist Worker,* July 20, 2007, http://socialistworker.org/2007–2/638/638_04_Arnove.shtml.

46. *The Charlie Rose Show,* PBS, February 21, 2008. See www.charlierose.com/shows/2008/02/21/2/a-conversation-with-samantha-power.

47. Paul Street, "Largely about Oil: Reflections on Empire, Petroleum, Democracy, and the Occupation of Iraq," *Z Magazine,* January 2008, pp. 38–42.

48. Juan Gonzales, Amy Goodman, and Jeremy Scahill, "Despite Antiwar Rhetoric, Clinton-Obama Plans Would Keep US Mercenaries, Troops in Iraq for Years to Come," *Democracy Now,* February 28, 2008, www.democracynow.org/2008/2/28/jeremy_scahill_despite_anti_war_rhetoric.

49. Jonathan Chait, "Entanglements: Ignore What Candidates Say About Foreign Policy," *The New Republic* (May 28, 2008), p. 5.

50. Jeremy Scahill, "Obama's Mercenary Position," *The Nation,* March 16, 2008.

51. Gonzales et al., "Despite Antiwar Rhetoric."

52. Scahill, "Obama's Mercenary Position."

53. Obama, *Audacity,* p. 317; Obama, "A Way Forward in Iraq"; Greg Borowski, "Obama Addresses State, U.S. Topics," *Milwaukee Journal-Sentinel Online,* February 13, 2008, http://www.jsonline.com/story/index.aspx?id=718193.

54. Anthony Arnove, *Iraq: The Logic of Withdrawal* (New York: New Press, 2006), pp. 28–29; Noam Chomsky, *Failed States: The Abuse of Power and the Assault on Democracy* (New York: Metropolitan, 2006), p. 164.

55. Council on Foreign Relations, "Lindsay: Successful Constitution Vote in Iraq Crucial to Bush Administration's Iraq Policy," October 11, 2005, http://www.cfr.org/publication/8998/lindsay.html?breadcrumb=%2Fbios%2F6800%2Fjames_f_hoge%3Fpage%3D1.

56. For some useful reflections on the pivotal role of oil in the occupation of Iraq, see Noam Chomsky, "There Is No War on Terror," *ZNet Magazine,* January 16, 2006; Chomsky, *Failed States,* pp. 36–37; Chomsky and Achcar, *Perilous Power,* pp. 53–60, 83–85. See also David Harvey, *The New Imperialism* (New York: Oxford University Press, 2003), pp. 18–25, 75; Joshua Holland, "Bush's Petro-Cartel Almost Has Iraq's Oil," *Alternet,* October 16–17, 2006, thirdworldtraveler.com/Oil_watch/Bush's_ OilCartel_IraqOil.html; Antonia Juhasz, "Spoils of War: Oil, the U.S.–Middle East Free Trade Area and the Bush Agenda," *In These Times,* January 2007; Michael Schwartz, "Why Did We Invade Iraq Anyway?" *Truthout,*

October 30, 2007, http://www.truthout.org/docs_2006/103107F.shtml; Greg Palast, *Armed Madhouse* (New York: Plume, 2007), pp. 51–141; A. K. Gupta, "Oil, Neoliberalism and Sectarianism in Iraq," *Z Magazine,* April 2007; Michael Klare, *Blood and Oil* (New York: Metropolitan, 2004); Michael Klare, "Beyond the Age of Petroleum," *The Nation,* November 12, 2007, http://www.thenation.com/doc print.mhtml?i=20071112&s=klare; Norman Solomon and Resse Erlich, *Target Iraq: What the News Media Didn't Tell You* (New York: Context Books, 2003), pp. 107–116; Paul Street, "Largely about Oil: Reflections on Empire, Petroleum, Democracy, and the Occupation of Iraq," *Z Magazine,* January 2008, pp. 38–42; Paul Street, "Blood for Oil Control," *ZNet Magazine,* April 16, 2007, http://www.zmag.org/content/showarticle.cfm?ItemID=12591; Paul Street, "It's about the Oil: Not-So Candid Comments from Ted Koppel," *ZNet Magazine,* February 25, 2006, http://www.zmag.org/content/showarticle.cfm?ItemID=9798; Paul Street, "Addicted to Empire, Not Middle Eastern Oil," *ZNet Magazine,* February 8, 2006, http://www.zmag.org/content/showarticle.cfm?ItemID=9689. In "Largely about Oil," I mention other and related motives besides oil control, including electoral considerations, the desire of "defense" contractors to increase profits, and the role of war in distributing wealth upward and diverting the populace from domestic inequities.

57. Harvey, *The New Imperialism,* pp. 26–81.

58. Chomsky, "There Is No War on Terror."

59. Stephen Zunes, "Behind Obama and Clinton," *Foreign Policy in Focus,* February 4, 2008.

60. Tom Engelhardt, "The Corpse on the Gurney: The Success Mantra in Iraq," Antiwar.com, January 18, 2008, www.antiwar.com/engelhardt/?articleid=12229.

61. Nir Rosen, "The Death of Iraq," *Current History,* December 2007, p. 31.

62. WIFR Television, CBS 23, Rockford, Illinois, "Obama Speaks at General Motors in Janesville," February 13, 2008, http://www.wifr.com/morningshow/headlines/15618592.html.

63. Noam Chomsky, "The Mechanisms and Practices of Indoctrination" (1984), in *Chomsky on Democracy and Education,* ed. C. P. Otero (New York: Routledge-Falmer, 2003), pp. 207–208.

64. Ibid.

65. Street, "'We've Done More Than Talk.'"

66. Engelhardt, "The Corpse on the Gurney."

67. Noam Chomsky, "Why Is Iraq Missing from the 2008 Presidential Election?" speech reproduced on Democracy Now! at http://www.democracynow.org/2008/2/26/noam_chomsky_why_is_iraq_missing (emphasis added).

68. Obama, "A Way Forward in Iraq" (emphasis added).

69. Michael Mann, *Incoherent Empire* (New York: Verso, 2005), p. xii; Arnove, *Iraq,* pp. 27–28; Paul Street, "Vilsacking Iraq."

70. Obama, "A Way Forward" (emphasis added); Rosen, "The Death of Iraq"; Mahajan, *The New Crusade,* pp. 15, 27, 28, 38, 46, 56, 105–107, 118–122, 133–135, 143; Blum, *Rogue State,* pp. 206–207. There were mass civilian casualties and widespread targeting of civilians and surrendered soldiers during the first open U.S military war on Iraq (the "Persian Gulf War" of 1991)—an assault whose expert management by George H.W. Bush Obama effusively praised in April 2008. See Devlin Barrett, "Obama Aligns Foreign Policy with GOP," Associated Press, March 29, 2008.

71. Obama, "A Way Forward in Iraq"; Gupta, "Oil, Neoliberalism, and Sectarianism." Karen de Young, "All Iraq Groups Blame U.S. Invasion for Discord," *Washington Post*, December 19, 2007. p. A14.

72. Obama, "A Way Forward in Iraq"; Robert Holdierene, "Down on the War," *Military Times,* December 29, 2006, http://www.militarycity.com/polls/2006_main.php; Paul Street, "'Without Question?' On Growing Military Opposition to the Cheney-Bush Occupation of Iraq," *Dissident Voice,* January 11, 2007, http://www.dissidentvoice.org/Jan07/Street11.htm.

73. For sources and reflections on the 2005 Durbin episode and Obama's distancing, see Paul Street, "Durbin, Daley, Democrats and the New American Militarism," *ZNet Magazine,* June 24, 2005; Alexander Cockburn, "Obama's Game," *CounterPunch,* April 24, 2006, www.counterpunch.org/cockburn04242006.html.

74. Glen Ford and Peter Gamble, "Obama Mouths Mush on War," *Black Commentator,* December 1, 2005; Lance Selfa, "The New Face of U.S. Politics," *International Socialist Review,* March-April 2007, p. 2.

75. Zunes, "The Foreign Policy Agenda of the Democratic Front-Runners"; Zunes, "Barack Obama and the Middle East"; Robert Naiman, "Obama Glosses Over Colombian Attack in Ecuador," *Common Dreams,* March 5, 2008; Nicholas Kozloff, "The Audacity of Vagueness," *ZNet*, March 5, 2008; Ali Abunimah, "How Barack Obama Learned to Love Israel," *Electronic Intifadah,* March 4, 2007; Turl, "Is Obama Different?"; Ralph Nader, "The Silent Violence of Gaza's Suffering That Candidates and Congress Ignore," *CounterPunch*, March 8–9, 2008; Justin Elliot, "Obama's Israel Shuffle," *Mother Jones,* February 1, 2008, http://www.mojones.com/commentary/columns/2008/01/obamas-israel-shuffle.html.

76. Barack Obama, "The War We Need to Win," speech to Woodrow Wilson International Center, August 1, 2007, http://www.barackobama.com/2007/08/01/remarks_of_senator_obama_the_w_1.php; Mike Dorning, "Obama Remark Angers Pakistan," *Chicago Tribune,* August 4, 2007, sec. 1, p. 1; Glen Ford, "Barack Obama the Warmonger," *Black Agenda Report,* August 8, 2007, http://www.blackagendareport.com/index.php?option=com_content&task=view&id=305&Itemid=34; On the often neglected moral and legal aspects of the ongoing Afghanistan incursion, see Noam Chomsky, *Hegemony over Survival*, pp. 199–206; Mahajan, *The New Crusade,* p. 2; Dr. Marc Herold, "A Dossier on Civilian Victims of United States Aerial Bombing of Afghanistan," March 2002, http://www.cursor.org/stories/civilian_deaths.htm; Murray Campbell, "Bombing of Farming Village Undermines U.S Credibility," *Toronto Globe and Mail,* November 3, 2001; Elizabeth Rubin, "Battle Company Is Out There," *New York Times Magazine,* February 24, 2008; Paul Street, "Obama's 'Good' and 'Proper' War," *ZNet Magazine,* March 5, 2008, http://www.zcommunications.org/znet/viewArticle/16760.

77. Barack Obama, "The American Moment: Remarks to Chicago Council on Global Affairs," April 23, 2007, http://www.thechicagocouncil.org/dynamic_page.php?id=64; Ibid.; Christopher Preble, "Barack Obama's American Exceptionalism," *The Globalist,* May 25, 2007, http://www.cato.org/pub_display.php?pub_id=8380; Remarks of U.S. Senator Barack Obama at the Knox College Commencement, June 4, 2005. For some very useful reflections on the toxic imperial consequences of elite American exceptionalism in relation to the Iraq War, see Howard Zinn, "Afterword: On American Exceptionalism," in Arnove, *Iraq,* pp. 107–117.

78. David Brown, "Iraq 'Excess' Death Toll Has Reached 655,000," *Washington Post,* October 11, 2006, p. A12; Zinn, *A People's History of the United States;* Chomsky,

Year 501; Elizabeth de la Vega, *The United States v. George W. Bush et al.* (New York: Seven Stories, 2006).

79. Obama, "The American Moment."

80. Robert Kagan, "Obama the Interventionist," *Washington Post,* April 29, 2007, p. B7.

81. Barack Obama, "Renewing American Leadership," *Foreign Affairs,* July/August 2007, http://www.foreignaffairs.org/20070701faessay86401/barack-obama/renewing-american-leadership.html.

82. Klare, *Blood and Oil,* pp. 3–6, 45–47, 50, 150; Klare, "Beyond the Age of Petroleum"; Schwartz, "Why Did We Invade Iraq?"

83. Obama, "Renewing American Leadership."

84. Ford, "Barack Obama the Warmonger."

85. Chicago Council on Foreign Relations (CCFR), *Global Views,* October 2004, www.ccfr/globalviews2004/sub/usa.htm; for an (I hope) useful summary of key findings, see Paul Street, "Americans' Progressive Opinions vs. The Shadow Cast on Society by Big Business," *ZNet Sustainer Commentary* (May 15, 2008), read at http://www.zcommunications.org/zspace/commentaries/3491.

86. Quoted in Arnove, *Iraq,* pp. 65–66.

87. Obama, "A Way Forward in Iraq."

88. Obama, "A Way Forward." Obama, *Audacity,* pp. 303–304.

89. CCFR, *Global Views;* Chomsky, *Failed States,* pp. 228–229.

90. Zunes, "Behind Obama and Clinton." The real reason for Dr. Power's popularity is her reflexive ignoring and denial of U.S. crimes. In her famous book *A Problem From Hell: America and the Problem of Genocide* (New York: Basic, 2002), those transgressions are nearly completely absent, and the small number of cases treated are selectively interpreted through the lens of her paradigm asserting that our sole blemish is failing to respond adequately to the sins of *others*. See Edward S. Herman, "The Cruise Missile Left, Part 5: Samantha Power and the Genocide Gambit," *ZNet Magazine* (May 17, 2004), read at http://www.zmag.org/znet/viewArticle/8538; Edward S. Herman, "Response to Zinn on Samantha Power," *ZNet Magazine* (August 27, 2007), read at http://www.zcommunications.org/znet/viewArticle/14622.

91. Juan Santos, *Dissident Voice,* February 13, 2008.

92. Barrett, "Obama Aligns Foreign Policy with GOP." For reflections on the murderous, imperial, and unnecessary first U.S. military assault on Iraq, see, among many sources, Mahajan, *The New Crusade*, pp. 15, 27, 28, 38, 46, 56, 105–107, 118–122, 133–135, 143; Blum, *Rogue State*, p. 206.

93. See, for example, Christopher Hayes, "The Choice," *The Nation,* January 31, 2008, and Zunes, "The Foreign Policy Agenda."

94. *The Charlie Rose Show*, PBS, February 21, 2008. See www.charlierose.com/shows/2008/02/21/2/a-conversation-with-samantha-power.

95. John Pilger, "After Bobby Kennedy.

Chapter 5

1. Ken Silverstein, "Obama, Inc.: The Birth of a Washington Machine," *Harper's,* November 2006.

2. John F. Kerry, "Truly Transformative," *Newsweek,* April 28, 2008, p. 34; Noam Chomsky, *What We Say Goes* (New York: Metropolitan, 2007), p. 95; John B. Judis, "American Adam: Obama and the Cult of the New," *The New Republic,* March 12,

2008; Larissa MacFarquhar, "The Conciliator: Where Is Barack Obama Coming From?" *The New Yorker,* May 7, 2007; Katherine Adams and Charles Derber, *The New Feminist Majority* (Boulder, CO: Paradigm, 2008), pp. 67–95; for relevant majority opinion data indicating the stark disconnect between "surprisingly" progressive U.S. majority policy opinion—shockingly irrelevant in the actual making of U.S. domestic and foreign policy—and U.S. politics and policy, see Jacob S. Hacker and Paul Pierson, *Off Center: The Republican Revolution and the Erosion of American Democracy* (New Haven, Conn.: Yale University Press, 2005), pp. 2, 15, 17, 21, 34–43, and passim (page citations too numerous to list); Noam Chomsky, *Failed States: The Abuse of Power and the Assault on Democracy* (New York: Metropolitan, 2006), pp. 204–250; Chicago Council on Foreign Relations (CCFR), *Global Issues,* October 2004, www.ccfr/globalviews2004/sub/usa.htm; Anthony Arnove, *Iraq: The Logic of Withdrawal* (New York: New Press, 2006), pp. 65–66; Noam Chomsky and Gilbert Achcar, *Perilous Power: The Middle East and U.S. Foreign Policy* (Boulder: Paradigm, 2007), pp. 116, 192. Benjamin Page and Marshall Bouton, *The Foreign Policy Disconnect: What Americans Want From Our Leaders But Don't Get* (Chicago: University of Chicago Press, 2006). For a summary of majority progressive public opinion in the U.S., see the Appendix: Americans' Progressive Policy Attitudes," Page and Bouton, *The Foreign Policy Disconnect.*

3. By which I simply mean a remarkable and often dedicated fan and voting base across the nation in 2007 and 2008.

4. Gallup Poll, December 16, 2004, www.gallup.com. It is unclear, however, that this reflects real preferences. The deeper reality may well be that that's all people see as available, since substantive policy issues are so systematically excluded from campaigns. For evidence that people prefer substance, see Pew Research Center for the People and the Press, "Public Sees Fair Fight," March 6, 2008.

5. Chomsky, *Failed States,* p. 223.

6. Eric Foner, *Give Me Liberty! An American History,* vol. 1 (New York: W. W. Norton, 2005), p. 377.

7. Gabriel Kolko, *Main Currents in American History* (New York: Pantheon, 1976), p. 306.

8. Alexander Cockburn, "The Spitzer Sting," *The Nation,* March 31, 2008.

9. Steven Hill, *Fixing Elections: The Failure of America's Winner Take All Politics* (New York: Routledge, 2002).

10. Paul Street, "Labor Day Reflections: Time as a Democracy Issue," *ZNet Daily Commentaries,* September 3, 2002, www.zmag.org/sustainers/content/2002–08/01street.cfm.

11. Associated Press, "Most Americans Say America on the Wrong Track," April 4, 2006, http://www.cnn.com/2008/US/04/04/dissatisfied.poll.ap/index.html.

12. John F. Kerry, "Truly Transformative," p. 34.

13. George Will, "The Problem with Populists," *RealClearPolitics,* January 6, 2008, http://www.realclearpolitics.com/printpage/?url=http://www.realclearpolitics.com/articles/2008/01/populist_campaigns_based_on_de.html.

14. MSNBC, "2008 Primary Results: Exit Polls," http://www.msnbc.msn.com/id/21225966.

15. Paul Street, "Barack Obama's White Appeal and the Perverse Racial Politics of the Post–Civil Rights Era," *Black Agenda Report,* June 20, 2007, http://www.blackagendareport.com/index.php?option=com_content&task=view&id=254&Itemid=34. Thus, Iowa City is loaded with middle-class white "progressives" who pro-

claim their willingness to vote for a black man but know or do nothing about the fact that their state ranks number one in terms of racially disparate mass incarceration. Paul Street, "The Deeper Racism in Iowa: Beneath the White Obama Craze," *Black Agenda Report* (May 14, 2008).

16. Kathleen Parker, "Obama Has U.S. Hooked on a Feeling," *Chicago Tribune,* January 11, 2008.

17. Steele is quoted in Joe Klein, "The Fresh Face," *Time,* October 17, 2006.

18. Kirk Johnson, "We Agreed to Agree and Forgot to Notice," *New York Times,* January 6, 2007, sec. 4, p. 4; Andrew Kohut, "Getting It Wrong," *New York Times,* January 10, 2008, p. A27; Karl Rove, "Why Hillary Won," *Wall Street Journal,* January 10, 2008, p. A15; Mike Dorning and Christi Parsons, "Race Emerging as an Issue in the Democrats' Campaign," *Chicago Tribune,* March 13, 2008, sec. 1. p. 6.; MSNBC, "2008 Primary Results: Exit Polls"; Patrick Healy and Jeff Zeleny, "Racial Issue Bubbles Up Again for Democrats," *New York Times,* March 13, 2008, pp. A1, A14; Dorning and Parsons, "Race Emerging." For more detailed reflections on race, class, and racial bloc voting in the 2008 Democratic primaries, see Paul Street, "Race and Class in the Democratic Primaries," *ZNet Magazine,* April 25, 2008, www.zcommunications.org.

19. For instructive historical reflections on DuBois, race, and white working-class consciousness, see David Roediger, *The Wages of Whiteness: Race and the Making of the American Working Class* (London: Verso, 1991); Martin Luther King, Jr., "The Drum Major Instinct," *A Testament of Hope*, p. 264.

20. So I argue in more detail in Street, "Race and Class in the Democratic Primaries," adding a critical point from Chapter 2 of this book—that the largely corporate-imposed narrowness of the policy and ideology contest between Hillary Clinton and Obama tended to enhance the significance of racial (and gender) identity in voters' struggle to make meaningful choices between those two candidates.

21. John Judis, "The Big Race: Obama and the Psychology of Color," *The New Republic* (May 28, 2008), p. 24; MSNBC Exit Polls, read at http://www.msnbc.msn.com/id/21660890, accessed May 20, 2009.

22. In addition to the sources cited in Chapter 1, see Glen Ford, "White Boys and Barack Obama," *Dissident Voice,* February 21, 2008. "The no-nonsense white men that rule society and cling to ownership of the world," Ford noted, "were harder nuts to crack; you've got to sign a prenuptial to get skin-tight with them. No problem. Before Obama even began to strut on the national runway, he'd won the approval of the Wall Street and military/industrial (and nuclear power) branches of the Money Family."

23. For the notion that there are serious hints of potential American fascism (highly informed by fundamentalist U.S. evangelical Christianity) behind the Bush II era, see Chris Hedges, *American Fascists: The Christian Right and the War on America* (New York: Free Press, 2006); Charles Derber, *Hidden Power: What You Need to Know to Save Our Democracy* (San Francisco: Berrett-Koehler, 2005), pp. 150–180; Chomsky, *Failed States,* p. 224; Henry A. Giroux, *The Terror of Neoliberalism: Authoritarianism and the Eclipse of Democracy* (Boulder: Paradigm, 2004), pp. 9–32, 147–148.

24. Juan Santos, "Barack Obama and the End of Racism," *Dissident Voice,* February 13, 2008.

25. Pilger, "After Bobby Kennedy.

26. Aurora Levins Morales, "Thinking Outside the Ballot Box," *Z Magazine,* April 2008.

27. James Traub, "Is (His) Biography (Our) Destiny?" *New York Times Magazine,* November 4, 2007; Liza Mundy, "A Series of Fortunate Events: Barack Obama Needed More Than Talent and Ambition to Rocket from Obscure State Senator to Presidential Contender in Three Years," *Washington Post Magazine,* August 12, 2007; See Paul Street, "Bush, Kerry, and 'Body Language' v. 'Message': Notes on Race, Gender, Empire and Mass Infantilization," *ZNet Magazine,* October 12, 2004, http://www.zmag.org/content/showarticle.cfm? SectionID=90&ItemID=6396%20; Kerry, "Truly Transformative."

28. Traub, "Is (His) Biography (Our) Destiny?"

29. A very useful and accessible compendium is William Blum, *Rogue State: A Guide to the World's Only Superpower* (Monroe, Maine: Common Courage, 2005). For examples from my own initial 2008 candidate John Edwards, see Paul Street, "Imperial Temptations: John Edwards, Barack Obama, and the Myth of Post–World War II United States Benevolence," *ZNet Magazine,* May 28, 2007, http://www.zmag.org/content/showarticle.cfm?ItemID=12928.

30. For reflections on the theory of cognitive dissonance and its relationship to American exceptionalism and Iraq War attitudes inside the United States, see Paul Street, "Loss, Class, Empire, and the Vicious Cognitive Consequences of Forced Compliance," Empire and Inequality Report No. 27, *ZNet Magazine* (July 6, 2007), read at http://www.zmag.org/content/showarticle.cfm?ItemID=13219.32.

31. For contemporary and historical reflections and sources, see Andrew Bacevich, *The New American Militarism: How Americans Are Seduced by War* (New York: Oxford, 2005).

32. This is a substantively accurate paraphrase of something I heard again and again from middle- and working-class voters in Iowa in the fall and winter of 2007.

33. Edward S. Herman and Noam Chomsky, *Manufacturing Consent* (New York: Pantheon, 1988); Norman Solomon and Resse Erlich, *Target Iraq: What the News Media Didn't Tell You* (New York: Context Books, 2003); Elizabeth de la Vega, *The United States v. George Bush et al.* (New York: Seven Stories, 2006); Street, *Empire and Inequality,* pp. 32–35, 67–83, 90–98, 110–134.

34. For relevant data and related reflections, see Paul Street, "Profit Surge," *ZNet Magazine,* February 10, 2007, http://www.zmag.org/content/showarticle.cfm?ItemID=12089.

35. Street, "Loss, Class, Empire."

36. Noam Chomsky, *American Power and the New Mandarins* (New York: New Press, 2002 [1967]), p. 313.

37. Andrew Ferguson, "The Wit and Wisdom of Barack Obama," *The Weekly Standard,* March 24, 2008.

38. Chomsky, *Failed States,* p. 215; Edward S. Herman, "How Market-Democracy Keeps the Public and 'Populism' at Bay," *ZNet Sustainer Commentary,* August 13, 2007, available online at http://www.zmag.org/sustainers/content/2007-08/13herman.cfm.; Edward S. Herman, "Democratic Betrayal," *Z Magazine,* January 2007.

39. Jacob S. Hacker and Paul Pierson, *Off Center: The Republican Revolution and the Erosion of American Democracy* (New Haven, Conn.: Yale University Press, 2005). The quotations come from p. 223 and the dust jacket.

40. Ibid.

Chapter 6

1. David Garrow, *Bearing the Cross: Martin Luther King and the Southern Christian Leadership Conference* (New York: 1986), p. 562; Michael Eric Dyson, *I May Not Get There with You: The True Martin Luther King, Jr.* (New York: Touchstone, 2000), pp. 82–89.

2. For some chilling reflections on U.S.-imposed mass death and devastation in Southeast Asia, see William Blum, *Rogue State: A Guide to the World's Only Superpower* (Monroe, Maine: Common Courage, 2005), pp. 66, 114, 117–118, 138–139, 174; Noam Chomsky, *Year 501: The Conquest Continues* (Boston: South End, 1993), pp. 251–274; Ward Churchill, *On the Justice of Roosting Chickens: Reflections on the Consequences of U.S. Imperial Arrogance and Criminality* (Oakland, CA: AK Press, 2003), pp. 132–149; Garrow, *Bearing the Cross,* p. 562.

3. Martin Luther King, Jr., "Where Do We Go from Here?" 1967, p. 250.

4. Adolph J. Reed, Jr., "Sitting This One Out," *The Progressive* (November 2007).

5. Ibid.

6. John K. Wilson, *Barack Obama: This Improbable Quest* (Boulder: Paradigm, 2008).

7. Manning Marable, "African-American Peacemakers—Dr. Martin Luther King, Jr., Barack Obama, and the Struggle against Racism, Inequality, and War," *Black Commentator,* April 13, 2008. By Obama biographer Mendell's account, the confusion between Dr. King and candidate Obama is significantly shared by Obama himself and his early Chicago community-organizing mentor Jerry Kellman. See David Mendell, *Obama: From Promise to Power* (New York: HarperCollins, 2007), pp. 72–74.

8. George Lakoff, *Don't Think of an Elephant: Know Your Values and Frame the Debate* (White River Junction, VT: Chelsea Green, 2004); During my years as a social policy researcher in the liberal academic and nonprofit worlds (1995–2005), I observed that other researchers and our funders often seemed to operate on precisely the assumption that Lakoff criticizes—that positive and progressive policy action would naturally ensue from the solid excavation and exposure of the empirical facts of poverty and inequality. There was often relatively little effort or compulsion to adequately explain or "frame" these terrible facts in a morally or politically relevant way and in relation to deeper structures of racial, socioeconomic, and imperial oppression. See George Lakoff, "What Counts as an 'Issue' in the Clinton-Obama Race," *Common Dreams,* January 31, 2007, www.commondreams.org/archive/2008/01/31/6760, where Lakoff claims that Obama's "vision is deeply progressive." Lakoff absurdly praised Obama for rejecting Hillary Clinton's "incrementalism"—her "belief in getting lots of small carefully crafted policies one at a time, step by small step, real but almost unnoticed." "Obama," Lakoff claimed, "believes in bold moves and in the building of a movement in which the bold moves are demanded by the people and celebrated when they happen." See Larissa MacFarquhar, "The Conciliator: Where Is Barack Obama Coming From?" *The New Yorker,* May 7, 2007, and the first chapter of the book for useful antidotes to these fantastic claims. Paul Street, "Time to Scrape the Kerry Sticker Off: On Democrats, Values, and the Lakoff Thesis," *ZNet Sustainer Commentary,* June 17, 2005, http://www.zmag.org/Sustainers/Content/2005–06/17street.cfm.

9. National Voting Rights Institute, "The Wealth Primary," http://www.nvri.org/about/wealth.shtml; Thomas Ferguson, *Golden Rule: The Investment Theory of Party Competition and Logic of Money-Driven Political Systems* (Chicago:

University of Chicago Press, 1995); Elizabeth Drew, *The Corruption of American Politics: What Went Wrong and Why* (Secaucus, N.J.: Birch Lane Press, 1999); Center for Responsive Politics, *A Brief History of Money in Politics* (Washington, D.C.: Center for Responsive Politics, 1995); Jamin Raskin and John Bonifaz, "The Constitutional Imperative and Practical Imperative of Democratically Financed Elections," *Columbia Law Review* 94, no. 4 (1994): 1160–1203; Charles Lewis, *The Buying of the President* (New York: Avon, 1996), pp 1–20.

10. Ali Abunimah, "How Barack Obama Learned to Love Israel," *Electronic Intifadah* (March 4, 2007).

11. See Paul Street, "The Audacity of Reaction: On Barack Obama, Jeremiah Wright, Jesus, James Madison, and Dr. Martin Luther King," *ZNet,* March 19, 2008, http://www.zcommunications.org/znet/viewArticle/16918.

12. Since early on—see the comments of close friend Valerie Jarrett, brother-in-law Craig Robinson, and Harvard professor Robert Putnam in Liza Mundy, "A Series of Fortunate Events: Barack Obama Needed More Than Talent and Ambition to Rocket from Obscure State Senator to Presidential Contender in Three Years," *Washington Post Magazine,* August 12, 2007; Mendell, *Obama,* p. 7.

13. Matt Gonzalez, "The Obama Craze: Count Me Out," *BeyondChron: San Francisco's Online Daily,* February 28, 2008, www.beyondchron.org/articles/index.php?itemid=5413#more.

14. Edward N. Wolff, *Top Heavy: A Study of the Increasing Inequality of Wealth in America* (New York: The New Press, 2002), p. 8; Robert W. McChesney, *Rich Media, Poor Democracy: Communication Politics in Dubious Times* (Urbana: University of Illinois Press, 1999), p. 261; National Voting Rights Institute, "The Wealth Primary," Available online at http://www.nvri.org/about/wealth.shtml.

15. G. William Domhoff, *Who Rules America? Power, Politics, and Social Change* (New York: McGraw Hill, 2006), pp. 136–139.

16. Richard Oestreicher, "Urban Working Class Political Behavior and Theories of American Electoral Politics, 1880–1940," *Journal of American History* 74 (March 1980); Domhoff, *Who Rules America?* p. 137.

17. Domhoff, *Who Rules America?* pp. 137–138.

18. Ibid.

19. Ibid., p. 139.

20. Noam Chomsky, *Failed States: The Abuse of Power and the Assault on Democracy* (New York: Metropolitan, 2006), pp. 205–209 (Dewey quoted on p. 206).

21. Wolff, *Top Heavy,* p. 8; Jeff Faux, *The Global Class War: How America's Bipartisan Elite Lost Our Future and What It Will Take to Win It Back* (New York: Wiley, 2006), pp. 126–200; Noam Chomsky, *Profit over People: Neoliberalism and Global Order* (Boston: South End, 1999).

22. See *Webster's New Twentieth Century Dictionary Unabridged* (New York: Simon and Schuster, 1979), p. 269: "capitalism, *n.*" Lester Thurow, *The Future of Capitalism* (New York: Penguin, 1996), p. 248.

23. For detailed reflections, see Ellen Meiksens Wood, *Democracy against Capitalism: Renewing Historical Materialism* (Cambridge: Cambridge University Press, 1995); David Montgomery, *Citizen Worker: The Experience of Workers in the United States with Democracy and the Free Market during the Nineteenth Century* (Cambridge: Cambridge University Press, 1993); Paul Street, "Capitalism and Democracy 'Don't Mix Very Well': Reflections on Globalization," *Z Magazine,* February

2000, pp. 20–24; Paul Street, "Hitchens, Orwell, Capitalism, and the Real Threat to Democracy," *Review of Education, Pedagogy, and Cultural Studies* 26, no. 1 (January-March 2004): 61–68; Chomsky, *Failed States,* pp. 205–209.

24. Chomsky, *Failed States,* p. 206.

25. Domhoff, *Who Rules America?* p. 208; Alfred Chandler, *The Visible Hand: The Managerial Revolution in American Business* (Cambridge: Harvard University Press, 1976); Louis Hartz, *The Liberal Tradition in America* (New York: Harcourt, Brace, 1955); Robert Weibe, *The Search for Order, 1877–1920* (Portsmouth, N.H.: Greenwood, 1967); Melvyn Dubofsky, *Industrialism and the American Worker, 1865–1920* (Arlington Heights, Ill.: AHM, 1975); Stephen Skowerneck, *Building the American State: The Expansion of Administrative Capacities* (Cambridge: Cambridge University Press, 1982); Montgomery, *Citizen Worker.*

26. Howard Zinn, "Are We Politicians or Citizens?" *The Progressive* (May 2007); Edward Palmer Thompson, *The Poverty of Theory* (London: Merline Press, 1978).

27. Reed, "Sitting This One Out."

28. Charles Derber, *Hidden Power* (San Francisco: Berrett-Koehler, 2005), p. 8; Richard Wolffe and Darren Briscoe, "Across the Divide: Barack Obama's Road to Racial Reconstruction," *Newsweek,* July 16, 2007; Tim Dickinson, "Machinery of Hope," *Rolling Stone,* March 20, 2008, p. 42; Cornel West, "The Role of Law in Progressive Politics" (1990), in David Kairys, ed., *The Politics of Law: A Progressive Critique* (New York: Basic, 1998) (emphasis added).

29. Noam Chomsky, *Interventions* (San Francisco: City Lights, 2007), p. 99.

30. Howard Zinn, "Election Madness," *The Progressive,* March 2008.

31. Derber, *Hidden Power,* pp. 8–9; Godfrey Hodgson, *The World Turned Right Side Up: A History of the Conservative Ascendancy in America* (New York: Houghton Mifflin, 1996), pp. 128–315.

32. Frank, *What's the Matter With Kansas?*

33. Jacob S. Hacker and Paul Pierson, *Off Center: The Republican Revolution and the Erosion of American Democracy* (New Haven, Conn.: Yale University Press, 2005), pp. 194–200. See also Frank, *What's the Matter with Kansas?* p. 246, for some interesting and important reflections on the powerful positive role (from a progressive Democratic perspective) of union membership in "framing" the political perspectives of white male workers. Derber, *Hidden Power,* pp. 21–67, 150–180; Henry A. Giroux, *Terror of Neoliberalism: Authoritarianism and the Eclipse of Democracy* (Boulder: Paradigm, 2004), pp. 1–53; Hacker and Pierson, *Off Center;* Chomsky, *Failed States,* pp. 205–250; Joe Conason, *It Can Happen Here: Authoritarian Peril in the Age of Bush* (New York: St. Martin's Press, 2007).

34. For some concrete examples, See Stephen Zunes, "The Foreign Policy Agenda of the Democratic Front-Runners: Comparisons on Some Key Issues," *Common Dreams,* January 25, 2008 (on intraparty candidate differences), and Paul Street, "Brother Can You Spare a Dime? Why Kerry Will Sweep the Black Vote," *In These Times,* November 15, 2004 (on interparty differences with regard to domestic racial justice).

35. Chomsky, *Interventions,* pp. 99–100.

36. Paul Street, "A Very Narrow Spectrum: Even John Edwards Is Too Far Left for the U.S. Plutocracy," *ZNet Sustainer Commentary,* August 29, 2007, http://www.zmag.org/sustainers/content/2007–08/29street.cfm; Laurence H. Shoup, "The Presidential Election 2008," *Z Magazine,* February 2008. For an extended

treatment using and justifying this metaphor in relation to the 2004 elections, see Paul Street, "Kerry Is Coke, Bush Is Crack," *ZNet Magazine,* March 24, 2004, http://www.zmag.org/content/showarticle.cfm?SectionID=33&ItemID=5204. On proto-fascism and American fascist tendencies, see Giroux, *The Terror of Neoliberalism,* pp. 1–53; Derber, *Hidden Power,* pp. 150–180; Chris Hedges, *American Fascists: The Christian Right and the War on America* (New York: Free Press, 2006).

37. Frank, *What's the Matter with Kansas?*, p. 245.

38. Ibid., p. 245.

39. See MacFarquhar, "The Conciliator." For more detailed reflections, see Paul Street, "'Angry John' Edwards v. KumbayObama," *SleptOn Magazine,* December 28, 2007, www.slepton.com/slepton/viewcontent.pl?id=1234.

40. Associated Press, "Heated Campaign Souring Democrats on Rival Candidates," www.yahoo.com, April 29, 2008.

41. Tariq Ali and Anthony Arnove, "The Challenge to the Empire," *Socialist Worker Online,* October 20, 2006.

42. Aurora Levins Morales, "Thinking Outside the Ballot Box," *Z Magazine,* April 2008; Pilger, "After Bobby Kennedy.

43. That call came in an essay whose title—"A Testament of Hope"—reminds us that the Obama campaign's master keyword, "hope," is subject to different meanings in accord with the moral and ideological standpoint of its user. See Martin Luther King, Jr., "A Testament of Hope" (1968), *A Testament of Hope*, p. 315.

44. David Moberg, "Obamanomics," *In These Times,* April 2008, p. 34.

45. Derber, *Hidden Power,* pp. 6–9.

46. Chomsky, *Interventions.*

47. Moberg, "Obamanomics."

48. Doug Henwood, "Would You Like Change with That?" *Left Business Observer,* no. 117 (March 2008).

49. Barrington Moore, Jr., *The Social Origins of Dictatorship and Democracy: Lord and Peasant in the Making of the Modern World* (London: Penguin, 1967); Barrington Moore, Jr., *The Social Basis of Obedience and Revolt* (White Plains, NY: M. E. Sharpe, 1978). For an earlier historical example of activism fed by a charismatic presidential candidate's unfulfilled campaign rhetoric, see Michael Schwartz, "Harvard Politics: The Careless Young Men," *The Harvard Crimson,* June 13, 1963. "The formation of disarmament and civil rights groups," Schwartz noted, "is very largely a response to the stirring rhetoric with which President Kennedy heralded the 'passing of the torch,' and to the dismal race he and the new generation have run since they took over in Washington. The candidate raised expectations that the President has not satisfied and the result has been the growth of organizations which aim at doing for themselves what Kennedy is unwilling or unable to do for them." The Schwartz article can be read at http://www.thecrimson.com/article.aspx?ref=248550.

50. Istvan Meszaros, *Socialism or Barbarism: From the "American Century" to the Crossroads* (New York: Monthly Review, 2001); Martin Luther King Jr., *A Testament of Hope: The Essential Writings and Speeches of Martin Luther King Jr.*, edited by James M. Washington (San Francisco: HarperSanFrancisco, 1986). According to Martin Luther King Jr., very near the end of his life: "Millions of Americans are coming to see that we are fighting an immoral war that costs nearly thirty billion dollars a year, that we are perpetuating racism, that are tolerating almost forty million poor during an overflowing material abundance. Yet they remain helpless to

end the war, to feed the hungry, to make brotherhood a reality. . . . In these trying circumstances, the black revolution is much more than a struggle for the rights of Negroes. It is forcing America to face all its interrelated flaws—racism, poverty, militarism, and materialism. It is exposing evils that are rooted deeply in the whole structure of our society. It reveals systemic rather than superficial flaws and suggests that radical reconstruction of society itself is the real issue to be faced."

51. Street, "Capitalism and Democracy 'Don't Mix Very Well'"; Ellen Meiksens Wood, *Democracy against Capitalism: Renewing Historical Materialism* (New York: Cambridge University Press, 1995); William T. Robinson, *Promoting Polyarchy: Globalization, U.S. Intervention, and Hegemony* (Cambridge: Cambridge University Press, 1996), pp. 10, 54, 339–363.

52. Howard Zinn, "Are We Politicians or Citizens?"

Afterword

1. Adam Nagourney, Carl Hulse, and Jeff Zeleny, "No Road Map for Democrats as Race Ends," *New York Times*, June 1, 2008, sec. 1, p.1.

2. Gallup Poll, "McCain Moves to 6-Point Lead Over Obama," read May 12, 2008, at www.gallup,com/poll/106966/Gallup-Daily-McCain-Moves-Point-Lead-Over-Obama.

3. MSNBC Exit Polls at /www.msnbc.msn.com/id/21660890/; Clarence Page, "Pursuing the Elusive White Voter," *Chicago Tribune,* May 11, 2008.

4. Yahoo News, "Election 08 Political Dashboard: West Virginia," read May 13, 2008, at http://news.yahoo.com/election/2008/dashboard/?d=WV.

5. David Espo and Matt Apuzzo, "Determined Clinton Wins West Virginia, Says Race Not Over," Associated Press (May 13, 2008).

6. MSNBC, "2008 Primary Results for Kentucky," read May 29, 2008, at http://www.msnbc.msn.com/id/21229208.

7. For Ohio, see http://www.msnbc.msn.com/id/21226001. For Pennsylvania, see www.msnbc.msn.com/id/21226004. For West Virginia, see www.msnbc.msn.com/id/21226014.

8. Quoted in Clarence Page, "Pursuing the Elusive White Voter," *Chicago Tribune*, May 11, 2008.

9. On the Republican use of the "elitism" charge to win white working-class, see (among many possible citations) Frank, *What's the Matter with Kansas?* and Michael Lind, *Up From Conservatism: Why the Right is Wrong for America* (New York: Free Press, 1996).

10. Page, "The Elusive White Voter."

11. Ellis Cose, "McCain's Hidden Advantage," *Newsweek* (May 5, 2008), p. 37. Sarpolus was certainly correct about the absence of a working-class message, but it is by no means clear that that absence trumps "race" (racism) in explaining white, working-class voting behavior. For further reflections, see Paul Street, "Race and Class in the Democratic Primaries," *ZNet Magazine* (April 25, 2008), read at http://www.zcommunications.org/znet/viewArticle/17313.

12. Karen Tumulty, "A Bitter Lesson," *Time* (April 28, 2008), p. 30.

13. Eric Foner, *Give Me Liberty! An American History*, volume 1 (New York: W.W. Norton, 2005), p. 350.

14. Thus, while I am technically from the South Side of Chicago, I would personally never use this designation to describe myself. I grew up as the child of middle-class professionals (a professor and a school teacher) and lived again in later

years (2001–2005) in the South Side neighborhood of Hyde Park—a very disproportionately middle- and upper-middle-class and largely academic neighborhood defined largely by the presence of the elite University of Chicago (UC). This has been Obama's neighborhood of residence since at least the mid-1990s, and he taught for many years at UC's law school.

15. Not surprisingly, given the Republican Party's attachment to wealth and militarism, Rove failed to add that Obama appeared to have absorbed the interrelated values of Wall Street, corporate America, and the foreign policy establishment. Karl Rove, "Dear Senator Obama . . .," *Newsweek* (May 5, 2008), p. 35.

16. Quoted in Glen Ford, "Obama Stumbles on His Own Contradicitions: Pop Goes the Race-Neutral Campaign!," *Black Agenda Report* (April 30, 2008).

17. John Judis, "The Big Race," *The New Republic* (May 28, 2008), p.24.

18. Ibid., p.24. Some of what an Obama nomination will be up against was suggested in a May 22, 2008, *New York Times* article on his troubles with older white Jewish voters in Florida. One such voter told *Times* reporter Jodi Kantor that he would not vote for Obama because the voter's mother was mugged and beaten by a black person in Chicago decades ago. Another Jewish Floridian cited his experience with black crime in Brooklyn after World War II as a reason to reject Obama. Florida resident Ruth Grossman, 80, told Kantor that many of her Jewish neighbors were being deceptive when they cited "Israel," "the minister [Reverend Wright] thing," and "the wife" as reasons not to support Obama and to vote for McCain. "The major issue," Ms. Grossman observed, "is color." See Jodi Kantor, "As Obama Heads to Florida, Many of Its Jews Have Doubts," *New York Times*, May 22, 2008.

19. Page, "Elusive White Voter."

20. Judis, "The Big Race," p. 24; Adolph Reed, Jr., "Obama No," *The Progressive* (May 2008).

21. Pickler, "'Hillary Democrats.'"

22. Along with the fact that I have long shared Adolph Reed, Jr.'s' long-standing characterization of Obama as a politician whose "fundamental political center of gravity, beneath an empty rhetoric of hope and change and new directions, is neoliberal" (Reed, "Obama, No"), the fact that a significant portion of the U.S. electorate remains too racially prejudiced to vote for a black candidate is quite frankly one of the reasons I did not support his campaign in Iowa. In my experience, some in Obama's camp will call you racist for daring to mention this terrible reality, which holds no small significance for election outcomes when the electorate is as closely divided as it currently is in the United States. The charge is, of course, absurd, analogous to calling someone a thief because they observe stealing. Reed's critique is a reminder that Obama has long met considerable criticism from within the black community—a basic fact that tends to get lost in America's binary political culture. During this campaign season, it has been interesting to see the (I think largely accurate) charge that Obama is "elitist" revolve (in "mainstream" media discussion) completely around his relationship to the white working class. During my five years working in Chicago's South Side black community, I commonly heard and saw that charge made against Obama from African American citizens and activists. See Ted Kleine, "Is Bobby Rush in Trouble?" *Chicago Reader* (March 17, 2000) for some interesting history and evidence on this. For consistent criticism of Obama from a black Left perspective, see the regular weekly reports of *Black Agenda Report* at *www.blackagendareport.com.*

23. For some deep and useful reflections, see Edmund S. Morgan, *American Slavery, American Freedom: the Ordeal of Colonial Virginia* (New York: W.W. Norton, 1975); Eric Foner, *Reconstruction: America's Unfinished Revolution, 1863–1877* (New York: Harper & Row, 1988); David Roediger, *The Wages of Whiteness: Race and the Making of the American Working Class* (New York: Verso, 1991); David Roediger, *Towards the Abolition of Whiteness: Essays on Race, Politics, and Working Class History* (New York: Verso, 1994); David Roediger, *Working Toward Whiteness: How America's Immigrants Became White* (New York: Basic, 2005); Theodore W. Allen, *The Invention of the White Race: Volume One: Racial Oppression and Social Control* (New York: Verso, 1994); Mike Davis, *Prisoners of the American Dream: Politics and Economy in the History of the U.S. Working Class* (New York: Verso, 1986); James R. Barrett, *Work and Community in the Jungle: Chicago's Packinghouse Workers, 1894–1922* (Urbana, IL: University of Illinois Press, 1987), pp. 188–239; Thomas Sugrue, *The Origins of the Urban Crisis: Race and Inequality in Postwar Detroit* (Princeton, NJ: Princeton University Press, 1996, 2005); Bruce Nelson, *Divided We Stand: American Workers and the Struggle for Black Equality* (Princeton, NJ: Princeton University Press, 2001); Godfrey Hodgson, *America in Our Times: From World War II to Nixon* (New York: Vintage, 1976); Godfrey Hodgson, *The World Turned Right Side Up: A History of the Conservative Ascendancy in America*; Godfrey Hodgson, *More Equal than Others: America From Nixon to the New Century* (Princeton, NJ: Princeton University Press, 2004); Jennifer L. Hochschild, *Facing Up to the American Dream: Race, Class, and the Soul of the Nation* (Princeton, NJ: Princeton University Press, 1995); Lind, *Up From Conservatism*; Michael Lind, *The Next American Nation: the New Nationalism and the Next American Revolution* (New York: The Free Press, 1995); Sheryl Cashin, *The Failures of Integration: How Race and Class Are Undermining the American Dream* (New York: Public Affairs, 2004); E. J. Dionne, *Why Americans Hate Politics* (New York: Touchstone, 1991); Greg Palast, *The Best Democracy Money Can Buy* (London, UK: Pluto Press, 2002), pp. 6–43; Wolin, *Democracy, Incorporated*, pp. 57–58, 102, 278.

24. See the Appendix: "Americans' Progressive Policy Attitudes."

25. It leaves out numerous critical policy areas like immigration, financial sector regulation, education, the home mortgage and foreclosure reform, and much more.

26. I rely here in a particularly strong way on Charles Derber's important book *Hidden Power: What You Need to Know to Save Our Democracy* (San Francisco: Berrett-Koehler, 2005).

27. Derber, *Hidden Power*, p. 257.

28. Sheldon Wolin, *Democracy Incorporated: Managed Democracy and the Specter of Inverted Totalitarianism* (Princeton, NJ: Princeton University Press, 2008, pp.59, 66. 286–287.

29. An indispensable source on this topic is Joel Bakin, *The Corporation: The Pathological Pursuit of Profit and Power* (New York: Free Press, 2004).

30. Derber, *Hidden Power*, pp. 260–261.

31. Ibid., p. 262.

32. Ibid., pp. 265–266.

33. Ibid., pp. 263–264. On media democratization, see Robert W. McChesney, *Rich Media, Poor Democracy: Communication Politics in Dubious Times* (New York: New Press, 1999).

34. Derber, *Hidden Power,* pp. 266–267. See also Faux, *Global Class War*, pp. 219–254, with related proposals in the context of a call for a North American Union.

35. For further reflections, see Paul Street, "The Nation's Leading Moral Issues: Empire and Inequality," *ZNet Magazine* (May 18, 2008), read at www.zcommunications.org/znet/viewArticle/17664.

36. Derber, *Hidden Power*, p. 268; Frank, *What's the Matter with Kansas*?, pp. 75, 132–137.

37. Calling among other things for the certification of union representations through employee check-card voting and for a revitalized government effort to crack down on technically illegal employer practices like the discriminatory firing of union members.

38. See Derber, *Hidden Power*, pp. 268–269.

39. For a devastating critique, see Glen Ford, "Obama's 'Race Neutrality' Unravels of its Own Contradictions," *Black Agenda Report* (April 30, 2008), at http://www.blackagendareport.com/index.php?option=com_content&task=view&id=603&Itemid=1.

40. See Chomsky, *Failed States*, p. 228, where the author notes that one major poll taken after the 2004 election found that the Iraq War placed first in the list of "moral issues" that most affected voters' decision. Forty-two percent of voters mentioned the Iraq War as the leading moral issue for them, compared to just 13 percent who named abortion and 9 percent who named gay marriage. The primary source is Glen Johnson, *Boston Globe*, November 27, 2004, citing surveys from Zogby International and Pax Christi.

41. As it most certainly was, just from an imperial perspective. See Jonathan Steel's brilliant study *Defeat: Why Britain and America Lost Iraq* (Berkeley, CA: Counterpoint, 2008), arguing that "the occupation itself was the [imperial] mistake."

42. King, Jr., "A Time to Break the Silence," p. 241 in *A Testament of Hope*; Paul Street, "The Spiritual Death of a Nation," *Black Commentator* (November 3, 2005), read at http://www.blackcommentator.com/157/157_think_street_spiritual_death_pf.html; Chalmers Johnson, *The Sorrows of Empire: Militarism, Secrecy, and the End of the Republic* (New York: Metropolitan, 2004); Paul Street, *Empire and Inequality: America and the World Since 9/11* (Boulder, CO: Paradigm, 2004). For brilliant, extensive, and haunting reflections on fundamental contradictions between democracy and Empire in U.S and world politics and history, see Wolin, *Democracy, Incorporated*, pp. 20, 49, 52, 70, 97, 100, 189, 191–192, 194, 239–241, 244–245, 247–248, and passim.

43. See Paul Street, *"Whose* Aims in *What* 'U.S. Global War on Terror?," Plenary Address to the Campus Antiwar Network (CAN), Iowa City, Iowa (April 19, 2008), read at http://www.zcommunications.org/znet/viewArticle/17218.

44. Derber, *Hidden Power*, pp. 270–271.

45. See the following essay by the British climate-change activist and author George Monbiot: "Here's the Plan" (October 31, 2006), www.monbiot.com/archives/200610/31/here's-the-plan.

46. Wolin, *Democracy, Incorporated*. For some instructive reflections on how little should be realistically expected from a progressive perspective even "if state power were to fall into the hands of a reform-minded Democratic administration," see Wolin, pp. 206–207.

47. For a haunting and virtuoso reflection on the possibility that a post-democratic United States has perhaps already "morphed into a new and strange kind of political hybrid, one where economic and state powers are conjoined and virtually unbridled," see Wolin, *Democracy Incorporated.*

48. As John Pilger notes, "none of the candidates represents so-called mainstream America. In poll after poll, voters make clear than they want the normal decencies of jobs, proper housing and health care. They want their troops out of Iraq and the Israelis to live in peace with their Palestinian neighbors. This is a remarkable testimony, given the daily brainwashing of ordinary Americans in almost everything they watch and read." Pilger, "After Bobby Kennedy."

49. Chomsky, *Interventions*, pp. 99–100.

50. Derber, *Hidden Power*, pp. 6–9, 97–98.

Appendix A

1. For sources, see note 40, pp. 266–267 in the present study.

2. And for what it's worth, Iraqis have wanted—and do want—U.S. troops out. "By 2004," Anthony Arnove noted in 2006, "a survey conducted by *USA Today*, *CNN*, and the Gallup Organization found that 71 percent of Iraqis considered foreign troops to be occupiers, a number that rises to 81 percent the autonomous Kurdish region in northern Iraq. A poll released by the Independent Institute for Administration and Civil Society Studies in May 2004 found that 92 percent of Iraqis viewed foreign troops as occupiers, and 2 percent saw them as liberators. In the same poll, only 7 percent of Iraqis expressed confidence in 'coalition forces' led by the United States ." A poll commissioned by the British Ministry of Defence in August of 2005 found that fully 82 percent of Iraqis were "strongly opposed" to the presence of foreign troops and that less than 1 percent believed the troops were "responsible for improvement in security." See Anthony Arnove, *Iraq: The Logic of Withdrawal* (New York : New Press, 2006), pp.28–29; Chomsky, *Failed States*, p. 164.

Appendix B

1. Pilger, "After Bobby Kennedy."

2. Susan Davis, "Obama Tilts Toward Center," *Wall Street Journal*, June 25, 2008; Michael Powell, "For Obama, a Pragmatist's Shift Toward the Center," *New York Times*, June 27, 2008; Janet Hook, "Obama Moving Toward Center: Democrat Edging Away From Left on Some Issues in Effort to Woo Independent Voters," *Los Angeles Times*, June 27, 2008.

3. The Hamilton Group is a leading "conservative" (business-friendly) economic think tank. Furman, 37, is linked closely to Robert Rubin, the top Wall Street financial mogul and former Clinton economics advisor and Treasury secretary. Rubin's regressive views on behalf of "free trade" (including the North American Free Trade Agreement, investor's rights, wages, welfare and "deficit reduction") gave the Clinton administration "credibility" in the halls of corporate and financial power.

4. See also Alexander Cockburn, "Change? What Change?," *CounterPunch* (June 13–15, 2008), read at http://www.counterpunch.org/cockburn06132008.html.

5. Sara Baxter, "Barack Obama May Recruit Defence Chief Robert Gates," *London Sunday Times*, June 29, 2008, read at http://www.timesonline.co.uk/tol/news/world/us_and_americas/us_elections/article4232070.ece.

6. Barack Obama, "Remarks of Senator Obama: Council for Faith-Based and Neighborhood Partnerships," Zanesville, Ohio (July 1, 2008), read at http://www.barackobama.com/2008/07/01/remarks_of_senator_barack_obam_86.php.

7. Leutisha Stills, "Obama Charges Rightward," *Black Agenda Report* (June 25, 2008), read at http://www.blackagendareport.com/index.php?option=com_content&task=view&id=674&Itemid=1.

8. Hook, "Obama Moving Toward Center;" Paul Street, "Obama's 'Shift to the Center' and the Narrow Authoritarian Spectrum in U.S. Politics," *ZNet Magazine* (July 1, 2008), read at http://www.zcommunications.org/znet/viewArticle/18052.

9. For a useful (if unoriginal) summary of relevant data, see Paul Street, "Americans' Progressive Opinions versus "The Shadow Cast on Society by Business," *ZNet Sustainer Commentary* (May 15, 2008), read at http://www.zcommunications.org/zspace/commentaries/3491.

10. A recent, brilliant, and haunting reflection is Sheldon Wolin, *Democracy Incorporated: Managed Democracy and the Specter of Inverted Totalitarianism* (Princeton, NJ: Princeton University Press, 2008).

INDEX